"This book opens essential conversations on the most complex and pressing issues of sustainable strategy. Its global perspective adds immense value, enabling practitioners and institutions to approach sustainability challenges with clarity and depth. By combining conceptual rigour with practical examples, it creates space for multiple voices to engage in this critical debate."

Roberto Vassolo, *Full Professor in Strategic Management and Long Range Planning Co-Editor-in-Chief, AE Business School, Universidad Austral, Argentina*

"Professor Phillips puts sustainability at the heart of strategic management. His latest book provides relevant insights for practitioners and students. It is a timely and welcome addition to the literature."

Catherine Robinson, *Professor, Dean of the School of Business and Law, University of Brighton, UK*

"Phillips delivers a disciplined account of sustainability as key element of a company's strategy – not just lofty CSR talk. With precise constructs, analytic frameworks, and intriguing cross-industry cases, he demonstrates how stakeholder outcomes translate into goals, capital allocation, and governance. A welcome playbook for executives and directors that links purpose to performance, improves risk posture, and provides credible metrics."

Roland Deiser, *Senior Drucker Fellow, Chairman of the Center for the Future of Organization at the Drucker School of Management, USA*

SUSTAINABLE STRATEGIC MANAGEMENT

Sustainable Strategic Management revolutionises strategic management by combining cutting-edge academic theories with the latest sustainable business practices.

Featuring a visionary framework for sustainable strategic management, this textbook offers practical strategies for aligning financial success with ethical and sustainable practice. It covers a spectrum of topics, from core principles of sustainable strategic management and technological disruptions to stakeholder engagement and the United Nations Sustainable Development Goals (UNSDGs). This book thoroughly examines the interconnected relationship between sustainability and practical strategic decision-making efficacy and offers case studies, strategy nuggets, and practical strategies throughout for integrating sustainable practices and reducing pushback from stakeholders.

Written for postgraduate students, executives, and practitioners, this forward-looking resource empowers readers to lead the sustainability **transition** within organisations, preparing them for the challenges and opportunities of a rapidly changing business landscape. Online resources include chapter slides and an instructor guide.

Paul A. Phillips is an Honorary Professor in Strategic Management and former Director of Kent Business School, UK.

SUSTAINABLE STRATEGIC MANAGEMENT

Leadership with Purpose

Paul A. Phillips

Routledge
Taylor & Francis Group
LONDON AND NEW YORK

Designed cover image: Eoneren / Getty Images

First published 2026
by Routledge
4 Park Square, Milton Park, Abingdon, Oxon OX14 4RN

and by Routledge
605 Third Avenue, New York, NY 10158

Routledge is an imprint of the Taylor & Francis Group, an informa business

British Library Cataloguing-in-Publication Data
A catalogue record for this book is available from the British Library

ISBN: 978-1-032-85144-0 (hbk)
ISBN: 978-1-032-84450-3 (pbk)
ISBN: 978-1-003-51677-4 (ebk)

DOI: 10.4324/9781003516774

Typeset in Optima
by codeMantra

Access the Support Material: www.routledge.com/9781032844503

I would like to express my deepest gratitude to my family members for their patience, understanding, and encouragement throughout this book-writing project.

Thank you all for your unwavering support during the long hours spent in my study, writing apart from you all.

CONTENTS

PREFACE

In boardrooms worldwide, a profound shift is underway. The once back-office sustainability function has taken centre stage with climate change and the net-zero crisis now at the centre of strategic decision-making. Companies that fail to acknowledge this fundamental shift will not only miss opportunities but also face being devalued by the capital markets and disrupted by stakeholder pressure.

Embracing a holistic view of sustainability that incorporates economic resilience and social equity in the context of environmental stewardship will enable firms to meet their sustainability targets and drive long-term value creation.

The rewards can be enormous, with Citadel, a US hedge fund, generating $12 billion in two years through sophisticated climate modelling. This demonstrates how forward-thinking organisations can move the dial from compliance to sustainability-driven value creation. This represents one of the most significant opportunities of the 21st century.

However, the significance of leadership in shaping how organisations proactively manage their trajectory during their sustainability journey remains immense. While estimates vary, surveys consistently report low rates of sustainable strategy implementation. Using a sample of 5,000 C-suite executives across 22 industries and 22 countries, IBM Institute for Business Value (2024) found that while many companies now pursue **innovation** sustainability strategies only 30% make significant progress in execution. In other words, 70% are falling short.

This book offers a blueprint for MBA and MSc postgraduate students, business executives, and practitioners seeking to position themselves and/or organisations at the forefront of sustainability-driven transformation. Drawing on research and practice from across academia, industries, markets, and geographies, this book presents actionable frameworks and toolkits that can help enhance the internal intelligence that drives stakeholder value and address pressing societal and environmental challenges.

This book seeks to make the **transition** from strategic management to sustainable strategic management by merging academic theories with contemporary sustainable business practices. The goal is to act as a conduit between the perspectives of sustainable and strategic management. Today, it is not the time for business as usual, where companies continue to destroy the planet, and the Chief Sustainability Officer sees colleagues treating the concept as a gimmick.

The hard truth many leaders face is that their organisation must be redesigned to be genuinely sustainable. Sustainability strategies are not merely costs but produce tangible benefits for stakeholders. Sustainability must be embedded across all strategic functions of the organisation. Sustainability professionals must speak the language of the CFO and work within agreed metrics. The journey will continue to be challenging, and this book will deliver the insights to ensure that a sustainable business has its strategy integrated with its North Star.

Targeting postgraduate students, MBA students, executives, and practitioners, this book provides insights to thrive in the dynamic realm of sustainable business. Established business practices require reevaluation, as actions must foster a more promising future for all. The overarching goals for *Sustainable Strategic Management: Leadership with Purpose* include:

1. Innovative Framework: This book presents a visionary framework for **transitioning** from strategy to sustainable strategic management. It then provides pragmatic tactics for adeptly navigating change, minimising employee pushback, seizing opportunities, and achieving success through integrating sustainable practices.
2. Profit and Purpose Integration in **Transition**: This book serves as a blueprint, envisioning a future where profit and purpose are unified. Theory and practice demonstrate how businesses can formulate strategies that integrate financial success with ethical and sustainable practices.
3. Comprehensive Coverage: The content encompasses a range of subjects, including fundamental principles of sustainable strategic management, technological disruptors, stakeholder involvement, and the UNSDGs. It rigorously analyses the interdependent relationship between sustainability and the effectiveness of practical strategic decision-making. It provides examples of resistance to change.
4. Pedagogical Approach: This book uses a vivid storytelling approach to guide readers through a transformative journey. It incorporates engaging case studies, thought-provoking activities, and practical examples to augment comprehension and promote experiential application.
5. Bridge between Theory and Action: This book effectively connects theoretical topics with practical applications. It emphasises the need to understand sustainable strategic management principles and their effective application in practical organisational contexts that demonstrate resilience.
6. Global Relevance: This book aims to engage readers from diverse cultural and geographical backgrounds by addressing international concerns and opportunities, particularly those pertinent to the Global South, and focusing on issues of **transition**.
7. Clarity over Complexity: Despite the voluminous nature of the written strategy literature, a key theme is maintaining clear and accessible content for all.

This book encourages readers to think holistically about sustainability through a business and management lens, deploying open-minded rather than closed-minded strategy thinking. Dynamic macro- and micro-environments will trigger changes in sustainable opportunities and threats. Promoting a comprehensive, integrated viewpoint enables organisations to question previous assumptions regarding flawed business models and expedite the implementation of innovative alternatives.

This book is a forward-looking resource that empowers readers to lead the sustainability **transition** and connect with society within and outside the organisations. It prepares them for the difficulties and opportunities of a swiftly evolving business environment. One of the features includes the use of a sustainable strategy toolbox consisting of toolkits that help readers navigate changes. The following topics are discussed throughout the chapters:

- Stakeholder capitalism
- Cost of sustainability
- Strategic thinking
- Strategy and design thinking
- Stakeholder engagement tools
- Biomimicry design principles
- Business and government non-profit interaction
- Artificial intelligence (AI) and Generative AI.

Making the **transition** from strategy to sustainable strategic management is a considerable task, which includes overcoming several hurdles in a business and societal context, some of which are included in Table 0.1

Audience

This book will serve as an essential guide to strategic management, catering to readers from diverse backgrounds, including learners and experienced professionals. MSc, MBA postgraduate students, business executives, and participants in executive education programmes can utilise this book. It elucidates the fundamental principles and frameworks

TABLE 0.1 Critical societal challenges impacting sustainability

Societal Challenge	*Examples*
1 Power asymmetries and economic justice	The concentration of economic power such as the so-called "Magnificent Seven," comprising the largest stocks Alphabet, Amazon, Apple, Meta, Microsoft, NVIDIA, and Tesla, creates tension with local communities and workers.
2 Worker rights	The move towards sustainable practices during periods of **transition** can raise questions about workers protection.
3 Cultural heritage preservation	In the rush to modernise, there is a need to balance modernisation with the practices of indigenous and local communities.
4 Knowledge democracy	Western scientific approaches create power imbalances in Global South knowledge production practices.
5 Quality of life	Moving away from a sole preoccupation with GDP to consider well-being, environmental health, and social cohesion.
6 Inclusive decision-making	Provide a voice for marginalised groups during strategy processes.
7 Community autonomy vs corporate control	The tensions between decentralised community-based economic solutions and traditional management models.

crucial for learning strategic management, ensuring accessibility for individuals without specialised knowledge. This book clarifies complex strategic topics through clear explanations and practical examples, including internal and external strategy frameworks, competitive advantage, and strategic planning procedures. Furthermore, it explores current strategic issues and industry trends, providing readers with the knowledge to manoeuvre through the constantly changing corporate landscape.

This book assumes no prior knowledge of strategy, strategic management, and sustainability, establishing a robust foundation for readers unfamiliar with these historical concepts. The accessible language and organised format guarantee that beginners can comprehend essential concepts without intimidation.

In today's world, readers new to these critical challenges can systematically develop core knowledge, guiding them through the intricacies of sustainable strategic decision-making and enabling them to implement strategic management principles successfully in practical situations. This book serves as an essential resource for those beginning their career in the industry or seeking to enhance their knowledge, equipping readers with the skills necessary to understand the complexities of strategic management.

Sustainable Strategic Management: Leadership with Purpose is well-suited for several taught courses across business, management, and entrepreneurship disciplines. Here is an assessment of the potential courses where students and business executives would find this text useful:

1 Strategic Management (Core):

- Given the focus on strategic management principles and the innovative sustainable strategic management framework presented in this book, it aligns well with core courses in strategic management. This could serve as a foundational text for students studying the core concepts of strategic decision-making.

2 Sustainability in Business (Core or Elective):

- The book's emphasis on integrating sustainability considerations into strategic decision-making positions it as a valuable resource for courses specifically dedicated to sustainability in business. This could be either a core component of a sustainability-focused curriculum or an elective for students interested in sustainable business practices.

3 Business **Innovation** and Entrepreneurship (Elective):

- The "Sustainable Strategy Toolbox," together with discussions on sustainable business models, makes the text relevant for elective courses on business **innovation** and entrepreneurship. It provides insights into how strategic **innovation** and sustainable practices can be integrated for success.

4 Leadership and Change Management (Elective):

- Sections on sustainable leadership, purpose-driven leadership, and leadership in sustainable ecosystems make this book suitable for elective courses focused on leadership and change management. It addresses the role of leadership in driving sustainable strategic initiatives.

5 Global Business Management (Elective):

- Chapters discussing the international dimensions of sustainable strategic management and considerations for global perspectives position this book as a beneficial resource for elective courses in global business management.

6 Strategic Planning and Implementation (Core or Elective):

- As this book covers the foundations of strategic management, strategic analysis, and case study analysis, it can be applicable to both core and elective courses on strategic planning and implementation.

7 Corporate Social Responsibility (Core or Elective):

- Given this book's strong focus on integrating sustainability and ethical responsibility into strategic decision-making, it aligns well with courses on corporate social responsibility, whether as a core component or an elective.

8 Environmental Management (Elective):

- The chapters addressing UNSDGs, sustainability assessment, and sustainability measurement and reporting make this book suitable for elective courses in environmental management and sustainability.

By offering relevant content across a range of courses, the proposed textbook demonstrates versatility and applicability to both core and elective modules, making it a valuable resource for students pursuing various aspects of business and management education.

Case Studies – Key Features and Benefits

Case studies and examples are a vital component of this textbook, and each chapter will include the following attributes (see Table 0.2).

TABLE 0.2 Case studies – key features and benefits

Features	*Benefits*
Sustainable strategy toolbox	Uncover five toolkits that blend strategic management with cutting-edge innovative approaches empowering readers to drive forward-thinking sustainable strategies.
Sustainability implementation	Gain insights into strategy and tactic gaps to help overcome the implementation deficit. Learn how to integrate sustainability considerations into every facet of strategic decision-making, creating resilient and ethically responsible organisations.
Real-world insights	Gain actionable insights from real-world case studies that spotlight organisations at the forefront of sustainable strategic management and globally showcase successes and challenges.

Pedagogical Features

This book addresses fundamental business and management subjects while integrating a sustainable agenda, encompassing:

1. Twelve interactive mini case studies illustrate real-world applications of innovative strategies and conceptual issues.
2. Eleven strategy nuggets are compact and encapsulated features of the sustainability phenomenon.
3. Comprehensive examination of critical business trends and their influence on strategic decision-making.
4. Stimulating tasks and introspective enquiries to enhance critical thinking and practical skill acquisition.
5. Learning strategic objectives.
6. Chapter introduction.
7. End-of-chapter key takeaways.
8. End-of-chapter self-reflection questions.
9. Tables and Figures.
10. References.

Online Support

The companion website features a short instructor manual, an overview and introduction to this book, author information, supplementary materials, including chapter-by-chapter PowerPoint slides, a test bank of questions, and outline solutions.

Diversity and Inclusion

A fundamental premise is the recognition of the urgent sustainability trends in low- and middle-income countries (LMICs), where distinct difficulties arise from growing urbanisation, population expansion, and resource constraints. It highlights the Global South, a heterogeneous collection of countries predominantly located in the southern hemisphere, encompassing Latin America, Africa, Asia, and Oceania. These regions have a history of colonisation, economic exploitation, and underdevelopment, persistently obstructing sustainable goals. Despite encountering considerable challenges, such as rapid population growth, resource limitations, climatic vulnerability, and socio-economic disparities, there remains an unwavering emphasis on **innovation** and advancement.

This book firmly adheres to inclusivity and diversity in all dimensions, encompassing contributors, references, case studies, and illustrations. It strives to amplify voices and experiences often marginalised in sustainability discourse, ensuring representation from women's networks, employee networks, and ethnic and cultural affinity groups. This book aims to foster a more inclusive understanding of sustainability challenges and solutions by intentionally incorporating diverse perspectives.

As an educator deeply familiar with the nuances of the Global South, I am dedicated to researching and compiling relevant material for this book. By utilising my academic networks and attending conferences, I aim to establish contacts with other academics and practitioners in the sustainability and business sectors. Through these relationships, I seek the most recent ideas, recommendations, and practical examples for tackling the complex sustainability challenges confronting LMICs and the Global South.

Why Sustainable Strategic Management?

Throughout my career in business schools, where I have taught strategy at undergraduate, postgraduate, and executive education levels, I have consistently endeavoured to assess each cohort's interpretation of the term strategy. This inquiry appears straightforward; nonetheless, dialogues may rapidly devolve into ambiguity. In the last 20 years, responses have been provided by individuals employed in organisations of various sizes, encompassing all major industries and a global reach. People's experiences and context limit the understanding of strategy.

My experiences reveal a recurring pattern in diverse situations, where initial enthusiasm succumbs to disillusionment due to unforeseen hurdles, and the absence of strategic thinking and agility obstructs advancement. Strategic adaptability is a key predictor of organisational effectiveness in a tumultuous climate characterised by market instability. This necessitates explicit guidance from the leadership team and organisational structural adjustments enabled by innovative methods.

Nonetheless, the difficulty of persuading individuals and management teams to go from a closed to an open mindset regarding strategy is substantial. As the late Donald Henry Rumsfeld stated, "We don't know what we don't know." So, we need to be explicit about the gaps in current strategy practice by focusing on what we know [that] we don't know!

"We are unaware of our ignorance." We must concentrate on what we acknowledge as unknown to identify deficiencies in the present strategic practices. By clearly addressing these uncertainties, we can more effectively navigate the intricacies of strategic management and achieve more innovative and resilient outcomes. This **transition** is a significant challenge but crucial for maintaining competitiveness in a volatile business environment.

Nonetheless, cultivating a mindset of "sustainability" exploration within businesses poses a considerable challenge. Leaders recognise the importance of sustainability in maintaining competitiveness in rapidly evolving markets. Conversely, **transitioning** from a conventional, insular "economic" perspective to a more open, societal paradigm may encounter opposition.

Conventional **performance** measurements increasingly integrate political, behavioural, psychological, humanistic, and sociological elements. This may generate multiple fault lines between traditional and contemporary methodologies. For-profit organisations must produce social metrics, whereas non-profit organisations should create revenue by implementing suitable tactics. In both cases, strategic management processes are recalibrated. Extended periods of uncertainty are detrimental.

Employees may fear the repercussions of failure or hesitate to relinquish established methods that have historically yielded success. Moreover, reconciling short-term **performance** indicators with the long-term advantages of sustainable projects requires considerable time and work. This tension can engender a paradox in which the behaviours essential for fostering future growth and resilience are hindered by a culture of risk aversion and an excessive focus on immediate outcomes.

Figure 0.1 depicts the strategic dilemma at the intersection of social, economic, and environmental perspectives. CEOs and their CFOs often face an investment paradox,

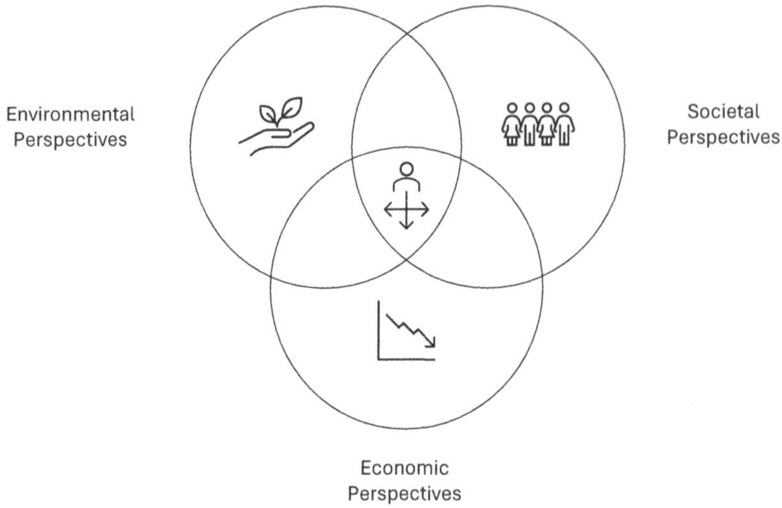

FIGURE 0.1 Sustainability strategy dilemma

where sustainability requires high upfront capital, and the capital markets tend to reward quarterly **performance**.

This emphasises the scenario where leadership teams manage and reconcile intrinsic tensions to fulfil their sustainability objectives. Although the significance of sustainable development is rising, achieving sustainable growth may be elusive, and we need to currently focus on the **transition** as we figure out in more detail what needs to be changed (the unknown, unknown).

Strategic management is essential; however, a primary focus of this book is on examining how businesses can implement creative methods to achieve their sustainability key **performance** indicators. The premise is that a modern approach is required to cultivate awareness and foster sustainable strategic management, enabling organisations to align their operations effectively with sustainability goals.

This book recognises that the strategic problem presents itself differently in diverse contexts, such as profit-driven corporations, non-profits, non-governmental organisations, governments, and markets, and seeks to offer customised solutions.

The premise asserts the necessity for a contemporary approach to fostering awareness to participate in **SSM**, which is potentially transformative. The proposed integrated strategy guarantees that sustainability is not a standalone objective but an essential element, promoting a resilient and equitable growth path for all stakeholders.

This requires fresh knowledge and insights to enable organisations to proactively cope with issues by formulating good rather than bad strategies. Rumelt's (2022) diagnosis of the strategy includes:

"The core of strategy work is always the same: discovering the critical factors in a situation and designing a way of coordinating and focusing actions to deal with those factors p2."

Strategy and sustainability need to converge, with the latter evolving from a mere ethical consideration to a fundamental component of central strategic management-related discourse. This symbiotic relationship now integrates ecological factors into mainstream decision-making, heightening expectations for organisations to assume responsibility for their impact on the planet.

Evidence suggests that for-profit, not-for-profit, and public sector organisations are more adept at adapting to changing conditions and future uncertainties by incorporating environmental and social concerns into their decision-making processes. This necessitates the identification of innovative, inclusive, and responsible solutions. The CEO of Mercedes-Benz has recently pledged to delay the cessation of fossil fuel-powered vehicles and to dilute its electric vehicle (EV) objectives. He contends that the prices of electric cars and petrol automobiles continue to be elevated, and consumers persist in questioning and resisting the value proposition of EVs, which justifies these premiums.

As a result, the major automotive manufacturers are reevaluating their EV forecasts. This underscores the triple dilemma of sustainability, economics, and society, which has heightened uncertainty, alongside the impact of Chinese automobile manufacturers entering European markets at highly competitive prices. Adaptive strategies are crucial for proactively responding to the continuous fluctuations of the external environment, thereby enhancing resilience and facilitating the long-term management of operational and financial risks.

Research indicates that effective stakeholder management is crucial; nonetheless, contemporary companies face pressure to balance the demands of stakeholders within their ecosystem. This balancing act requires a nuanced understanding of each stakeholder group's distinct expectations, goals, and levels of influence. Achieving sustainability goals requires managing complex relationships with investors, employees, customers, and stakeholders across societal and environmental spheres. Meeting the needs of each group while maintaining overarching strategic objectives requires an approach that incorporates stakeholder feedback into strategic decision-making processes.

References

IBM Institute for Business Value, Research Insights (2024). Beyond checking the box. Available at: https://www.ibm.com/downloads/documents/us-en/10a99803fbafdc95 (Accessed: 26 August 2025).

Rumelt, R., (2022). *The Crux: How leaders become strategists*. Profile Books.

ACKNOWLEDGEMENTS

Sustainable Strategic Management: Leadership with Purpose

From my first international Master's teaching Cohort in Athens in 1999, I have taught more than 2,000 MBA Business executives and 3,000 MSc students, which has allowed me to share my strategic management ideas and learn from each of their experiences.

In recent years, sustainability has become a growing topic of conversation and planted the seed of the idea for this book. I am grateful to all of them, as they pushed me towards writing *Sustainable Strategic Management: Leadership with Purpose*.

With regard to the subject of sustainable strategic management, I am hugely grateful for the reviewers of my book proposal, who were able to shape my ideas into a more accessible, academically rigorous, and practitioner-oriented book. Their invaluable and perceptive thoughts on the interface of the sustainable and strategic management phenomenon made this book far better as a result.

Specifically, this book could not have reached this stage without the support, cooperation, and guidance of numerous colleagues. I am grateful to all of them for their willingness to give me their time, wise counsel, and acting as a critical colleague when required during my career.

I am indebted to all my colleagues at the Universities of Wales, Surrey, and Kent and beyond, who helped strengthen my original ideas over the years in joint teaching, research, and consultancy projects. These exchanges have shaped my thoughts on sustainable and strategic management into a more solid academic and practical discourse.

Recently, specific colleagues who contributed to reading draft sections of this book, including Professor May Seitanidi, Professor Rajendra Shirole, Dr Dongmei Coa, Dr Krystin Zigan, and doctoral student Perla de la Caridad Errasti Hernández, also contributed to the primary case studies. Members of the Association of Sustainable Practitioners and the RSA (Royal Society of Arts, Manufactures and Commerce) provided valuable feedback on some of my ideas, making certain sections more accessible to readers.

To the CEOs, CFOs, CSOs, HR directors, and Heads of learning and development in profit and not-for-profit firms who allowed me to validate and test some of my ideas over the years, I owe a special debt of gratitude. I am grateful for the countless hours of conversations with my collaborators during consulting assignments. I look forward to continuing these collaborations, as the ideas presented in this book get deployed in practice.

Editorial Support

I extend my sincere appreciation to Sophia Levine, Senior Editor at Routledge, for believing in my book idea and guiding me through the early stages of the book commissioning process. I would like to thank Sarah Rae, Editor, who took over from Sophia Levine during the later stages, as well as the other staff at Routledge for their support. Nicole Doyle, Editorial Assistant, was a pillar of support, addressing my many queries during the writing of this book and getting the text ready for the production stage.

PAP
07/12/25

PART I

Foundations of Sustainable Strategic Management

1

HISTORY AND IMPLICATIONS OF SUSTAINABILITY TO BUSINESS AND SOCIETY

1.1 Learning Strategic Objectives

Upon completing this chapter, you will have the ability to:

1. **Knowledge-Based Objectives:**
   - Understand the key events that have shaped the historical development of sustainability over the past six decades.
   - Appreciate the implications of how sustainable strategic management affects business and society.
2. **Skill-Based Objectives:**
   - Identify and analyse the leading sustainability issues organisations face in the future.
   - Link the phenomenon of sustainability to economic and societal issues with the constraints of environmental degradation.
3. **Attitude-Based Objectives:**
   - Appreciate the necessity of integrating sustainability practice with strategic management for long-term success.
   - Feel motivated to implement sustainable practices and support sustainability policies in their professional lives.

1.2 Introduction

At its core, the sustainability phenomenon comprises two key pillars: limiting global warming to 1.5°C and **transitioning** to a low-carbon economy. If left unmanaged, the aftereffects of worldwide warming and the use of fossil fuels will disrupt the delicate ecosystems that are pivotal to the planet's foundational aspects. Rising average temperatures cause ecosystem disruption, as evidenced by the freak weather experienced globally.

DOI: 10.4324/9781003516774-2

Sustainability is at a crossroads (Lee, Mascena, Rüegger, and Miller, 2025). With academics stressing that the business should be a force for good (McPhail, Kafouros, McKiernan, and Cornelius, 2024), operating smartly with planetary boundaries and resources (Lahneman, Walls, Unter, and Howard-Grenville, 2025).

Using a planetary boundaries framework, which consists of nine Earth system boundaries, and seeing how this gets integrated into business and management is a challenge (Williams, Perego, and Whiteman, 2025). The urgency of this ecological crisis demands a fundamental transformation in how academics theorise, measure, and engage with the sustainability phenomenon.

Businesses cannot be complicit in perpetuating human behaviour that leads to planetary destruction. However, deniers of sustainability, which include industry incumbents with stranded asset exposure, financial market sceptics, and those who are ideologically opposed, can also represent opportunities. Their resistance can create opportunities for sustainability leaders to capitalise on. Those in denial are losing out on talent acquisition, customer capture, capital access, and success.

The 47th President of the United States, Donald Trump, is at best sceptical about embracing policies that reduce emissions and promoting renewable energy. As soon as Trump was elected, the market sentiment changed, with green stocks suffering. However, experts still advocate for a diversified portfolio approach, which includes green stocks in clients' investment portfolios. So, Trump's action should be seen more as a blip in 60 years of progress rather than as an ongoing trend.

Financially, the figures are staggering; climate change costs the planet $60 million per hour. By 2100, it is expected to represent 7.4% of UK GDP, far exceeding the cost of implementing corrective measures. Governments face the challenge of adopting long-term strategies that will require raising taxes on the public. The "hard yards of governing" related to long-term decision-making for the greater good are now being quantified through a financial perspective when considering autopoietic-based solutions.

The pandemic had a profound influence but arguably accelerated inequality and the pace towards sustainable development. However, these headwinds, including inflationary pressures, economic uncertainties, fragmented trade patterns, and geopolitical events, have dampened growth, and transformational change is now requisite.

Despite sanguine attitudes not being universal, sustainability provides an enormous opportunity to escape the trough induced by the post-pandemic slowdown. However, despite the optimism behind the sustainability phenomenon, there are growing signs of friction as organisations fail to plan for their long-term future. The planet will look and operate very differently in 2100.

Transitioning from anthropocentrism to regenerative business models will require reconceptualising organisations' relationships with nature. This pivot requires us to adopt a fiduciary duty that prioritises environmental stewardship in our decision-making. The sustainability phenomenon requires a Gestalt approach to organisational strategy, recognising that the whole system can present properties more significant than the sum of its parts.

Against this backdrop of climate change, new thoughts and actions have emerged. Sustainability activists look for solutions from businesses, governments, and non-governmental organisations (NGOs), but practices can be complex as organisations have differing stakeholder needs. Most stakeholder approaches overlook the last two, which

FIGURE 1.1 Key stakeholders

are increasingly critical: customers, employees, investors, commercial partners, the community, and, lastly, the environment (see Figure 1.1).

Simultaneously, a catalytic race is underway to **transition** to a low-carbon economy and discover alternative energy sources. Large companies play a crucial role in navigating the dual challenge of generating economic profits while pursuing sustainability goals.

A case in point is Google, a member of the Magnificent Seven Stocks, which is accelerating its power purchase agreements to acquire 1.5 GW of renewable energy in 12 months to power its data centres. Walmart, the world's largest supermarket, is working at pace to be 100% powered by renewable energy by 2035 through its solar projects. L'Oréal, the global cosmetics company, is captivating audiences with its awards for its sustainability and has been awarded a Triple A rating by the international environmental non-profit carbon disclosure project (CDP) for eight consecutive years.

But this is only the tip of the iceberg. Seeking a symbiotic relationship, activists want to see signs of a shared responsibility for the planet. Drawing on shareholder wealth maximisation, the organisation's CFO is also accountable to the capital markets and finance providers. Critics would view this as misguided, given the increasing evidence of exploitation of employees, communities, and the environment. Understanding and appreciating biogeochemical cycles disrupted by 21st century industrial activity provides a context for creating truly regenerative approaches.

1.2.1 Reflection

In stark contrast to conventional practice, sustainability thinking embraces the past, present, and future, necessitating a paradigmatic shift in strategy and practice (Kopnina, 2017). Current strategic planning practice is increasingly counterproductive, with management teams making decisions through abstruse reasoning. Moreover, the desiderata for organisational transformation now extend well beyond carbon reduction to include social equity.

Within planetary ecosystems, countries around the globe have spent more than six decades innovating about how they handle sustainability, but it's time to accelerate progress. There are increasing comments in the media on how companies make once-in-a-lifetime decisions, which is attributed to one of the two core pillars. However, as realities become increasingly apparent, organisations often reengineer their endogenous (internal) activities and align with the exogenous (external) forces. This phenomenon is increasingly prevalent in the highly competitive automotive industry.

More than a decade after its $12 billion emission scandal, Volkswagen faces a tsunami of strategic issues, resulting in drastic decision-making. Volkswagen competes with Toyota as the world's largest car company, so any issues it faces highlight implications that can be applied to this and other industries. This time last year, Volkswagen was considering halting Polo car production in Europe due to the higher cost of producing fossil fuel-driven smaller cars. For the first time in its 87-year history, the Volkswagen leadership team is considering closing factories in Germany, accompanied by a severe reduction in headcount.

The scalable challenge of maintaining a growth trajectory and adhering to sustainability principles now applies to many organisations pursuing strategic renewals for themselves and their stakeholders. Small and medium-sized enterprises (SMEs) are also feeling immense supply chain pressure with little influence over suppliers. Such action is increasing SME compliance costs, which in turn further reduces profit margins. SME business owners need to develop tailored solutions appropriate for their scale of operations.

The strategic implications of shifts have reverberated through the management consultancy industry. The development of sustainability has provided the industry with fresh revenue opportunities. With the demand for sustainability professionals surging, management consulting firms have stepped into the breach, reporting significant growth in their sustainability offerings.

In the same vein, McKinsey, the strategy consultant, forecasts that "in a 2.0°C world, roughly a billion more people would be exposed to climate hazards than in a 1.5°C world." This will hinder the ambition to respect the environment, promote social inclusion, and achieve equality. Correspondingly, net-zero carbon emissions have evolved from their physical climate science origins to be operationalised through organisational economic, social, and political systems.

In today's increasingly complex world, heightened geopolitical risk presents both challenges and opportunities. Pursuing the global sustainability agenda requires insights into how political risks affect business operations, necessitating the redesign and implementation of new processes to help manage these risks. Understanding the interplay of geography and strategy can help contextualise shifts in the global markets. Modern approaches, such as geostrategy, can help serve as a guiding framework for coping with the complexities. The strategist can formulate and implement cross-functional processes to address growing pockets of hostility around the globe. Leadership teams must navigate an era of liminality as their businesses **transition** between the industrial business paradigm and the emergent regenerative models.

Otherwise, vulnerable members of society will be exposed and displaced, resulting in severe economic consequences.

1.2.2 Looking Forward

Net-zero is an inclusive 2050 target (Fankhauser et al., 2022). Still, the scientific question is, what will it take to halt the global average surface temperature increase? Elevated CO_2 levels are not just a function of anthropogenic warming but also include other greenhouse gases. The **transition** towards net-zero will pose challenges to governments worldwide as they create legislation aimed at changing behaviours to achieve their targets.

For change to take place, organisational calcification merits close attention. Strategies now go beyond recycling and balancing carbon use with nature. For instance, energy-intensive sectors such as chemicals, iron and steel, oil refineries, cement, and concrete must decrease emissions by at least 25% by 2030. While renewable refineries play a significant role in reducing the carbon footprint, their higher cost base compared to conventional fuels hinders their adoption.

Ethanol, Fatty Acid Methyl Ester biodiesel, renewable diesel, bioethanol, and sustainable aviation fuel are the five most common renewable fuels in the market. The processing of biomass yields renewable fuels that produce fewer carbon emissions over their lifetime compared to carbon-based fuels. Therefore, the perpetual movement to decarbonise biofuels has led to the conversion of traditional refineries into renewable ones. However, a significant disadvantage of cost competitiveness with conventional fuels is that it requires policy shifts and achieving economies of scale in production to make biofuels more attractive (Marketline, 2023).

The neoliberal assumption that markets left to themselves can self-correct to address environmental externalities is not without its challenges. Developing countries face a financial sustainability challenge due to the scarcity of funds resulting from higher levels of debt and constrained government budgets, which limit the funds available for sustainability initiatives. This results in calls for high-income countries to step up and help provide the necessary funding for Global South projects.

One of the significant pledges of the UN's Climate Change Conference, COP29, held in November 2024, was for developed countries to commit $300 billion a year to aid emerging countries in combating climate change. Dubbed the "finance COP," experts reveal that this is still $2.3 to $2.5 trillion short of the desired amount. The International Monetary Fund advocates a broad mix of policies to unlock private capital in developing economies, thereby creating a more positive and broader climate impact.

Sustainability creates an exigency for financial model **innovation** that overrides the current banking system. Despite limited local sources, risk perception, combined with high interest rates, can render viable projects unviable due to investment capital appraisal methods such as net present value and internal rates of return.

Leaders of developing economies make the call at international forums for the need for consilience with innovative funding mechanisms and robust international cooperation to meet these substantial financial demands. This is particularly problematic in underdeveloped internal financial markets, where nascent institutions are vulnerable to capital flight and external pressures.

Moreover, developing countries must be frugal, as infrastructural and societal barriers hinder decarbonisation interventions. These can include skilled labour constraints, which limit decarbonisation options. For example, carbon capture and hydrogen are essential for direct carbon emissions from energy-intensive production processes, but limited access to specialised workers creates obstacles for the Global South. In these environments, sustainability strategies must incorporate innovative, bricolage-type ideas to deliver value for money to stakeholders (Mateus and Sarkar, 2024).

The following section of this chapter explores the foundation for sustainability, tracing its origins and examining the impact of limiting global warming to 1.5°C, as well as progressing towards a low-carbon economy. Next, the focus is on the importance of sustainability in modern business and societal contexts. This chapter concludes by providing an overview of this book, which helps readers plan their way through *Sustainable Strategic Management: Leadership with Purpose*.

Mini Case Study

Citadel's Climate-Driven Strategy

In 2018, Citadel's founder and CEO, Kenneth Griffin, identified a market opportunity for his hedge fund to elevate weather predictions to the next level to generate significant profits.

The strategy led to the hiring of a 20-member team, including PhD-level atmospheric scientists together with a high-**performance** computing scientist team, to harness data and spot market opportunities. The team's brief being to develop actionable strategies to create in-house weather forecasting capabilities that surpass the market.

The spirit of the strategic vision was recognising that accurate climate predictions could provide a competitive advantage in commodities trading. Citadel's approach includes four pillars:

1 Data Evaluation: Using supercomputers to run multifaceted weather models to explore, create, and determine their value and provide insights.
2 Algorithms and Models: The team developed novel models to predict the behaviour of thunderstorms and tropical cyclones.
3 Strategy Development: Conceptualising new strategies from ideation to final output.
4 Research and Analysis: The interdisciplinary integration of the meteorological expertise with financial acuity provided a rethink of first principles thinking. These fresh solutions to old challenges generated superior long-term returns.

The results were most impressive. The CEO, Kenneth Griffin, and his team's commodities trades generated approximately $8 billion in 2022 and $4 billion in 2023.

Possessing a strategic vision and the ability to implement illustrates the root of Citadel's success, such as:

1 Climate Risk: Sustainability-themed business strategies can help unlock environmental threats by spotting market opportunities.
2 Data-Driven Decision-Making: By leveraging big data and advanced analytics, the firm cultivates new capabilities. These can deliver synergistic effects that enhance strategic decision-making.
3 Interdisciplinary Approach: Instead of operating in disciplinary silos, the integration of expertise from meteorology, computing, and finance creates a compelling value proposition.
4 Long-Term Vision: Although investing in bought-in capabilities may hit short-term returns, the new strategic asset positions the organisation well for the long term.
5 Adaptive Strategy: A prerequisite for real-world impact is the ability to develop agile strategies that respond to market threats and opportunities.

Applications across Industries

Financial investment trading lies at the heart of Citadel's business model. Integrating climate intelligence into strategic decision-making has transferable applications to other sectors:

- Agriculture: Sophisticated data evaluation techniques can be used to enhance long-term forecasts, optimising crop selection and planting times in climate-challenged environments.

- Insurance: Proactive use of new risk-based models can help spot global climate change patterns.
- Real Estate: Making long-term investment decisions based on climate change projections can benefit vulnerable geographical locations.
- Energy: Creating new renewable energy infrastructure to reduce the carbon footprint.
- Supply Chain Management: Anticipating and mitigating climate-related disruptions in global trade.

Challenges and Ethical Considerations

As organisations adopt climate-intelligent strategies, they must navigate several challenges:

1. Data Reliability: Ensuring the accuracy and reliability of climate data and models to provide differentiated investment decisions.
2. Ethical Use: Balancing profit motives with broader societal and environmental responsibilities to ensure that execution does not harm nature.
3. Regulatory Compliance: Adhering to evolving climate-related regulations and financial disclosures will maintain compliance.
4. Talent Acquisition: Attracting and retaining interdisciplinary talent that can bridge climate science and business strategy requires Human Resources to have a continuous recruitment mode.

Questions

1. Explain how Citadel's founder and CEO, Kenneth Griffin, established a competitive advantage by building a 20-member team of atmospheric scientists and computing experts to exploit environmental opportunities.
2. Select an industry and develop a strategic framework for how a specific company in that industry could operationalise climate intelligence to create a competitive advantage while simultaneously addressing sustainability challenges.
3. Analyse the potential tensions that could arise when an organisation develops superior climate intelligence primarily for competitive advantage.

1.3 Evolution of the Sustainability Concept

A well-cited definition of sustainability is provided by the World Commission on Environment and Development (1987):

Sustainable development is the development that meets the needs of the present without compromising the ability of future generations to meet their own needs.

Building upon the earlier foundations and responding to the growing sustainability phenomenon, Crutzen and Stoermer (2000) noted that the human race had entered a new geographical period termed the Anthropocene. One of the ripple effects is that the Earth is entering an irreversible moment, marking the end of the Holocene period. Sustainability should now be viewed as more than a bolt-on activity for strategic management.

Accepting this fact reinforces the emergence and necessity of integrating sustainable and strategic management, which need to fuse to identify relevant and effective novel strategies. Yet progress towards the sustainability development holy grail is slow, suggesting the need for concrete guidance (Baumgartner and Rauter, 2017). Caradonna (2022) traces the evolution of sustainability, which has led to its ubiquity, by incorporating an economic perspective of the growth of sustainability since the 18th century.

1.3.1 The Evolution

The extant literature reveals that the sustainability landscape began well before the 2015 United Nations Sustainable Development Goals (UNSDGs) and originated in the 1960s and 1970s. Examining institutions and institutional fields, including government agencies, international organisations, NGOs, and multinational agreements and treaties, will help to understand emerging signals in the external environment. Leadership teams must prioritise market signals and operationalise the knowledge base to inform policy and decision-making. This critically exposes individuals and the organisation to opportunities and vulnerabilities.

Rachel Carson's seminal 1962 publication, *Silent Spring*, shocked the middle classes with its exposure of the harm caused by DDT and other contaminants to animal life and human safety. By emphasising these dangers, interest shifted from a scientific debate to a public political issue, inspiring environmentalists to form grassroots organisations. The actions led to the inauguration of Earth Day celebrations in 1970. The epistemological concepts of indigenous cultures offer a valuable guide for understanding grassroots activism.

This signalled a profound awakening in public awareness regarding the imperative for environmental preservation and conservation efforts in the evolving landscape. Rallies took place across the United States, and by the end of the year, the government had established the Environmental Protection Agency. Over five decades later, Earth Day is celebrated on April 22, serving as a wake-up call for all. During the 1970s, Munich Re, the insurer, published a paper citing ancient diluvial stories urging better monitoring of climate variations.

With climate change fuelling natural disasters, the insurance industry is most alert to natural catastrophes. In terms of numbers, the last four years have rocked the industry with claims exceeding $100 billion. The juxtaposition of punctuated environmental changes and record temperature levels against a deteriorating planetary ecosystem creates dissonance among stakeholders.

Moving to the next decade, the 1987 Brundtland Commission's influential work, led by Norwegian Prime Minister Gro Harlem Brundtland, initiated the bringing together of the business and society discourse. Innovative business models began to emerge at the intersection of business, society, and the environment. The Brundtland Report introduced the definition of sustainable development as meeting "the needs of the present without compromising the ability of future generations to meet their own needs."

The hegemonic positioning of countries creates "sustainability camps" that operate in economic and environmental silos, thereby perpetuating a fragmented approach to sustainability. During the 1990s, sustainability started gaining traction in the public arenas and business practices. The changing philosophical self-reflections have led to the reset button being pressed. The Global South's limited resources for deployment, combined with the increasing consumption patterns of the North, create an uneven playing field when pursuing sustainability strategies.

Intriguingly, three decades later, the Global South still needs to identify development roadmaps, while the Global North needs to be more frugal in its use of resources and minimise its ecological impact. The 1992 Earth Summit in Rio de Janeiro was another catalyst for

TABLE 1.1 Evolution of significant sustainability-themed events

Year	*Landmark Event*
1962	*Silent Spring* – Rachel Carson's seminal 1962 publication.
1972	United Nations Conference on the Human Environment. The first major international conference devoted to environmental issues, held in Stockholm, leading to the creation of the United Nations Environment Programme.
1987	The Brundtland Report ("Our Common Future") – This report introduced the definition of sustainable development, and fundamentally transforming the global environmental thinking and discourse.
1992	Earth Summit in Rio de Janeiro – Also known as the UN Conference on Environment and Development, it resulted in the adoption of Agenda 21, a comprehensive plan of action for global sustainable development.
1997	Kyoto Protocol – An international treaty that commits its parties to reduce greenhouse gas emissions, acknowledging that global warming exists and is largely caused by human-made CO_2 emissions.
2000	Millennium Development Goals (MDGs) – Eight goals established following the Millennium Summit of the United Nations, aimed at addressing poverty, health, education, and environmental sustainability.
2015	Sustainable Development Goals (SDGs) – Seventeen goals adopted to succeed the MDGs, addressing a wide range of global challenges including climate change, economic inequality, sustainable cities, responsible consumption, and peace and justice.
2015	Paris Agreement – A landmark environmental accord to combat climate change and its impacts, aiming to keep the global temperature rise this century well below 2°C above pre-industrial levels and pursue efforts to limit it to 1.5°C.
2018	Greta Thunberg – Swedish activist inspired millions of young people around the world to participate in climate strikes to demand stronger action on climate change. These protests, part of the "Fridays for Future" movement, highlighted the urgency of the climate crisis and increased public awareness and political pressure.
2020	European Green Deal – An EU initiative aimed at making Europe climate neutral by 2050 through comprehensive measures that include cutting greenhouse gas emissions, investing in **innovation**, and preserving Europe's natural environment.
2021	COP26 (2021) – Pivotal climate conference in Glasgow where world leaders discussed and committed to more ambitious climate actions to achieve the goals of the Paris Agreement.
2023	The Global Sustainable Development Report 2023 written at the midpoint between 2015 and 2030 highlighted the incremental and fragmented change taking place, which is insufficient in its pace to attain SDG targets in 2030.
2024	COP29 – Emphasise on agreeing a new climate finance goal. The EU's Corporate Sustainability Reporting Directive subjected the first set companies to its rules.
2025	World Development Summit 2025 – Took stock of current sustainability efforts and emphasised partnerships for accelerating progress towards SDG and climate change.

pursuing sustainable development and global partnership approaches. Leaders in attendance adopted and signed Agenda 21, a 300-page plan to achieve sustainable growth in the 21st century. This was followed by the Kyoto Protocol, which began the implementation of the United Nations Framework Convention on Climate Change. However, the evidence today suggests that, despite such agreements, carbon dioxide levels in the atmosphere continue to rise, which in turn heats the Earth. As I write, parts of northern and central India are scorching under a severe, record-breaking heatwave, with temperatures exceeding 52°C. This temperature is the highest recorded in India, reinforcing the need for action.

In September 2000, effective governance mechanisms led to leaders of 189 countries signing the historic Eight Millennium Development Goals. These were ushered in to reverse societal needs relating to poverty, primary education, gender equality, child mortality, maternal health, aids, environmental sustainability, and development. The eight issues led to the proposal of the landmark 17 Sustainable Development Goals (SDGs) for the global development agenda from 2015 to 2030.

A series of landmark events during the last decade have continued to fuel the advancement of sustainability (Table 1.1).

1.3.2 The Need to be Dynamic, Resilient, and Capable

Although there are many different interpretations of the term sustainability, when placed in the context of strategic management, guidelines for operationalising it in organisational settings are needed. But the modern world is constantly changing. To illustrate the overall conditions of *volatility, uncertainty, complexity,* and *ambiguity*, the acronym **VUCA** was introduced in 1985. However, in 2018, professional futurist Jamais Cascio (2020) introduced a new framework that better addresses modern phenomena, named **BANI**, Brittle, Anxious, Non-Linear, and Incomprehensible (Figure 1.2).

Artificial intelligence (AI) has influenced business and management practice. The escalation of AI is restructuring industries at an unparalleled pace. As AI continues transforming employment and jobs, many professionals question: *Which jobs are safe, and where are the highest-paying opportunities in this new era?*

A recent *Telegraph* (2025) article examines the impact of AI on employment, shedding light on sectors that stand to benefit and those that might be disrupted. It's clear that AI is

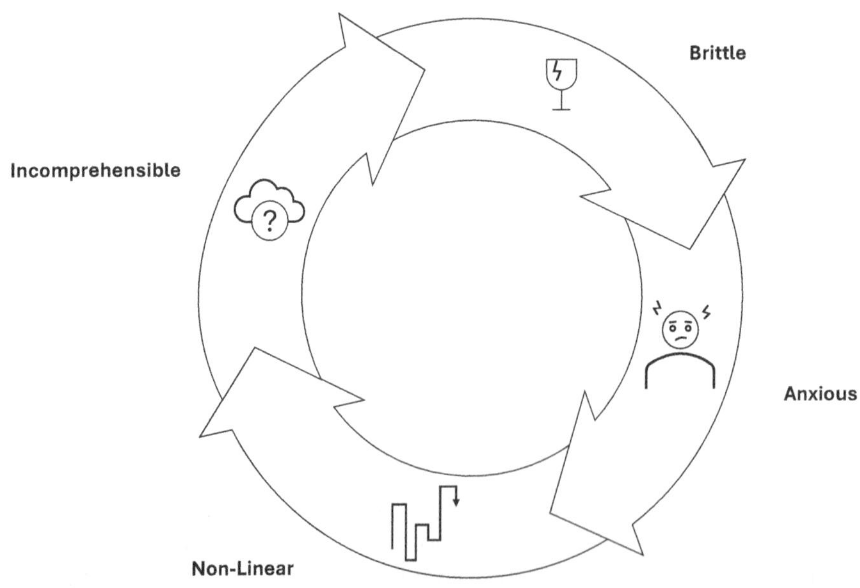

FIGURE 1.2 BANI (Brittle, Anxious, Non-Linear, and Incomprehensible) framework

not just about automation and increasing productivity, but it's about creating entirely new job roles, augmenting existing ones, and even creating more flexible careers that didn't exist a decade ago.

While nothing is safe in this turbulent world, senior roles that require complex decision-making, **innovation**, creativity, and human interaction will be resilient. Sectors such as healthcare, technology, finance, and engineering will continue to thrive, with the demand for some skilled professionals affected. AI engineers, data scientists, and cybersecurity experts are more essential than ever. Nascent technologies will become influential, and lifelong learning, upskilling, and continuous learning will be vital to staying ahead of the curve in this AI-driven world.

Holistically, three perspectives allow us to make observations: technology is reshaping how firms compete, strategies, and reorganising operations. Not only are large language models changing the landscape of data science, cybersecurity, and generative AI, but they are also now heavily influencing organisational strategy.

For example, NVIDIA, a San Francisco-based manufacturer of AI super chips, has experienced a meteoric surge in the global stock markets. At the time of writing, its market capitalisation was more than $4 trillion, placing it ahead of the dominant players. By taking first-mover advantages in its AI field, it is well-positioned to continue to exploit opportunities. Interestingly, DeepSeek, a Chinese AI company, has thrown the market into disarray, with its low-cost manufacturing capability rattling stock markets.

This illustrates the power of new business models and pathways for value creation. Staff need to appreciate and understand the long-term strategy and have a sense of purpose and direction. Perception can change daily based on the market sentiment. Those charged with implementing the strategy move from having a good day to a bad day, and then to the next.

However, new heuristics are scarce, and the perceptual changes have taken their toll on staff, resulting in higher staff burnout and worse work-life balance levels. Chief sustainable officers (CSOs) are not immune, as research has shown that burnout rates are higher when leading a sustainability-themed strategy than when pushing through a traditional approach.

1.4 Importance of Sustainability in Modern Business and Societal Context

Drawing on the earlier sections of this chapter, the historical trajectory of sustainability in a modern business and societal context is pivotal for success. Prescience is necessary for identifying winning strategies and understanding past failures.

Regarding industrial decarbonisation, commentators are drawn between "sunset" and "sunrise" firms and their sectors. Being carbon-intensive, industries such as oil and gas, mining, and petrochemicals have benefited from historical advantages (Verrier and Strachan, 2024). Still, they are now under pressure to change their operations to align with today's sustainable world. The latter are low-carbon or zero-carbon industries that are attractive to green investors but possess low levels of business relationships to capitalise on the available funds.

1.4.1 Modern Business

The markets have witnessed that most of the world's largest companies prepare and present strategic plans underpinned by sustainability goals. This is well encapsulated by Morgan

Stanley (2025), which noted that 80% of CEOs view sustainability as a driver of value creation and seek to integrate it into their strategic plans. This implies that sustainability is no longer viewed as merely a compliance chore. A winning modality incorporates a combination of economic, societal, and environmental realities. Interestingly, Morgan Stanley (2025) also asked their research sample, "Why are companies pursuing sustainability strategies?" and respondents were twice as likely to cite value creation rather than pressure from civil society.

Encouragingly, this is likely to increase as the EU's Corporate Sustainability Reporting Directive (CSRD) presents more work, but also a business opportunity. This EU legislation will require companies to provide detailed disclosures about sustainability **performance** and strategy-related issues. This conversation continues in Chapter 7.

Companies must think critically and explain how their strategies address sustainability, market perturbation, and the critical issue of materiality. For example, suppose a major clothing retailer identifies water use as a material resource, they must demonstrate this by aligning their strategy and goals with potential such impacts, which can be both harmful and beneficial to the environment.

The implications for companies are considerable, with organisation structures and processes integrating sustainability into strategic planning. Benefit corporations, also known as B-Corps, are for-profit businesses that meet high standards of economic, societal, and environmental **performance**. They are certified by the non-profit B Lab, which ascribes a five-point evaluation framework. Areas include customer, staff, governance, community, and environment. Patagonia is one of the most well-known B-Corps, with its unwavering commitment to sustainability, with customers willing to pay premium prices for its high-quality products.

Clear objectives must be embedded in strategic plans, involving a cross-functional business-wide approach to collecting high-quality, verifiable sustainability data. Transparency is key. The Board needs to be comfortable with the current sustainability impacts and the journey the business is undertaking; otherwise, key market **performance** indicators will suffer.

However, the payoff can be noteworthy for those leadership teams that can reinvent their business. Senior management teams and their boards need to be sapient, operating in a complex environment and needing clarification on sustainability objectives to deliver value for end-users. The rate at which organisations progress along their sustainability trajectory has been a considerable debate.

Critics are clamouring about the pace at which senior management teams are addressing planetary challenges. This sluggish pace can be attributed, in part, to the complex environment in which leaders operate. The increasing regulatory frameworks further complicate their efforts. Notwithstanding these challenges, there is a growing recognition that accelerating the pace of sustainability initiatives is crucial for achieving a competitive advantage.

We can witness several organisations seizing the sustainability opportunity:

- Despite battery problems, the automotive industry has seen a rapid growth in electric car stock. Goldman Sachs (2024) projects that Electric Vehicles are forecast to make up 50% of global new car sales by 2035.
- Future Marketing Insights reports that the global plant-based food market is projected to expand by three times, increasing from $11.3 billion in 2023 to $35.9 billion by 2033.

Plant-based food sales are poised to surge at a stunning compound annual growth rate (CAGR) of 12.2% between 2023 and 2033.
- Nike's Flyknit Trainer generates an average of 60% less waste than traditional footwear. For example, the luxury brand Stella McCartney is pioneering the use of regenerative cotton to create high-end fashion without harming the planet. Such companies are supporting the movement towards a more sustainable fashion industry.

The case for how sustainability drives value continues to gather pace. The broader view of value offers a theoretical and practical lens through which stakeholders can interact with the firm. In this sense, stakeholders can be a valuable focus for a sustainability strategy. If successfully performed, organisations can achieve several successes.

In their research, the Boston Consulting Group (2025) asserts six ways to link sustainability and value creation:

- Price premium
- Customer retention
- Reducing the cost base
- Accessing new profit pools
- Mitigating regulatory risk
- Market expansion.

They note that 80% of corporate sustainability-related announcements fail to meet best practices. In a piece of 2023 research reported in their 2025 study covering mining, automotive, and consumer goods, they observed that the market disproportionately rewarded firms when they included at least five of the following in their announcement:

- Material to sector
- Clear on funding
- Connected to core strategy
- Include tangible goals
- Third-party verified
- Materiality to the firm
- Linked to value creation.

The last bullet point provides evidence that sustainability extends beyond regulatory compliance.

1.4.2 Societal

Amidst all the writings, a salient question to address is the role of business in society. This presents opportunities for business leaders to develop impactful strategies that outlast the initial feel-good factor of the launch. Successful sustainable strategies can drive job creation and contribute to societal progression in terms of quality of life. Societal solutions can bridge the inequality gaps and make access equitable for all. Healthcare is a prime example that can save lives.

The interface between business operations and societal needs can facilitate the translation of external social challenges into business priorities. The CSO can manage the tensions of competing stakeholders' requests. Otherwise, it will be challenging to prioritise decisions about what to address and defer. The power dynamics can affect the concerns of marginalised communities, and the CSO must be vigilant about who gets heard. With the CSO functioning effectively, this interface can drive meaningful change, but resource limitations must be acknowledged.

The latticed nature of sustainability and improved quality of life is discussed in many arenas, from health to economic stability. This now requires a historical, political, and social consciousness for radical change. In this context, movements for worker empowerment, environmental sustainability, and social justice often challenge the concentration of economic power in large Western firms. The sustainability agenda posits a more decentralised and community-based model of economic organisation. Uncovering the interrelationships among and between actors and the market is advisable when faced with numerous opportunities. To investigate these issues, this section will consider two examples: quality of life, inclusive growth and social justice.

Pursuing sustainable practices can yield multiple benefits. These can include better quality of life, cleaner air and water, a reduction in the incidence of diseases, and enhanced public health outcomes. Additionally, a balanced, sustainable development will create jobs, increase job security, and improve living standards for all strata of society.

A new sense of inclusive growth and social justice is manifesting in sustainability. Organisations such as the United Nations, with economists working alongside the unemployed and youth groups to create realistic growth initiatives, are embracing this globally.

The World Bank seeks to resolve the dilemma of the missing ingredient for inclusive growth. Such a situation affects public services, lowers wages and salaries, and perpetuates inequality. This is not merely a matter of economic statistics, but a profound transformation that impacts the very fabric of society. These organisations are fostering a more equitable allocation of scarce resources by addressing the root causes of inequality and providing marginalised communities with access to essential services and opportunities.

By integrating sustainability into their financing operations, development financial institutions (DFIs) have assisted developing countries in unlocking capital flows and providing technical assistance in sustainable economic development.

DFIs comprise National Development Banks (NDBs), Multilateral Development Banks (MDBs), and Bilateral Development Banks (BDBs). These banks differ as NDBs focus on financing projects within a respective state to support their economic growth, usually capitalised and owned by national governments. MDBs are supranational institutions established and owned by multiple governments, with their shareholders defining their purpose. Lastly, BDBs are also capitalised by national governments but specifically focus on bilateral cooperation and economic development in developing countries and emerging markets.

Looking into the future, the following will impact societal challenges that impact sustainability in modern business and society (see Table 1.2). Each of the following seven challenges represents a complex intersection of social, economic, and environmental factors that companies must attempt to ameliorate while pursuing sustainability goals.

TABLE 1.2 Societal challenges impacting sustainability in modern business and society

Societal Challenge	*Example*
1 Power asymmetries and economic justice	The concentration of economic power such as the so-called "Magnificent Seven," being the largest stocks Alphabet, Amazon, Apple, Meta, Microsoft, Nvidia, and Tesla, creates tension with local communities and workers.
2 Worker rights	The move towards sustainable practices during periods of **transitions** can raise questions about workers' protection.
3 Cultural heritage preservation	In the rush to modernise, there is a need to balance modernisation with the practices of indigenous and local communities.
4 Knowledge democracy	Western scientific approaches will create power imbalances in Global South knowledge production practices.
5 Quality of life	Moving away from sole preoccupation with GDP to consider well-being, environmental health, and social cohesion.
6 Inclusive decision-making	Provide a voice for marginalised voices during strategic planning processes.
7 Community autonomy vs corporate control	The tensions between decentralised community-based economic solutions with traditional management models.

1.5 Summary of Benefits

When sustainability and strategy are intertwined, advantages can include (see Figure 1.3):

1. Corporate Reputation: Stakeholders view branding as a key marketing asset. This can increase customer loyalty, especially among Millennials and Gen Z, who prefer to have relationships with firms that have strong social and environmental commitments. Building deeper social trust will help to create more authentic relationships.
2. Financial **Performance**: Pursuing sustainability strategies can deliver higher financial market metrics. Some organisations can charge premium pricing through differentiation strategies. More substantial financial **performance** can enable cheaper access to green finance and sustainable investment.
3. **Innovation** and New Market Opportunities: Sustainability-led **innovation** can create new products/services that are attractive to existing and new markets. Driving long-term shareholder value through sustainable business models can create industry ecosystem leadership.
4. Operational Efficiency: Organisations can lower operational costs by closely scrutinising resource and waste strategies. Creating regenerative business practices will strengthen resilience.
5. Attracting and Retaining Talent: An authentic commitment to sustainability can attract the younger workforce, who are increasingly prioritising societal, environmental, and social issues. The more mature workforce can be better prepared for senior leadership roles.
6. Resilience: By considering robust, sustainable processes, organisations are better positioned to adapt to future uncertainties. Enhancing climate change adaptation capabilities will help the organisation meet its targets. A more proactive risk management culture will future-proof the organisation.

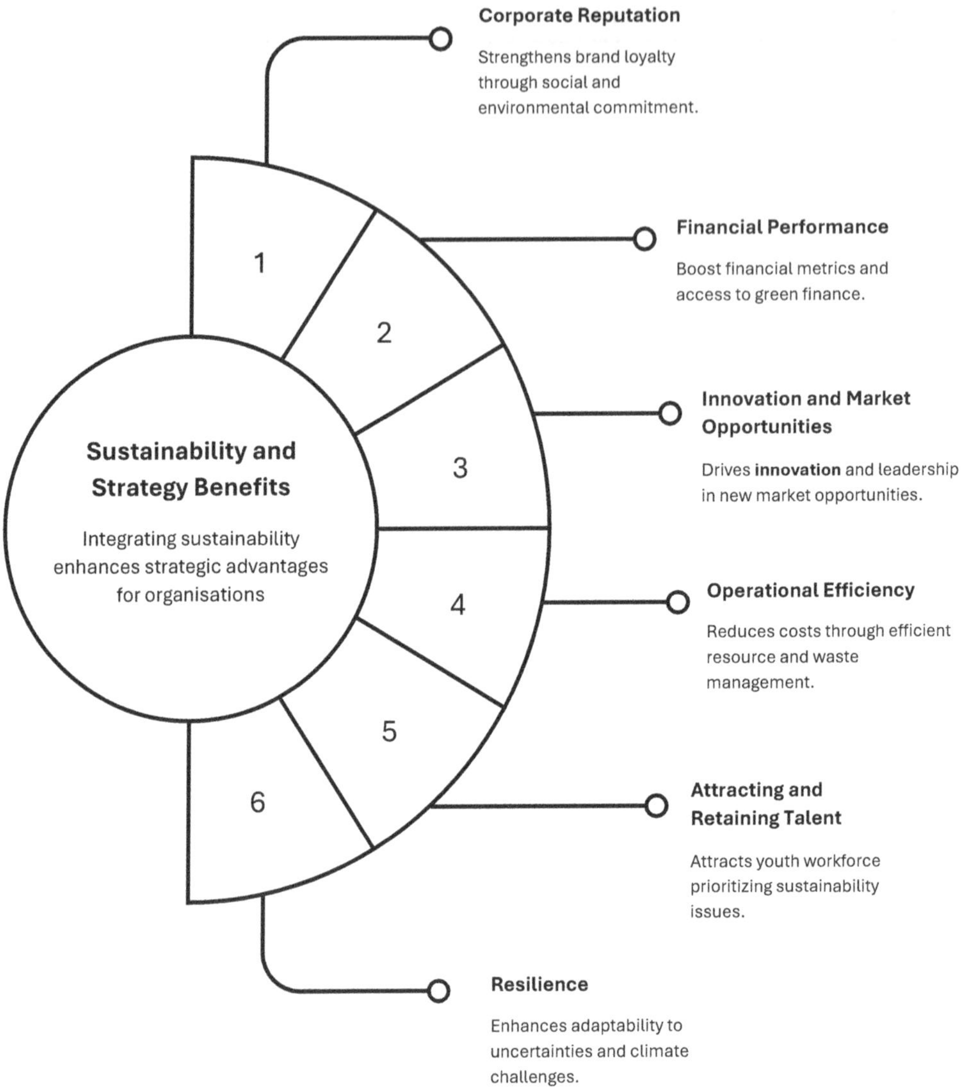

FIGURE 1.3 Sustainability and strategy benefits

1.5.1 Pathways to Sustainable Development

Sustainable development facilitates the transformation of critical pathways across various industries. In global industries, the pursuit of net-zero is increasingly viewed as a driver of new business models for value creation and capture. The raw materials of production processes must allow natural systems to regenerate. It is worth critically analysing connectivity issues across the UNSDGs. A strategic rather than a silo perspective will shed light on the interconnections, where an improvement in one area will catalyse improvements in other areas. These various pathways will help organisations to rewrite their sustainability playbooks. Organisations can **transition** from a singular focus to a more effective approach for enhancing value creation and capture.

At the industry level, organisations are in various states of **transition**, which occurs when the end-user expects sustainable solutions for their needs and is reluctant to overpay for products and services.

1.6 Overview of Textbook

1.6.1 Introduction

In *Sustainable Strategic Management: Leadership with Purpose*, we explore the transformative power of integrating sustainability with strategic management. A key theme throughout is demonstrating how **SSM** not only benefits the environment and society but also drives long-term business success. By adopting an interdisciplinary approach that draws on socio-economic, political, and environmental studies, we provide a critical lens through which to view the phenomenon under investigation, inspiring you to make a positive impact in your field.

The organisation's current state requires baseline assessments, with a focus on changing existing habits and mindsets to achieve authentic change. Sustainable Strategic Management is the desired state, representing ambitious thinking for the future, which is encapsulated into a vision, goals, and objectives. But in my experience, the elephant in the room is the tension, which multiplies the effort and resistance to change. Otherwise, these pushbacks prevent leadership teams from achieving their desired state.

1.6.2 Changing the Mindsets of Organisations and Individuals

This book prepares current and future leaders with the mindset to understand conflict dynamics and provides frameworks and tools to tackle the most crucial sustainable grand challenges. Solving grand challenges requires a differentiated set of problem-solving skills.

Problem solving is not when the leader has a hammer and sees every problem as a nail. Recent years have shown that organisations operate in complex environments, involving multiple stakeholders, and across global boundaries (George et al., 2016). Leaders must be able to inspire and lead their followers towards strategic aspirations. This textbook breaks new ground by shifting the emphasis from business sustainability to its practical implementation. From a leader's perspective, this modern textbook introduces sustainability topics and applies the lens of strategic management to provide solutions. This textbook covers the fundamental principles of **SSM**, including how to use it within various profit and non-profit contexts.

This book champions diversity by considering a breadth of perspectives and ethical implications. It then embeds sustainability into real-world applications, positioning you to address these challenges in an emerging context. By providing insights into integrating sustainability into strategic decision-making, this book equips the reader with the knowledge and tools to implement these strategies effectively. Each chapter aims to foster an understanding of sustainability through theoretical and practical perspectives, offering a comprehensive guide to integrating sustainability into your strategy.

This book aims to revolutionise strategic management by integrating cutting-edge academic theories with the latest sustainable business practices. The aim is to focus on postgraduate students, executives, and practitioners, equipping them with insights to thrive in the ever-evolving landscape of sustainable business. Stakeholder perspectives provide the context for strategic management, highlighting the multifaceted benefits of integrating sustainability into business strategies. This holistic approach addresses economic, social, and governance (ESG) responsibilities and drives **innovation**, efficiency, and competitive advantage.

Sustainability lies at the heart of today's organisational strategies, but its definition can vary widely to reflect the diverse challenges and priorities specific to each context. Organisational endeavours can view sustainability as a normative goal, whereas ambition does not equate to a strategy. Focusing on ambition may appear to incumbents as the way to lead, but there is little guidance on what to do for followers. Such aspirations will highlight the schism between the "North Star," a metaphor for the ultimate goal, and operational activities.

This book will focus on integrating sustainability into strategic management practice, identifying the strategies, structures, and processes to overcome bottlenecks. Ambition is a key organisational and individual attribute, but it is insufficient to attain the desired state.

Arguably, today's strategic management theory and practice require a holistic perspective that enables organisations to transform their current trajectory towards a multidimensional understanding of sustainability. This book offers a modern perspective anchored in the realism of current strategy formulation, implementation, and evaluation practices. Accordingly, the sustainability message is getting lost as organisations face choices with trade-offs in crafting their strategies.

1.6.3 Diversity and Inclusion for Readers

This book recognises the critical importance of sustainability within low- and middle-income countries, where unique challenges persist. Persistent inequality, poverty, and inequity in core services can be matters of life and death among the diverse populations of the Global South. By highlighting these challenges, we aim to foster a sense of empathy and awareness of the global impact of sustainability.

Moreover, this book is committed to inclusivity and diversity coverage across all aspects and builds on these issues by including material from diverse races, ethnicities, genders, and sexual orientations.

My experiences through academic networks and active participation in conferences and forums provide me with contextual and contingent knowledge of the Global South. This has benefited from connecting with fellow experts and practitioners in the strategy and sustainability fields.

We can link the fissure between theory and practice to deliver measurable, meaningful impact for tomorrow's world (see Figure 1.4). If you strive to understand the emerging "New Game" of sustainable impact, improve outcomes, and influence people, policy, practice, and communities, then this book is for you.

1.6.4 Book Structure

This book was written during a time of monumental generational shift in the commercial landscape. With this book, the aim is to create an army of professionals who can lead organisations to make the **transition** from sustainability aspirations to implementation.

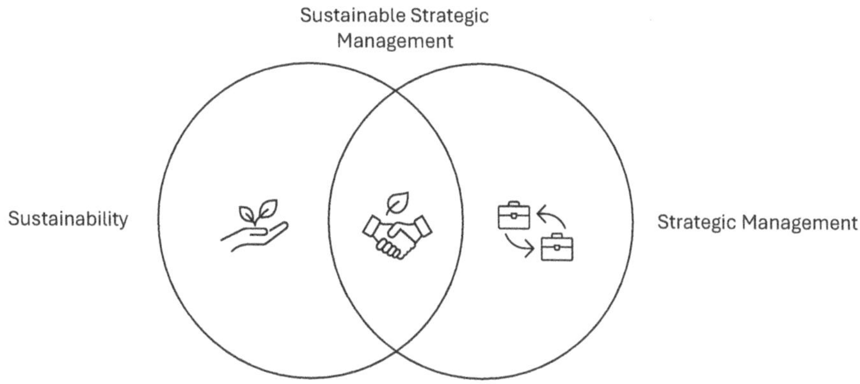

FIGURE 1.4 Sustainable strategic management overview

Strategy and sustainability must coexist. Their growing integration will require a shift from passive action to active collaboration.

Understanding how to nurture a generation of sustainable strategists and specialists will require equipping them with the appropriate frameworks, tools, and experiences from modern practice. Through academically supported, practical, and action-oriented content, *Sustainable Strategic Management: Leadership with Purpose* will help readers gain confidence to tackle new challenges and continue to drive their career and outcomes for organisations.

Forging new paths during these uncertain times will help overcome some of our planetary problems. In my work, one sees large- and small-scale organisations become paralysed with legacy self-inflicted rules. This book will help readers return to first principles thinking and improve their problem-solving capabilities.

You will learn to ask the right questions, use the appropriate set of frameworks and/or tools, and involve key stakeholders to make informed, sustainable strategy decisions. **SSM** shows a way out of the current dilemma of integrating sustainability into strategy, creating bolder options.

This book consists of four parts (see Table 1.3), which serve as building blocks that provide the reader with insights into four key areas. First, it equips the reader with insights into strategy through the lens of **SSM**. Second, it offers practical guidance in organisational analysis and reporting to assess how organisations are ready for the next stage of growth and fulfil reporting standards. Third, it addresses how sustainability assessment, sustainable business model, and organisational culture for sustainability align with each other. Finally, the last part draws upon the key ingredient of leadership, which can pull everything together. Without purpose, followers don't follow, and the transformational experience will fail to materialise. This capstone section prepares students and business executives for senior leadership roles where strategic vision must be translated into organisational transformation.

1.6.4.1 Part I: Foundations of Sustainable Strategic Management

1.6.4.1.1 Chapter 1: History and Implications of Sustainability to Business and Society

Climate change costs the world $60 million per hour, and new rules, such as the EU's CSRD, require businesses to be more transparent than ever before. The race to limit global warming to 1.5°C and **transitioning** to a low-carbon economy is on.

TABLE 1.3 Chapter structure overview – Sustainable Strategic Management: Leadership with Purpose

Section	*Chapter*	*Title*	*Focus*
Part I: Foundations of Sustainable Strategic Management	1	History and Implications of Sustainability to Business and Society	Traces the evolution of sustainability and its strategic implications for business and society.
	2	Strategy	Reviews strategic theory and challenges in the context of sustainability.
	3	Sustainable Strategic Management	Introduces dimensions and frameworks integrating sustainability into strategic thinking.
	4	The Seven Schools of Sustainable Strategic Management	Compares traditional and sustainability-focused schools of strategic thought.
Part II: Organisational Analysis and Reporting	5	Strategic Analysis	Applies internal and external analysis tools within a sustainability context.
	6	Case Study Analysis	Provides a step-by-step framework for evaluating sustainability case studies.
	7	Sustainability Measurement and Reporting	Covers ESG reporting standards, frameworks, and implementation challenges.
Part III: Aligning Sustainability, Models, and Culture	8	UNSDGs and Sustainability Assessment	Links strategic planning with UNSDGs and impact assessment tools.
	9	Sustainable Business Model **Innovation**	Explores how organisations can create sustainable value through innovative models.
	10	Leveraging Organisational Culture for Sustainability	Addresses cultural enablers and barriers to embedding sustainability.
Part IV: Sustainable Leadership	11	Purpose-Driven Leadership	Emphasises the role of values and purpose in driving sustainable change.
	12	Leadership in Sustainable Ecosystems	Investigates leadership strategies in multi-stakeholder ecosystems.
	13	Overcoming Organisational Pushbacks	Identifies resistance patterns and strategies for effective implementation.

Abbreviations: ESG, economic, social, and governance; UNSDGs, United Nations Sustainable Development Goals.

This foundational chapter provides essential historical context by illustrating how sustainability has progressed from Rachel Carson's seminal environmental awakening in 1962 to the planetary boundary frameworks of today. It demonstrates how environmental awareness has evolved from a minority concern to one of the most significant strategic priorities facing us all.

Salient pedagogical features include thorough frameworks for understanding the shift from shareholder primacy to stakeholder capitalism, as well as real-world examples from companies like Google and Walmart that demonstrate how to gain a long-term, sustainable competitive advantage. This chapter provides numerous examples of organisations that have seized the sustainability opportunity. The speed of development is illustrated in the Citadel's $12 billion climate intelligence Mini Case Study, which demonstrates how to swiftly convert a market opportunity and utilise weather forecast data to inform sustainability decision-making.

This chapter presents the book's methodical four-part structure, which is designed to provide leaders with valuable thoughts and tools for transforming and enhancing the **performance** of their organisations.

1.6.4.1.2 Chapter 2: Strategy

The strategic implications of the pandemic reverberate throughout modern organisations. Together with the imperative for sustainability, a fundamental reimagining of strategy formulation is now imperative. A pragmatic and flexible leadership approach is crucial for managing change and connecting corporate strategy with sustainability objectives.

As traditional strategy frameworks prove inadequate for today's fast-paced sustainability challenges, business leaders are confronting a fundamental paradigm shift. Sustainable strategic management is briefly introduced.

This chapter systematically examines the evolution of strategy from the 1960s to the 2020s, illustrating the challenges faced by leadership teams as they navigate uncertainty in their marketplaces. This chapter then considers the various perspectives of strategy, which provide a base for thinking about how to gain a competitive advantage. No review can ignore the seminal work of Mintzberg's ten schools of strategy. Challenges and reasons for falling behind **performance** targets have led to an increased emphasis on the implications, which can increase long-term risk. This is pertinent to the UNSDGs 2030 and net-zero 2050 deadlines.

Critical pedagogical features include the shareholder capitalism vs stakeholder capitalism Strategy Nugget. The Oxfam Mini Case Study presents a not-for-profit perspective, examining the capital allocation process and considering factors such as the number of billionaires.

1.6.4.1.3 Chapter 3: Sustainable Strategic Management

Today's strategist recognises the need to tackle the grand sustainability challenges. Yet, many still use the old, trusted causal models of the past that seek to optimise **performance.** This chapter asserts that for organisations to make the **transition** from strategy to **SSM** practice, it needs to be dynamic for the new normal. To make the **transition** will require a reconfiguration of expert action and processes within a context of inter-, cross-, and multidisciplinary thinking.

Changes in the external environment have motivated the need for sustainability in business education. This book contributes to this void. To tackle societal concerns, a multidimensional perspective is adopted. A strategic management spectrum illustrates the differences between the old and new ways, which differ from a top-down to a more distributed and consultative decision-making culture. A starting point is to gauge the organisational positioning in terms of old and new practices.

This chapter provides two sustainable strategy toolkits: the seven dimensions of strategic management (1) and the five **transition** levels of the **SSM** journey (2).

The Nigerian Geregu Power Plc Mini Case Study illustrates the momentum towards net-zero in the natural-gas-fired combined cycle gas turbine facility. The BT Strategy Nugget features the principal shareholder, billionaire telecoms tycoon Sunil Bharti Mittal, who orchestrated a two-day strategy meeting with the BT Board.

1.6.4.1.4 Chapter 4: The Seven Schools of Sustainable Strategic Management

This chapter delves into the specific schools of thought within **SSM**. Various approaches exist reflecting the multidimensional nature of sustainable and strategic decision-making. Adopting a similar style to Mintzberg's Strategy Safari, with its ten schools of strategy, this chapter critically analyses the following seven "Schools":

1 Traditional strategic management
2 Corporate social responsibility approach
3 Environmental sustainability and green strategies
4 Social **innovation** and inclusive business
5 Circular economy and cradle-to-cradle design
6 **Innovation** and disruption
7 Global South perspectives.

"Sustainable Strategy Toolkit (3) – The **SSM** typology" offers a structured approach to understanding the phenomenon under investigation. By prioritising different constructs, this reduces complexity and highlights areas of focus by adopting a shared vocabulary for discussing **transition**, strategy, and **performance.**

NVIDIA's $4 Trillion Mini Case Study illustrates a blueprint for the AI winner-take-all **performance**-driven economy. The Strategy Nugget shows how the seven schools of **SSM** interconnect to form a holistic approach.

This chapter closes with an **SSM** definition, together with a table that reinforces the applicability to practitioners through the translation of each school. The competitive logic is that organisations focus on two to three dimensions (financial, stakeholder, and environmental), but mastering all seven dimensions creates a competitive advantage. The sustainability challenge is to develop strategies that achieve solutions within both business and planetary constraints.

1.6.4.2 Part II: Organisational Analysis and Reporting

1.6.4.2.1 Chapter 5: Strategic Analysis

Today's BANI business environments require leaders to possess sophisticated analytical capabilities that integrate sustainability considerations with classical strategic thinking.

This chapter considers the popular salient strategy frameworks and tools taught in most postgraduate strategic management/strategy modules.

Sometimes, the discrepancy between a student's effort and outcome may stem from differences in their backgrounds. While this diversity enriches classroom discussions, it also means that such students may lack a foundational understanding of strategic management concepts. Without prior exposure to strategic frameworks and tools, students can find it challenging to identify the **innovative** intricacies of strategic analysis.

This chapter will equip students with the adaptability and foresight required to confront the strategic uncertainties looming on the horizon, fostering a culture of creative imagination. A good starting point for strategic analysis is to address the 5Ws and H (who, what, when, where, why, and how) to gain the overall picture.

Students can create bold case study solutions by meticulously analysing the internal and external environments and leveraging third-party insights to guard against bias. Instead of becoming overly fixated on extrapolating existing paradigms, the student should look forward and try nurturing a new projectile for the organisation. New and ambitious aspirations to enhance **performance** are vital. Readers are also introduced to the spectacular Mini Case Study collapse of Builder AI.

1.6.4.2.2 Chapter 6: Case Study Analysis

Analysing case studies is a part of the business school curriculum. However, students may need help with engaging in case study analyses within their studies. Students may consume the case study, but may require more real-world experience in decision-making and **performance** improvement. So, applying theoretical knowledge to business scenarios can be arduous at the beginning of the module.

Balancing multiple perspectives on sustainability within the classroom and reconciling conflicting opinions is becoming increasingly challenging. These require facilitated discussions, critical thinking exercises, and fostering an open-minded approach. The need for standardised evaluation metrics for sustainable strategies poses difficulties in objectively assessing case study analyses. This chapter provides a ten-step framework for performing case study analysis in the era of sustainability. The Chinese Tencent Mini Case Study illustrates the strategic implications of partnerships for universities.

Analysing a business situation needs a formalised plan of action. The case study analyst should strive to understand all elements of a particular business situation to recommend actions that can improve it. The entire process must be systematic. In an **SSM** case study analysis, there should be an organised set of principles and procedures for examining a particular situation and making appropriate recommendations. The case study method becomes an effective teaching device when students are encouraged to analyse the presented data and formulate their recommendations.

1.6.4.2.3 Chapter 7: Sustainability Measurement and Reporting

Moving beyond the economic lens, the focus is on the growing awareness of environmental and social impacts. Principles and standards now underpin the measurement and reporting agenda. CEOs and their leadership teams increasingly recognise the need to keep stakeholders informed about levels of **performance.**

For measurement, this chapter examines three indicators: economic, social, and governance. Key frameworks and standards for sustainability measurement are considered. Some principles and approaches to measuring sustainability, including International Financial Reporting Standards (IFRS), IFRS S1, and IFRS S2, are analysed. The CSRD, which came into effect in January 2023, was introduced, marking a significant shift as compliance and reporting are now mandatory. Consideration is given throughout this chapter to some of the current problems of Sustainability Measurement and Reporting, including a lack of standardisation, materiality determination, integration with financial reporting systems, and stakeholder engagement.

The Mini Case Study of Singapore Airlines and the Strategy Nugget of HSBC sustainable risk management provide global perspectives of two multinationals. These help the reader gain insights into the now-mandatory reporting for organisations.

The final section of this chapter stresses the need for companies to use a comprehensive and multifaceted approach as they begin to deliver the required reports.

1.6.4.3 Part III: Aligning Sustainability, Models, and Culture

1.6.4.3.1 Chapter 8: UNSDGs and Sustainability Assessment

Before delving into the UNSDGs, it is essential to have a clear understanding of their historical development, which dates back to the late 18th century. The term Industrial Revolution provides a context for transformations since the late 18th century. Over the last 250 years, human existence has witnessed and benefited from numerous breakthroughs.

Today's organisations refer to the 17 UNSDGs. Their sustainability environmental reports emphasise the critical role of strategy in shedding light on the environmental consequences of organisational strategic endeavours. Critical sustainable assessments are explored, including ecological footprint analysis, carbon footprint measurement, and life cycle assessments (LCAs).

This chapter integrates sustainability with strategic planning. By intertwining sustainability into strategic frameworks, organisations enhance their operational **performance** and contribute to advancing the UNSDGs.

Specific assessments considered are as follows LCA, Environmental Impact Assessment, Social Impact Assessment, Carbon Footprint Assessment, Ecological Footprint Analysis, Biodiversity Impact Assessment, SDGs Alignment Assessment, Social Return on Investment Analysis, Triple Bottom Line (TBL) Assessment, Circularity Assessment, Supply Chain Sustainability Assessment.

The Mini Case Study of Barbados' UNSDG and Strategy Nugget of counting the cost of EU sustainable supply chains provide some rich insights into both practical contexts.

1.6.4.3.2 Chapter 9: Sustainable Business Model Innovation

Business models combined with AI are a transformational combination with profound implications for sustainability. Integrating AI into business operations, organisations can optimise resource allocation, reduce waste, and enhance decision-making.

Moreover, with markets in flux, business model interest continues to gain momentum as organisations adopt strategies around value capture and managing the supply and demand side of operations.

This chapter explores the integration of sustainability and business model, examining how organisations can enhance **performance** while advancing their sustainable goals and mission. It discusses innovative business models using a value proposition framework. By re-envisioning products, services, and processes, organisations can eliminate waste generation, extend product life cycles, and foster the regeneration of natural systems. Innovative business models are assessed using a UNSDG focus value proposition framework. A business model canvas is proposed with sustainability and **SSM** issues.

The concept of value is a fundamental premise in strategy, and an overarching framework of value capture, destruction, and missed opportunity is considered. From this perspective, the CEO can ensure the organisation is actually delivering meaningful outcomes for its stakeholders.

Higher education is the focus of the Mini Case Study, which explores the concept of unlocking value through a multi-sided business model. Jaguar Land Rover's *Reimagine* strategy delivers a Strategy Nugget with a sustainability-rich vision of modern luxury by design.

1.6.4.3.3 Chapter 10: Leveraging Organisational Culture for Sustainability

This chapter is not an exhaustive comparative study of organisational culture, but considers the phenomenon of implementation deficits. Organisational culture is a multidimensional field of research and practice. Multiple perspectives in the literature offer a richer understanding of the phenomenon; however, CEOs continue to complain about resistance to change, competing priorities, and resource constraints.

Indeed, organisational culture should be treated as a behavioural process involving staff at all levels. For instance, staff who can operate across silos in their boundary-spanning roles are pivotal. They play a vital role in breaking down silos, which create blockages to the change journey and necessary **performance** attainment. By bridging internal and external boundaries, boundary spanners help organisations respond effectively to changing market conditions, customer needs, and competitive pressures.

The Competing Values Framework has stood the test of time, with slight variations that can help leaders. Gamification strategies can help overcome cultural inertia; a table illustrates the salient relationship. **SSM** and organisational culture challenges are discussed to act as a conduit between the two concepts. Cultural issues in emerging regions, as seen through the lens of the Caribbean, help to overcome historical and structural legacies.

The seven myths of organisational culture in sustainability strategy development Mini Case Study are based on consulting engagements. The Strategy Nugget on Patagonia, the sustainability champion, enables the reader to delve into its success.

1.6.4.4 Part IV: Sustainable Leadership

1.6.4.4.1 Chapter 11: Purpose-Driven Leadership

In terms of purpose, leaders need to possess a laser-like focus on providing direction to guide their followers. However, with AI being a disruptive force that transforms work, calls are being made for a fundamental and **innovative** rethink of how leaders make the **transition**.

This chapter emphasises the essential elements of purpose-driven leadership, which is emerging as a transformative force for modern firms. The role of purpose-driven leadership emphasises aligning organisational goals for each actor concerning ESG. In this context, change management is persistent, but strategy, technology, and market offer can cause leaders to suffer fatigue.

Serendipitous inspiration is often one of the missing ingredients that can impose huge costs, but deliver unexpected **performance** benefits. Change management can buckle under the strain without staff buy-in to the purpose. Failure to address this can erode followers' faith and may lead to a slow-motion catastrophe. Organisational trauma, the influence of AI, ethics, and UNSDGs are discussed.

"Sustainable Strategy Toolkit (4) – Triple A Leadership Framework" outlines three essential dimensions of leadership – Accountability, Authenticity, and Agility.

The Hitachi Mini Case study, which refers to its PLEDGES sustainability plan, provides some valuable insights. The Unilever and Accenture Strategy Nugget shows how AI can enhance productivity.

1.6.4.4.2 Chapter 12: Leadership in Sustainable Ecosystems

Operating as a leader within an ecosystem requires a multifaceted approach that is adaptive to address the complex environment. This applies in biology and now business organisations, and the bioeconomy deploys renewable resources to produce food, energy, and goods.

Today's pro-growth strategies require value propositions that are attractive to stakeholders. Times have moved beyond the old economic model of **performance**; we now operate in a multi-stakeholder ecosystem marketplace. A crucial currency is one of value; this chapter considers several examples of leadership value creation along the **transition** journey.

As discussed in this book, **SSM** requires leaders to detect emerging trends and changes in ecosystems. This will provide early warning signs about shifts in stakeholder behaviour, AI, and regulatory changes. Strategic foresight tools are used to prepare for multiple futures, enabling leaders to create contingency plans that strengthen their resilience.

Leadership for sustainable ecosystems will involve how formal organisational design impacts the **innovation** of its members. In addition, managing cooperative strategy with other businesses and collaborative endeavours between industry and government are mentioned.

The Green Banks Mini Case Study takes a brief stock of the provision of green finance. Coca-Cola Corporation is used as a Strategy Nugget to illustrate another example of corporate backtracking.

1.6.4.4.3 Chapter 13: Overcoming Organisational Pushback

Organisational pushback in a sustainability context costs organisations considerable sums in their TBL **performance** metrics. The last chapter provides insight into some of the challenges that leaders can face when attempting to implement **innovative** sustainability-related projects.

These may occur in various guises, such as active or passive resistance. Leaders may face pushback during sustainability change management **transition** programmes for familiar reasons, including fear of the unknown and a lack of trust. Such pushback can be associated with adverse behaviours that include sabotage.

At the individual level, flagrant denial of responsibility must be tackled head-on. Otherwise, the change management project could get pushed into the long grass. Internal resistance may stem from entrenched positions among the leadership team, where traditional profit-centric mindsets clash with the perceived bloated costs and uncertainties associated with sustainability initiatives. Symptoms of organisational resistance are examined.

The term EDI (Equity, Diversity and Inclusion) gets used, but the term comes with baggage. The bandwagon has existed for decades, but attaining diversity is not always meaningful. Staff brought in with an EDI mission can leave if lived experiences in the organisation are not in alignment.

Moving beyond ESG compliance is the final Strategy Nugget, which highlights blind spots. The final Mini Case Study, The €60 Billion Novo Nordisk Wake-Up Call, reinforces the turbulent nature of the markets.

"Strategy **Innovation** Toolkit (5) – Sustainability Strategy Matrix" maps the organisation's approach and current positioning along strategic focus and governance integration.

1.7 Self-Reflection Questions

1 How does limiting global warming to 1.5°C compared to 2°C impact global economic stability, and what are the potential benefits for businesses and societies?
2 What are the main challenges and opportunities for businesses **transitioning** to a low-carbon economy, and how can they effectively address them?
3 Provide a detailed synopsis of one significant event in tracing the evolution of the sustainability concept from its inception to the present day, highlighting key events and milestones that have shaped its development.
4 Why is sustainability increasingly considered a critical component of strategic management in modern businesses, and how does it influence corporate decision-making?
5 How do corporate sustainability initiatives impact societal well-being, and what role do businesses play in advancing social equity and environmental justice?

References

Baumgartner, R.J. and Rauter, R., (2017). Strategic perspectives of corporate sustainability management to develop a sustainable organisation. *Journal of Cleaner Production, 140*, pp.81–92.

Boston Consulting Group (2025). Six ways to link sustainability and value creation. Available at: https://www.bcg.com/publications/2025/six-ways-link-sustainability-value-creation (Accessed: 15 January 2026).

Caradonna, J.L., (2022). *Sustainability: A history*. Oxford University Press.

Cascio, J., (2020). Facing the age of chaos. medium.com/@ cascio/Apr, 29.

Crutzen, P.J. and Stoermer, E.F., (2000). Global change newsletter. *The Anthropocene, 41*, pp.17–18.

Daily Telegraph (2025). The careers that will survive the AI revolution – and pay the highest. Available at: https://www.telegraph.co.uk/money/jobs/ai-revolution-what-jobs-are-safe-highest-paying-salaries/ (Accessed: 26 August 2025).

Fankhauser, S., Smith, S.M., Allen, M., Axelsson, K., Hale, T., Hepburn, C., Kendall, J.M., Khosla, R., Lezaun, J., Mitchell-Larson, E. and Obersteiner, M., (2022). The meaning of net zero and how to get it right. *Nature Climate Change, 12*(1), pp.15–21.

George, G., Howard-Grenville, J., Joshi, A. and Tihanyi, L., (2016). Understanding and tackling societal grand challenges through management research. *Academy of Management Journal, 59*(6), pp.1880–1895.

Goldman Sachs (2024). The future of four wheels is all electric. Available at: https://www.goldmansachs.com/intelligence/pages/the-future-of-four-wheels-is-all-electric.html#:~:text=Electric%20vehicles%20could%20make%20up,supply%20chains%2C%20and%20commodity%20markets (Accessed: 26 August 2025).

Kopnina, H., (2017). Sustainability: New strategic thinking for business. *Environment, Development and Sustainability, 19*, pp.27–43.

Lahneman, B., Walls, J.L., Unter, K.M.M. and Howard-Grenville, J., (2025). EXPRESS: (Re) focusing on planetary boundaries for corporate sustainability research. *Strategic Organization*, p.14761270251315632.

Lee, J.Y., Mascena, A., Rüegger, S. and Miller, E.M., (2025). Sustainable development at a temporal crossroads: Learning from the past while focusing on the future. *Journal of Business Research, 190*, p.115232.

Marketline (2023). Renewable refineries are crucial in advancing sustainability, Report Code: MLCS00004–033, August.

Mateus, S. and Sarkar, S., (2024). Bricolage–a systematic review, conceptualisation, and research agenda. *Entrepreneurship & Regional Development, 36*(7–8), pp.833–854.

McKinsey's (2021). COP26 made net zero a core principle. Here's how leaders can act. Available at: https://www.mckinsey.com/capabilities/sustainability/our-insights/cop26-made-net-zero-a-core-principle-for-business-heres-how-leaders-can-act (Accessed: 26 August 2025).

McPhail, K., Kafouros, M., McKiernan, P. and Cornelius, N., (2024). Reimagining business and management as a force for good. *British Journal of Management, 35*(3), pp.1099–1112.

Morgan Stanley (2025). Morgan Stanley Sustainable signals Corporates 2025. Available at: https://www.morganstanley.com/assets/pdfs/MS_Institute_for_Sustainable_Investing_Sustainable_Signals_Corporate_report_2025.pdf (Accessed: 26 August 2025).

Verrier, B. and Strachan, N., (2024). Sunset and sunrise business strategies shaping national energy transitions. *Renewable and Sustainable Energy Reviews, 195*, p.114330.

WCED, S.W.S., (1987). World commission on environment and development. *Our Common Future, 17*(1), pp.1–91.

Williams, A., Perego, P. and Whiteman, G., (2025). Boundary conditions for organisations in the Anthropocene: A review of the planetary boundaries framework 10 years on. *Journal of Management Studies, 62*(4), pp.1811–1846.

2

STRATEGY

2.1 Learning Strategy Objectives

Upon finishing this chapter, you will have the ability to:

1 **Knowledge-Based Objectives:**

- Elucidate the foundational theories and models of strategy.
- Appreciate the strategy nuances that can cause organisations to fail.

2 **Skill-Based Objectives:**

- Learn how to apply strategy at key organisational levels through theory and practice.
- Analyse and critically identify the leading sustainability challenges that organisations currently face and will face in the future.

3 **Attitude-Based Objectives:**

- Develop and cultivate a proactive and adaptive mindset to integrate sustainability into strategic management processes, fostering long-term success.
- Cultivate a leadership mindset during the change management initiative.

2.2 Introduction

The strategic implications of the pandemic reverberated throughout modern organisations, and together with the imperative for sustainability, a fundamental reimagining of strategy formulation is imperative.

Yet, sustainable approaches are normative in that they seek to prescribe the morally correct way of doing things for the planet. But after 60 years, more is needed to bring about faster and enduring change. Critically, analysing this approach exposes the limitations of current approaches to complex sustainability issues.

In contrast to conventional thinking, this book adopts a post-normative approach that goes beyond pronouncements and technical interventions, seeking to engage with

DOI: 10.4324/9781003516774-3

value-driven and socially challenging issues. **SSM** provides a critical lens for this thinking. Making the **transition** from strategy to **SSM** within new frameworks and tools will influence practice. However, the extant literature makes it clear that it is not just new frameworks and tools that will engender change, but solutions that incorporate a dynamic field influenced by cultural, social, and political factors.

As Schmieg et al. (2017) highlight, normative frameworks in sustainability often intersect with socio-technical systems, reinforcing our approach. Koff et al. (2022) also observe that complex norms are codified through legal measures too.

Post-normative sustainability establishes an overarching framework that integrates the economic, social, and governance (ESG) principles of sustainability. It encourages engagement by all actors with diverse values, norms, and practices that collectively help to make the **transition** in a context, understanding that these elements are interdependent and ever-changing in a globalised planet.

These concerns about global sustainability have led to intense conversations about problems and potential solutions. The rapid advancement of digital technology in the strategy literature and practice has led to the emergence of numerous platforms (Wang, Zhao, and Wang, 2024). The so-called magnificent seven of large American firms – Apple, Amazon, Microsoft, Nvidia, Meta, Tesla, and Alphabet – have been high-performing stocks and dominating investor portfolios.

But President Donald Trump's global tariff polices have created increased uncertainty, and chaos for strategists. Understanding sustainability demands a Gestalt approach to strategy formulation, which views organisations as part of an interconnected ecosystem where ESG outcomes are inextricably linked. At first glance, a paradigmatic approach to strategy provides a vision for the future, although it needs to be defined in terms of positioning and differentiation.

Leadership teams need to move the organisation forward while appreciating the strategic opportunities of a global marketplace. However, one of the pandemic's key takeaways is the necessity for leaders to be catalytic in preparing for the next crisis, which involves developing best-case and worst-case scenarios. Sustainability-themed strategies are no exception (Cai et al., 2024; Syväri, Tähtinen, and Nordberg-Davies, 2025).

Strategic management has not yet unified into a single paradigm and remains fragmented. Its interdisciplinary nature is increasingly broad, creating both richness and complexity in its foundations. However, this presents challenges in developing a unified framework. Its evolution is shaped by exogenous forces, including sustainability that transcends boundaries.

This book does not intend to delve into the diverse paradigms of scholarship and practice in a granular manner. It aims to inspire the practice of **SSM** within a global framework focused on sustainability. Pushing the narrative beyond lip service requires change with roadmaps towards tackling grand challenges.

In terms of sustainability outcomes, utilitarianism, which is premised on moral decisions that enable the greatest amount of good for the greatest number of people affected by the action, a humanitarian ultimate goal prevails (Crane, Matten, Glozer, and Spence, 2019).

Nonetheless, a cautionary message for researchers suggests that public, private, and non-governmental organisations (NGOs) seek outcomes that align with stakeholder interests. Such pluralist conceptualisation goes beyond the pure utilitarian message of the hedonists' view of pleasure and pain.

Regrettably, environmental pressures necessitate a revision to utilitarianism in today's post-pandemic, complex, fast-paced digital world. Leaders need to rethink their futures and identify critical bottlenecks in a more agile, dynamic, and flexible approach to achieve success.

2.2.1 What's Next?

The following section will provide a concise review of key strategy terminology and the challenges encountered by academics and practitioners. A suitable initial approach is to examine the core lexicon in use and taught during introductory business school modules in strategy. While strategy and strategic management are not synonymous, they are often conflated. Schendel (1994) asserts that strategic management constitutes a distinct field of study, with strategy as its primary focus. Comprehending how organisations identify, create, and capture value, and why some outperform others, remains the holy grail.

Nonetheless, additional areas have become of interest, leading to the fragmentation of strategy and strategic management fields with increasing disquiet (Durand, Grant, and Madsen, 2017) and in examining the origins of strategic management, Rumelt, Schendel, and Teece (1995) posed four essential questions that have influenced the discipline.

What is the behaviour of firms? What accounts for the differences among firms? What is the function of, or value added by, the headquarters unit in a multibusiness firm? What factors influence a firm's success or failure in international competition?

This chapter examines the underlying philosophies and evolution of strategy, from Sun Tzu's military doctrines to modern sustainability viewpoints. Subsequently, we examine the critical views of strategy from a comprehensive standpoint, including positioning, emergent, resource-based, and stakeholder approaches. Mintzberg, Ahlstrand, and Lampel (2008) delineated their ten schools of strategy in Strategy Safari. This chapter considers the unit of analysis of organisations and outlines their difficulties in managing regenerative strategy processes.

Differing strategy levels indicate that the context varies and influences strategic decision-making. Overseeing the transformation process requires that all aspects must adapt, regardless of the changes' unpopularity. Multi-modal activities will lie at the heart of stakeholder engagement.

The chapter concludes by emphasising the global significance of these strategies, particularly within the framework of a swiftly evolving economic and environmental milieu.

STRATEGY NUGGET

Shareholder Capitalism vs Stakeholder Capitalism

The crux of the sustainability challenge is the increasing evidence of the prominence of two contrasting paradigms in business.

The former is long established through Milton Friedman's seminal writings on maximising profit for shareholders. The latter expands the firm's responsibilities to all stakeholder groups. Edward Freeman argues that businesses should create value for all. This swing in thought continues to gain momentum in response to climate change and net-zero initiatives.

Stakeholder capitalism provides a contemporary approach to addressing systemic risks. For the strategist, implementation requires new forms of governance, accountability, and a cultural shift throughout the organisations. Balancing stakeholders' demands and organisational success beyond the financial narrative remains the challenge.

As the sustainability agenda gains ground, investors are becoming more concerned about social and environmental issues in global capital markets. These changes will have a profound impact on traditional strategic management practices, which are deeply rooted in shareholder capitalism. Leadership teams often struggle to adapt to this stakeholder capitalism, revealing a critical gap in organisational strategies.

Tackling this dichotomy requires making sacrifices in such a way that it instils sustainability into legacy strategic decision-making processes. However, media reports indicate that some leaders appear to be swimming against the tide.

Questions

1 How should the CEO redesign sustainability capital allocation processes to attain the financial returns demanded by the CFO?
2 What are the salient governance mechanisms that the CEO should implement to prevent stakeholder capitalism from being a performative rather than value-creating?
3 During the **transition** to stakeholder capitalism, what actions should the CEO take to maintain investor confidence?

2.3 Evolution of Strategy

The initial book on strategy stems from the writings of Sun Tzu. His book *The Art of War* was authored over 2,500 years ago, and many of Sun Tzu's insights and techniques remain pertinent in today's marketplaces. Sun Tzu theorises that strategy devoid of tactics is the slowest route to victory, and his four principal categories of warfare strategy – offensive, defensive, flanking, and guerrilla – have persisted in shaping the latest scholarly inquiry. The ancient Chinese adage, "The marketplace is a battlefield," remains pertinent for leaders. The military strategy provides a framework that enables strategists to distinguish between strategy and tactics.

Military strategy involves allocating resources to secure an advantageous position, while tactics focus on outmanoeuvring the adversary on the battlefield. This distinction is crucial; nonetheless, several instances exist where it's overlooked, leading to tactics being conflated with strategy. An often-referenced case study used in business schools is Apple vs Nokia. The rise and fall of Nokia were due to its failure to pivot fast enough in a rapidly changing smartphone market.

Over the past six decades, the evolution of business strategy can be categorised into the following periods (Figure 2.1).

2.3.1 1960s: The Birth of Strategic Management

The 1960s signified the establishment of strategic management as a separate discipline within the broader management domain. Key works, such as Chandler's (1962) *Strategy*

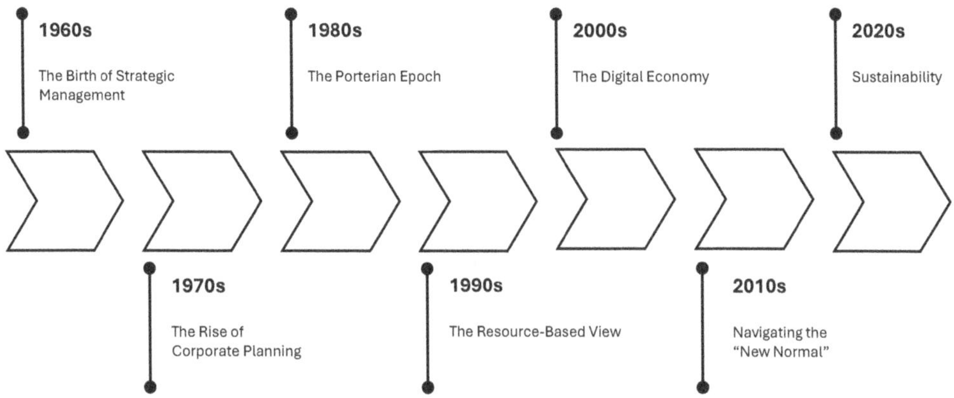

FIGURE 2.1 Drivers of the strategic management evolution 1960–2020s

and Structure, Ansoff's (1965) *Corporate Strategy,* and Andrews' (1971) *The Concept of Corporate Strategy,* laid the foundational theories of strategic planning. Chandler proffers three fundamental strategies: horizontal expansion in local, national, or multinational markets; vertical integration by acquiring suppliers or moving forward towards the end-user; and diversification into related or unrelated markets. Ansoff authored his seminal book, which is widely regarded as the inception of strategic planning. Andrew's work was a comprehensive model for developing and implementing corporate strategy.

This era witnessed the rise of strategic planning as a distinct activity, independent of other business operations, such as accounting and marketing. The emphasis was on financial budgeting, highlighting the necessity of adhering to annual budgets and making investment decisions grounded on capital budgeting protocols. The dominant value system in companies was "meeting the budget," resulting in the regular practice of multi-year forecasts and projections.

2.3.2 The 1970s: The Rise of Corporate Planning

During the 1970s, organisations began developing more scientific approaches to strategy, leading to the establishment of corporate planning departments. These departments developed five-year long-range plans and diversification initiatives. The 1973 oil crisis was a substantial disruption that highlighted the limitations of long-range planning, as it altered business conditions and rendered numerous forecasts inaccurate. Boards adopted a more prudent approach to their long-range planning. From a sustainability standpoint, it highlighted the weaknesses of over-reliance on oil, leading to measures aimed at improving energy efficiency, diversifying energy sources, mitigating risks, and fostering **innovation**.

This period highlighted the importance of maintaining ongoing alignment with the external environment and adopting a strategic mindset. This decade saw significant contributions, notably agency theory (Meckling and Jensen, 1976) and transaction cost economics (Williamson, 1979), which emphasised the significance of governance structures and efficiency in economic transactions. Organisational success hinges on profit maximisation, with strategic typologies – prospector, analyser, defender, and reactor (Miles et al., 1978) – illustrating how organisations can adapt to their contexts.

2.3.3 1980s: The Porterian Epoch

The 1980s saw the groundbreaking contributions of Michael Porter and his significant impact on strategic management. Michael Porter's influence grew as strategic planning declined in favour. Porter's *Competitive Strategy* (1980) and the Five Forces model became essential tools for analysing industry attractiveness and achieving competitive advantage. The **transition** from strategic planning to strategic management altered the understanding of industry structures and the execution of competitive advantage to surpass rivals. This era saw a shift away from diversification strategies and a greater emphasis on profitability and business-level strategy. Porter's frameworks remain a cornerstone of business school strategic management education, underscoring the importance of firms strategically positioning themselves within their industries to achieve a competitive edge.

Notwithstanding its extensive recognition, the academic literature advocates for more dynamic, context-specific approaches, which are problematic to operationalise, and raises concerns about the framework's validity. More recently, there is a need for moderate changes to incorporate sustainability.

2.3.4 1990s: The Resource-Based View

The resource-based view (RBV) emphasises firm-specific resources over industry structure (Penrose, 1959; Schumpeter, 1934). The 1990s marked a shift in emphasis to internal resources and capabilities. The RBV stream of research, defined by Wernerfelt (1984) and subsequently refined by Barney (1991), emphasises the connection between firm's resources and **performance**. Their emphasis is on how the firm's assets and capabilities can be a source of advantage over its peer group. RBV emphasises the importance of valuable, rare, inimitable, and non-substitutable resources as key to organisational **performance**.

Eminent researchers Prahalad and Hamel (1990) questioned the dominance of industry-level determinants of **performance**, arguing that firm-level resources and capabilities were crucial for sustained competitive advantage. This decade witnessed the emergence of dynamic capabilities theory (Teece et al., 1997) and knowledge-based approaches (Grant, 1996), highlighting the importance of leveraging internal strengths in response to changing environments. Mintzberg, Ahlstrand, and Lampel's (2008) analysis of the ten schools of strategy afforded a comprehensive overview of the evolution and diversification of strategic theory.

2.3.5 2000s: The Digital Economy

Organisations took advantage of the internet and digital technologies to innovate and streamline operations. The dot-com crash of 2001 marked a pivotal juncture in the evolution of business strategy, signalling a shift from a speculative mentality to a more disciplined and sustainable approach. This crucial moment compelled organisations to reevaluate and cultivate skills appropriate for the digital age (Phillips, 2003). The failure of numerous early internet ventures, which lacked a clear value proposition, prompted organisations to reassess their strategic foundations. This period of introspection led to the widespread adoption of e-business models, which offered the agility and flexibility necessary to navigate dynamic markets. Companies acknowledged the need for robust digital strategies to support long-term growth and resilience, setting the stage for the comprehensive digital transformations that would follow in the coming decades.

Conventional business practices were transformed as organisations leveraged the internet and digital technologies to innovate and streamline operations. Digital technologies expedited the rate of change, as online commerce facilitated new ways of engaging with customers and introduced novel value delivery methods. Strategy involves making choices and generating alternatives. Insights from the early 2000s profoundly influenced modern strategic methods, facilitating corporate success in a complex and dynamic environment.

Companies today continue to build on these foundational principles, integrating advanced digital technologies and data-driven insights to maintain competitiveness and drive sustainable growth.

2.3.6 2010s: Navigating the "New Normal"

The 2008 financial crisis and the ensuing worldwide economic downturn ushered in the 2010s, a decade defined by significant transformations in global economic trends. This constituted the second-worst financial crisis in the United States, culminating in severe strategic and policy issues. Following the crisis, businesses had to navigate significant shifts in consumer behaviour and market dynamics. The "new normal" was characterised by a downturn in household and corporate budgets, leading to prudent expenditure and an increased emphasis on value and necessity rather than luxury and excess. The era of conspicuous consumption came to an end, as individuals and businesses prioritised financial stability and resilience. This shift led to a rise in demand for affordable, high-quality goods and services, driving **innovation** and competition in the market. As CEOs recognise that substantial restructuring was occurring in their markets, the old business ways would not return. Survival was paramount; however, due to increased debt and a credit bubble, strategies had to deliver meaningful productivity gains.

Therefore, organisations need to be nimble, consistently adjusting their strategies to accommodate changing customer needs and preferences. This period witnessed an increase in regulatory scrutiny and financial reforms aimed at averting future economic downturns, necessitating organisations to implement more rigorous risk management frameworks and enhance transparency and compliance. The new normal demands that strategy be more dynamic, technology-driven, customer-centric, and resilient.

Over the last decade, the significance of strategic purpose has reached new heights due to ongoing threats from climate change and geopolitical instability. Strategic purpose offers a definite direction and a sense of meaning that guides organisations through tumultuous periods. It helps organisations maintain focus on their long-term objectives while navigating short-term uncertainties. This clarity is crucial for maintaining stability and resilience in the face of ongoing disruptions.

Strategic management in this period requires a focus on resilience, agility, and sustainability. By comprehending and adapting to the changing landscape, businesses can address obstacles and capitalise on the opportunities inherent in the new normal, thereby preparing themselves for future growth and success.

2.3.7 2020s: Sustainability

The ongoing coevolution of strategic management with the development of the Fifth Industrial Revolution, ESG initiatives, social justice movements, and the Next Normal pose both complications and opportunities. Businesses, policymakers, and educational institutions must unite to develop sustainable, inclusive, and resilient strategies that guarantee a balanced and prosperous future for all.

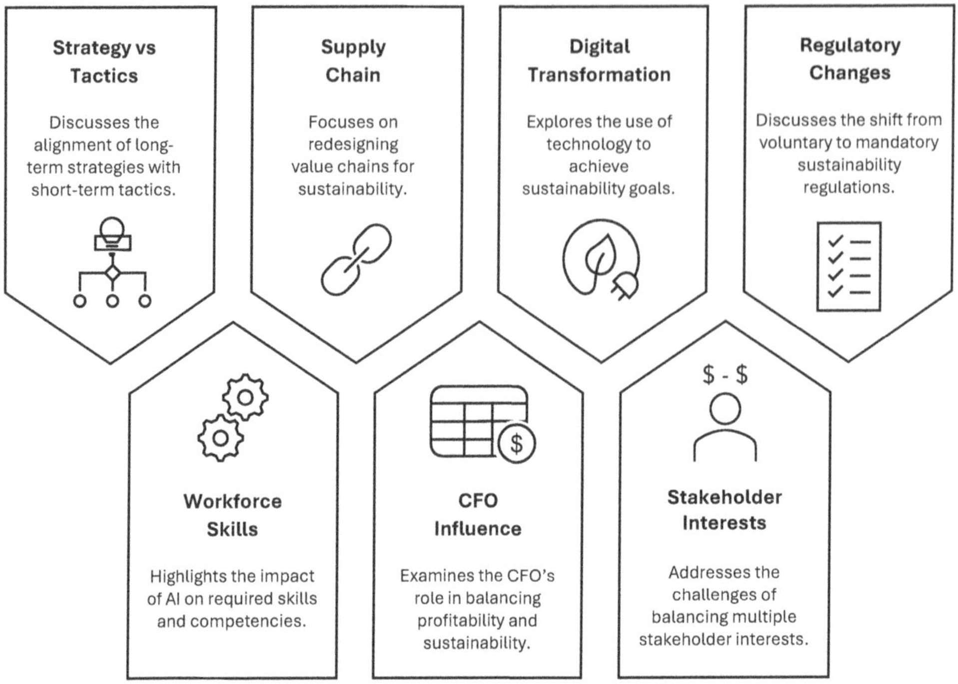

FIGURE 2.2 Sustainability strategy challenges

An example of where entities are changing their specific roles can be illustrated. The private sector is known for its skills in generating surpluses, the public sector provides welfare, and NGOs direct resources to social or environmental issues. However, in a sustainability landscape, businesses face legal constraints in profit maximisation, the public sector struggles with debt-laden balance sheets, and NGOs need partners to help address their issues.

We can observe that solutions are sought for new challenges (see Figure 2.2), but with old tools. The World Economic Forum's (2024) concept of "sustainomy" proposes a transformative way of generating economic impact. Governments can pivot from being just regulators to facilitators of change.

Sustainability leadership will continue to emerge through praxis, which translates strategy into practice. However, sustainability regulations and reporting will hinder business operations. Implementing rule-based systems can be challenging, especially in a rapidly evolving ecosystem. Indeed, effective sustainability governance systems will have to function as a holarchy supported by systems of accountability.

Geopolitical uncertainties and human rights issues will need to be closely monitored. Shifts in **innovations**, artificial intelligence (AI), resource use, and societal priorities will drive change. However, as developments unfold, the pace of change gathers pace. Major trends will include decarbonisation, circular thinking, urbanisation, curbing growth forecasts, and balancing food and consumption. Navigating these trends will be a rollercoaster ride, with leaders having to ensure long-term resilience and success for their stakeholders.

In conclusion, a pertinent question to consider is whether the strategy aims to achieve its aspirations; if so, why do many organisations formulate strategies that suggest they are planning to fail?

2.4 Perspectives of Strategy

After more than 50 years, strategy is no longer an unnecessary luxury. Most senior executives are educated in their fundamentals, and large corporations possess proficient strategy personnel and in-house strategy expertise. Nevertheless, the business world is replete with instances of bad strategies. Why is this? What compels a senior executive to back them when so much know-how is available? Often, leadership teams have vested interests, and implementing change can be expensive, so they are reluctant to do so.

However, despite the evolving landscape, which includes increased regulation, threats of terrorism, more demanding customers, changing technology, and the growth of the silver economy, excessive ambition, avarice, and other corporate vices may serve as potential catalysts.

In addition, the expansion and population-related demands of emerging markets, coupled with the ongoing digital revolution, prompt politicians to act with alacrity. This presumes that there is a sufficient level of long-term vision, human resource capability, and incentive alignment in practice.

Traditional three- to five-year strategic planning cycles may be inadequate to capture the nuances of each emerging market. However, any bloated bureaucracy may impede the effectiveness of strategic planning, which is viewed by some as endangered.

Certain observers, including Henry Mintzberg, contend that strategic planning is dead. Mark Twain, upon discovering that reports of his demise were erroneous, stated, "The reports of my death are greatly exaggerated." This book asserts that such missives tend to be based on inaccurate assumptions.

Strategy is the essence of the strategic management domain. The absence of a widely accepted definition has muddled theory and practice. Strategy definitions may encompass various categories. According to Rumelt (2022), strategy constitutes a method of problem-solving, and one cannot resolve a problem that is not understood (p. 13). It is noteworthy that if a strategy is to benefit an external stakeholder, it must be sustainable (Henry, 2021).

Table 2.1 focuses on some influential keywords and definitions of strategy.

2.5 Ten Schools of Strategy

"Strategy Safari," authored by Henry Mintzberg, Bruce Ahlstrand, and Joseph Lampel (2008), is universally recognised as an influential work in strategic management.

TABLE 2.1 Keywords and definitions of strategy

Category	*Definition of Key Works and Strategy*
Positioning	Porter (1996) Deliberately choosing a different set of activities to deliver a unique mix of value.
Emergent	Mintzberg (1987) Pattern in a stream of decisions.
Resource-based	Barney (1991) Conceptualises the firm as a bundle of resources, which include all assets.
Stakeholder approach	Chaffee (1985) As orienting metaphors or frames of reference that allow the organisation and its environment to be understood by organisational stakeholders.

Mintzberg, Ahlstrand, and Lampel integrate their extensive knowledge of strategy formulation with an authoritative catalogue of the ten schools (see Table 2.2) of strategy that have emerged over the decades. Their work elucidates and offers significant insights into the diverse approaches that constitute strategic management today, making it an indispensable guide for those seeking to navigate the complex landscape of business strategy.

The authors allocate ten chapters to investigating the book's different "schools of thought" on strategic management. They apply the metaphor of ten blind men, each endeavouring to describe an elephant, to exemplify these diverse methods. This imaginative framework not only makes the complex subject matter more accessible but also highlights the diversity and richness of strategic management practices. Strategic management is characterised by varying opinions, represented by the ten schools of strategy.

The introductory and concluding chapters, "And Over Here, Ladies and Gentlemen: The Strategic Management Beast," "Hang On, Ladies and Gentlemen," and "You Have Yet to Meet the Whole Beast," employ the safari analogy to introduce and summarise the journey through strategic management. Their work provides clarity and offers invaluable insights into the diverse approaches to contemporary strategy.

The complexity in terms of strategy and unit of analysis is illustrated in Table 2.3, which impacts their sustainability aspirations for their stakeholders.

2.6 Strategy Levels

A strategy will derive from an organisation's vision and mission. Nonetheless, multiple strategies may be necessary. Organisations must be prepared to pivot and consider backup options in the rapidly changing external environment. Possessing a plan B to pull out of the back pocket can be a helpful ploy when confronting threats in the marketplace. The

TABLE 2.2 Mintzberg, Ahlstrand, and Lampel (2008) Ten Schools of Strategy

School	*Approach*
1 Design	As a process of conception. Despite being widely advocated, it possesses weaknesses that are exposed in turbulent environments.
2 Planning	As a formal process. Strategy can be too static, which makes prediction difficult.
3 Positioning	As an analytical process. Ignores the soft management areas such as power, politics, and culture and is the approach for large firms.
4 Entrepreneurial	As a visionary process. Being the architect is an extremely demanding approach for the CEO.
5 Cognitive	As a mental process. Problems occur beyond the initial conceptual stage.
6 Learning	As an emergent process. Runs the risk of not adopting a clear strategy.
7 Power	As a process of negotiation. Can be a divisive process where muddling along becomes the norm.
8 Cultural	As a collective process. The vagueness of culture can make it difficult to know how things should be done.
9 Environment	As a reactive process. The complexity of the environment makes it difficult to know the salient force affecting the firm.
10 Configuration	As a process of transformation. Within the top management team there may be differing views of the reality facing the firm – pattern is in the eye of the beholder.

TABLE 2.3 Organisational types pursuing a sustainability mission

Strategy Unit of Analysis	*Category*	*Sustainability Strategies Dilemmas*
Energy companies Manufacturing companies Retail and consumer goods companies	For-profit	**Transition** to renewable energy, reduce regulatory risks, and access new markets in clean energy. Reduce production costs, minimise waste, enhance brand reputation, and drive long-term profitability. Meet consumer demand for eco-friendly products, optimise supply chains, and increase customer loyalty.
Healthcare organisations Charities Mutual financial institutions	Non-profit	Minimise waste and energy use to lower operating expenses and improve patient care services. Diversify income streams (e.g., through social enterprises or commercial partnerships), but doing so might risk diluting focus on the core mission. Profits are reinvested into the business or returned to the members, rather than being distributed as dividends.
City councils County councils Public transport	Government	Improve urban infrastructure, reduce environmental impact, and enhance residents' quality of life. Reduce the carbon footprint of operations, promote green jobs, and drive national progress towards climate goals. **Transition** to electric or low-emission vehicles, optimise routes, and reduce energy consumption.
Environmental Humanitarian and development Equality and human rights advocacy	NGO	Reduce environmental impact, enhance credibility, and attract donors focused on environmental stewardship. Promote sustainable practices in programme delivery and align with global sustainability goals. Advocates for equal opportunities for all citizens in the UK, regardless of gender, race, disability, sexual orientation, or age.
Worker cooperative Fairtrade CIC	Social enterprise	John Lewis Employee ownership can lead to a profound socially responsible business, providing both economic and personal benefits to its employees. Divine Chocolate Social mission to prevent exploitation of workers. The Big Issue Operates as a social enterprise and a CIC, with the mission to provide opportunities for people in poverty to earn a legitimate income.
B Corps There are over 6,000 Certified B Corps in 80 countries across 153 different industries	Hybrid organisation	Nespresso B Corps are certified companies that use the power of business to build a more inclusive and sustainable economy.

Abbreviations: CIC, community interest company; NGO, non-governmental organisation.

components of strategic management – position (context), choices (content), and action (process) – are essential aspects of the field.

The academic and practitioner literature suggests that, in certain instances, what is perceived as a strategy may not be a strategy (Vermeulen, 2017). Compo (2022) identifies five disqualifiers of strategy that serve as a powerful diagnostic for analysing strategies. He poses five fundamental questions that address the essence of the topic:

1 Is the opposite of the strategy statement true?
2 Are numbers and dates evident?
3 Is the strategy statement the same as the parent strategy?
4 Is there any part of the system that the strategy statement does not relate to?
5 Is the strategy statement a list of aspirations?

If you respond affirmatively, your strategy fails the test. But if you answer yes, your organisation may still have a good plan.

Strategy applies to various levels under different circumstances. The "Why" question is strategic, the "What" question is tactical, and the "How" question is operational. The CEO and their team must formulate strategies at various levels of the firm, including alliance, corporate, business, and functional levels. In terms of implementation, structure, processes, and culture are core enablers that can result in higher levels of strategic **performance**. A brief critique now follows.

2.6.1 Alliance-Level Strategy

In recent decades, the imperative for alliances has significantly escalated as organisations address the problems posed by market globalisation. Alliances are crucial for firm growth and survival, as they provide access to scarce resources. To achieve their corporate objectives, many firms are implementing collaborative strategies to maintain their competitive edge in the marketplace. Competition at both regional and global levels has shifted from individual firms to alliance networks.

Alliances constitute a substantial portion of an organisation's value, as evidenced by metrics such as revenue, assets, or market capitalisation. Discussions at the alliance level have now gained significant relevance, shifting from their original place at the periphery of corporate strategy. The prospects and challenges of the digital revolution have altered the commercial landscape, necessitating that leadership teams comprehend the emerging paradoxes affecting cooperation strategies (He et al., 2020).

2.6.2 Corporate-Level Strategy

A corporate-level strategy establishes objectives and formulates suitable structures and processes to achieve them. CEOs face ongoing pressure to maintain revenue growth, and an excessive focus on external positioning may result in organisations pursuing prospects for which they lack the necessary competencies to thrive. Furthermore, pursuing excessive opportunities may result in the depletion of resources. Contemporary successful businesses identify their core competencies and link their strengths with market prospects. The prospects sought are determined by external market analysis through financial measurements and internal capabilities, including personnel, knowledge, processes, systems, and interventions that might augment organisational value.

CEOs must spearhead corporate-level initiatives, making essential decisions to enhance business value. Mergers, acquisitions, and divestitures can erode shareholder value. Corporate scope decision-making transpires within companies; in addition to execution deficits, the strategy may not effectively address the fundamental grand challenge. Feldman's (2020) diagnosis of corporate strategy encompasses three essential components: leaders orchestrating decision-making within the organisation's confines, establishing contacts beyond the organisation's periphery, and delineating which firms function within the organisation's parameters (and which do not).

2.6.3 Business-Level Strategy

At this level, marketplace conflicts are determined, underscoring the essential importance of decision-making concerning the services and goods the organisation should provide. At this strategic level, organisations must recognise and leverage competitive advantages to distinguish themselves in the market. The emphasis is on understanding consumer needs, anticipating market trends, and innovating to maintain a competitive edge. Decisions have a direct impact on the company's market standing, revenue streams, and profitability. Consequently, a profound understanding of market dynamics and a proactive strategy are vital for success.

Strategic business units (SBUs) can be categorised according to product lines, divisions, and profit centres. Each SBU functions as a semi-autonomous unit inside the broader business structure, enabling focused strategies that address particular market niches. Nonetheless, decision-making at this level may be perplexing due to internal rivalry and the extensive variety of strategic typologies in the literature. These typologies encompass cost leadership, differentiation, focus, and other approaches. This variety of strategic alternatives necessitates that managers meticulously evaluate their internal and external contexts, identify their strengths and weaknesses, and choose the most suitable strategic method. The challenge lies in navigating this complex environment to develop and execute plans that align with the company's goals while effectively addressing competitive pressures.

2.6.4 Functional-Level Strategy

A functional-level strategy formulates the action plans required to fulfil the objectives specified in the corporate- and business-level strategies. Functional strategies translate overarching strategic objectives into precise operational objectives, ensuring that each department effectively contributes to the mission. These action plans can enhance efficiency, elevate quality, stimulate **innovation**, and augment client responsiveness. When all functional areas are linked with strategic objectives, the organisation may function cohesively and respond more swiftly to market changes.

Numerous leaders candidly assert that they operate within siloed organisations. Information is perceived as a source of power and is not disseminated for the advantage of others. This behaviour diminishes efficiency, morale, and output. CEOs must adopt authentic, customer-centric practices that are incorporated throughout all business processes, rather than existing in isolation. Numerous departments, including marketing, human resources, and accounting, undergo scrutiny, analysis, and thorough evaluation. They can no longer evade the influence of contemporary management theories about organisational operations, which eschew rigid functional silos. The current emphasis on isolated functions should be supplanted with a more flexible, cross-functional, and integrated approach to work.

Mini Case Study

Takers, Not Makers Oxfam 2025

Introduction

This case study examines the two-tiered world through the eyes of the Takers, Not Makers Oxfam 2025 report. With the business world still prioritising a growth mantra, this case considers the ripple effect on those living in poverty.

Government leaders create policies that address inequalities through both indirect and direct taxation. The aim is to improve the well-being of all societal segments. Often, pronouncements are made to convey the message that better days are ahead and persuade voters to stick with them.

Unfortunately, we are witnessing that it has never been better to be a billionaire, while vulnerable communities face multiple crises.

Addressing such a situation is one of Oxfam's core strategic pillars, so reading about this inequality through the lens of a leading international NGO committed to mitigating global poverty and injustice is interesting.

Oxfam Background and Context

Oxfam was founded in 1942 to address poverty and injustice globally. Over the decades, it has broadened its mandate to address rising global concerns, including climate change, conflict, women's work, and humanitarian crises.

Strategic Actions:

- Humanitarian assistance and resilience development
- Advocacy and campaigns
- Collaborations and community leadership
- Economic and social empowerment.

Oxfam's strategic initiative exemplifies a thorough commitment to address poverty and injustice via direct humanitarian assistance, advocacy, and sustainable development. Oxfam has made considerable progress in aiding vulnerable communities and championing a more just society by emphasising local leadership, tackling systematic injustices, and advancing climate justice. Oxfam's strategic initiatives highlight the importance of collaboration, creativity, and dedication to social justice in the ongoing fight against global poverty and injustice.

Growth of Billionaire Wealth

According to the report, 204 new billionaires were created in 2024, resulting in a wealth increase of $2 trillion. Growth in 2024 was three times faster than in 2023. Governments appear powerless to halt this trend. However, according to the World Bank, the number of people living in poverty has remained relatively stable since the 1980s.

So, where is billionaire wealth coming from? Oxfam cites that 60% of billionaire wealth either comes from inheritance, cronyism, corruption, or monopoly power. Despite such rampant growth, it looks like we will witness a trillionaire in the next couple of years, with Elon Musk in pole position.

The Global South lobbies for efforts to close the gap, but current financial systems curtail the responses. The Oxfam results include the startling figures that in 2023, the wealthiest 1% of the Global North received $263 billion from the Global South, which equates to over $30 million an hour.Some strategic implications that will keep recurring throughout this book:

- Changing stakeholder expectations, which give rise to societal expectations.How should resource allocation processes change with the rise of billionaires who are concentrating the planet's capital?
- Since wealth is not always generated by market competition, on-market strategising is crucial for governments.
- Those billionaires who possess market monopolies, such as Amazon, control 70% of online purchases in several European markets.
- Financial system asymmetries need to be addressed for the benefit of all members of society.

Questions

1 What role should Oxfam play in advocating informed decisions about equitable redistribution?
2 As monopoly power is a significant source of billionaire wealth, how should business strategists distinguish between unwarranted and beneficial market dominance?
3 How should Oxfam incorporate awareness of historical colonial relations into its strategic and operational plans?

Source: Oxfam (2025).

2.7 Sectors in Upheaval

Universities exemplify a sector under upheaval, necessitating transformative adjustments to enhance resilience and secure strategic advantage. Universities can rigorously match their strategic changes with sustainability goals in the external marketplace. Even prestigious universities like Oxford are not exempt from this trend.

Modern universities must progress by investing in bold plans to maintain their leadership in research, education, and public involvement. **Innovation** is essential to effectuate such transformation and advancement. Nonetheless, the fundamental assertion is that numerous aspects must change and evolve, even if such adjustments are not universally accepted at the outset.

Resolving this paradox presents a challenge; it is imperative. Global higher education institutions are persistently impacted by the educational cost crisis, a decline in international student enrolment, diminishing public support in real terms, and the cost-of-living challenge. The higher education model must adjust to the learner's decision-making psychology regarding study methods and locations. The current global transformations hold promise for the next generation of leaders, executives, politicians, and entrepreneurs. The current era of escalating expenses and diminished relative income renders the option to work and study concurrently, viewed through the prism of sustainability and social justice, a compelling opportunity for colleges.

Leadership teams now recognise the necessity to alter their existing strategies and embrace the new rules of engagement before it is too late. Contemporary organisations must function as catalysts for change to capitalise on opportunities. The organisational-level impact is significant, necessitating a robust value proposition, a value-creating process, a value exchange, and value capture related to sustainability efforts. This occurs in a realm where all sectors are transforming. For instance, local leaders at all levels operating within an evolving industry experiencing transformation may explicitly encompass the following industries:

- Financial services
- Tourism
- Renewable energy
- Green economy
- Blue economy
- Health
- Agritech
- Transport
- Public sector.

During the journey, organisations must prioritise customer-centricity, focusing on the human experience, and customers are at the heart of their decision-making. However, strategy should incorporate elements of familiarity and novelty, especially in the B2C marketplace. Strategy distinctiveness for consumers will have differing aspects in the B2B market. The former focuses more on products and services, while the latter focuses more on the vision and strategy (Figure 2.3).

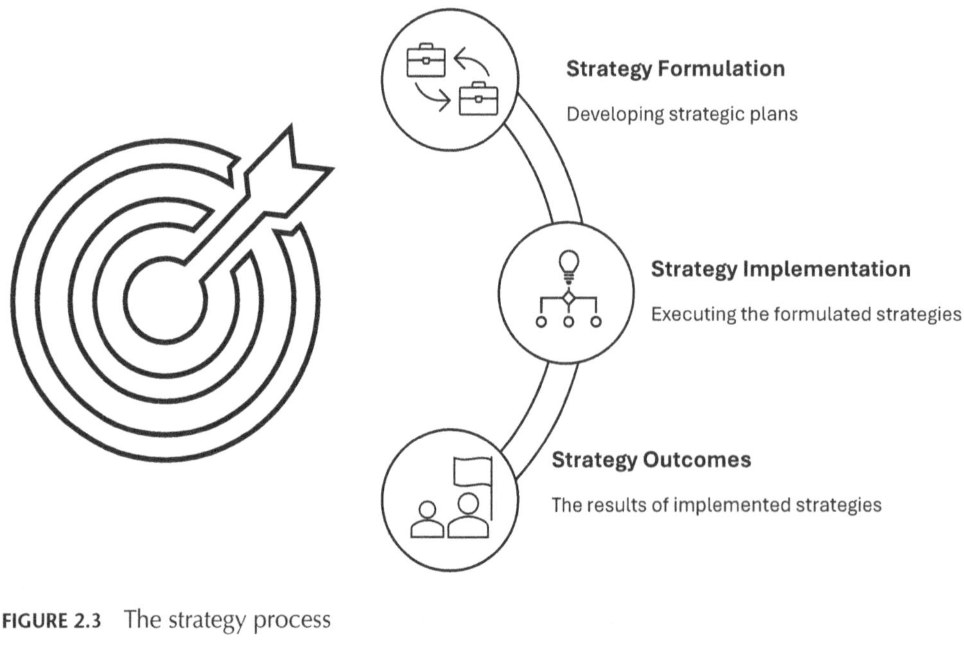

FIGURE 2.3 The strategy process

In the B2 marketplace, the onus is on creating a sense of urgency to encourage impulse purchases through limited time offers and discounts. A classic one is when you sign up for a free offer and then find that you have also signed up for an ongoing subscription, which you soon forget at your peril! The B2B focuses more on long-term relationships and creating bespoke solutions. The gestation period for achieving a sale can be much longer. The business will have a more sophisticated procurement process, which will increase the sales cycle. Organisations can foster growth and long-term prospects by creating strategies tailored to their specific context.

Strategy-as-practice (SAP) offers a fresh perspective on how to study strategy (Jarzabkowski, Lê, Seidl, and Vaara, 2025). But for any new contribution, generating insights is pivotal. Therefore, creating an **SSM** typology with an understanding of the microfoundations of sustainable strategies is apt. Making the **transition** involves strategising and organising activities involving actors in workshops.

SAP is now being recognised as a legitimate stream of process research. With its development marked by more than 500 publications (Jarzabkowski, Seidl, and Balogun, 2022), it provides opportunities to investigate how organisations can better address sustainability challenges.

Finally, a question worth considering is whether the new normal (strategy) today is tomorrow's (old) strategy?

2.8 Chapter Key Takeaways

The key takeaways from Chapter 2 on strategy are as follows:

1 **Fundamental Theories of Strategy:**

- This chapter outlines the progression of strategic management, emphasising significant theories and models from historical perspectives, including Sun Tzu's military strategies, to modern sustainability-oriented methodologies. It highlights the importance of understanding how companies generate and capture value, as well as the reasons behind some companies' superior **performance** compared to others.

2 **Strategic Management vs Strategy:**

- A distinction is made between strategic management (the formulation, implementation, and evaluation of strategies) and strategy (the overarching plan to attain goals or objectives), emphasising that a thorough comprehension of both is essential for effective leadership.

3 **Sustainability Integration:**

- This chapter emphasises the necessity for businesses to incorporate sustainability into their strategic management to address present and future challenges associated with ESG factors.

4 **Leadership Mindset:**

- It promotes a pragmatic and flexible leadership approach, crucial for managing change and connecting corporate strategy with sustainability objectives.

5 **Historical Contextual:**

- The evolution of strategy is delineated throughout specific periods (the 1960s to the 2020s), each posing distinctive problems for strategists. The emergence of corporate planning in the 1970s and the advent of the digital economy in the 2000s are illustrated.

6 **Strategic Levels:**

- This chapter examines many tiers of strategy – corporate, business, functional, and alliance – emphasising that each tier necessitates specific enquiries for the strategist.

7 **Practical Applications:**

- Practical instances, such as Jaguar Land Rover's sustainability strategy and Oxfam's initiatives, demonstrate how organisations can successfully implement strategic frameworks that prioritise sustainability.

2.9 Self-Reflection Questions

1. The extant literature makes it clear that it is not just new frameworks and tools that will engender change, but solutions that incorporate a dynamic field influenced by cultural, social, and political factors. What are the implications for sustainable strategists?
2. Outline the evolution of business strategy from the 1960s to the 2020s, and what are the principal distinctions among the strategic methodologies of each decade? What are the ramifications as we near 2030?
3. Analyse the similarities and differences between the prescriptive and emergent viewpoints of strategy.
4. Summarise one of Mintzberg's ten schools of strategy and elucidate its contribution to your comprehension of strategic management.
5. How should leadership teams reconcile the tensions between AI, **innovation**, ESG compliance, and long-term value creation to remain competitive?

References

Barney, J., (1991). Firm resources and sustained competitive advantage. *Journal of Management, 17*(1), pp.99–120.

Cai, Q., Wu, J., Wu, T., Chang, P.C. and Mardani, A., (2024). The impact of digital leadership on hidden champions' competitive advantage: A moderated mediation model of ambidextrous innovation and value co-creation. *Journal of Business Research, 182*, p.114819.

Chaffee, E.E., (1985). Three models of strategy. *Academy of Management Review, 10*(1), pp.89–98.

Compo, P., (2022). *The emergent approach to strategy: Adaptive design & execution*. Business Expert Press.

Crane, A., Matten, D., Glozer, S. and Spence, L.J., (2019). *Business ethics: Managing corporate citizenship and sustainability in the age of globalization*. Oxford University Press.

Durand, R., Grant, R.M. and Madsen, T.L., (2017). The expanding domain of strategic management research and the quest for integration. *Strategic Management Journal, 38*(1), pp.4–16.

Feldman, E.R., (2020). Corporate strategy: Past, present, and future. *Strategic Management Review, 1*(1), pp.179–206.

Grant, R.M., (1996). Toward a knowledge-based theory of the firm. *Strategic Management Journal, 17*(S2), pp.109–122.

He, Q., Meadows, M., Angwin, D., Gomes, E. and Child, J., (2020). Strategic alliance research in the era of digital transformation: Perspectives on future research. *British Journal of Management, 31*(3), pp.589–617.

Henry, A., (2021). *Understanding strategic management*. Oxford University Press.

Jarzabkowski, P., Lê, J.K., Seidl, D. and Vaara, E., (2025). Two decades of revolutionizing strategy research: How strategy-as-practice illuminates the complex, dynamic and consequential ways of doing strategy. *Academy of Management Collections, 4*(2), pp.55–76.

Jarzabkowski, P., Seidl, D. and Balogun, J., (2022). From germination to propagation: Two decades of strategy-as-practice research and potential future directions. *Human Relations, 75*(8), pp.1533–1559.

Koff, H., Challenger, A., Cuellar, J.R., Orea, R.A., and López, M.D.S.L., (2022). How green are our laws? Presenting a normative coherence for sustainable development methodology. *Environmental Policy and Governance, 33*(1), 90–109. https://doi.org/10.1002/eet.1998

Meckling, W.H. and Jensen, M.C., (1976). Theory of the firm: Managerial behavior, agency costs and ownership structure. *Journal of Financial Economics, 3*(4), pp.305–360.

Miles, R.E., Snow, C.C., Meyer, A.D. and Coleman Jr, H.J., (1978). Organizational strategy, structure, and process. *Academy of Management Review, 3*(3), pp.546–562.

Mintzberg, H. (1987). *Crafting strategy*. Harvard Business School Press.

Mintzberg, H., Ahlstrand, B. and Lampel, J., (2008). *Strategy Safari* (2nd ed.). Financial Times Prentice Hall.

Oxfam (2025). Takers, not Makers. Executive Summary. Available at: https://oi-files-d8-prod.s3.eu-west-2.amazonaws.com/s3fs-public/2025-01/English%20-%20Davos%20Executive%20Summary%202025.pdf (Accessed 24 January 2026).

Penrose, E.T., (1959). *The theory of the growth of the firm*. Wiley.

Phillips, P.A., (2003). *E-business strategy: Text and cases*. McGraw-Hill.

Porter, M.E., (1996). What is Strategy? *Harvard Business Review, 74*(6), pp.61–78.

Prabalad, C.K. and Hamel, G., (1990). The core competence of the corporation. *Harvard Business Review, 68*(3), pp.79–91.

Rumelt, R.P., (2022). *The crux: How leaders become strategists*. Profile Books.

Rumelt, R.P., Schendel, D. and Teece, D.J., (1995). Fundamental issues in strategy: A research agenda. *Administrative Science Quarterly, 41*(1), pp.196–198.

Schendel, D. (1994). Introduction to the summer (1994) special issue – 'Strategy: Search for new paradigms'. *Strategic Management Journal, 15*(S2), 1–4.

Schmieg, G., Meyer, E., Schrickel, I., Herberg, J., Caniglia, G., Vilsmaier, U., Laubichler, M., Hörl, E. and Lang, D., (2018). Modeling normativity in sustainability: A comparison of the sustainable development goals, the Paris agreement, and the papal encyclical. *Sustainability Science, 13*, pp.785–796.

Schumpeter, J.A., (1934). *The theory of economic development. Harvard University* (7th ed.). (R. Opie, Trad.) Harvard University Press.

Syväri, M., Tähtinen, J. and Nordberg-Davies, S., (2025). Enacting 'true business sustainability'– Market shaping for environmental impact. *Journal of Business Research, 186*, p.114949.

Teece, D.J., Pisano, G. and Shuen, A., (1997). Dynamic capabilities and strategic management. *Strategic Management Journal, 18*(7), pp.509–533.

Vermeulen, F., (2017). Many strategies fail because they're not actually strategies. *Harvard Business Review, 11*, pp.1–5.

Wang, T., Zhao, X. and Wang, X., (2024). Making platform firms' competitive advantage sustainable: The roles of network orchestration capabilities and collaborative innovation. *Journal of Business Research, 183*, p.114854.

Wernerfelt, B., (1984). A resource-based view of the firm. *Strategic Management Journal, 5*(2), 171–180.

Williamson, O.E., (1979). Transaction-cost economics: the governance of contractual relations. *The Journal of Law and Economics, 22*(2), pp.233–261.

World Economic Forum (2024). It is time to create an economy that works for all. Available at: https://www.weforum.org/stories/2024/04/it-is-time-to-create-an-economy-that-works-for-all/ (Accessed: 26 August 2025).

3

SUSTAINABLE STRATEGIC MANAGEMENT

3.1 Learning Strategy Objectives

Upon finishing this chapter, you will have the ability to:

1 **Knowledge-Based Objectives:**

- Understand why sustainable strategic management is so essential today and in the future.
- Appreciate and understand the seven dimensions of strategic management to facilitate organisational and digital transformation.

2 **Skill-Based Objectives:**

- Appreciate and understand the nuances of sustainable strategic management within organisations.
- When considering profit and societal decision-making, make strategic decisions to overcome the "sustainability" dilemma.

3 **Attitude-Based Objectives:**

- Foster a sense of ethical responsibility in strategy decision-making.
- Embrace open and collaborative thinking while addressing sustainability challenges.

3.2 Introduction

A question posed by researchers, consultants, and practitioners for more than six decades in strategy research includes: How do organisations change? Why do they stay the same? What makes them change for the better? Within the strategy literature, numerous theories have grown up around these perennial concerns.

However, what remain lacking are theoretical and practical perspectives on sustainable strategy. What is particularly important now is that we do not live in an ergodic world, where change occurs, but after a sustained period, the state returns to its original state

DOI: 10.4324/9781003516774-4

(North, 1999). The Brittle, Anxious, Non-linear, Incomprehensible (BAINI) environment suggests that we now live in a non-ergodic world, where change does not revert to its original state (Hitt, Arregle, and Holmes, 2021).

Our contention is that for organisations to make the **transition** from strategy to **SSM** practice, it needs to be dynamic for the new normal. To make the **transition** will require a reconfiguration of expert action and processes within a context of inter-, cross-, and multidisciplinary thinking. This will flow from the country level down through institutions to groups of individuals with varying needs and wants.

Shove, Watson, and Pantzar (2012) provide excellent examples for the reader in their *Dynamics of Social Practice* book, which includes the instance of car-driving and its impact on society, commencing with horse wagons in the late 18th century. The rules of the road were based on horse riders. Then, cars with their gas-powered internal combustion engines overtook their steam-powered counterparts. The car industry created a new infrastructure of practice. Those skilled in working with horses had to reskill to remain competitive in the job market.

The horse-to-automobile **transition** provides an analogy for understanding the imperatives of **SSM** in modern organisations. So, we liken **SSM** to requiring a new skillset of practice to create the competence to move organisations forward in their sustainability journey. What is required is novelty with a continual flow of disruptive changes in the modern car industry, such as multi-lane dual carriageway roads (Merriman, 2006).

Such insights suggest that today's organisations face similar profound transformations in core competencies and operational practices. **SSM** offers a way of making a difference, and of the most vibrant areas of contemporary and organisations; strategy-as-practice can offer a practice-theoretical perspective (Jarzabkowski, Lê, Seidl, and Vaara, 2025). Also, **SSM** is not only a critical perspective, but its impact also goes beyond the closed academic environment.

In academic and professional contexts, workshops often pose a fundamental issue to students and executives: Why do specific strategic management initiatives fail despite being supported by comprehensive top-down and bottom-up approaches? This inquiry frequently reveals a fundamental flaw in the problem-solving capabilities of organisations. The essence of strategic problem-solving for organisations is predominantly tactical, usually requiring actions to be clarified and aligned with the overarching strategy goal. Instead, strategic projects are established with staff accountable, requiring greater authority and dedicated resources and personnel to effectuate the necessary changes, which frequently run into roadblocks.

In this circumstance, strategic management objectives are unlikely to be realised, hence diminishing the ensuing value-added. When strategic efforts are misdirected or inadequately resourced, the anticipated value creation may devolve into value destruction for stakeholders.

Some of my recent projects have revealed a strategic management value dilemma observed across various businesses. This paradox extends to all levels, underscoring the need for a more profound understanding and a novel approach to strategic management.

Establishing ambitious objectives necessitates sufficient resources and a harmonious connection between strategy and execution that underpins these objectives. By addressing essential gaps, companies can strive to deliver significant value in today's complex and interconnected environment, where strategic insights and leadership will be crucial for navigating the forthcoming challenges.

Grounded in this context, **SSM** compels organisations to establish a more socially and ecologically responsible framework, aiming to achieve long-term resilience. This can help navigate the changes within the sustainability-focused ecology. The gap between strategy and tactics in sustainability projects has diminished organisations' capacity to implement creative solutions to mitigate climate change and ecological degradation.

Addressing this gap necessitates re-evaluating conventional strategic management, current organisational processes, and activity arrangements. Innovative strategies will enhance the narrative and re-establish the value proposition by organising communication with stakeholders, engaging with customers and end-users, and being socially responsible.

The social dimension will provide legitimacy challenges, which, if addressed, will facilitate the realisation of untapped value-creation potential. As outlined in Chapter 1, the chapter's theoretical foundation will significantly rely on sustainability disciplines. This novel mindset has been accelerated as enterprises seek to establish a competitive advantage following the pandemic.

A contemporary examination of strategic narrative across the sustainability landscape suggests that organisations should be more explicit about their purpose. Leadership teams must be aware of sustainability's emerging contexts and applications.

Notwithstanding such challenges, public sector organisations typically formulate effective policy-oriented responses to their external environment. An ideological divide may persist between the open, outward-orientated world and the closed, inward-orientated environment in which they function. The emphasis has shifted from an internal focus on policy changes to an outward orientation, linking initiatives to end-users. Developing key skills and competencies is appropriate for advancing strategic management practice.

The triangle of pressures on strategic leaders consists of stakeholder demands (market), governmental expectations, and stakeholder interests. Any technique must be implemented within these parameters. The leadership realism is "Leaders don't know what they don't know," so in this instance, they may not understand or appreciate the "New World."

3.2.1 Multidimensional Perspective

From a multidimensional perspective, transdisciplinary methods provide opportunities to address significant societal concerns. This will necessitate collaboration and strengthening of relationships among business partners and vendors in the years to come. Engaging stakeholders at the outset of sustainability-focused projects facilitates reciprocal learning within interdisciplinary and transdisciplinary teams and practice communities, hence promoting the co-evolution of conventional strategic management towards sustainability outcomes.

This method of practical collaboration can help tackle intricate, intractable issues. This book aims to develop a community of educators, researchers, and leaders across many disciplines, sectors, and national boundaries, fostering a professional network for transformation. By disseminating skills, methodologies, and instruments for the co-production of novel knowledge, this book can help leaders navigate this tumultuous landscape with intention. However, concerns exist regarding obstacles and the risk of not meeting objectives.

Corporate boardrooms recognise the importance of sustainability and its potential to impact long-term economic and societal outcomes. However, a UN Global Compact–Accenture (2022) study, utilising survey and interview data from 2,600 CEOs across 18 industries and 128 countries, revealed that a substantial majority, 93%, are grappling with ten or more challenges, and 87% will restrict the achievement of United Nations Sustainable Development Goals (UNSDGs). This may pose a significant obstacle for both business and society.

These issues are illustrated by some large private sector corporations, including Unilever, Bank of America, and Shell, which have recently dropped or missed goals for cutting emissions or reducing ties with the most polluting sectors. Governments have issued pronouncements such as missed decarbonisation targets, with Scotland's devolved and Germany still deliberating their 2030 targets. These patterns highlight substantial obstacles and explain why organisations are not making progress towards their 2030 net-zero targets.

The situation was effectively conveyed by former BP CEO Lord John Browne (FT.com, 2024), who urged investors to reflect on Aesop's fable of the rider who ceases to feed his horse during peacetime, only to discover it unfit when conflict arises. Nevertheless, despite the intellectual allure of the climate change objective, the soldier in the analogy symbolises organisations opting to pull back on their climate initiatives. This decision exacerbates long-term risks for ecosystem constituents. Collectively, these undermine the momentum needed to drive significant change, such as:

1 Political and Regulatory Factors: Governments must assume a leadership role, but they encounter challenges and, in certain instances, lack the necessary political will, financial incentives, coherent policies, and adequate resources to drive substantial progress.
2 Ambition versus Feasibility: Excessive optimistic rhetoric can result in the establishment of unrealistic expectations, leading to stakeholder disillusionment when these targets are inevitably missed, and undermining overall trust and progress in sustainability efforts.
3 Measurement and Standards Issues: Organisations frequently encounter difficulty identifying the standards necessary for attaining net-zero standards due to their abstract nature. This abstraction complicates the measurement and demonstration of progress. The absence of definitive benchmarks undermines initiatives and obstructs transparent reporting.

3.2.2 What's Next?

This chapter builds upon and expands Chapter 2 by incorporating sustainability into the strategic management framework, addressing the shortcomings of conventional methods. In light of the CFO's insistence, businesses are increasingly acknowledging that achieving financial objectives is not the sole focus, prompting the CEO to seek a reset.

Regrettably, implementing change via strategic management is proving problematic. This chapter will explore diverse organisational views to enhance the organisational attitude for a proactive response and prosperity. Examining the traditional and contemporary/proactive paradigms will enable readers to recognise the forthcoming challenges and implement suitable strategies.

The strategic analysis begins by identifying the key facets of strategic management. This entails re-evaluating the events, histories, and partnerships that shaped the current strategy. Subsequently, focus on the emerging paradigms that will reveal an enhanced decision-making framework for implementing tactics that create or distinguish a new offering.

This chapter examines how researchers must articulate several hypotheses on how to model today's sustainability concerns effectively. It is essential to investigate interdisciplinary perspectives across academic fields of study. Matters are complicated in the turbulent sustainability environment, where new products and services emerge, and the CEO must ensure they effectively manage stakeholders and regulatory pressure. The Seven Dimensions of Strategic Management and the **SSM Transition** Journey are introduced to help guide the leadership team during their sustainability deliberations.

3.3 Strategic Management Spectrum

Strategic management involves decision-making, with optimal choices arising from a methodical evaluation of alternatives within the framework of an evolving situation. The efficient arrangement of resources and relationships will provide value for internal and external stakeholders rather than solely for themselves.

Unfortunately, certain unique internal traits related to **innovation**, inclusion, and communication hinder some businesses from effectively transforming and capitalising on exciting opportunities. These can manifest as more symbolic than strategic activities. The proposed approach often assumes that existing strategic management processes, which evolve into strategies, are culturally influenced by financially driven metrics.

This book postulates that a structured approach is necessary for implementing change, despite the absence of a universal method applicable to all organisational circumstances, including size, internal resistance, and desired transformation. This book also aims to facilitate sustainable initiatives characterised by the ongoing change, with strategic management evolving into an emerging process. This entails exploring different techniques that assist organisations in **transitioning** from a rational to an emergent worldview. A wider array of organisational viewpoints in strategic management will enhance businesses' ability to adjust and thrive proactively.

A robust foundation empowers leaders and their teams to develop bold strategies that outline precise, explicit, and quantifiable approaches to achieve tangible change. Some will remain anchored in the traditional, while others will fail to acknowledge the traditional and predominantly exhibit the new qualities (see Figure 3.1). My observations indicate considerable discrepancies in the focus of organisations on various paradigms.

Organisations may be polarised by occupying a spectrum bounded at one end by a top-down, command-and-control budgeted culture and at the other by a much more distributed and consultative decision-making culture.

Examples of strategic management practices are illustrated by type in Table 3.1. Strategic management remains a prominent topic, and attention should be drawn to the practices within large companies and civil society. We can see how the practices with civil society organisations are more akin to some of our **SSM** insights.

Table 3.1 reinforces the view that strategic management is context-dependent, with no one-size-fits-all panacea. Large companies have the resources to hire consultants to tailor such systems, supported by dedicated personnel. The CEO and the board must recognise that merely copying "best practices" can be likened to buying an ill-fitting suit.

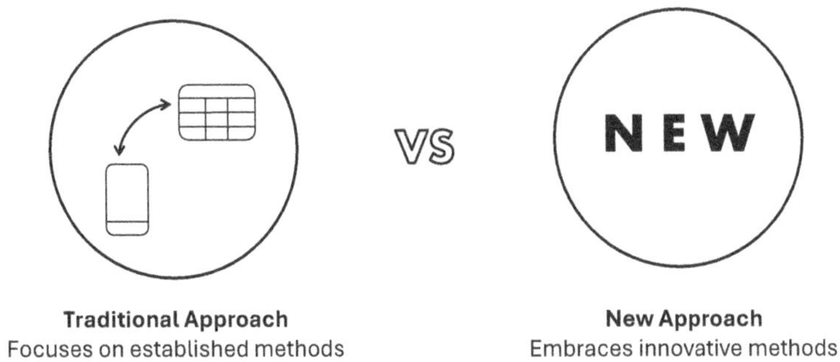

FIGURE 3.1 Strategic management: traditional vs new approach

Civil society affords superior stakeholder-oriented integration models. Engagement approaches, such as participatory, can enhance the corporate strategy formulation and implementation processes. Large companies may operate with rigid systems, which are dependent upon the organisational behaviours, artefacts, and cultural practices. They have funds for structures for strategy retreats, **innovation** labs, and scenario planning. In the public sector and civil society organisations, it is a much more social process that requires investment in human-related challenges.

The distinctiveness of mission clarity is illustrated by the civil society organisations that have the greatest alignment between strategic priorities and social practices. This contrasts with large companies that tend to pursue shareholder value maximisation, while small companies may focus on survival strategies in the current economic climate.

3.3.1 Priorities for Strategic Management

Recent research in strategic management has examined various approaches to social inquiry, including positivist, postpositivist, interpretivist, postmodernist, and critical theory (Rabetino, Kohtamäki, and Federico, 2021). Scholars now articulate several hypotheses on how to best cope with today's sustainability concerns. Considering the stances adopted, it is essential to examine interdisciplinary perspectives. Strategy is a multidisciplinary theory grounded in economics, management, sociology, and psychology, importing concepts and theories from ecology and biology, systems science, philosophy (Durand, Grant, and Madsen, 2017), and the context of sustainability science. In addition to sustainability and initiatives, other recent priorities for strategic management include:

- Artificial intelligence (AI) (Keding, 2021)
- Roles of leadership (Ateş et al., 2020)
- Design and strategy (Grimsgaard, 2022)
- Digital transformation and **innovation** (Appio, Frattini, Petruzzelli, and Neirotti, 2021)
- Global supply chain resilience (Salama and McGarvey, 2023)
- Data analytics and business intelligence (Mikalef, Pappas, Krogstie, and Pavlou, 2020)
- Crisis management and resilience planning (John-Eke and Eke, 2020).

Finally, looking at the organisational ecosystem, the CEO of a public sector firm may face a fragmented landscape of multiple agencies. This can create a complex web of

TABLE 3.1 Strategic management practices by organisational type

Analytical Dimension	*Large Company*	*Small Company (SMEs)*	*Public Sector*	*Civil Society Organisation (CSO)*
Strategic management priority	Maximising shareholder value and long-term competitive advantage; integrating ESG and **innovation** into growth models.	Ensuring survival, profitability, and market differentiation; responding rapidly to external shocks.	Delivering public value, maintaining policy alignment, and ensuring service accountability to citizens.	Achieving mission impact, social legitimacy, and long-term sustainability within donor constraints.
How strategic management is managed	Formalised, top-down processes with annual strategy reviews, KPIs, dashboards, and dedicated strategy teams.	Informal and adaptive; often led by owner-manager or small leadership team; short-term planning cycles dominate.	Bureaucratic, compliance-heavy, often driven by political cycles and policy mandates; medium- to long-term strategic frameworks.	Participatory and consensus-based, involving boards, funders, and stakeholders; strategy evolves with cause-based mandates.
Key social practices	Strategic retreats, **performance** reviews, **innovation** labs, stakeholder engagement, ESG reporting, scenario planning.	Customer feedback loops, informal networks, bootstrapped **innovation**, lean planning, agility in execution.	Stakeholder consultation, public reporting, policy alignment reviews, cross-departmental steering committees, programme audits.	Community co-creation, advocacy campaigns, fundraising cycles, multi-stakeholder dialogues, transparency practices.

Abbreviations: ESG, economic, social, and governance; KPIs, key **performance** indicators.

overlapping mandates with conflicting priorities. The strategic picture is illustrated in Figure 3.2, which depicts some of the UN/multilateral bodies, including UN agencies, development banks, specialised programmes, intergovernmental organisations, and non-governmental organisations (NGOs). This presents a style of strategic management behaviour that seeks to achieve goals, conforming to the needs of society (Stead and Stead, 2014).

We have now briefly examined the strategic management spectrum. The following will focus on the development of **SSM**, commencing with assessing the baseline for strategic management.

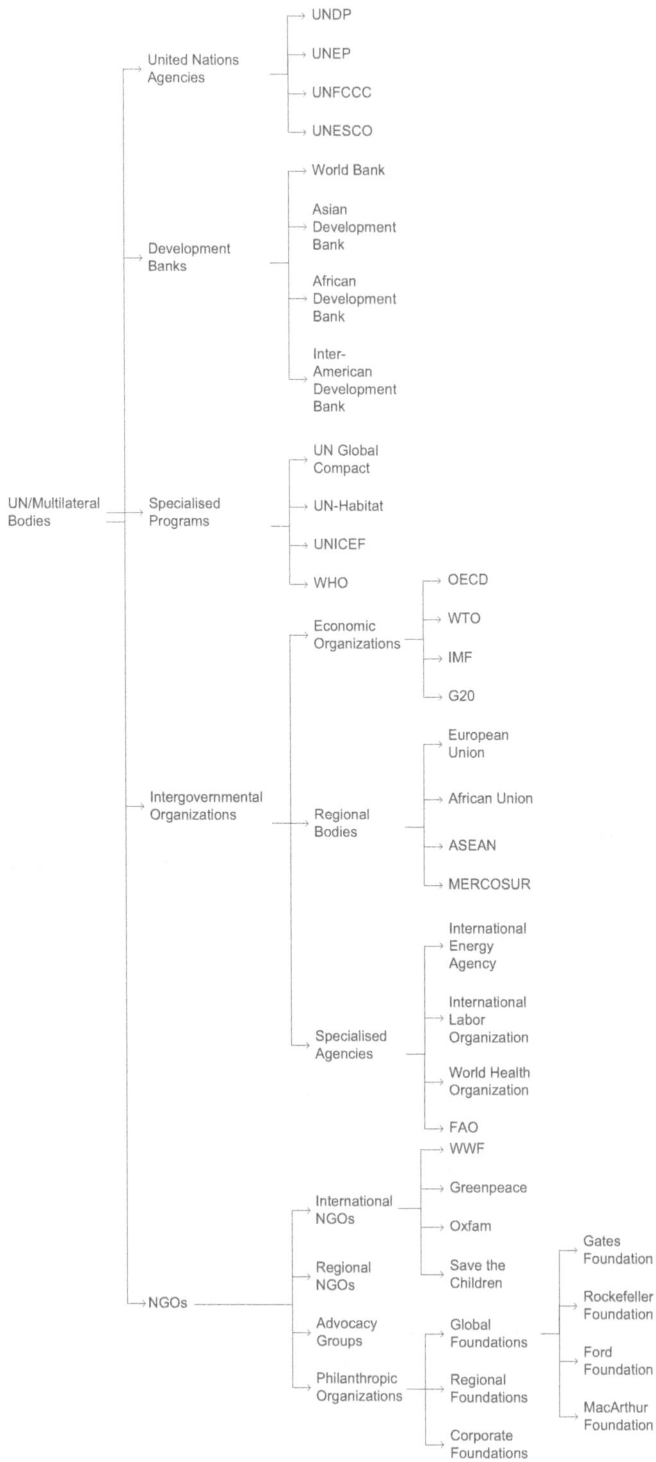

FIGURE 3.2 Some UN/multilateral bodies

3.4 Sustainable Strategy Toolkit (1) – Seven Dimensions of Strategic Management

This section draws on my practical observations in strategic management practice spanning over three decades. CEOs need to convey a sense of certainty throughout their organisation, especially as stakeholders yearn for certainty and will have varying levels of risk tolerance. However, to succeed in this sustainability-driven world, organisations will need to challenge the status quo. Instead of relying on the programmed practices that have culminated from six decades of research and practice, there is a need to look ahead and adopt new practices.

In addition to ensuring that strategies align with the context, organisation, and circumstances, it is crucial to use frameworks and tools that are most appropriate. Their use in themselves will not develop strategies that harness the power of uncertainty. Ideally, the strategic analysis commences with an understanding of the dimensions of strategic management.

This entails re-evaluating the events, histories, and collaborations that created existing strategies. Then, direct attention to the emergent paradigms, which will reveal a better decision-making platform for pursuing strategies that make or differentiate a new offer.

This requires a strategic management framework that enables the organisation to move away from traditional approaches. The following section considers the "Old and New" games that organisations can undertake to facilitate their **transition**.

Practice reveals that some organisations fail to **transition** from traditional approaches and consequently fail to achieve their goals. The proposed Seven Dimensions of Strategic Management framework demonstrates that there is no single right answer, but it provides valuable insights into the key dimensions of strategic management.

What differentiates this approach is the unbundling of seven salient dimensions of strategic management, which provides concise, comprehensive, and invaluable insights for those responsible for managing the sustainability change agenda.

Visually, the framework can help develop and assess an organisation's preparedness to embark on or adjust its strategic management journey. Each of the seven dimensions in Figure 3.3 should be mapped against the organisation's current practices.

Playing the New Game will require organisations to assess the state of their legacy thinking, processes and activities that are holding them back. The leadership team will need to consider what changes in behaviour or approach are necessary to overcome the existing paradigm, the problems they identify, and the potential consequences.

Shown in greater detail, the Old–New Game approach in Table 3.2 assesses the relative fit (alignment) of the organisation within its context, its desired market positioning. The approach needs to be open, incorporating the views of stakeholders.

The appropriate balance between the Old and New Games will depend on the sector's volatility and where organisations are in relation to these paradigms. Some will be rooted in the old, whereas others will not recognise the old and will broadly display the characteristics of the new. In more turbulent sectors, firms will occupy a spectrum bounded at one end by top-down, command-and-control approaches and at the other, a more distributed and consultative decision-making style.

The emergent paradigm will provide a stronger foundation for organisations to develop a robust and agile strategic management philosophy. The organisation's raison d'être will

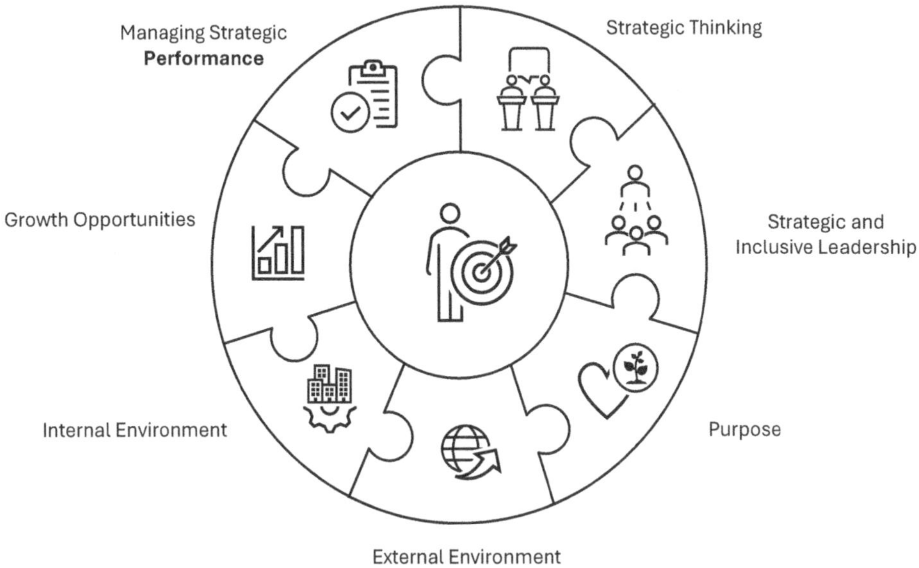

FIGURE 3.3 Seven dimensions of strategic management

TABLE 3.2 Seven dimensions of strategic management

Seven Dimensions of Strategic Management	*Rational Paradigm (Old)*	*Emergent Paradigm (New)*
1 Strategic thinking	Top-down policy-driven to maximise operational efficiency	Sensemaking relationships among staff rather than being top-down and driven by a few powerful individuals. Ideally, top-down and bottom-up approaches for the creation of knowledge inform the institutional strategy. Need to develop resilience, focus on peer group/ competition, customers (core and outliers, stakeholders, etc.); the offer (old and new) investment (what do we stop investing in?) and infrastructure/media for delivering value.
2 Strategic & inclusive leadership	Managing within a closed environment	Leadership within a networked ecosystem environment crosses traditional closed boundaries and firmly enters the emerging marketplace. To be successful, the focus needs to also include diversity, equality, and inclusion in an authentic manner to unlock inherent capabilities and seize external opportunities.
3 Purpose	Self-focus	Being there for others, as well as themselves. Is the style leading inwards or outwards? Is there evidence of social legitimacy (all stakeholders)/ positioning and differentiation? The circular system should address the "Why" do I exist?

(*Continued*)

TABLE 3.2 *(Continued)*

Seven Dimensions of Strategic Management	*Rational Paradigm (Old)*	*Emergent Paradigm (New)*
4 External environment	Evaluate past and current macro-environmental forces	Evaluate past, current, and future scenarios of micro/macro-environmental forces. This involves dealing with future issues – challenges/opportunities. Who are the disrupters, facilitators/change agents for this? What are the new defining characteristics of the marketplace?
5 Internal environment	Resource strengths	Dynamic capabilities/values and culture are driven throughout the organisation. There are a number of blockages due to contextual factors, some of which are unknown to the leadership team, which came to prominence during and after the pandemic.
6 Growth opportunities	Globalisation	Organisational and national culture will mean a one-size approach will not work. Surprising many mergers and acquisitions still fail on these grounds. The Australian Hilco capital 2018 acquisition of the UK Homebase being an example.
7 Managing strategic **performance**	Budget attainment, accreditations, and rankings	Value attainment of all core missions. This goes beyond traditional financial metrics.

lie at the heart of the strategy and provide the foundation for developing insights and understanding of the key processes of the Old and New Game, creating a roadmap for growth.

Mini Case Study

Geregu Power Plc – Nigeria

Introduction

Geregu Power Plc, a subsidiary of Amperion Power Distribution Co Ltd, is a corporation that provides power plant operation services. The corporation produces energy through the efficient and safe operation and maintenance of its facilities. It offers a range of production and maintenance services, including mechanical, electrical, **performance**, procurement, and laboratory services.

The Geregu Power Plant is a natural gas-fired combined cycle gas turbine facility. The organisation utilises a computerised maintenance management system to maximise efficiency and minimise the human planning of plant maintenance activities. Its facilities function on grid and island models. Geregu Power is based in Victoria Island, Lagos, Nigeria.

Goal: Accelerating economic growth through sustainable power generation in Nigeria.

Background and Context

The company reported revenues of (Nigeria Naira) NGN82,908.8 million for the fiscal year ended December 2023 (FY2023), an increase of 74.1% over FY2022. In FY2023, the company's operating margin was 37.6%, compared to an operating margin of 31.1% in FY2022. In FY2023, the company reported a net margin of 19.4%, compared to 21.4% in FY2022. The company reported revenues of NGN50.428 billion for the first quarter, which ended March 2024, representing an increase of 85.7% over the previous quarter.

Strategic Issues

CEO Akin Akinfemiwa stated: "Ongoing global changes that focus on climate change, disruptive technologies, global peace, and prosperity demand that businesses play an active role in pursuing broader objectives beyond profitability, encompassing societal and environmental goals and objectives for a more sustainable future."

The new government's initiatives, particularly the Electricity Act of 2023, are expected to enhance the viability of the Nigerian Electricity Supply Industry. This presents opportunities throughout the entire value chain. This legislation enables the utilisation of resources in the transmission and distribution subsectors, promoting the vision of being a comprehensive energy solutions provider.

The momentum towards Nigeria's goal of achieving net-zero status by 2050 necessitates a comprehensive re-evaluation of its business model for renewable energy solutions. In the medium term, the aim is for a seamless energy **transition** that minimises disruptions to customers and the environment.Strategic Actions TakenTo leverage membership in the West African Power Pool and increase share in the regional electricity market. Geregu Power Plc is committed to developing a world-class workforce and robust risk management frameworks.

In 2024, the plan is to launch a pioneering initiative to foster the growth and development of young engineers through a specialised young engineering scheme. This programme will provide a structured career path for emerging engineering talent by offering mentorship, skill enhancement, and practical experience.

Questions

1 How should the Geregu Power Plc CEO, Akin Akinfemiwa, balance their current reliance on natural gas with Nigeria's 2050 net-zero ambitions?
2 What opportunities does the Electricity Act of 2023 present to Geregu and its board?
3 Assume you are a strategy consultant. You are to outline three capabilities that Geregu Power needs to develop to succeed in its sustainability strategy while maintaining financial **performance**.

Source: Geregu Power (2023).

3.5 Sustainable Strategic Management

Contrary to common perception, the calls for organisations to consider financial returns and environmental issues originated in the 19th century. The Industrial Revolution prompted environmentalists like John Muir (1817–1862) and Henry David Thoreau (1838–1914) to express concerns. In the preceding chapter, we examined how governments and institutions implement policies in reaction to environmental degradation. Likewise, implementing pollution control measures in rapidly growing industrial cities marked the beginning of a long road towards sustainable development. These early endeavours established the foundation for environmental policies, demonstrating that integrating economic and ecological considerations has deep historical roots.

The sustainability landscape, as illustrated in Chapter 1, remains in a state of flux. The interconnected micro and macro contexts influence change, with many components enhancing or mitigating the impact. The marketplace is dynamic and complex; leaders' primary objectives should enhance societal value. The time has come to move from pledges to progress, necessitating an understanding of where sustainability lies, which requires knowing which sustainable efforts will deliver the most significant impact.

Organisations' ability to deploy renewal strategies that can solve problems and build and run the business provides a powerful platform for change. In turbulent sustainability environments where new products and services emerge, one of the primary components is managing stakeholders and regulatory pressure.

3.5.1 Stakeholders

Heightened stakeholder and regulatory demands for sustainable **performance** compel modifications in strategic planning, core operations, legal frameworks, measurements, and reporting. More than 70% of investors (MorningStar, 2022) now assert that organisations with robust sustainability policies represent prudent investments, indicating a growing body of data. This presents a distinctive opportunity for strategists to develop and evaluate models with ramifications for significant societal transformations. Each sector's unique traits and life cycles will likely call into question the suitability of conventional baseline assumptions and methodologies.

Identifying an organisation's stakeholders may appear straightforward. Nonetheless, my workshop experiences indicate that they are typically presented as a list, with challenges accurately characterising the customer. Current concepts are manifesting within the academic sector. Tensions escalate when a typical consumer purchases a product or service and reaps benefits with little to no effort. Higher education differs in that when an individual pays tuition, they must engage in a course of study that may not yield successful outcomes.

The varied interests of stakeholders necessitate a more comprehensive evaluation of their concerns. A comprehensive approach should involve illustrating and critically evaluating the significant transactions with stakeholder groups (Kenny, 2023).

Active collaboration necessitates emphasising value development and realisation, with benefits that benefit ecosystem members. Organisational assets, encompassing intellectual capital, can facilitate the discovery and realisation of stakeholder value; nevertheless, the value narrative must be comprehensive, addressing creation, opportunities, destruction, and value propositions.

These challenges must be articulated more clearly when evaluating options and cultivating connections, which requires a significant amount of time. Multiple enquiries necessitate consideration, hence questioning the Porterian (Porter, 1980, 1985) industry structure and value generation models, as elaborated in Chapter 2.

While today's strategists face many new challenges and opportunities, there is growing concern that organisations must invest significant sums in sustainability-themed projects.

Consequently, academics are tasked with generating theoretical insights that advance in tandem with practice.

Over the last four decades, scholars have sought strategic management tools to apply in enhancing sustainability-themed projects. The area is still emerging, attracting interest from several disciplines, such as environmental science, engineering, and strategic management. The emphasis has shifted from ecological concerns at the macro policy level to the practicalities of management efforts in advancing the business. This paradigmatic shift has led to questioning of the concept of the narrow lens of **performance**.

3.5.2 Strategic Management Clusters

As strategic management undergoes a paradigmatic shift, leadership teams can capitalise on opportunities within their business ecosystems. A recurring theme of this book is that the external environment can be complex, requiring rapid changes and greater collaboration in strategy practice. Traditional strategic management practices remained within the firm's boundaries, with strategists "peering over the wall" without serious thought about the broader ecological repercussions (Sulich and Soloducho-Pelc, 2024).

The sustainable strategic management literature reveals several concepts. Rao and Shukla's research identifies four clusters, as presented in Table 3.3.

Given the long-term objectives established for 2050, the organisation, as a dynamic organism, necessitates strategic thinking with foresight (Suriyankietkaew and Petison, 2019). Stead and Stead (2013) stated, "Strategic planning spiralled into strategic management in response to an increasing need for environmental vigilance." More recently, Stead (2025) still calls for a revolutionary approach that harnesses business resources in dealing with humanity issues.

Transformations in the ecosystem can trigger changes in the opportunities and threats facing the organisation and cascade through the environmental layers. Such changes will include building healthy relationships with regulators and policymakers who shape the environment in which organisations operate. Their role as enablers of success is fundamental, and efforts in creating a regulatory framework that supports growth and **innovation** in the sustainable sector will deliver value.

Also, the societal dimension requires building healthy interactions with communities where organisations operate. At times, these communities can be difficult to locate. Facilitating assistance and gaining trust in operations will be essential for success. Being a

TABLE 3.3 Breadth of research interests in sustainable strategic management

Clusters	*Research Interests*	*Key Author*
1	Strategic management, sustainable competitive advantage, corporate environment **performance**, and strategic resources	Barney (1991), Kiefer (2019), Teece (2007)
2	Competitive strategy, resource-based view, integrated strategy, and sustainable advantage	Barney (1991), Porter (1980), Teece (1997)
3	Economic stability, resource dependency theory, sustainable supply chain management, and strategic management	Esfahbodia (2016), Ahi (2013), Carter (2008)
4	Corporate sustainability management, strategy, strategic sustainable development, and sustainable development	Baumgartner (2014), Galbreath (2009), Porter (2006)

responsible corporate citizen who contributes positively to the socio-economic development of communities presents a solid platform for stakeholder management.

The phrase co-evolution denotes that two or more terms are somehow interrelated. In this case, strategic management and the external environment are key considerations. Explanations of problem-solution "co-evolution" either overtly or subtly compare strategic management design processes to biological evolution processes.

Business strategy theory has not remained static; however, a fundamental premise of this book is that it has not fully incorporated the robust practice of sustainability management. Some authors have made this observation, with Stead and Stead (2019) asserting that the changes in the business environment warrant a new paradigm of **SSM** that is more aligned with what leaders face in their strategising activities.

Today's strategist recognises the need to tackle the grand sustainability challenges, yet many still use the old, trusted causal models of the past that seek to optimise **performance**. Such models tend to simplify complexity to a manageable level, which often results in a static rather than dynamic approach (Grewatsch, Kennedy, and Bansal, 2023).

STRATEGY NUGGET

BT Passive vs Active Shareholders

An interesting case study emerges at BT involving its principal shareholder, the billionaire telecoms tycoon, Sunil Bharti Mittal, who has orchestrated a two-day strategy meeting with the board. Many issues mentioned are prime examples of dilemmas facing today's organisations.

Five strategic implications can be derived from the BT context:

1 Such encounters indicate a possible strategy realignment. Mittal's intensive two-day meeting with BT's management team contrasts with Patrick Drahi's more passive strategy. Mittal's actions may expedite BT's transformation initiatives and cost-reduction strategies.
2 BT's international portfolio restructuring may escalate with an increased emphasis on UK operations. BT strategists may focus on market repositioning opportunities within the telecommunications industry.
3 Workforce **transition** is anticipated to accelerate. BT's CEO, Allison Kirkby, aims to decrease the workforce from 130,000 to between 75,000 and 90,000 by 2030. Mittal's cost-reduction influence will result in more effective automation, outsourcing, and in its organisational reconfiguration.
4 A divergent long-term strategic planning horizon arises. This may necessitate re-evaluating BT's current business model to develop new capabilities. As Mittal perceives himself as a long-term investor, BT is in a state of flux, as it will need to emphasise sustainable growth rather than short-term budget cuts.
5 BT's CEO, Allison Kirkby, focusing on inclusion and diversity amid contraction, signals a positive step. BT's talent management strategy will be under scrutiny.

Questions

1 Using the BT case, how should incumbent telecommunication companies balance aggressive cost reduction with long-term competitive positioning when facing activist shareholder pressure?

2 Outline your thoughts on Sunil Bharti Mittal, a majority shareholder taking an active role in corporate strategy? What are your thoughts on this pivotal moment in BT's transformation journey?
3 What do you think the future holds for BT? How long can BT survive on cutting costs rather than growing revenue?

Source: FT.com (2025).

3.6 Sustainable Strategy Toolkit (2) – Sustainable Strategic Management Transition Journey

To build a sustainability-enabled organisation for the future, the organisation must understand its current trajectory and path. As sustainability becomes an integral part of everyday operations, understanding the maturity level reached and identifying opportunities for improvement will be crucial strategy differentiators.

Some stakeholders may express cynicism about the utility and value of the proposed levels of sustainability investment. However, the CEO and leadership team recognise that ongoing assessment exercises of their proposed journey will have a significant impact on influencing, shaping behaviour, and delivering rewards.

The following section introduces a **transition** framework for **SSM**, outlining how organisations can navigate their journey. During the journey, organisations' sustainability efforts can stall and appear to be heading towards a roadblock. Common causes can relate to an unclear strategy that has not been effectively communicated throughout the organisation's layers. Critical thinking is required to ensure the organisation knows what sustainability means to them, i.e., its purpose.

Symptoms include common phrases heard in such situations: "We don't understand our sustainability strategy." Management says we must adopt sustainable principles, but where is the budget?

Against the backdrop of previous discussions on the criticality of internal and external alignment, overcoming these issues can be addressed through the use of a sustainability integration framework. Key benefits of the approach include:

1 Mapping the sustainability journey across time frames to deliver system-level change.
2 Ensuring a balance between short-term metrics and long-term value creation.
3 Develop the necessary capabilities and competencies to engender change.
4 Help to work closely with key stakeholders, including conversations across the network.
5 Be a catalyst for **innovation** and growth.

Collectively, these will help form a sustainable value proposition for any organisation.

This approach is designed to help visualise the **SSM transition** across five levels.

During the evolution, a tailored and insightful approach to each sustainability project is apt.

Understanding and embracing sustainable strategy throughout the organisation is the foundation of core values. This alignment ensures the sustainability identity in the marketplace not only appeals to potential stakeholders but also represents the mission and vision of tomorrow's firm.

Key elements, such as organisational excellence and **innovation** in economic, social, and governance (ESG), will be at the forefront of this approach.

3.6.1 Branding and Naming

Before commencing or assessing the existing journey, the following branding and naming activities can kick-start the **transition**:

1 Target Audience Analysis and Engagement: Identifying and understanding the needs and aspirations of primary audiences within the firm ecosystem is key. Ideally, the approach includes a level of audience research to inform a branding strategy that speaks directly to these groups. The focus should be on showcasing the organisation as a beacon for sustainability impact in the selected marketspace.
2 Innovative and Adaptive Branding Approaches: The sustainability space is dynamic, and an impactful brand must reflect this. Now with AI and Gen AI, modern approaches in digital marketing, storytelling, and visual identity development ensure that the brand is not only contemporary but also adaptable to changing trends. The ongoing strategy should involve building a robust online presence, creating memorable marketing materials, and offering an overall brand experience that distinguishes the firm in the competitive landscape.
3 Create and Develop a Brand: For the sustainability journey that resonates with core values, appeals effectively to the target audience, and remains vibrant and relevant in the ever-evolving business landscape.
4 Collaborative Workshops: For key participants to engage key participants. Interventions can include a series of online 30-, 60-, and 90-minute interactive events. These should capture the pre-agenda version and a semi-completed document based on group participation. The latter documents should be extensively used to debate further and to unify the direction of travel.
5 From the activities in workshop sessions in 1 to 4, summaries should be presented, and the creative approach considered. The creative process should incorporate presentation, hands-on feedback, and extend to the final design of the sustainability journey. Once approved, brand and naming guidelines are established under agreed-upon parameters.

3.6.2 Practical Guidance for Sustainability Leaders at Varying Maturity Levels

Once the organisation is ready, the maturity levels need to be articulated. Reasons include:

- Resource allocation and return on investment optimisation.
- Internal and external benchmarking and market position.
- Risk management and future-proofing the organisation.

In terms of the sustainability **transition**, this can be broken down into five levels (see Figure 3.4):

- Level 1 Compliance and Reporting: The journey begins with meeting external regulatory requirements to establish credibility.
- Level 2 Strategic Partnerships: In these situations, a good starting point is to revisit the basics and clarify purpose and vision. Then, focus on and invest in relationships based on demand, delivering the value stakeholders want.

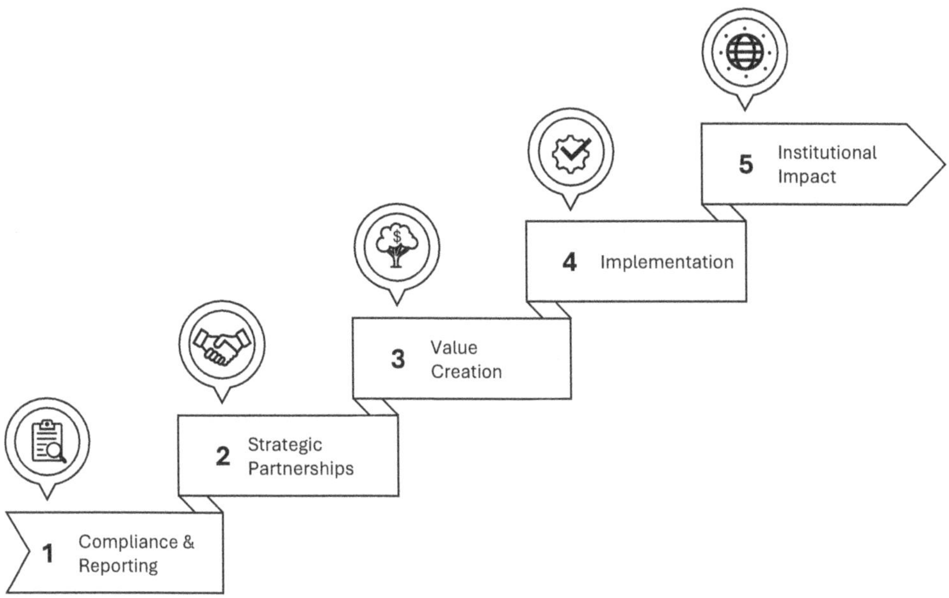

FIGURE 3.4 The five-level **transition** journey

- Level 3 Value Creation: Shifts sustainability from being seen as a separate initiative to being fully integrated into operations and strategic decision-making processes, creating value.
- Level 4 Implementation: An implementation deficit is hindering economic and societal improvements. Successfully crossing this chasm requires overcoming the missing link between strategy and tactics.
- Level 5 Institutional Impact: Evidence with quantitative and qualitative impactful outcomes in economic, societal, and environmental real terms.

Business sustainability leaders must traverse a systematic progression via five maturity levels, evolving from compliance-oriented strategies to institutional impact. The following provides practical suggestions at each phase to facilitate the adequate maturation of organisations.

3.6.2.1 Level 1: Compliance and Reporting

Objective: Enhance credibility via regulatory compliance and fundamental reporting.

Key Actions:

- Conduct a sustainability audit to identify compliance opportunities, deficiencies, and risks.
- Establish a systematic framework for sustainability and ESG reporting.
- Establish a precise reporting mechanism to keep external stakeholders informed.
- Implement a governance framework that ensures board-level responsibility for sustainability.
- Educate essential personnel on sustainability legislation, rules, and optimal practices.
- Utilise technology, such as automated reporting systems, to optimise compliance procedures and improve data integrity.

3.6.2.2 Level 2: Strategic Partnerships

Objective: Integrate sustainability with corporate mission and utilise partnerships to move forward from a compliance and reporting exercise.

Key Actions:

- Establish a specific sustainability vision that is congruent with the corporate strategy.
- Identify key stakeholders (clients, suppliers, regulatory bodies, and NGOs) to develop collaborative solutions that deliver benefits for all.
- Establish strategic alliances with industrial organisations, public sector organisations, academic institutions, and research think tanks.
- Establish supplier sustainability standards that incorporate ESG factors into procurement processes.
- Implement a materiality evaluation procedure to highlight areas of significant influence.
- Utilise co-investment and collaborative actions with partners to enhance sustainability efforts without requiring substantial financial investment.

3.6.2.3 Level 3: Value Creation

Objective: Embed sustainability into fundamental business operations to foster long-term value generation.

Key Actions:

- Integrate sustainability into business decision-making and risk management systems to accelerate the **transition** to a more sustainable future.
- Establish **transition** from corporate social responsibility to ESG-driven business models.
- Assess financial and non-financial impacts (e.g., carbon footprint, social capital).
- Establish sustainability key **performance** indicators linked to executive remuneration.
- Promote **innovation** via circular economy initiatives and sustainable product design.
- Establish cross-functional sustainability task forces to break down silos and foster enterprise-wide collaboration.

3.6.2.4 Level 4: Implementation

Objective: Connect the sustainability strategy with tactical implementation.

Key Actions:

- Enhance sustainability proficiency throughout operational teams via training and leadership development.
- Surmount implementation obstacles by obtaining C-suite endorsement and financial commitment.
- Utilise digital technologies (e.g., AI, Gen AI, blockchain) to improve supply chain transparency.
- Implement a sustainability-focused budgeting strategy to prioritise eco-friendly investments.
- Establish internal accountability systems to monitor advancement and guarantee implementation.

- Utilise agile project management methodologies to test sustainability efforts before comprehensive implementation.

3.6.2.5 Level 5: Institutional Impact

Objective: Exhibit quantifiable, extensive influence across economic, social, and environmental spheres, which demonstrates sustainability not as a bolt-on activity but a key driver of value creation.

Key Actions:

- Cultivate sustainable leadership beyond the organisation (e.g., industry coalitions, policy advocacy).
- Establish comprehensive impact measurement frameworks (e.g., UNSDG Impact Standards).
- To demonstrate long-term advantages, use evidence-based reporting that incorporates both quantitative and qualitative data.
- Foster public-private collaborations to facilitate systemic transformation.
- Establish a culture of sustainability through effective governance, robust policies, and ongoing education.

Practical Recommendation: Disseminate impact reports using authentic case studies to enhance credibility and motivate action throughout the sector.

3.6.2.6 Final Assessment

Sustainability leaders must acknowledge that maturity is a continuous journey rather than a single initiative. By adhering to organised advice throughout all five stages, businesses can go from fundamental compliance to industry leadership, ensuring that sustainability is integrated as an essential driver of long-term success.

However, the **SSM transition** journey may be oversimplified, potentially obscuring the nuanced reality of how organisations emerge and evolve in practice. Users must be aware of such limitations, and a more nuanced approach may need to be adopted to incorporate the following:

- Maturity scores need to align with actual ESG **performance** outcomes, value creation or competitive advantage.
- The framework suggests a linear progression assumption. Organisations may not evolve in a fixed sequential path, with experiences being more dynamic and iterative.
- The sectoral, cultural, and context will suggest that a one-size-fits-all will not be appropriate.
- Strategy models often suffer from being snapshot assessments. However, with Aland Gen AI, real-time versions can be adopted.
- The attainment of level 5 is not the end, and the organisation must keep pace with the evolving external environment.

The following section considers a range of metrics that can be incorporated into the **transition** journey (see Tables 3.4–3.7).

TABLE 3.4 Environmental impact metrics

Metric Category	*Key **Performance** Indicators*	*Measurement Tools/ Methods*	*Industry Examples*
Carbon footprint	Scope 1, 2, 3 GHG emissions (tCO_2e)	GHG protocol	Manufacturing: BMW tracks emissions per vehicle produced
	Carbon intensity ratio	Carbon accounting software	Tech: Microsoft's carbon negative commitment tracking
	Renewable energy adoption rate	Energy management systems	
Resource efficiency	Water consumption per unit	Smart metres	Food & beverage: Coca-Cola's water stewardship metrics
	Waste diversion rate	Waste audit tools	Retail: H&M's textile recycling measurements
	Material recycling rate	Life cycle assessment software	

Abbreviation: GHG, Green House Gases.

TABLE 3.5 Social impact metrics

Metric Category	*Key **Performance** Indicators*	*Measurement Tools/ Methods*	*Industry Examples*
Community impact	Local employment rate	Community surveys	Mining: Rio Tinto's indigenous employment rates
	Community investment ROI	Social impact assessment tools	
	Stakeholder engagement level	Stakeholder mapping software	
Labour practices	Worker satisfaction score	Employee surveys	Tech: Salesforce's equality metrics
	Health & safety incidents	OSHA reporting tools	Manufacturing: Toyota's safety metrics
	Training hours per employee	HR management systems	

Abbreviations: OSHA, Occupational Safety and Health Administration; ROI, return on investment.

TABLE 3.6 Economic **performance** metrics

Metric Category	*Key **Performance** Indicators*	*Measurement Tools/ Methods*	*Industry Examples*
Financial returns	Green revenue percentage	Financial reporting systems	Banking: JP Morgan's green financing targets
	Sustainable product margin	ERP systems	
	ESG-linked cost savings	Cost-benefit analysis tools	
Innovation	Sustainable product pipeline	R&D tracking systems	Automotive: Tesla's battery **innovation** metrics
	Green patent applications	IP management systems	
	Circular economy initiatives	**Innovation** management platforms	

Abbreviation: ERP, Enterprise Resource Planning.

TABLE 3.7 Governance and compliance

Metric Category	*Key **Performance** Indicators*	*Measurement Tools/ Methods*	*Industry Examples*
Risk management	ESG risk score	ESG rating platforms	Insurance: Allianz's climate risk assessment
	Supply chain sustainability score	Supplier assessment tools	
	Environmental compliance rate	Compliance management systems	
Transparency	ESG disclosure score	GRI reporting framework	Consumer goods: Unilever's sustainability reporting
	Stakeholder communication frequency	Communication tracking systems	
	Third-party verification coverage	Audit management platforms	

Abbreviation: GRI, Global Reporting Initiative.

3.7 Chapter Key Takeaways

The key takeaways from Chapter 3 on Sustainable Strategic Management are as follows:

1 **Problem-Solving Character of Organisations:** Understanding why specific strategic management initiatives fail despite being supported by a comprehensive top-down and bottom-up approach.

2 **Importance of SSM:** Addresses the challenges businesses face in a rapidly changing environment, emphasising the need to integrate long-term social, environmental, and economic goals. This approach helps organisations achieve resilience, adaptability, and alignment with societal demands.
3 **Public Sector Organisations:** Typically formulate effective policy-oriented responses to their external environment. An ideological divide may persist between the open, outward-orientated world and the closed, inward-orientated environment in which they function.
4 **Strategic Management Spectrum:** Organisations can be located between traditional and emergent paradigms. The conventional approach focuses on top-down policy-driven methods, while the emergent paradigm emphasises inclusive leadership, resilience, and future-oriented strategies. Leaders need to adopt more inclusive and flexible decision-making processes.
5 **Balancing Profit with Sustainability:** The sustainability dilemma often pits profit against societal responsibilities. However, **SSM** emphasises that financial returns and social impact are not mutually exclusive. Organisations can achieve long-term success by embedding sustainability into core business functions.
6 **Collaboration and Partnerships: SSM** promotes cooperation among businesses, governments, and stakeholders to address complex challenges, including climate change, resource management, and inequality. This transdisciplinary approach enables mutual learning and the development of innovative solutions to today's and tomorrow's grand challenges.
7 **Stakeholders:** Engaging stakeholders at the outset of sustainability-focused projects facilitates reciprocal learning within interdisciplinary and transdisciplinary teams and practice communities.

3.8 Self-Reflection Questions

1 Outline some of the limitations of traditional strategic management assumptions.
2 Discuss the strategic management spectrum in the context of sustainability. How do different approaches within this spectrum influence the integration of sustainability with corporate strategy?
3 Why is it crucial for strategic management to balance financial returns to achieve this balance?
4 Discuss whether profitability and sustainability can coexist. Provide an overview of some salient issues and discuss their relevance and application in formulating sustainable strategies.
5 Organisational leadership teams recognise the need to tackle the grand sustainability challenges, yet many still rely on the old, trusted causal models of the past that seek to optimise **performance**. Outline a strategic management approach to overcome this issue.

References

Appio, F.P., Frattini, F., Petruzzelli, A.M. and Neirotti, P., (2021). Digital transformation and innovation management: A synthesis of existing research and an agenda for future studies. *Journal of Product Innovation Management, 38*(1), pp.4–20.

Ateş, N.Y., Tarakci, M., Porck, J.P., van Knippenberg, D. and Groenen, P.J., (2020). The dark side of visionary leadership in strategy implementation: Strategic alignment, consensus, and commitment. *Journal of Management, 46*(5), pp.637–665.

Durand, R., Grant, R.M. and Madsen, T.L., (2017). The expanding domain of strategic management research and the quest for integration. *Strategic Management Journal, 38*(1), pp.4–16.

FT.com (2024). How companies are starting to back away from green targets. Available at: https://www.ft.com/content/c9fee776-1471-442c-aae8-8d78fe60faeb (Accessed: 31 August 2025).

FT.com (2025). BT braces for two-day strategy meeting with billionaire investor Mittal. Available at: https://www.ft.com/content/b19d93cd-43ca-41bd-9794-1518cd3a4c6a (Accessed: 15 December 2026).

Geregu Power (2023). Annual report and financial statements. Available at: https://www.geregu-powerplc.com/wp-content/uploads/2024/03/2023-Annual-Reports-and-Accounts.pdf

Grewatsch, S., Kennedy, S. and Bansal, P., (2023). Tackling wicked problems in strategic management with systems thinking. *Strategic Organization, 21*(3), pp.721–732.

Grimsgaard, W., (2022). *Design and strategy: A step-by-step guide*. Routledge.

Hitt, M.A., Holmes Jr, R.M. and Arregle, J.L., (2021). The (COVID-19) pandemic and the new world (dis) order. *Journal of World Business, 56*(4), p.101210.

Jarzabkowski, P., Lê, J.K., Seidl, D. and Vaara, E., (2025). Two decades of revolutionizing strategy research: How strategy-as-practice illuminates the complex, dynamic and consequential ways of doing strategy. *Academy of Management Collections, 4*(2), pp.55–76.

John-Eke, E.C. and Eke, J.K., (2020). Strategic planning and crisis management styles in organisations: A review of related literature. *Journal of Strategic Management, 5*(1), pp.36–46.

Keding, C., (2021). Understanding the interplay of artificial intelligence and strategic management: four decades of review research. *Management Review Quarterly, 71*(1), pp.91–134.

Kenny, G., (2023). *Strategy discovery: Achieving business resilience, engagement and performance*. Taylor & Francis.

Merriman, P., (2006). Mirror, Signal, Manoeuvre: Assembling and governing the motorway driver in late 1950s Britain. *The Sociological Review, 54*(1_suppl), pp.75–92.

Mikalef, P., Krogstie, J., Pappas, I.O. and Pavlou, P., (2020). Exploring the relationship between significant data analytics capability and competitive performance: The mediating roles of dynamic and operational capabilities. *Information & Management, 57*(2), p.103169.

Morningstar (2022). Yes, Sustainability is important to investors. Available at: https://www.morningstar.com/sustainable-investing/yes-sustainability-is-important-investors (Accessed: 31 August 2025).

North, D.C., (1999). Dealing with a non-ergodic world: Institutional economics, property rights, and the global environment. *Duke Environmental Law & Policy Forum, 10,* p.1.

O'Reilly III, C.A. and Tushman, M.L., (2013). Organisational ambidexterity: Past, present, and future. *Academy of Management Perspectives,* 27(4), pp.324–338.

Porter, M.E., (1985). Technology and competitive advantage. *Journal of Business Strategy, 5*(3), pp.60–78.

Porter, M.E. and Strategy, C., (1980). *Competitive strategy: Techniques for analyzing industries and competitors*. Free Press.

Rabetino, R., Kohtamäki, M. and Federico, J.S., (2021). A (re) view of the philosophical foundations of strategic management. *International Journal of Management Reviews, 23*(2), pp.151–190.

Salama, M.R. and McGarvey, R.G., (2023). Resilient supply chain to a global pandemic. *International Journal of Production Research, 61*(8), pp.2563–2593.

Shove, E., Watson, M. and Pantzar, M., (2012). *The dynamics of social practice: Everyday life and how it changes*. SAGE Publications Ltd.

Stead, J., (2025). Revolutionizing business with sustainable strategic management. *Open Access Government, 45*(1), pp.414–415. https://doi.org/10.56367/oag-045-11820

Stead, J.G. and Stead, W.E., (2013). The coevolution of sustainable strategic management in the global marketplace. *Organization & Environment, 26*(2), pp.162–183.

Stead, J.G. and Stead, W.E., (2014). *Sustainable strategic management*. Routledge.

Stead, J.G. and Stead, W.E., (2019). Why Porter is not enough: Economic foundations of sustainable strategic management. In T. Wunder (ed.), *Rethinking strategic management: Sustainable strategising for positive impact,* pp.67–85. Springer.

Sulich, A. and Soloducho-Pelc, L., (2024). Strategic management and business ecosystem scientific relations—key areas review. *International Journal of Innovation Studies, 8*(3), pp.287–296.

Suriyankietkaew, S. and Petison, P., (2019). A retrospective and foresight: Bibliometric review of international research on strategic management for sustainability, 1991–2019. *Sustainability, 12*(1), p.91.

UN Global Compact/Accenture (2022). 12th UN Global Compact – Accenture CEO Study. Available at: https://www.unglobalcompact.org.uk/ceo-study/ (Accessed: 31 August 2025).

4

THE SEVEN SCHOOLS OF SUSTAINABLE STRATEGIC MANAGEMENT

4.1 Learning Strategy Objectives

Upon finishing this chapter, you will have the ability to:

1 **Knowledge-Based Objectives:**

- Understand the criticality of sustainable strategic management as a framework for the sustainability leader.
- Appreciate and understand the seven schools of sustainable strategic management to facilitate the organisational journey.

2 **Skill-Based Objectives:**

- Appreciate and understand the necessary skills to apply the seven schools of sustainable strategic management.
- Overcome the "sustainability" dilemma when considering profit and societal decision-making.

3 **Attitude-Based Objectives:**

- Foster a sense of ethical and nature-based responsibility in strategy decision-making.
- Embrace open and collaborative strategy thinking while addressing sustainability challenges.

4.2 Introduction

Sustainability is an overarching framework for strategists to generate value, rather than just focusing on compliance and reporting activities. *Sustainable Strategic Management: Leadership with Purpose* aims to integrate concepts from several theoretical frameworks. Rather than rigidly adhering to a single school of thought, this chapter presents seven schools of **SSM**, highlighting their strengths and limitations.

DOI: 10.4324/9781003516774-5

The structure enables readers to explore various approaches to developing rational and integrated strategies. The configuration of available resources and relationships will affect the ability to implement strategy, to make the world a fairer place for all and in balance with nature. The rise in the practice of **SSM** will bring concomitant increases in the re-imagination of sectors built upon value-based partnerships.

The media highlights the bifurcation between organisations that attempt to adopt a regenerative business philosophy, with varying degrees of success, and those that cling to traditional ways of doing things. Environmental catastrophe is a pressing concern of today's society, and strategists play a crucial role in offering solutions.

Organisational isomorphism tells us of the rapid spread of sustainability strategies, regardless of the impact. New practices are driven in part by stakeholder pressure and shared norms within a sector. They can take three forms:

- Normative Isomorphism: Sustainability reporting frameworks are being adopted to influence behaviour.
- Mimetic: During uncertain times, the organisation may imitate the successful sustainability practices of its peers or industry leaders.
- Coercive: Organisations may feel pressured to implement sustainability strategies due to pressure from their stakeholders.

Collectively, these may act as stimulants for the **transitions**. Nonetheless, actions may not correlate with improvements in expected outcomes.

A deeper examination reveals some core challenges of applying strategic management in a sustainability context. Current approaches fail to capture the nuances, necessitating a more integrative and dynamic model. To achieve this, this chapter proposes the seven schools of sustainable strategic management, which have been derived from a synthesis of the existing literature and practical observations.

This chapter will feature insight into the **SSM** phenomenon and integrate theory with real-world examples. It will also consider the leverage points in embracing the spectrum of **SSM** approaches. The existing literature suggests that companies face complex ecosystems when **transitioning** towards sustainability (Stead and Stead, 2019). It recognises the criticality of sustainability in management and business education, exploring various schools of thought. **SSM** includes several styles, illustrating its multifaceted character and effect on strategic decision-making processes.

Each of the seven schools forms an integral part of the **SSM** system. This chapter acts as a bridge between the worlds of sustainability and strategy. Figure 4.1 illustrates how strategy is plagued with ambiguity of approaches. **SSM** enhances conventional strategy thinking and incorporates greater agility, resilience, and responsibility in business practices for adopters. Integrating strategy and sustainability will alter organisational posture and competitive dynamics. The primary objective of this chapter is to act as a bridge between these two domains.

The conventional strategic management approach has been essential throughout the decades, framing how business schools teach and practitioners deliver strategy. The tripartite approach of economic, social, and governance (ESG) provides an inclusive perspective on organisational success by merging traditional financial **performance** with

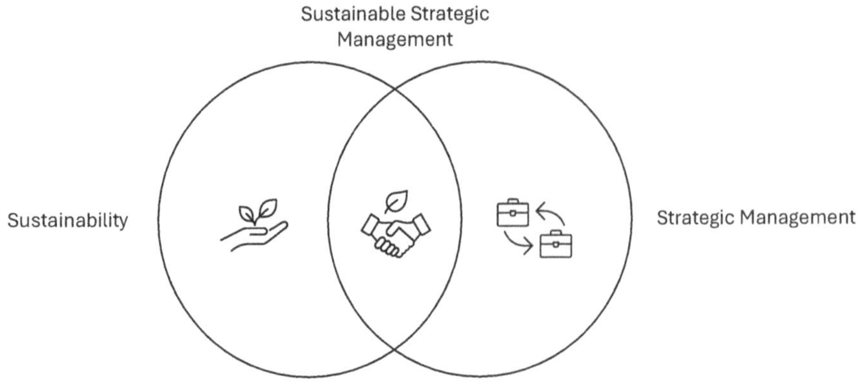

FIGURE 4.1 Sustainable strategic management overview

TABLE 4.1 The seven schools of sustainable strategic management

School	*Approach*	*Tactics for Integration*
1 Traditional strategic management	Emphasises conventional business strategies, focusing on financial **performance** and competitive advantage. Sustainability may be considered an auxiliary concern rather than a core element.	Use a variety of external and internal strategy frameworks and tools to integrate sustainability metrics.
2 Corporate social responsibility (CSR)	At its core this involves integrating social and environmental considerations into everyday business practices. CSR-focused approaches include emphasising citizenship, ethical behaviour, stakeholder engagement, and creating a better society.	Appoint dedicated CSR leadership roles and linking rewards with CSR **performance** metrics.
3 Environmental sustainability and green strategies	Focus on differing aspects of lessening environmental impact and promoting an ecological balance.	Encourage use of environmentally sustainable models, which align with strategic plans.
4 Social **innovation** and inclusive business	Incorporate societal challenges in business models. There needs to be balance among generating social impact alongside financial returns, fostering **innovation** for inclusive and sustainable development.	Collaborative solutions with underserved communities and consumers.
5 Circular economy and cradle-to-cradle design	The circular economy approach contrasts with traditional linear approaches. Keeping products, components, and material in use for as long as possible.	Redesign products with circularity to make more sustainable and efficient.
6 **Innovation** and disruption	Leverage and exploit **innovation** and disruptive technologies. The organisation should possess the capability and capacity to embrace technological changes.	Make measured investments in emerging and green technologies for stakeholder impact.
7 Global South perspectives	Recognition of the unique challenges faced and opportunities available to developing nations. Then develop strategies that exploit opportunities.	Participate in global conversations but develop localised strategies that promote resilience and equity in resource-limited contexts.

environmental stewardship and social impact. The conventional strategic management paradigm, which emphasises competitive advantage and market positioning, frequently overlooks these factors. Integrating sustainability into strategic management enables organisations to address the daily challenges of contemporary markets with greater efficacy and consideration of ethics.

The expansionist goals of the corporate world were once well-suited to the workforce. Now, organisations must rethink their strategy as Gen Z values and behaviours transform the workplace, with issues of work-life balance, purpose-driven work, and flexible working methods becoming increasingly important. Within this dynamic, **SSM** needs to stretch minds and be transformative. A mantra of doing things differently with less can help succeed. This long-term perspective needs to align with the planetary boundaries and utilise renewable resources. Real change often occurs when we shed tightly held mindsets.

The seven schools of sustainable strategic management are presented in Table 4.1. The opening contention is that such an integrative approach offers untapped potential for organisations to make the **transition** from strategy to **SSM**.

STRATEGY NUGGET

How the Seven Schools Interconnect to Form a Holistic SSM Approach

The seven schools, as presented in Figure 4.2, should not be viewed as operating in silos, but rather as complementary and integrative. When considered holistically, these schools can create a synergistic approach that achieves strategic goals.

The traditional strategic management school can serve as the foundational element, as essential tools such as SWOT (Strengths, Weaknesses, Opportunities, and Threats), Porter's, and PESTLE can initiate the analysis. More sophisticated tools will be presented in Chapter 5. To do this properly, C-suite executives and boards should consider the time dimension – short, medium, and long-term – and how to **transition** along each dimension. Net-zero targets are 2050 and beyond. To move the organisation forward without disrupting nature's balanced ecosystem is a moral step.

Two of the seven pillars can aid this. A corporate social responsibility (CSR) approach, combined with environmental sustainability and green strategies, can help shift the focus from shareholders to a broader perspective, moving beyond a siloed lens. This broadens the scope of stakeholders and ecological parameters. This reinforces the thought of value creation beyond financial returns. Carefully blending CSR, environmental sustainability, and green strategies will create the proper context for strategic decision-making.

As organisations **transition** from compliance to a source of competitive advantage, the circular economy (CE) and cradle-to-cradle (C2C) design will serve as catalysts for transformation. Executives will seek solutions beyond linear models. The work of Kate Raworth (2018), with her Doughnut Economics development paradigm, can provide a mantra for meeting the needs of all within the means of the planet. Figure 4.3 depicts the components within which organisations should operate. The inner ring provides the social foundation,

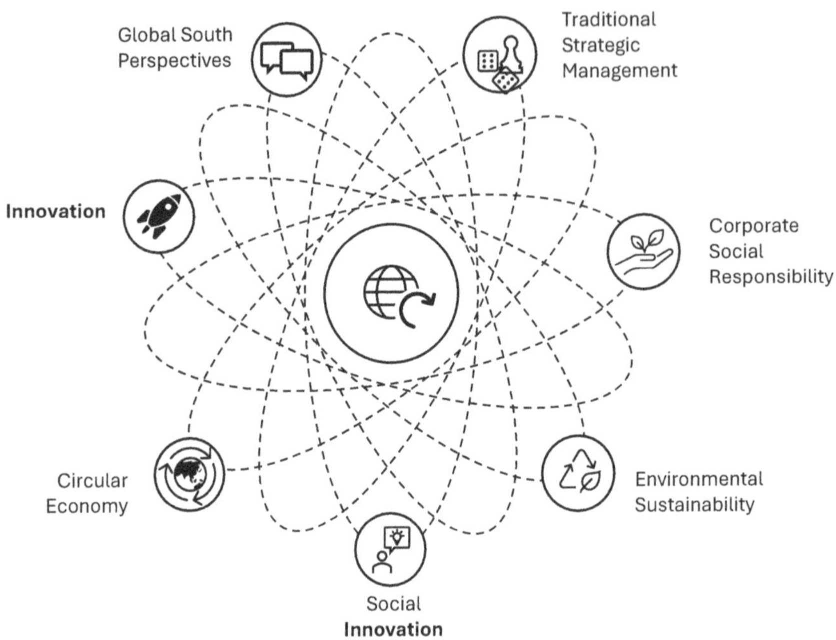

FIGURE 4.2 The integrative nature of the seven schools of **SSM**

and the ecological ceiling lies in the outer ring. Raworth's model can help strategists to work within a safe space.

A persistent gap in strategy processes is due to overlooking two critical elements: social **innovation** and inclusive business, as well as Global South perspectives. For organisations that pursue a societal agenda and cross borders, this can help strategies be locally relevant and impactful. Both epistemological frameworks can offer powerful insight into sustainability for marginalised groups. The structural power in balances created by Western hegemony creates an environment where both voices are at the periphery. Including both groups is not only morally right but also creates market-based opportunities.

Organisations can transform sustainability from a peripheral idea into a core driver of long-term value creation by orchestrating these seven schools into a coherent strategic planning approach.

1 Which of the seven schools offers the most untapped potential for organisations to make the **transition** from strategy to **SSM**?
2 What are the opportunities and strategic risks of pursuing "net-zero targets for 2050" in the current business environment?
3 How can organisations effectively balance their CSR strategies without creating a strategic paralysis or conflicting priorities?

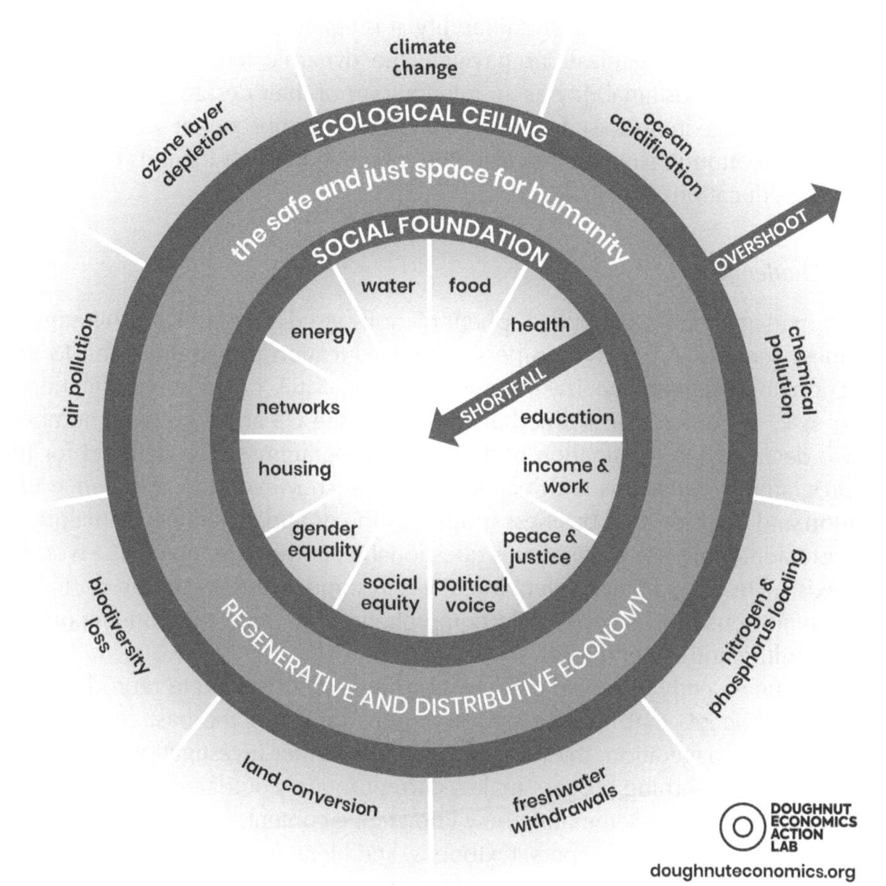

FIGURE 4.3 Raworth's Doughnut development paradigm (Credit: Kate Raworth and Christian Guthier. CC-BY-SA 4.0)

Source: Raworth (2017).

4.3 SSM School 1 – Traditional Strategic Management

4.3.1 Setting the Scene

Large and medium-sized organisations employ skilled MBAs who are professionals and are run by boards with strategic competence. Nevertheless, the corporate realm is replete with insufficient or flawed strategies and exemplary concepts performed ineffectively.

What are the fundamental causes of this failure? What factors contribute to CEOs making poor decisions despite abundant accessible expertise? Is it solely the result of numerous elements that must be navigated within a complicated, evolving landscape? Issues can be characterised partly as geopolitical dangers, increasingly demanding consumers, technological advancements, the expansion of the silver economy, excessive ambition, avarice, internal political manoeuvring, and other corporate vices.

Given the enduring nature of sustainability, it is essential to prepare current and future leaders to help their organisations navigate the dynamic terrain. University curricula should incorporate sustainability as an integral part of their design, producing graduates equipped to engage in the sustainability ecosystem. The subsequent section will examine the current situation in strategic management practice through the lens of an MBA business school education.

4.3.2 Challenge

Strategic management is an applied, phenomenon-based, and critical programme taught in business schools. Arguably, business school education programmes fail to embed a connection to sustainability. The premier full-time MBA business certification is currently at risk, as numerous esteemed institutions in the US and a growing number in the UK have declared the termination of their MBA programmes. The demand for full-time MBA programmes fluctuates with economic cycles; however, the prevalence of digital disruption and double-sided business models as the dominant strategy is making the relevance of traditional MBA programmes questionable, as they are rooted in a world that no longer exists. Despite some excellent initiatives in some business schools, critics question whether many business schools truly comprehend and value the connection between their curriculum and the end user.

A colleague recently observed that most business schools tend to reproduce the same models and concepts that have existed in various forms for the past century. Although this may be an exaggeration, the message warrants further investigation. The continuous digitisation of the learning process makes current models outdated, requiring increased agility in creating and disseminating new knowledge content.

Moreover, the plethora of papers, textbooks, and literature on MBA curricula addresses the overarching principles of strategic management. Yet, only a select few concentrate on how businesses generate value in sustainable contexts. Nevertheless, companies consistently seek to capitalise on specialisation, differentiation, and cost advantage. However, knowledge-intensive organisations will perform an increasingly influential role in innovating strategic management capability at the expense of new MBA hires. For organisations that fail to deliver value from their strategies, the above scenario creates uneasiness among senior management.

Strategic planning evolves and, if carried out appropriately, will help organisations solve increasingly complex problems. This requires a shift from purely analytical to creative approaches (consider McKinsey's reputation for analysis but its lack of ability to reinvent itself).

Current practices suggest that improving strategic management capability involves a series of iterative cycles that encompass business ecosystems, value propositions, digital environments, people, and the flow of knowledge. These cycles include leveraging data to obtain actionable insights and strategy, data-driven marketing, and fast new-product development processes. Iterations occur during the strategic process, and the subsequent sections delineate some of the critical imperatives that need to be managed and integrated into a redesigned, relevant programme for the enterprise.

The MBA product has relied on the capstone strategic management course, but commentators have been critical of the need for more alignment with the changing nature of the business world. Specific strategic management issues include:

- Traditional approaches often involve long-term planning; however, when it comes to implementing revisions and renewal strategies, these long-term plans must be more flexible to respond to changing circumstances.
- Predictable market conditions with incremental changes to products and services are no longer apt.
- The product-centric focus often overlooks the customer.
- Technology is no longer separate but is intertwined with strategic management.
- External-facing ecosystems are now superseding the internal focus on capabilities and resources for collaboration.

Sustainability is no longer viewed as a peripheral issue; it has become a fundamental component, albeit without a straightforward answer. When stakeholders perceive sustainability as an ancillary activity, they doubt the organisation's dedication to authentic, long-term environmental and social responsibility. This perception may erode trust and credibility, potentially damaging the company's reputation. Stakeholders are becoming increasingly astute at differentiating between superficial sustainability initiatives and genuine, integrated strategies.

Furthermore, when sustainability is regarded as an afterthought instead of an integral element of strategy planning, the organisation must capitalise on many possible advantages. Incorporating sustainability into strategic plans can foster **innovation**, enhance operational efficiencies, and provide new market opportunities. Organisations that neglect to adopt this comprehensive strategy may encounter opposition from discerning stakeholders and fall behind rivals who utilise sustainability as a key distinction.

Key components that differentiate from other schools:

- Corporate mindset sees sustainability as a cost centre instead of a value creation opportunity.
- Short-term quarterly financial targets override the longer-term sustainability goals.
- The integration of ESG is at best tenuous.

4.4 SSM School 2 – CSR Approach

4.4.1 Setting the Scene

This school advocates integrating social and environmental considerations into business practices. By integrating CSR and strategic management, leadership decision-making can be informed by stakeholder perspectives and ethical considerations. While CSR consciousness is one matter, the capability to analyse complex strategy-related issues is paramount. CSR-focused approaches can include ethical behaviour, stakeholder engagement, and the triple bottom line (people, planet, profit).

In a ground-breaking paper, Milton Friedman (1970) championed the concept of a business's social responsibility. His extensively referenced article, "The social responsibility of business is to increase profits," strengthened the division between corporations and managers. He vigorously argued against the notion of social responsibilities for corporations:

- Human beings, not corporations, have a moral responsibility for their actions.
- Managers have a fiduciary responsibility to act in the interests of their shareholders.
- Rather than corporations, the state is responsible for social issues and problems.

A prevalent perspective today, and the foundation of this book, is that firms, as corporate citizens, bear a dual duty for their economic and social objectives. But how did we arrive at this contemporary viewpoint, and what are the implications for **SSM**?

4.4.2 Evolution

The concept of CSR extends beyond a mere 20th-century phenomenon in the US. Husted (2015) provides a comprehensive analysis of CSR from 1800 to 1914, drawing on data from the UK, US, Japan, India, and Germany. Some antecedents of CSR were revealed, but in his words, "Current CSR practice seems relatively tepid" (p. 138).

The landmark decision, Dodge v. Ford Motor Co (1919), established that for-profit corporations must operate to make a profit. Socially responsible activities became permissible when serving a business purpose. Building on this, Milton Friedman's (1970) article shifted the imperative of corporations' objectives.

During the 1980s and 1990s, the ripple effects of CSR expanded to encompass broader concerns, including environmental sustainability, ethical employment practices, and community involvement. This era witnessed the emergence of voluntary standards and reporting frameworks, including the Global Reporting Initiative (GRI) and ISO 14001.

The GRI offers a thorough and standardised framework for sustainability reporting, encompassing diverse economic, environmental, and social aspects, enabling organisations to present a comprehensive overview of their sustainability **performance**. ISO 14001 provides a systematic framework for ecological management that helps organisations identify, control, and mitigate their environmental impacts through a structured methodology.

The next phase of evolution, marked by increasing adoption in the 21st century, saw CSR integrated with strategic management. The goal was to harmonise economic development with social and environmental conservation. Nonetheless, despite advancements, numerous difficulties remain. The increasing need for openness and accountability necessitates companies investing in comprehensive data collection and reporting systems.

Moreover, incorporating CSR into business culture continues to pose a considerable problem. Although high-level commitment is crucial, integrating CSR ideals across the organisation requires continuous training, communication, and incentives to ensure that all employees understand and support the company's CSR goals. CSR can propel strategic initiatives that generate competitive advantage and elevate reputation and brand recognition. Equally, CSR seeks to transform corporations into proactive social and sustainable partners, providing social, environmental, and economic benefits. This dual perspective has attained validity by endorsing Michael Porter's research on competitive advantage. Debates concerning the correlation between CSR theory and practice exist, with a current emphasis on inclusive value creation (Donaldson, 2023).

Some questions to contemplate about value creation:

- What do you bring regarding orchestration, people, practices, information, services, and governance?
- What assets (technologies, processes, relationships, products, industrial/professional, regional bodies) can we connect with?
- What are the benefits and costs?
- How to connect and provide value opportunities for all members?
- How can members be usefully mobilised?
- What can members do for you? Remember reciprocity. There has to be something in it for them, too.

Key components that differentiate from other schools:

- Formulated CSR leadership roles and supporting structures.
- Partnership strategies to strengthen environmental sustainability, ethical employment practices, and community involvement.
- Measurable community impact through dedicated investment programmes.

4.5 SSM School 3 – Environmental Sustainability and Green Strategies

4.5.1 Setting the Scene

As sustainability matures, organisations can focus on environmental impact, considering ways to mitigate adverse effects and foster innovative sustainable practices. This strategy fulfils regulatory obligations and societal expectations while offering opportunities for **innovation**, cost reduction, and a competitive edge.

Policies often consist of statements for stakeholders to understand, as well as a separate set of objectives. Commitments to environmental sustainability are established, and the organisation can help its stakeholders become more effective ecological stewards. This typically involves a consortium of partners to enhance their ecosystem.

As demand increases, energy companies have garnered significant media attention due to modifications in their green plans; nonetheless, they face challenges in implementing these changes for their shareholders. The UK Shell oil conglomerate has recently released an update to its **transition** strategy, postponing its carbon intensity targets for 2030 and increasing its reliance on liquefied gas. This amendment to its decarbonisation strategy received over 75% approval from shareholders.

4.5.2 Evolution

During the early 1990s, environmental laws were comparatively lax, with a predominant focus on pollution control and waste management. Governments primarily concentrated on establishing fundamental rules for emissions and effluents, with compliance often motivated by a desire to avoid penalties rather than a genuine commitment to sustainability.

As scientific information regarding the detrimental impacts of industrial operations on the environment accumulated, the regulatory framework began to tighten. The deficiencies of conventional modelling resulted in a miscalculation of the dangers of climate change and the **transition** to a low-carbon economy. This led to the development of a more comprehensive approach to environmental sustainability.

As the 2000s commenced, more rigorous legislation and international agreements were established to reduce carbon emissions, promote renewable energy, and promote resource efficiency. The fallacy of the "grow now, clean up later" mindset, as implemented in industrialised nations, has come under scrutiny. This reflects a lack of appreciation for the benefits of economic expansion that benefit populations, while certain social groups often encounter disasters related to environmental and natural resource issues. The escalating inequities among emerging countries, both internally and externally, coupled with the heightened risk to various species and air and water pollution, render an exclusive focus on expansion detrimental.

Implementing sustainable strategies involves integrating environmental considerations into all aspects of corporate operations. **SSM** strategy can aid CEOs in decision-making and improve organisational positioning in a competitive external environment. Today's automobile industry is seeking electric automobiles in collaboration with battery manufacturers, which are essential for achieving a competitive advantage. The rapid expansion of the electric vehicle market has intensified competition, prompting Tesla to reduce its pricing strategies. The automotive sector is challenged to achieve lower production costs while enhancing environmental **performance**. Tesla has lately declared that its growth will be notably lower.

Key components that differentiate from other schools:

- Environmental compliance goes beyond the minimum.
- Ring-fence investment in renewable energy and clean technology.
- Science-based **performance** targets for emission reduction.

4.6 SSM School 4 – Social Innovation and Inclusive Business

4.6.1 Setting the Scene

Integrating social **innovation** and inclusive business strategies provides innumerable benefits to stakeholders. Such approaches can enhance the quality of life for communities. However, the decline in trust in global corporations and governments following the 2008 financial crisis impeded societal-oriented initiatives. Nonetheless, the risk has decreased due to the increasing influence of non-governmental organisations (NGOs), with authors such as Osburg (2013) presenting a compelling argument that **innovation** is a vital catalyst for societal change.

The hybrid concept can present numerous obstacles. This hybridisation can generate difficulties by amplifying goal variation within leadership teams, frequently necessitating the adaptation of existing organisational processes and structures. Social **innovation** can allow organisations to address social challenges while creating economic value by enhancing workforce productivity. Employees can build enthusiasm by being involved in social **innovation** practices.

An inclusive business model seeks commercial sustainability while producing social benefits by focusing on the base of the pyramid (BoP), the most extensive yet poorest socio-economic group (Prahalad, 2005). The BoP refers to the approximately 4 billion individuals living on less than $2.50 per day.

The extant literature highlights the obstacles associated with **transitioning** to inclusive business models, which can be encapsulated as insufficient incentives for change, the need for new competencies, conflicts in goals and identity, and the issue of obtaining legitimacy (Lashitew, Bals, and van Tulder, 2020).

4.6.2 Evolution

Drucker (1975) noted that social **innovation** dates back nearly two centuries, predating technological **innovation**, yet technological **innovation** is of greater interest to scholars. The infrequent references originate from the 1920s, and to examine this progression, we reference the review by Edwards-Schachter and Wallace (2017) on the phenomenon of social **innovation**. They derived 252 definitions of social **innovation** and concluded:

"Our findings show that SI was introduced as an analytical concept by incipient academic communities and has spread in the last decades as a normative concept fuelled by development and **innovation** policies."

Inclusive business has made significant progress in recent decades, **transitioning** from peripheral societal initiatives to become a central strategic pillar for many organisations. As worldwide awareness of social injustices and environmental degradation grew, so did the recognition of the crucial role these challenges play in shaping our world.

As inclusive business models evolve, they will deliver social impact and commercial success, which can be mutually reinforcing. Businesses have increasingly adopted more sophisticated approaches to engage with BoP communities. Creating value for society and achieving business success is compatible and necessary for long-term sustainability in a rapidly changing world.

NGOs can benefit from collaborating with enterprises that prioritise social **innovation** and inclusivity. These partnerships can furnish NGOs with additional resources, technological expertise, and market access, enabling them to scale their impact more effectively. NGOs can enhance service delivery and reach more beneficiaries by leveraging the private sector's business acumen and logistical capabilities. Furthermore, fostering a more integrated approach to tackling social problems will help to bridge the gap between humanitarian efforts and market-driven solutions.

Coherent social **innovation** and inclusive business practices can serve as a competitive differentiator for Small and Medium-sized Enterprises (SMEs). Firms often operate near their communities, affording them a unique understanding of local needs and challenges. By integrating social objectives into their business strategies, SMEs can foster stronger relationships with customers and suppliers, enhance brand loyalty, and expand into new markets.

Impact investors who progressively pursue enterprises that provide financial returns and social benefits are attracted. Integrating social **innovation** and inclusive business strategies for major organisations can improve corporate reputation, mitigate risks, and ensure long-term viability. These corporations can participate in corporate social **innovation** (Dionisio and de Vargas, 2020), utilise their scale and resources to effect systemic change, shape industry norms, and advance global development objectives.

Social **innovation** and inclusive business have extensive ramifications, promoting a more inclusive and equitable global economy. By catering to the requirements of marginalised groups and advocating for sustainable practices, these strategies create social value and foster economic growth and resilience throughout all sectors of society.

Social **innovation** and inclusive business are essential elements of **SSM**. Organisations can achieve substantial social impact by addressing major social issues through innovative and inclusive strategies, while ensuring economic sustainability.

Key components that differentiate from other schools:

- **Innovation** processes incorporating co-creation.
- Partnerships with social enterprises and impact investors.
- Explicit employment strategies, such as targeting vulnerable communities for employment.

4.7 SSM School 5 – Circular Economy and Cradle to Cradle Design

4.7.1 Setting the Scene

The significance of the circular model is exemplified by its implementation by numerous national governments, including the European Union. Conversations, spearheaded mainly by practitioners, policymakers, associations, and corporations, have intensified regarding the constraints of conventional linear economic models, characterised by an extract-produce-use-dump approach. The realisation of not being sustainable has prompted the creation of sustainable financial models, including the CE and C2C design principles. The difficulties in developing more sustainable solutions have led to frameworks establishing closed-loop systems, wherein resources and products are perpetually repurposed, thereby minimising waste and environmental effects.

As a result, the CE concept stresses the significance of designing products and systems for durability, reuse, remanufacturing, and recycling. A prominent subject in sustainability discourse is the capacity to maintain resource utilisation for an extended duration, maximising value extraction before the recovery and regeneration of materials after their service life. This strategy minimises environmental impact and promotes economic resilience by mitigating the risks associated with resource shortages and volatility.

The C2C design emphasises the creation of goods and systems that emulate natural processes, ensuring that every output serves as either a technical or biological nutrient. Braungart and McDonough (2009) initiated this design philosophy founded on three core principles: eradicating waste, using renewable energy, and celebrating diversity. C2C aims to establish a regenerative economy that promotes human and environmental well-being by ensuring that all materials can be safely reintegrated into the environment or permanently recycled through industrial processes.

Both approaches facilitate collaborative conversations among stakeholders, easing tensions and encouraging organisational transformation that will lessen environmental harm.

4.7.2 Evolution of the Concept

Since 1972, the Kalundborg Symbiosis project in Denmark has exemplified the notion by establishing and implementing the world's first industrial symbiosis with a circular approach to production. This project demonstrated how waste materials from one industry can be utilised as inputs for another, creating a network of resource exchange that reduces waste and enhances economic efficiency. Collaboration in this form enhances resilience and yields financial benefits while also reducing environmental impact and expenses.

The academic literature reveals advancements that align with practical applications. The origins of the CE can be traced back to industrial ecology. This discipline originated in the 1980s, concentrating on the movement of materials and energy within industrial systems. Building on this linear process will exhaust the planet's limited resources, necessitating organisations of all sizes to unite to mitigate the adverse effects of discarded products inside the Technosphere. The therapeutic use of resources expands the domain of waste management and holds the possibility for transformative models with diverse growth and sustainability goals. Embracing both offers a foundation for leadership activity; paradoxically, they can be highly apparent and deliberately ambiguous. The advantages transform into a generic truth instead of being realised.

The CE literature extensively references the concept (Geissdoerfer, Savaget, Bocken, and Hultink, 2017; Korhonen, Honkasalo, and Seppälä, 2018; Murray, Skene, and Haynes, 2017; Raworth, 2018). The authors acknowledge the associated concepts of the CE. Ogunmakinde, Sher, and Egbelakin's (2021) semi-systemic review identified 14 circular concepts. Such interdisciplinary approaches optimise resource use and reduce environmental impact by treating industrial systems as part of the broader ecological system.

Popular CE definitions include the Ellen MacArthur Foundation (2016): "A circular economy is restorative and regenerative by design and aims to keep products, components, and materials at their highest utility and value at all times, distinguishing between technical and biological cycles."

C2C design concepts were established in 2002 with the publication of Braungart and McDonough's 2009 book, *Cradle to Cradle: Remaking the Way We Make Things*. The book challenged conventional design practice by promoting materials that could be recycled without losing quality.

The biomimicry approach emphasises the creation of systems where waste becomes obsolete and becomes a valuable resource for new production. The focus is on minimising waste and creating positive ecological footprints. Shifts in strategic thinking resulted in new forms of product design, supply chain management, and business models that prioritise resource efficiency and sustainability.

Key components that differentiate from other schools:

- Designing products and systems for durability, reuse, remanufacturing, and recycling.
- The biomimicry approach emphasises the creation of systems where waste becomes obsolete and becomes a valuable resource for new production.
- Product as a service aligns with sustainability principles.

4.8 SSM School 6 – Innovation and Disruption

4.8.1 Setting the Scene

The pandemic compelled organisations to acquire additional resources to achieve optimal outcomes. Following decades of admonitions on sustainability concerns, their current problem is augmented by the need for transformation: **transitioning** from a profit- and growth-centric model to one emphasising **innovation**, industry collaboration, value, and sustainability.

Organisations must embrace **innovation** and disruption to leverage value. This is one of the key emergent strategic differentiators, but the social challenges within market frictions must maintain justice and fairness. The positive aspect of sustainability is that doing things differently can help exploit opportunities for all. Organisations must prioritise utilising **innovation** and disruptive technologies to promote sustainability. With the planet's population exceeding 8 billion, this places a strain on resources and requires alterations in their utilisation.

Innovative literacy and architecting skills must be part of the CEO's leadership toolkit. One of the best books that should be compulsory reading for any MBA and business executive is the seminal book by the late Christensen, 2015, *The Inventor's Dilemma*. He raises the pertinent question: Why do technologies cause the best firms to fall? This ground-breaking work analyses in great depth how technology shifts can change the status quo, often without incumbents realising. **Innovation** and disruption lie at the crux of the phenomenon.

This perspective challenges the prevailing assumptions that size alone confers sustainable competitive advantage. Today's organisations that pursue sustainability strategies may possess a technical solution to a problem, but are unable to realise their return on investment and need a business model to create value. This theme will be explored in Chapter 9.

4.8.2 Evolution of the Concept

Business expansion, resilience, and sustainability depend on enhancing productivity and establishing faster routes to **innovation**. This frequently necessitates acquiring new knowledge, skills, and innovative thinking. The **innovation** process should be regarded as a sequence of alterations within a comprehensive system, encompassing internal resources and the organisation's external market.

Many publications have examined the discourse surrounding scholarly outputs, which encompass a wide range of themes. While sometimes used interchangeably, terms such as eco-**innovation**, sustainability-oriented, and green **innovation** encapsulate the notion of transcending mere economic objectives.

Using a bibliometric methodology involving analysis of 1,108 papers to elucidate the temporal progression of information about sustainable **innovation**, Afeltra, Alerasoul, and Strozzi (2023) identified five themes:

- Influence of regulation
- Markets and technology
- Determinants of eco-**innovation**
- Green **innovation**
- Interaction of policy, legislation, and green **innovation**.

Bower and Christensen (1995) introduced the seminal concept of "disruptive **innovation**." This phrase is well-used in business circles, considering how small companies with fewer resources can successfully challenge dominant businesses. It emphasises the importance of being willing to cannibalise one's products and embrace change, even at the risk of short-term losses, to stay competitive in the long run.

Sustainability is a long-term phenomenon, and disruptive **innovation** has proven to be a powerful approach to **innovation**-led growth. Yet, fascinatingly, Christensen, Raynor, and McDonald (2013) suggest that the concept of disruptive **innovation** is sometimes misused.

Intriguingly, a specific proposition by Kahn (2018) is that to reap the benefits of **innovation**, a practitioner must recognise three things: **innovation** is a process, an outcome, and a mindset.

Addressing these difficulties is a concern for numerous organisations seeking a competitive advantage. Within the context of sustainability, **innovation** is a social and political act that requires management. Questions that need to be addressed include:

What is the type of **innovation** our sustainability solution is based on?

- Challenges that help underserved customers.
- New Market: The product/service enables customers to complete tasks faster and more cost-effectively.
- Operational: Moving from linear to circular approaches, which can rethink existing value chains.
- Disruptive: Using artificial intelligence (AI) to disrupt prevailing business operations.

Innovation-driven research and development have led to the creation of sustainable, durable, repairable, and recyclable products. Such creativity can help organisations achieve their goals and delight customers. Today's customers increasingly prioritise environmental consciousness and are likely to prefer to build a relationship with organisations committed to sustainability.

Key components that differentiate from other schools:

- **Innovation** labs are addressing sustainability challenges within their respective sectors.
- Partnerships and ecosystems involving tech startups and research institutions.
- Business model **innovation** that explores the concept of **innovation** as a process, an outcome, and a mindset.

4.9 SSM School 7 – Global South Perspectives

4.9.1 Setting the Scene

The Global South's standpoint acknowledges the distinct issues emerging nations face and highlights measures that address their socio-economic and environmental circumstances.

This observation fosters inclusive and sustainable development worldwide. The Global South comprises nations, primarily in Africa, Latin America, Asia, and the Middle East, characterised by a legacy of colonialism, socio-economic challenges, and developmental aspirations. In contrast to their affluent counterparts in the Global North, these nations contend with distinct issues stemming from past inequities and current global dynamics.

The Global South encompasses geographical and socio-economic dimensions, reflecting the inequalities in prosperity and power within the international context. In recent years, the discourse around the Global South has evolved to emphasise the development of theoretical frameworks and practical approaches to enhance opportunities for all. This necessitates a more nuanced understanding of the sustainability phenomenon, which, from a Global South perspective, includes:

- Economic Vulnerabilities: Reliance on volatile natural resource exports that can create boom-cycles.
- Resource Constraints: Financial and workforce capital are insufficient to meet needs.

- Institutional Constraints: Unclear responsibilities between national and regional authorities.
- Governance Challenges: Limited monitoring systems to track sustainability key **performance** indicators.
- External Pressure: Disproportionate exposure to climate risks.
- Socio-Cultural Dimensions: Immediate concerns can overshadow long-term sustainability concerns.
- Technology Transfer: Intellectual property laws hinder incorporation and **transition** to green technology.

Then, to operationalise solutions, the structural impediments include:

- Government-Led Approaches: Embed sustainability in national strategic and development planning.
- Multi-Stakeholder Mechanisms: Integrate public-private partnerships (PPPs) under controlled oversight.
- Innovative Financial: Integrate concessional funding with commercial investment.
- Governance Integration: Develop tools to assess policy contradictions across sectors.
- Knowledge Systems: Enhance levels of sustainability literacy through education systems.
- Implementation Deficits: Identify ways to overcome sustainability strategy blockages.
- Resilience Building: Comprehensive assessment of climate and environmental risks.

4.9.2 Evolution of the Concept

The discussion on strategic management in the Global South requires greater industrialisation, especially concerning sustainability. Although there is a pressing need for sustainable development solutions, academic research on this topic requires more work. The absence of academic frameworks leads to a limited understanding of how businesses in these areas can successfully integrate industrialisation and sustainability into their strategic management practices.

The necessity for a more rigorous examination of the historical development and distinct issues encountered by enterprises in the Global South intensifies this gap, obstructing the creation of contextually pertinent frameworks and strategies. Without a solid intellectual basis, governments and business leaders in the Global South lack the essential knowledge to navigate the intricate relationship between economic growth and sustainability.

This neglect creates a strategy black box, wherein general strategic management frameworks are utilised without regard for local peculiarities, leading to inefficient or counterproductive results. To promote sustainable economic growth in the Global South, there is an immediate requirement for focused research that connects historical analysis with modern strategic management, highlighting the distinct pathways and needs of firms functioning in these varied and dynamic contexts.

The practical perspective is illustrated by the World Economic Forum summit in Davos, Switzerland, in January 2018, themed "Creating a Shared Future in a Fractured World," which raised significant concerns, especially regarding the current conditions of Global South nations and the pursuit of the 2030 UN Sustainable Development Goals.

Notwithstanding all policies and interventions, the chasm between the populace and governmental institutions is increasing. The government remains distanced from the populace, necessitating the inclusion of many individuals due to inadequate leadership and marginalisation.

Uplifting the impoverished and rectifying leadership disjunction involve more than merely instituting absent, targeted human capital development frameworks for sustainable development. It currently encompasses implementing a novel governance model and institutional leadership that embodies a new developmental agenda through inclusive and effective PPPs that are substantive and focused on the populace.

In contrast to their counterparts in the Global North, developing states in the Global South have populations with larger percentages of young people than older individuals. This demographic offers both an opportunity and a problem for sustainable development. The youthful demographic may be a significant catalyst for **innovation**, economic expansion, and social change.

Conversely, **SSM** is essential for the possibility of underutilising its potential. The disparity between academic research and practical frameworks specific to the Global South necessitates the development and implementation of robust strategies to leverage this demographic advantage in a sustainable manner.

Organisations must, therefore, proactively adapt their human capital strategies to address their sustainable challenges. This calls for capacity-building projects that can steer the future strategic pathways in research, **innovation**, and technology for the sustainable development of societies, sustainable strategic management and its practical applications, along with how it surpasses the traditional approach to strategic management.

Key components that differentiate from other schools:

- Characterised by a legacy of colonialism, socio-economic difficulties, and developmental ambitions.
- Characterised by the use of multilateral funding for core sustainability projects.
- In contrast to their Global North counterparts, the Global South possesses populations with a greater youth demographic than older people.

Table 4.2 contrasts the seven schools of **SSM** with traditional strategic management and illustrates the areas of benefit.

TABLE 4.2 Comparison of the seven schools of **SSM** with traditional strategic management

School	*Practical Applications*	*Advantages over Traditional Strategic Management*
1 Traditional strategic management	Leverage tools like SWOT and PESTLE with sustainability metrics. Integrate ESG factors into resource allocation and strategy.	Adds long-term resilience to short-term financial goals. Considers environmental and social risks.
2 Corporate social responsibility (CSR)	Develop shared value initiatives (e.g., ethical sourcing, community programmes). Adopt stakeholder engagement strategies.	Expands beyond shareholder value to benefit multiple stakeholders. Aligns with UNSDGs for global credibility.
3 Environmental sustainability	Adopt green supply chains. Invest in renewable energy and carbon reduction technologies.	Prepares for future regulatory changes. Enhances **innovation** with eco-friendly products/services.

(Continued)

TABLE 4.2 (*Continued*)

School	*Practical Applications*	*Advantages over Traditional Strategic Management*
4 Social **innovation** & inclusive business	Design solutions for underserved markets (e.g., microfinance, affordable healthcare). Build partnerships with NGOs.	Creates shared value by addressing societal challenges. Expands market reach and fosters trust in communities.
5 Circular economy & cradle-to-cradle	Design products for reuse, repair, and recycling. Establish closed-loop systems in supply chains.	Reduces waste and optimises resource use. Improves cost-efficiency and mitigates resource scarcity risks.
6 **Innovation** & disruption	Use AI and IoT for operational efficiency. Deploy blockchain for transparent supply chains.	Encourages proactive transformation instead of resisting change. Opens new revenue streams and competitive advantages.
7 Global South perspectives	Develop localised strategies tailored to specific socio-economic and environmental contexts. Build resilience in underserved markets.	Tailors strategies to regional needs, fostering equitable growth. Creates long-term opportunities in emerging markets.

Abbreviations: AI, artificial intelligence; ESG, economic, social, and governance; NGOs, non-governmental organisations; SWOT, Strengths, Weaknesses, Opportunities, and Threats; UNSDGs, United Nations Sustainable Development Goals.

Mini Case Study

Nvidia's $4 Trillion Valuation Isn't Just about Chips: It's a Blueprint for AI's Winner-Take-All Economy

On 9 July 2025, this seismic event pushed its valuation to $4 trillion, a market value greater than the GDPs of the UK, France, and India, which is truly mind-boggling.

If one looks at this Nvidia milestone through a strategic lens, then here are five critical implications for leaders navigating the AI transformation:

1 The AI Infrastructure Race Is Winner-Take-All: Nvidia's $4 trillion valuation isn't just about its core product of chips; it's about controlling the foundational layer of the AI economy. Leaders need to decide: Are you building your business on someone else's infrastructure or creating your competitive moat?

The story suggests that organisations controlling AI infrastructure will extract disproportionate value from the entire ecosystem.

2 "Sovereign AI" Is Reshaping Global Market Dynamics: The increase in Middle East deals and European "sovereign AI" initiatives signal a changing global landscape.

CEOs should recognise that AI capabilities are becoming matters of national importance, not solely a matter of competitive advantage.

This creates significant opportunities in regions seeking technological independence, but they face enhanced geopolitical risks.

3 The Demand Sustainability Question Will Define Valuations: While Nvidia projects 55% revenue growth, the DeepSeek disruption at the beginning of the year shows how quickly the AI landscape can pivot.

CEOs need to be continually stress-testing their AI investments and assumptions against the possibility that their computing requirements could plateau or become less efficient.

4 Margin Expansion through AI Is the New Competitive Battlefield with 70%+ Gross Margins: Nvidia demonstrates that AI leaders can achieve huge margins and levels of profitability.CEOs should focus less on AI adoption and more on leveraging AI to drive margin expansion. The question isn't whether to use AI, but how to utilise it to fundamentally improve your cost structure and pricing power.

5 The Trump Administration's Trade Policy Creates both Opportunity and Risk: The original China export restrictions initially negatively hurt Nvidia's stock price, but they were a catalyst in driving fresh **innovation** and new market development.

CEOs must build resilience into their AI strategies, treating geopolitical constraints as catalysts for **innovation** rather than insurmountable barriers.

Questions

1 The winner-take-all proposition of Nvidia looks compelling, so what are the threats to the leaders of the G7 countries?
2 What strategies can CEOs take to achieve AI-driven margin expansion rather than just cost reduction?
3 Given global trade policy volatility, how should global organisations build geopolitical resilience into their AI strategies?

4.10 Sustainable Strategy Toolkit (3) – The SSM Typology

Strategy typologies, such as the highly influential Miles and Snow (1978), offer a structured approach to understanding the phenomenon under investigation. By prioritising different constructs, this reduces complexity and highlights areas of focus by adopting a common vocabulary for discussing strategy. The shared language will improve communication of complex concepts.

For instance, **SSM** looks at the planet through a different lens, but the critical thinking and creativity may not come naturally to organisational leaders. Too much baggage may stifle what Varol (2020) refers to as first-principles thinking. Knowledge can be a virtue, but also a vice. These forces (namely, culture) may hold back the leadership team. The corporate mantra of "we have always done it this way," prevails, maintaining the status quo.

Beyond being anchored in a single mindset, **SSM** draws from an interdisciplinary practice-theoretical approach. When considering practice, it's no good waiting for the next crisis to commence playing the new game. In such instances, comparative analysis and benchmarking will enable a systematic comparison between different strategic approaches, which may lead to varying levels of success.

Organisations are confronted with uncertainty, which affects their ability to strategise. The adoption of **SSM** and its impact on sustainability outcomes, while pervasive, is dependent on a set of resources that grow as the sustainable organisation evolves. If resources are what an organisation possesses, then competencies are what set it apart. My observations from theory and practice suggest to consider three areas: focus, ambidexterity, and absorptive capacity.

- **Focus**: Achieving an equilibrium balance between economic, societal, and governance metrics. Balancing short-term and long-term profits can lead to the preservation of quality of life. The triple bottom line helps provide a more balanced approach to measuring **performance** (Elkington and Rowlands, 1999). Traditionally, this has been static from quarter to quarter. However, dynamic adaptation requires temporal cycles. These will be short-term operational, medium-term strategic, and long-term transformational. However, there still appears to be an over fixation with the financial aspects (Elkington, 2018).
- **Ambidexterity**: Ability of an organisation to simultaneously explore and exploit. These competing activities require different structures, processes, and strategies. Questions to consider – what are the internal and external organisational factors that affect ambidexterity, and what are the moderators of **performance**? The competence trap is a threat to responding adequately to external changes. Failure to balance the trade-off can lead to organisational trauma and failure (O'Reilly III and Tushman, 2013). Encouragingly, ambidexterity together with a green culture can unleash innovative capabilities (Hafeez et al., 2024).
- **Absorptive Capacity**: Gaining external knowledge to exploit opportunities such as emerging digital technologies to enhance economic, societal, and environmental **performance**. Sustainable knowledge learning system and cooperation in the ecosystem to make the desired **innovation** happen. Zahra and George (2002) define absorptive capacity as the ability to capture the value of new, external knowledge, integrate it, and apply it to economic objectives. Kerstens and Langley (2025) introduce "awareness capability" as a precursor to absorptive capacity, fostering curiosity and knowledge-seeking behaviours.

To plot the organisation on the **SSM** typology matrix, the roadmap should include actions for time scales:

Immediate action

- Map the current sustainability strategy.
- Map stakeholders in the organisation's ecosystem.
- Assess core material artefacts and Gen AI tools supporting the sustainability strategy.

Medium-term

- Create hybrid strategy processes encapsulating sustainability and ESG.
- Create capacity-building programmes to train key staff in sustainability practices.
- Effective technology integration with core strategy.

Long-term

- Implement effective ecosystem orchestration processes.
- Establish regenerative sustainable strategy practices that deliver impact.

- Establish the adaptive capacity for continuous change.

SSM reinvigorates strategising and organising as practice by forging new connections as **transition** evolves.

This can be mapped as follows with nine archetypes:

High focus (long-term)

1 Visionary Strugglers: Low ambidexterity, high absorptive capacity.
2 Sustainable Balancers: Moderate ambidexterity, high absorptive capacity.
3 Sustainable Innovators: High ambidexterity, high absorptive capacity.

Balanced focus

4 Cautious Adapters: Low ambidexterity, moderate absorptive capacity.
5 Strategic Optimisers: Moderate ambidexterity, moderate absorptive capacity.
6 Agile Transformers: High ambidexterity, moderate absorptive capacity.

Short-term focus

7 Reactive Compliers: Low ambidexterity, low absorptive capacity.
8 Efficiency Seekers: Moderate ambidexterity, low absorptive capacity.
9 Dynamic Exploiters: High ambidexterity, low absorptive capacity.

The **SSM** typology matrix (see Table 4.3) maps these archetypes across three dimensions:

- Focus: Long-term → Balanced → Short-term (vertical axis).
- Ambidexterity: Low → Moderate → High (horizontal axis).
- Absorptive Capacity: Low → Moderate → High (underlying dimension).

TABLE 4.3 SSM typology matrix V1.0

Focus	*Low Ambidexterity*	*Moderate Ambidexterity*	*High Ambidexterity*
Long-term	**Visionary Strugglers** ambitious long-term goals, but poor execution	**Sustainable Balancers** balanced long-term strategies and execution	**Sustainable Innovators** innovative transformational strategies
Balanced	**Cautious Adapters** cautious approach to sustainability efforts	**Strategic Optimisers** balancing short-term and long-term priorities	**Agile Transformers** dynamic balancing short- and long-term goals
Short-term	**Reactive Compliers** reactive compliance with sustainability trends	**Efficiency Seekers** focused on short-term gains through efficiency	**Dynamic Exploiters** exploiting short-term opportunities effectively
	Low Absorptive Capacity	**Moderate Absorptive Capacity**	**High Absorptive Capacity**

By utilising quantitative metrics and sector-specific adaptations, the **SSM** typology can be effectively integrated into the strategic planning process to drive sustainable competitive advantage.

Specifically, users of the **SSM** typology can create a 0–10 scale for each dimension, and as usage increases, sector benchmarks can be developed. Sector groups will be able to define specific actions and investments for the archetype trajectory.

Example Populations for the Matrix:

- **Visionary Strugglers:** A small business pledging carbon neutrality by 2050 without clear resources or expertise to achieve it.
- **Sustainable Innovators:** Patagonia or Unilever, integrating sustainability into their core strategy while achieving profitability.
- **Reactive Compliers:** Fast fashion brands implementing surface-level "green" initiatives in response to public pressure.
- **Efficiency Seekers:** Supermarkets that optimise their supply chain for cost savings and environmental benefits without a broader sustainability vision.

4.11 SSM Definition

The proposed definition helps to position **SSM** as the next evolution of strategic thinking, moving beyond traditional trade-offs to value creation in a regenerative context (Table 4.4).

Adopting a business-impact definition:

*Sustainable Strategic Management creates a competitive advantage by simultaneously mastering seven schools of critical, interconnected business dimensions in a regenerative context: financial **performance**, stakeholder capital, environmental optimisation, social **innovation**, operational circularity, technological disruption, and global market access.*

*Making the **transition** from sustainability challenges to economic, societal, and environmental benefits will help create a future-proof competitive moat, ensuring systemic, transformational change.*

TABLE 4.4 The seven schools reframed as business dimensions and corporate mantra

School	*Business "Dimension"*	*Corporate Mantra*
Traditional strategic management	**Financial performance**	Produce the highest level of ROI, market share, and profitability
Corporate social responsibility	**Stakeholder capital**	Build strong and enduring customer/employee/community loyalty
Environmental sustainability	**Environmental optimisation**	Outcomes of green initiatives should lead to tangible and positive benefits for the planet and CFO
Social **innovation**	**Social innovation**	Create new markets and revenue streams by solving society's biggest challenges
Circular economy	**Operational circularity**	Achieve zero-waste efficiency that competitors find hard to match
Innovation & disruption	**Technological disruption**	Be a leader in industry transformation through breakthrough solutions
Global South perspectives	**Global market access**	Unlock growth in emerging markets through inclusive strategies

Abbreviations: CFO, Chief Financial Officer; ROI, return on investment.

4.12 Chapter Key Takeaways

The key takeaways from Chapter 4 on the seven schools of sustainable strategic management are as follows:

1. **Traditional Strategic Management:** This emphasises financial **performance** and positioning as essential goals, with sustainability often viewed as an add-on rather than integral to strategy.
2. **CSR:** Engaging stakeholders with entities crucial for the organisation to achieve its long-term strategy, CSR goals, and attainment of the triple bottom line.
3. **Environmental Sustainability and Green Strategies:** This school emphasises minimising environmental impact through green technologies and innovative business models, promoting a long-term ecological balance.
4. **Social Innovation and Inclusive Business:** Developing solutions that address societal needs for the most vulnerable individuals. By fostering a mindset that promotes inclusivity and sustainable development.
5. **CE and C2C Design:** These approaches advocate for **transitioning** from linear to closed-loop systems, aiming to reduce waste and enhance resource efficiency, thereby supporting ecological sustainability.
6. **Innovation and Disruption:** These approaches have already led to the exciting application of disruptive technologies. This school encourages adaptability and resilience in new initiatives, enabling organisations to embrace novel solutions.
7. **Global South Perspectives:** These acknowledge the distinct issues of emerging nations and highlights measures that address their socio-economic and environmental challenges.

4.13 Self-Reflection Questions

1. What are the key limitations of the traditional strategic management approach in fostering sustainability?
2. Summarise one of the seven schools of sustainable strategic management and explain how it contributes to developing a comprehensive sustainability strategy.
3. How can countries in the Global South leverage their unique strengths and opportunities to overcome sustainability challenges and drive sustainable growth?
4. Explain how a CE model can benefit an organisation financially and environmentally.
5. In what ways does the "**Innovation** and Disruption" school promote sustainability within a strategic management framework?

References

Afeltra, G., Alerasoul, S.A. and Strozzi, F., (2023). The evolution of sustainable innovation: From the past to the future. *European Journal of Innovation Management*, 26(2), pp.386–421.

Bower, J.L. and Christensen, C.M., (1995). Disruptive technologies: Catching the wave. *Harvard Business Review*, *73*(1), pp.43–53.

Braungart, M. and McDonough, W., (2009). *Cradle to cradle*. Random House.

Carroll, A.B., (1991). The pyramid of corporate social responsibility: Toward the moral management of organizational stakeholders. *Business Horizons*, *34*(4), pp.39–48.

Christensen, C.M., (2015). *The innovator's dilemma: When new technologies cause significant firms to fail*. Harvard Business Review Press.

Christensen, C.M., Raynor, M.E. and McDonald, R., (2013). *Disruptive innovation*. Harvard Business Review.

Dionisio, M. and de Vargas, E.R., (2020). Corporate social innovation: A systematic literature review. *International Business Review, 29*(2), p.101641.
Dodge v. Ford Motor Co. (1919). 170 N.W. 668, 684 (Mich. 1919) ("A business corporation is organized and carried on primarily for the profit of the stockholders. The powers of the directors are to be employed for that end.").
Donaldson, T., (2023). Value creation and CSR. *Journal of Business Economics, 93*(6), pp.1255–1275.
Drucker, P.F., (1975). Economic realities and enterprise strategy. In Ezra F. Vogel (ed.), *Modern Japanese organization and decision-making*, pp.228–248. University of California Press.
Edwards-Schachter, M. and Wallace, M.L., (2017). 'Shaken, but not stirred': Sixty years of defining social innovation. *Technological Forecasting and Social Change, 119,* pp.64–79.
Elkington, J., (2018). 25 years ago I coined the phrase triple bottom line heres why its time to rethink it. *Harvard Business Review, 25*(2–5), p.6.
Elkington, J. and Rowlands, I.H., (1999). Cannibals with forks: The triple bottom line of 21st century business. *Alternatives Journal, 25*(4), p.42.
Ellen MacArthur Foundation (2015). *Towards a circular economy: Business rationale for an accelerated transition.*
Friedman, M., (1970). A Friedman doctrine: The social responsibility of business is to increase its profits. *The New York Times, 13*(1970), p.17.
Geissdoerfer, M., Savaget, P., Bocken, N.M. and Hultink, E.J., (2017). The Circular Economy–A new sustainability paradigm?. *Journal of Cleaner Production, 143*, pp.757–768.
Hafeez, M., Yasin, I., Zawawi, D., Odilova, S. and Bataineh, H.A., (2024). Unleashing the power of green innovations: The role of organizational ambidexterity and green culture in achieving corporate sustainability. *European Journal of Innovation Management, 28*(6), pp.2304–2336.
Kahn, K.B., (2018). Understanding innovation. *Business Horizons, 61*(3), pp.453–460.
Kerstens, A. and Langley, D.J., (2025). An innovation intermediary's role in enhancing absorptive capacity for cross-industry digital innovation: Introducing an awareness capability and new intermediary practices. *Journal of Business Research, 196*, p.115426.
Korhonen, J., Honkasalo, A. and Seppälä, J., (2018). Circular economy: The concept and its limitations. *Ecological Economics, 143*, pp.37–46.
Lashitew, A.A., Bals, L. and van Tulder, R., (2020). Inclusive business at the base of the pyramid: The role of embeddedness for enabling social innovations. *Journal of Business Ethics, 162*(2), pp.421–448.
Miles, R.E. and Snow, C.C., (1978). *Organizational strategy, structure, and process.* McGraw-Hill.
Murray, A., Skene, K. and Haynes, K., (2017). The circular economy: An interdisciplinary exploration of the concept and application in a global context. *Journal of Business Ethics, 140,* pp.369–380.
Ogunmakinde, O.E., Sher, W. and Egbelakin, T., (2021). Circular economy pillars: A semi-systematic review. *Clean Technologies and Environmental Policy, 23*, pp.899–914.
O'Reilly III, C.A. and Tushman, M.L., (2013). Organizational ambidexterity: Past, present, and future. *Academy of Management Perspectives, 27*(4), pp.324–338.
Osburg, T., (2013). Social innovation to drive corporate sustainability. In T. Osburg and R. Schmidpeter (eds.), *Social innovation: Solutions for a sustainable future*, pp.13–22. Springer Berlin Heidelberg.
Prahalad, C.K., (2005). *The fortune at the bottom of the pyramid.* Wharton School Pub.
Raworth, K., (2017). *Doughnut economics: Seven ways to think like a 21st century economist.* Penguin Random House.
Raworth, K., (2018). *Doughnut economics: Seven ways to think like a 21st-century economist.* Chelsea Green Publishing.
Stead, J.G. and Stead, W.E., (2019). Why Porter is not enough: Economic foundations of sustainable strategic management. In T. Wunder (ed.), *Rethinking strategic management: CSR, sustainability, ethics & governance*, pp.67–85. Springer. https://doi.org/10.1007/978-3-030-06014-5_4.
Varol, O., (2020). *Think like a rocket scientist: Simple strategies for giant leaps in work and life.* Random House.
Zahra, S.A. and George, G., (2002). Absorptive capacity: A review, reconceptualization, and extension. *Academy of Management Review, 27*(2), pp.185–203.

PART II

Organisational Analysis and Reporting

5

STRATEGIC ANALYSIS

5.1 Learning Strategic Objectives

After completing this chapter, you will be able to:

1 **Knowledge-Based Objectives:**

- Identify, apply, and explain the concepts of external and internal strategic analysis.
- Appreciate that strategic analysis is foundational to achieving long-term success.

2 **Skill-Based Objectives:**

- Perform strategic analysis from the CEO, board, and stakeholder perspectives.
- Identify and develop creative strategies based on the results of strategic analysis.

3 **Attitude-Based Objectives:**

- Cultivate a proactive attitude towards strategic analysis, recognising the need to be adaptive to dynamic environments.
- Adopt ethical considerations in strategy decision-making regarding economic, societal, and environmental issues.

5.2 Introduction

Strategic analysis is a recurrent concern for business school students, strategists, and executives. Frameworks such as volatility, uncertainty, complexity, and ambiguity (VUCA) and brittle, anxious, non-linear and incomprehensible (BANI) highlight the forces in the evolving external environment. The speed, scale, and scope impose new strains on leadership teams, and traditional solutions are no longer effective and warrant closer consideration.

As business crisis reverberates throughout global markets, corporate strategies are closely scrutinised and risk assessed, emphasising the need for a more comprehensive approach. CEOs must now navigate the recovery of profitability and address the evolving expectations of stakeholders, who demand greater transparency, ethical practices,

DOI: 10.4324/9781003516774-7

and social responsibility. The external and internal environments provide the context for developing strategies. By rigorously using analytical methods and tools, the CEO can answer the critical questions posed during the strategy formulation process.

Despite the increasing importance of strategic analysis in degree curriculum and practice, students often find the experience daunting. Insight into the salient factors within organisations needs to be identified. The over-dependence on Strengths, Weaknesses, Opportunities, and Threats (SWOT), PESTEL, and Porter's Five Forces is at the core of this challenge for some students. This chapter covers critical strategy frameworks and tools, providing a starting point for readers to build and apply theory in practice. A practical strategy analysis must incorporate the perspectives of multiple stakeholders.

5.3 External Environment

CEOs select strategies they hope will allow the organisation to deploy its scarce resources effectively. The selection is reliant on external and internal analysis. The uncertain environment makes spotting new opportunities and anticipating threats much more difficult. Over the last six decades, the strategy pendulum that swings from an external to an internal orientation illustrates the need to incorporate both perspectives. Today, discourses that impact the external environment now cover a myriad of issues, which, in addition to sustainability, include geopolitical dynamics, technology **innovation** and digital transformation, regulatory changes, and supply chain resilience.

Strategic analysis can be expanded to consider diverse discourses in contrast to traditional paradigms, and the incorporation of a strategic management perspective can enable organisations to be more proactive. The rest of this chapter will provide insight into the core strategy frameworks and tools and explain how they can help readers achieve their goals. Strategic analysis is a systematic process of asking and answering the most crucial issues. If done successfully, users can recommend a change of strategy direction and enhance the level of organisational **performance**.

5.3.1 Macro-Environment

Against the backdrop of previous discussions on **SSM**, the macro-environment now comprises complex ecosystems. Changes in the macro-environment can be cyclical or structural. The former requires a temporary tactical response, while the latter necessitates a more permanent one. No firm can control the macro-environment, but may seek to stay abreast of external shifts.

During workshops, my starting point is to state that no firm is an island and does not operate in isolation. The firm can take the form of any enterprise – small, medium, large, private sector, public sector, and third sector – and will be affected differently. Even public sector organisations face competition from peers vying for scarce resources, including funding. The charity sector has seen fluctuations in income, compelling organisations to innovate. Organisations must stay ahead of the curve by spotting what megatrends are gaining momentum.

Looking forward, strategic analysis should identify the current stage of the industry life cycle. This will impact the type and timing of the products/services brought to the marketplace. Unfortunately, external factors are uncontrollable.

5.3.2 Micro-Environment

The micro-environment consists of firms, their suppliers, and buyers. Other actors, such as the public, employees, media, and shareholders, are essential to a firm's local environment. Any problems in the micro-environment are usually noticed almost immediately, so these should be closely monitored. A more precise understanding of the micro-environment can provide better insights into higher levels of firm **performance**. The firm can influence the micro-environment with full appreciation of the unique characteristics of each factor and force.

Concurrent with these approaches, analysis of the industry and market enables opportunities to leverage core competencies in other industries and markets. To better illustrate these points, markets can be defined by product, utility (or need), or customer identity. Market segmentation supports the assertion that a firm cannot be all things to all buyers. The one-size-fits-all approach no longer works. Understanding the needs and wants of a smaller group of potential customers is more efficient.

From a resource perspective, it is easier to compete in fewer markets. Intermediaries now affect all markets, playing roles such as travel, financial resellers, physical distributors, and market service agencies. These intermediaries can scale extremely rapidly. Digital platforms are ubiquitous, and firms are looking to form trusted relationships and become valuable partners for the likes of Google, Microsoft, and Amazon. The easier connection between buyers and sellers via digital platforms has resulted in some firms needing to pay more attention to online frictionless options for the customer.

Synthesising the many approaches to external analysis reveals the following approaches.

5.4 SWOT Analysis

A key attribute of SWOT analysis is that it is straightforward and can be effective. It is also widely taught and used in practice, and durability and longevity remain compelling. The popularity and ease of use can quickly condense many issues identified into manageable and essential points. Nevertheless, knowing what is and is not relevant is subjective and debatable. Like any tool, it should guide the strategy process rather than being prescriptive.

Users find it a valuable tool for commencing brainstorming sessions and initiating discussions. A good SWOT analysis will critique both the internal perspective (strengths and weaknesses) and the external perspective (opportunities and threats) from the customer's point of view. The user can identify and address weaknesses, enhance strengths, maximise opportunities, and overcome threats. Inherent "strengths," such as old and established, can be a "weakness" in the organisation's ability to respond to new and agile competition. Management should address weaknesses, as being left unattended may prevent the firm from achieving its mission and goals.

A significant limitation is the underlying simplistic nature of SWOT analysis (see Figure 5.1). During consulting workshops, the SWOT analysis suffers when the language lacks specificity. Statements like "we sell great products" make it challenging to derive meaningful strategies without listening to the customer's voice. Insufficient and untimely data can lead to inaccurate assessments. Additionally, corporate culture biases can skew the results. Factors beyond management's control can also affect the analysis. The economic environment may adversely affect demand for a product or service but increase demand for another.

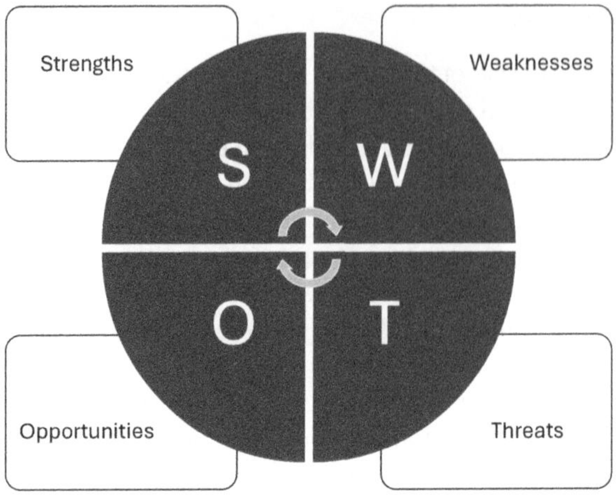

FIGURE 5.1 SWOT (Strengths, Weaknesses, Opportunities, and Threats) analysis

For example, during times of economic slowdown, organisations seek to reduce spending on overnight hotel accommodations for employees. They may trade down from a four-star to a three-star or even a budget hotel. Thus, the budget hotel sector can thrive during an economic slowdown to the detriment of mid-scale hotels. Another constraint to potential opportunities that may not be pursued is a lack of skilled labour. Threats can harm the organisation, its ventures and products/services. The organisation cannot avoid threats and must decide how to deal with them. The CEO must create intelligence to monitor threats regardless of size and sector focus. But remember that SWOT analysis should be a continuous process with timely reviews and involve different stakeholders to obtain diverse and balanced feedback.

One critical test of SWOT analysis is whether the organisation pursues a strategy and capability that is not a competitor's strength. Organisations use SWOT analysis as part of their strategy review processes when **performance** exceeds what influential stakeholders expect. Making the SWOT analysis actionable by providing top-down clarity will help formulate renewal strategies.

5.5 PESTEL

The macro-environment can be systematically assessed by PESTEL analysis (see Table 5.1) for OXFAM International. An appreciation of the fundamental forces in the macro-environment can aid understanding and enable the prediction of how an industry might change and evolve. This will allow users to make informed strategic decisions.

The confluence of exogenous factors makes PESTEL useful in providing a comprehensive assessment of the environment and market in which the firm operates. However, users sometimes need to pay more attention to its limitations. External factors

TABLE 5.1 PESTEL analysis for OXFAM International

PESTEL Factor		*OXFAM International Issues*
Political	1	Government policies on international aid and NGOs
	2	Geopolitical instability in regions where OXFAM operates
	3	Regulatory changes impacting NGO funding and operations
	4	Changing political agendas on humanitarian aid
	5	Diplomatic relations affecting cross-border initiatives.
Economic	1	Economic recessions, cost of living crisis reducing public donations
	2	Volatile currency exchange rate fluctuations affecting international funds
	3	Unequal climate finance to crisis regions
	4	Impact of economic inequality on vulnerable populations
	5	Rising operational costs due to inflation.
Social	1	Rising inequality undermines action of poverty, climate change, and economic transformation
	2	Public trust and perception of NGOs
	3	Availability and engagement of volunteers
	4	Impact of social media on awareness and activism
	5	Cultural sensitivities and differences in programme implementation.
Technological	1	AI and Data Science
	2	Cybersecurity threats to data and operational integrity
	3	Use of ICT to enhance quality, accessibility, and efficiency of global operations
	4	Adoption of technology for remote operations and virtual collaboration
	5	Technological disparities in target regions affecting programme delivery.
Environmental	1	Effects of climate change on vulnerable populations
	2	Environmental regulations influencing operational practices
	3	Resource availability and sustainability in aid distribution
	4	Impact of natural disasters on humanitarian efforts
	5	Implementation of eco-friendly practices within OXFAM's operations.
Legal	1	Compliance with international and local laws governing NGOs
	2	Legal issues related to challenging injustices
	3	Intellectual property rights for educational and advocacy materials
	4	Employment laws affecting staff and volunteer management
	5	Legal barriers to operating in certain countries.

Abbreviations: ICT, information and communications technology; NGOs, non-governmental organisations.

can change over time, and monitoring needs expert analysis in complex environments. Overfocusing on merely listing constituent parts can lead to blind spots to real-world challenges. Simplistic approaches will be dangerous. In such instances, there will be a failure to capture the critical signals in the external environment. The quality of PESTEL will also depend on the quality of the data. Primary and secondary data may be subjective, and one could question its relevance and applicability. Factors need to be prioritised and implemented. However, as such factors are beyond the firm's control, they represent risks.

Strategy Nugget

The Rise and Fall of Builder AI

The Rise

Builder artificial intelligence's (AI) quest for the democratisation of building apps ended abruptly on 20 May 2025, when the unicorn private tech firm, worth more than a billion dollars, appointed administrators. Builder AI founder Sachin Dev Duggal had previously stepped down in February 2025.

The British $1.5 billion AI–powered development platform promised to make app creation "as easy as ordering pizza." Sector coverage included financial services, retail, education, and healthcare, and was trusted and backed by big global brands and entrepreneurs. High-pedigree investors bought into this vision by providing $500 million, including Microsoft and Qatar's sovereign wealth fund.

The Fall

Financial restatements revealed systematic revenue inflation, with 2024 revenues declining from $220 million to $55 million, a 75% write-off. Similar patterns emerged in 2023 figures, dropping from $180 million to $45 million. The creditor Viola Credit, which lent $50 million in 2023, seized $37 million from Builder AI's accounts after it defaulted. Lawyers' internal investigations focused on questionable "reseller" relationships. Those in the Middle East were under scrutiny.

A deeper dive revealed that Builder AI owed $88 million in cloud fees to Amazon. Also, question marks relate to how much Builder AI products were AI-driven. Natasha, an AI-focused app development service, was promoted to replace human involvement; however, it was reported that offices had been set up in India and over 700 engineers had been recruited to handle all the coding responses.

Governance Deterioration

Against this backdrop, Founder Sachin Dev Duggal made the **Transition** from CEO to ceremonial "chief wizard," retaining board representation. The concurrent departure of both the CEO and CFO raised eyebrows in financial governance circles.

Builder AI's demise demonstrates the classic agency problem where management interests diverge from shareholder value maximisation. Information asymmetries appear to prevent accurate market signalling despite sophisticated institutional investors being involved.

While Builder AI possessed a unique value proposition, AI resources and premium investor relationships, organisational dysfunction prevented effective resource deployment, illustrating that sustainable competitive advantage requires ethical organisational systems alongside superior capabilities.

Questions

1 How could investors have identified revenue quality issues earlier?
2 What governance changes could have prevented systematic revenue inflation?
3 Why did possessing robust resources fail to create a sustainable competitive advantage?

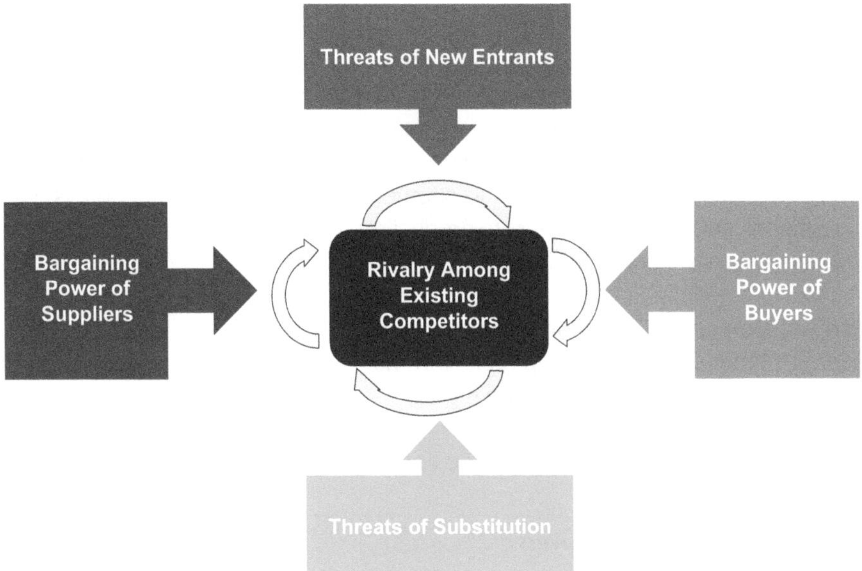

FIGURE 5.2 Porter's Five Forces

5.6 Michael Porter's Five Forces Model

Michael Porter's (1980) classical Five Forces framework depicts the threat of substitutes, the threat of new entrants, the intensity of rivalry, supplier power, buyer bargaining power, and complementors, which is sometimes mentioned as the sixth force in core readings within MBA programmes. When proposing his model, Porter argued that a strong force limits the ability of established companies to increase prices and earn a greater return. A strong competitive force can be likened to a threat as it reduces profits. The picture that emerges from the analysis depends on several variables. Heterogeneity in the strength of each force is derived from the horizontal and vertical levels of competition, as shown in Figure 5.2. Horizontal levels of competition encompass the threat of new entrants, substitutes, and competitive rivalry, with vertical competition characterised by the power of suppliers and buyers. The bifurcation of forces in turbulent markets can assist the strategist.

5.6.1 The Threat of New Entrants

Deconstructing profitable markets that produce high returns for incumbents will attract new firms. If new firms enter unabated, the high returns will normalise. As more firms compete for market share, profits will tend to fall. If incumbents block new firms, they can maintain their profits. Threats of new entrants are high when:

- Existing firms do not have established brands, patents, and trademarks.
- Low amount of capital is required to enter the market.
- Customer switching costs are low.
- Economies of scale are relatively easy to achieve.
- Lack of firms to retaliate.
- Products are similar.
- Scarce government regulation.

5.6.2 Bargaining Power of Suppliers

Through the analytical lens, suppliers can uncover and exert differing influences based on their strengths. If we consider the idea that suppliers have high bargaining power, then suppliers can sell higher-priced or lower-quality raw materials. In the supermarket sector, many small suppliers are a weak threat to the larger retailer firm. With low switching costs, management can switch from one supplier to another. However, with few suppliers, switching costs are higher, and if the item is vital to product quality, then the firm is in a weak position.

Suppliers have strong bargaining power when:

- There is high concentration of suppliers.
- There is a limited number of suppliers, but many buyers.
- Switching costs of raw materials are high.
- Suppliers possess scarce resources.
- A large number of suppliers possess the ability to forward integrate.

5.6.3 Bargaining Power of Buyers

The position of buyers is opposite to that of suppliers for the firm. If buyers' bargaining power is high, then they can demand low prices and higher quality simultaneously. The drive towards lower prices and higher quality will likely reduce the firm's margins. In the clothing industry, newer firms with an online presence are quicker and more flexible in getting their products to customers and employ aggressive pricing strategies.

Buyers have strong bargaining power when:

- A small number of buyers exist.
- Switching costs to other suppliers are low.
- Buyers are price-sensitive.
- Buyers possess the ability to integrate backwards.

5.6.4 Threat of Substitutes

If potential buyers can locate substitute products, then switching costs are low. Substitute products may come from outside the industry, too. This places the firm in a relatively weak position. If the substitute is in a strong position, then buyers will be price-sensitive and switch to the substitute in response to price increases. Also, buyers will switch if the substitute is of better quality and at a similar cost. Disruptive technology, such as the internet, provides many sources of substitute products with increased competition. Firms operating in the travel, newspaper, sports, and telecommunications industries have had to rethink their strategies over the last decade. In the newspaper sector, substitute products include online news, iPads, mobile phones, and 24-hour news channels.

The threat of substitute products is higher when:

- There are low switching costs.
- Products are lower price.
- Products have higher quality.
- Products have better **performance**.

5.6.5 *Intensity of Rivals*

These set the stage for determining how competitive and profitable an industry is. As the firm evolves within a mature industry, the strategic posture has to be aggressive to maintain and increase market share. In such environments, profit margins are slim. Firms strive to achieve a competitive advantage over their peers. The level of intensity varies within each market in which the firm competes. Industries that are concentrated are more intense than their fragmented counterparts. Several strategic postures are available to the firm, a vital feature of this textbook. Typical moves include increasing value for money, improving product differentiation, and enhancing distribution channels and supply relationships. Within the supermarket sector, a common consequence is price wars, aggressive advertising campaigns and customer-oriented **innovations**.

The intensity of rivals is intense when:

- There is a high number of competitors.
- Competitors are of similar size.
- There are low levels of customer loyalty.
- Products are mainly commodity type (i.e. not differentiated).
- There are high exit barriers.

5.6.6 *Complementors*

The sometimes forgotten six force–complementors have the opposite effect of substitutes. Complementors provide another mechanism for adding value. They will not be competitors in an industry, but a contractual relationship can influence demand. Complementors increase the demand for a primary product. Complementary product examples include a hotdog and the hotdog bun, as a consumer would tend not to buy one without the other.

Similarly, smartphones and apps serve as modern complements; the availability of diverse and useful apps enhances the value of smartphones and drives their sales. Another example is electric vehicles (EVs) and charging stations; the proliferation of charging infrastructure increases the convenience and attractiveness of owning an EV, thus potentially boosting EV sales. Lastly, gaming consoles and video games illustrate how complementary products can create a synergistic effect, with popular games driving console purchases and vice versa.

Delineating Porter's six forces will assess the macro-environment quickly, but the analysis should form only part of the overall strategy checklist of frameworks and tools to use.

5.6.7 *Limitations of Porter's Five Forces*

These include:

- Level of strategy analysis
- Assumes homogenous firms
- Assumes largely antagonistic relationships
- Cross-sectional, one moment in time
- Disregards the behavioural aspects within the firm

Role of governmental regulations:

- The internet and e-commerce
- Globalisation
- Changes in PESTEL affect "five forces"
- Green issues and green awareness
- Competition law
- Changes in industry growth rate.

The misuse of Porter's Five Forces escalates if the user ignores the unit and level of analysis and that the tool assumes homogeneity, so it will not suit highly diversified companies. A typical large UK FTSE company may operate across several industries; the analysis must focus on discrete business units. The analysis is also static, akin to the balance sheet and only depicts the organisation at that moment. Thus, given the long-term strategy perspective, Porter's Five Forces' timescale is too short. Most strategy tools should only be used as part of the beginning of a discussion.

The CEO should disentangle the complex interplay between strategic leadership and decision-making. In Chapter 2, part of the narrative focused on the new normal environment created following the 2008 crisis. Industries have been affected differently by the events of 2008, and Porter's framework does not account for changes in industry growth rates.

In addition to the fundamental changes in the use of debt leverage, the trajectory of globalisation, the nature of consumption patterns, and the appetite for risk-taking affect the competitive landscape. AI and Gen AI now increase the importance of globalisation, and deregulation fundamentally changes the basic conditions of any industry. The behavioural issues of strategy will affect implementation, and government regulation can change the structure and conduct of industries. Those organisations operating in the airline, railway, electricity, and telecommunication sectors are acutely aware of government policy. Responses to regulations are demanding, as organisations must consider complicated trade-offs between profit maximisation and broader social factors.

Intriguingly, Dobbs (2014) queries the use of the five forces model when users deploy it superficially. He asserts that this lack of depth is dangerous, as it can at best lead to incomplete, inaccurate, and unhelpful analysis. He mentions that users of Porter's Five Forces model, including academics, students, and practitioners, face several additional challenges: a lack of structural analysis, a lack of strategic insight, and the preferences of the Millennial generation. Porter (2008) does lament the lack of quantitative measures in typical applications of the five forces model. The qualitative measures are often arbitrary and serve as poor substitutes for rigorous analysis. This lack of structural analysis diminishes the quality of the output.

A lack of strategic insight is another disappointment, which Porter (1980) acknowledges. This is partly due to the tool being perceived by users as a means to assess attractiveness levels of industries rather than to gain strategic insight into how to compete more effectively. I can attest to these observations, as when marking student assignments at the postgraduate and undergraduate levels; the comments of lack of insight are frequently mentioned. The contextual setting for any classroom exercise should indicate that blueprint solutions are inappropriate (just like in the business environment).

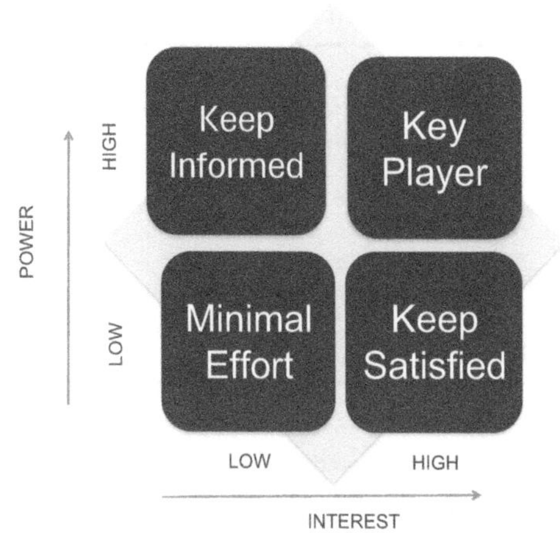

FIGURE 5.3 Stakeholder analysis

5.7 Stakeholder Analysis

As a result of the sustainability phenomenon, values among business and society are being recast. From a corporate perspective, firms need to show that they have a conscience and profit and growth can no longer be the sole justification for "immoral actions." Hence, stakeholders are now becoming increasingly influential during the decision-making process. The board must be aware of, understand, and manage stakeholder interests. Stakeholder analysis is a crucial plank of the strategy narrative. Kenny (2024) states that leaders may not fully appreciate how stakeholders impact strategy and fail to detail their roles in sustaining the enterprise. Determining which stakeholders are key will help strategy development and strategic planning.

Technological disruptions, such as social media, enable small stakeholder groups to impact organisational affairs quickly. The other dimension that should be proactively managed is stakeholder power. When interests and power are considered together, they provide management with an indication of the type of relationship to form with each group. This becomes pertinent when the CEO wishes to push specific projects. Quickly identifying who is essential and who can positively and negatively influence the project is desirable. A classic example, often mentioned, is when an organisation wishes to expand its footprint and must get the local council planning committee and local community on board to identify primary stakeholders, those who are ultimately affected, and secondary stakeholders who act as intermediaries. Mendelow's (1981) stakeholder mapping matrix (see Figure 5.3) provides the user with a way to depict, understand, and manage stakeholder power.

5.8 Mendelow's (1981) Stakeholder Mapping Matrix

Aligning strategy with stakeholders fosters mutual understanding and support during organisational change and challenges (see Table 5.2). By actively involving stakeholders in the strategic planning process, management can ensure that these critical players comprehend the underlying issues and traumas the organisation may face. This transparency

TABLE 5.2 Mendelow's stakeholder analysis matrix

Stakeholder	*Stakeholder Interests (H), (M), (L)*	*Assessment of Impact (+), (−), (?)*	*Potential Strategies*
Primary – directly affected – employees & shareholders			
Secondary – indirectly affected – govt & media			
Key – most significantly affected			

helps stakeholders appreciate the necessity of specific strategies and actions, leading to greater empathy and cooperation. Additionally, stakeholders may differ for different reasons and at other times. Also, when stakeholders, including employees, customers, and partners, see their interests reflected in the company's strategic decisions, they are more likely to offer their full support. This alignment not only aids in mitigating resistance but also strengthens the overall commitment to the organisation's goals, enhancing the effectiveness of strategic initiatives and fostering a more resilient organisational culture.

Talent management remains high on the CEO's agenda, so ensuring the organisation's values are explained to employees is crucial. Also, trade unions, which remain strong in some developing economies despite being of less influence than in the past, can still create havoc for the CEO, leading management of a change agenda. Although stakeholder analysis may be subjective, it is helpful to perform it continuously with a focus on the most important stakeholders for each particular situation. The end column of Table 5.2 considers potential strategies, including strengthening stakeholders' commitment to the project, addressing their sensitivities, maintaining support, converting neutral views into support, and coping with resistance. Specific strategies can benefit key stakeholder groups and enhance communication, involvement, and marginalisation levels.

5.9 Scenario Analysis

Scenario analysis provides practical, plausible, and alternative views that can be integrated with strategy assumptions. The robustness of a strategic plan can be stress-tested by using a variety of "what-if" analyses. Organisations should test their financial resilience to macroeconomic or market-driven scenarios. Each sector will have its salient operating models, risk methodologies, and investment priorities for the next decade and beyond. The scenario analysis matrix (Figure 5.4) is a deductive method for illustrating scenarios in uncertain and volatile situations. Four scenarios are depicted in the matrix. The two uncertain x-axis and y-axis dimensions form the analysis context. Timeframes should align with the duration of the strategic planning exercise. Four steps can be employed to perform practical scenario analysis: identification of salient factors for inclusion in the scenario analysis, which scenarios to analyse for each factor, estimation of asset cash flows, and assignment of probabilities.

Well-run scenario planning exercises can involve subject matter experts coming together to debate various issues such as economic, technological, and increasingly geopolitical futures. Essentially, scenario analysis can enable the board to consider multiple plausible futures and inherent risks. Scenarios can be for periods well over a decade.

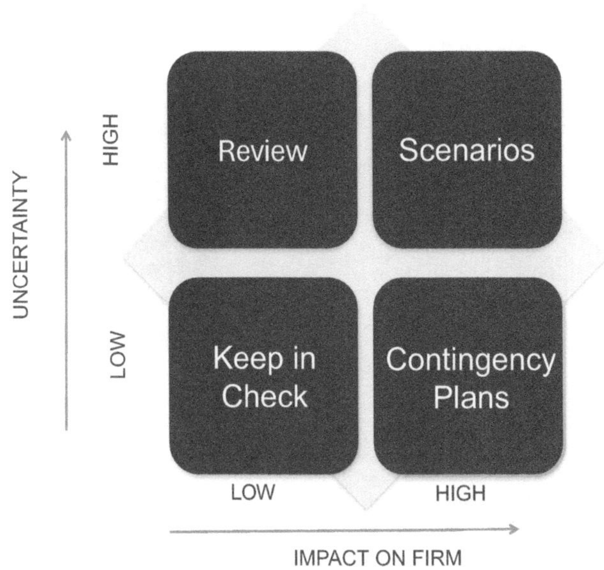

FIGURE 5.4 Scenario analysis

For example, in a comprehensive communiqué issued after the 2023 G20 summit in New Delhi, under the theme "One Earth, One Family, One Future," the G20 leaders reinforced their commitment to the Paris Agreement and called for accelerated action to reduce global greenhouse gas emissions by 45% by 2030. The overarching goal is to achieve net-zero emissions by 2050.

Given the high uncertainty and high impact level, businesses and governments must develop integrated scenario models that highlight the effects of decarbonisation. International cooperation will be necessary at the individual, community, organisational, government, and country levels. At the country level, those countries chiefly responsible for the carbon crisis should be leading in seeking a solution based on their past behaviour. In some quarters, matters are better as the technology is available to revolutionise clean energy. Still, the global legislative frameworks and the capital investment models must evolve to facilitate implementation. **Transitioning** to net zero will entail simulating plausible hypotheses to inform action.

5.10 Strategic Groups

A widespread theme in strategic analysis is that of strategic groups which exist within an industry and comprise members that possess similar strategic characteristics, pursue similar strategies, or compete on similar bases. From Hunt's (1972) doctoral thesis, the link between strategic groups and **performance** has been a popular research theme with tenuous findings.

Nevertheless, economic and cognitive theories suggest that there may be differences between the **performances** of firms that belong to different groups. We know that some organisations remain stable core members of strategic groups over time, while others may switch. Such observations appear to be moderated by organisational situational

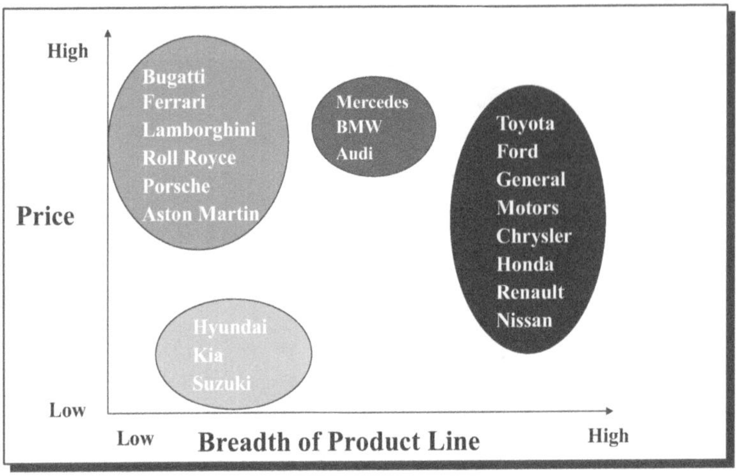

FIGURE 5.5 The world automobile industry

variables, including the degree of profitability. What has become evident is the emergence of resource-based theory at the expense of strategic group theory, with Barney and Hoskisson (1990) arguing that strategic groups, in some cases, may be merely artefacts of the algorithms utilised to generate clusters.

Despite the dissatisfaction with strategic groups, there is a benefit to integrating the two perspectives (Leask and Parnell, 2005). The different but complementary perspectives of strategic groups and Resource Based View (RBV) on competitive strategy and **performance** present a synergistic insight into how clusters of organisations compete. Over the last five decades, the strategy-conduct-**performance** paradigm has been evident in research, including strategic groups. Today's business will unlikely operate in a discrete environment but will be part of a strategic group. Understanding the intra-industry strategic groupings can enhance the **performance** of the CEO. From a research perspective, insight can be gained at the firm and industry level. As businesses tend to be multiproduct and sell in more than one market, blurring occurs, and depicting and understanding strategic groups may assist in understanding the salient drivers. If the CEO considers a strategic group, a cluster of firms with similar behaviours, then mobility barriers and technology can enable meaningful comparative analysis.

Strategic group mapping can help illustrate the salient differentiating forces. For example, start by identifying the peer group in the selected industry. Then, choose two critical variables for the y and x-axes. Using the appropriate axis, plot each organisation with the size of the circle being proportional to market share or another crucial dimension. Then, assess the overall map. The different groups should offer a different valuable proposition to the customer, which requires the CEO to create a compelling strategy. Figure 5.5 provides an overview of the world automobile industry.

5.11 Internal Analysis

The success of strategies depends on external and internal issues. The previous section provides tools to help the CEO gain sufficient knowledge about the external environment, anticipate changes in the external environment, and determine some competitive actions. In contrast to external analysis, internal analysis identifies and evaluates resources, capabilities, and competencies available for strategy implementation and attaining strategic objectives. The internal analysis process should closely examine the alignment of vision, mission, strategic objectives, and strategies.

The shift in the corporate landscape towards a more caring society is undermining the traditional efforts of organisations of all shapes and sizes. Executives spend more time at work than pursuing any other activity, and the behavioural aspects of strategy can lead to blockages. From a strategic management perspective, the literature needs behavioural rigour and practical relevance. Powell, Lovallo, and Fox (2011), in their special issue of the *Strategic Management Journal* on the psychological foundations of strategic management, comment that behavioural strategy merges cognitive and social psychology, but the topic still needs clarification. Recent research reveals that cognition and traits remain crucial internal factors (Hesselbarth, Alnoor, and Tiberius, 2023).

Individuals responsible for strategic analysis need to evaluate the organisation's internal environment. The strengths and weaknesses of the SWOT analysis provide an initial snapshot view of activities. In addition to the vision and mission statements, the internal environment consists of management, employees, organisational structures, culture, other intangible and tangible resources, and capabilities and competencies. The following topics are essential during strategic planning but will be covered briefly to demonstrate practical relevance.

5.12 Organisational Structure

CEOs need to acquire high-**performance** levels by simultaneously exploring and exploiting their internal environment. Figure 5.6 depicts the key elements of organisational structure. Arranging the organisational architecture in terms of formal structures is one of the keys to success. The traditional organisational structure is hierarchical, with the CEO at the top and tasks and people allocated in decision-making power flows. One dilemma is the balance between centralisation and decentralisation. Decision-making is best associated with authority, which can rest with senior management or be delegated down the hierarchy, and the 20th century belonged to a scenario of centralising capital, resources, and decision-making. We are now experiencing a shift in the 21st century to

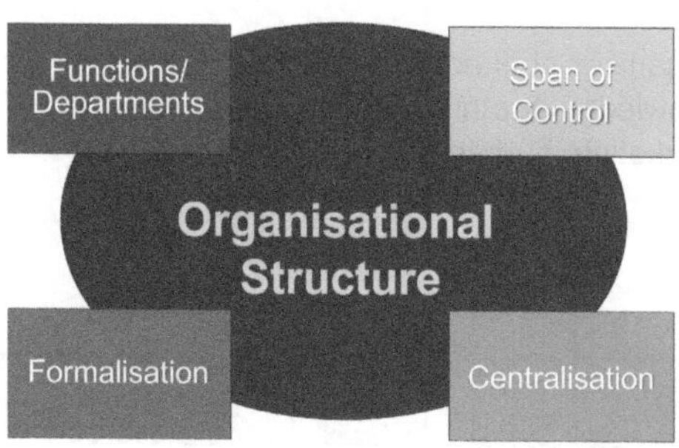

FIGURE 5.6 Organisational structure

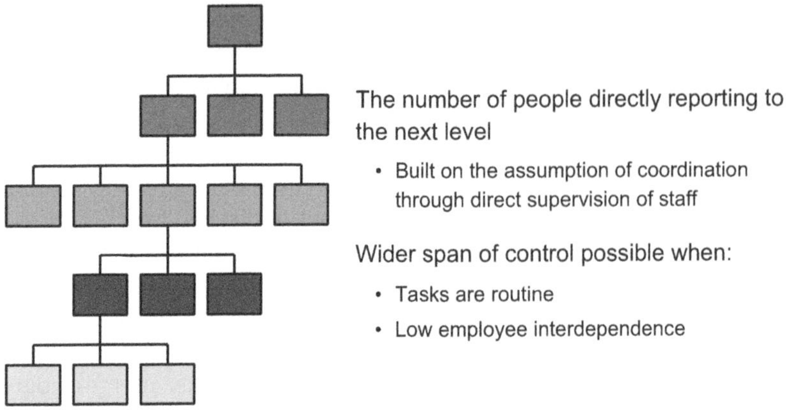

FIGURE 5.7 Span of control

decentralisation. But there are organisations that pivot between the two when the strategy does not achieve objectives. The challenge today is finding the right balance; how the CEO navigates these conflicting pressures will have economic and societal consequences for their organisation.

Since the 1980s, as organisations strive for better customer service, the number of direct relationships between managers and subordinates has increased. This has led to the widening of the span of control (see Figure 5.7). Factors such as external environmental turbulence, the nature of the job task, and budgetary constraints may affect the span of control. The formal structure clearly shows the organisation's official lines of enquiry and communication. Figure 5.8 illustrates a typical formal organisational chart, which features a deliberate division of labour, with each employee being aware of the rules, policies, and procedures.

The formal organisational structure (see Figure 5.6) should encourage informal structures, such as communities of practice, which are prevalent in learning organisations. Such structures can help crosslink organisational units and are thematic rather than hierarchical. It provides linkages between the individual, group, and the broader strategy themes. Wenger and Snyder (2000) state that the economy runs on knowledge. Despite the use of

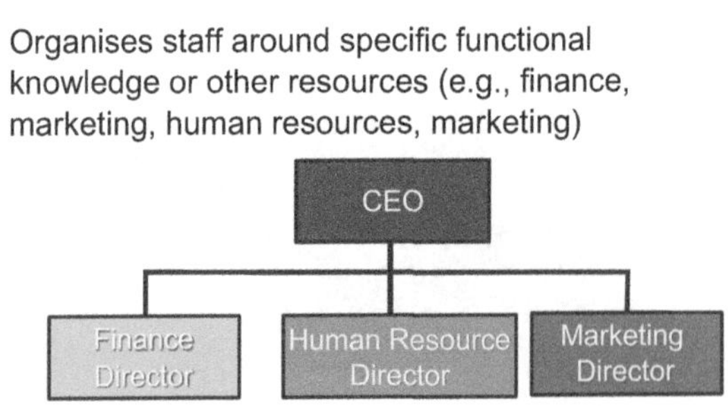

FIGURE 5.8 Formal organisation chart

cross-functional teams, customers of product-focused business units and the community of practice radically galvanise knowledge sharing, learning, and change. The impact of the digital age has accelerated the benefits of the community of practice. New theories can be located in the *Learning in Landscapes of Practice* textbook (see Wenger-Trayner and Wenger-Trayner, 2014).

The functional structure (see Figure 5.8) departmentalises activities into core business functions. Each department enables specialisation by grouping employees with shared skills and knowledge and is easily scalable as the organisation grows. Typically, this works best in environments involving routine operations with slight variations of the end product. Organisations may deploy structures regarding product/service line, customer, and location depending on their strategic posture. Functional structures do possess several benefits and limitations. A functional structure enables economies of scale, reduces unit costs, and is a conduit for career aspirations regarding promotions and paths. Limitations include the provable silo mentally, which can lead to dysfunctional conflict and less coordination.

Working in teams has become influential in problem-solving, increasing productivity, and product **innovation**. Advocates like Henry Ford and the late Steve Jobs have emphasised that collaboration is the key to success. Due to the decentralised structure, members should decide how to work together. Self-directed work teams are usually organic and organised around salient work processes. This flexible and responsive structure increases staff commitment to tasks and enables quicker management decisions. However, limitations include higher interpersonal training costs, slower startup efficiency due to the learning curve effect, and, in some situations, higher stress levels.

Matrix structures (see Figure 5.9) tend to evolve when there is a need to utilise the skill set of a functional structure without affecting day-to-day operations. Staff are appointed to specific projects to meet the project criteria: time, cost, and quality. Resources can be allocated efficiently, and staff can move from project to project in case of delays. Developing a cadre of experts can be deployed in highly complex environments using the latest state-of-the-art techniques, which can focus on clients and products. However, conflicts may arise due to split loyalties between the project manager and the departmental manager. There can be more conflict, organisational politics, and stress in complex environments.

As organisations seek to position themselves in global markets and leverage AI, their network structure (see Figure 5.10) has evolved to coordinate and delegate tasks among multiple parties with a common goal. This can be a specific product or service. Collaboration is vital, as it is a key to achieving a competitive advantage. The network's organisational structure is highly flexible and efficient. Each party is carefully selected and has responsibility for a specific task. This can operate across borders and utilise skills and technology to optimise product development. Limitations include being exposed to external forces and being over-reliant on each party, which can reduce synergistic effects.

Flat organisational structures may emerge due to delaying, reengineering, and creating cross-function teams to empower lower-level staff. Functional silos become blurred and cross-functional activities enhance the flow of communication. Moreover, informal employee networks can help bind the newer type of structures. In addition to strengthening staff satisfaction, morale, and talent retention, they are crucial in knowledge-intensive industries. Informal structures can be conduits for official rules to be negotiated or subverted by staff. From a strategic perspective, informal structures can enhance the flow of

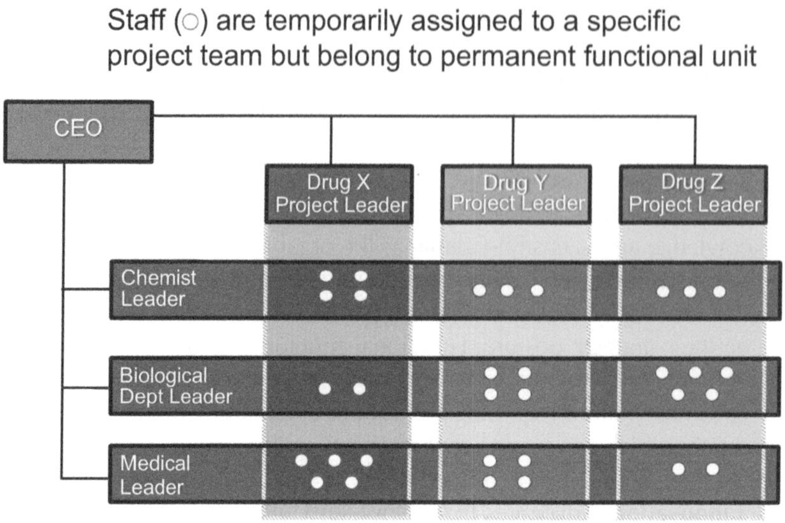

FIGURE 5.9 Matrix structures (project-based)

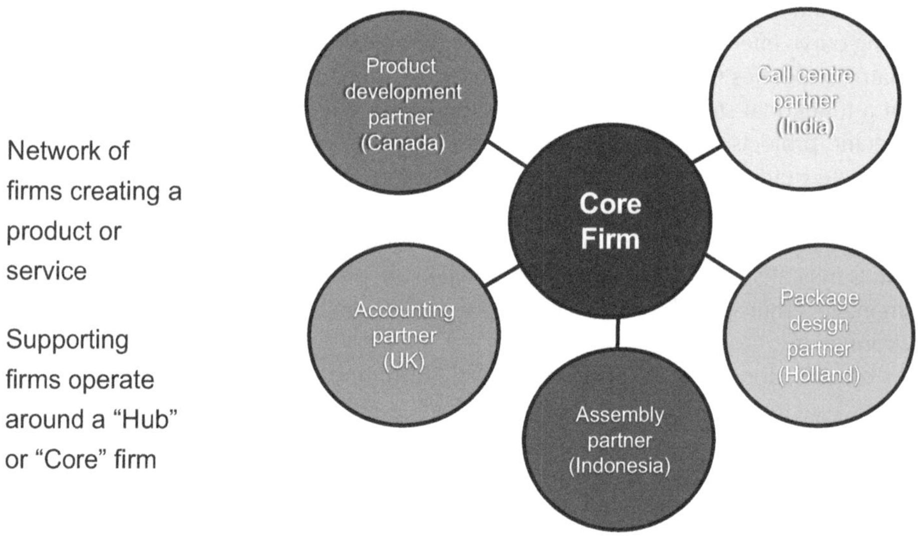

FIGURE 5.10 Network structure

communication and help address the challenges faced by management staff. Debates about tall versus flat organisational structures continue (see Figure 5.11). Tall organisations can provide a career path for newly appointed ambitious employees, but flat structures can work successfully in large firms. Structures are created to regulate and deliver control mechanisms for management and employees.

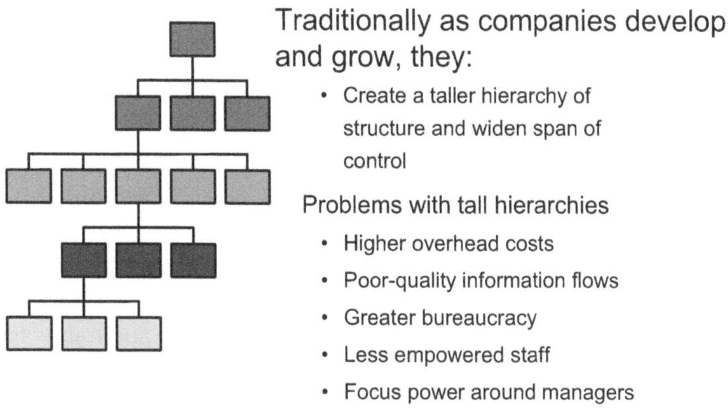

FIGURE 5.11 Tall vs flat structures

5.13 Organisational Culture

CEOs hugely influence culture, and this interaction is related to consequential organisational outcomes. Culture represents a system of shared values and beliefs of organisational members. Leaders shape culture and send signals via informal and formal mechanisms to reinforce desired behaviours and prevent undesired behaviours. Culture is passed from generation to generation and shapes behaviour and perceptions. Defining and analysing culture is problematic, and as pronounced by Williams (1983), it is one of the two or three most complicated words in English. Schein (1992) suggests that the confusion in defining culture is due to a failure to differentiate the levels at which culture permeates the organisation. Values underlie norms and artefacts and lead to consistent behaviour (Hogan and Coote, 2014). If the CEO wishes to pursue an innovative strategy, then innovative behaviours must be developed via norms supporting new processes. These can derive from values and manifest in artefacts from stories, rituals, and symbolic behaviour.

Organisations realise that being old and traditional is not necessarily a strength but can be a potential weakness. Being slow to respond to imminent danger has brought some organisations to a quick demise. Using the analogy of an iceberg, the image of culture above the water can be seen as how staff look, dress, and communicate, being the observable elements. However, the values, beliefs, norms, customs, and nonverbal behaviour can lead to difficulties in implementing a change management strategy, which are non-observable elements. In addition, organisational culture may be misaligned with the external environment, and if solid cultures exist, they may suppress dissenting subcultures.

One form of organisational culture is bureaucratic, and this textbook's theme is the need for **innovation**. Part of being innovative involves taking calculated risks and being creative. A bureaucratic culture perpetuates stability and works best for organisations that produce standardised goods and services. Hogan and Coote (2014) provide an overview of how organisational culture can support **innovation**. Value dimensions mentioned in the literature include success, openness and flexibility, internal communication, competence and professionalism, inter-functional cooperation, responsibility, appreciation, and risk-taking.

5.14 Organisational Resources

Intangible and tangible resources are recognised as crucial drivers of organisational success, as they can help gain competitive advantage and lead to higher **performance** levels. Intangible assets relate to non-financial assets without a physical presence, which are used to generate products or services, which in turn generate revenue. Successful brands tend to be easily recognised and have strong innovators, longevity, and strong balance sheets. Hence, the mismanagement of intangible assets in the knowledge era can be costly. Management of organisations needs to identify critical groups of tangible and intangible assets to ascertain their precise value drivers. As Kaplan and Norton (2004) state, intangible assets are the primary drivers by which a firm can establish its identity and frame its strategy.

Intellectual capital is often treated as synonymous with intangible assets. It defines "intellectual capital" as "all non-monetary and non-physical resources that are fully or partly controlled by the organisation and contribute to its value creation." Despite the disagreement of the literature on categorisation approaches, the tri-partite taxonomy of human, structural, and relational capital is employed in the literature. Human capital comprises the intangible resources embodied by individuals (e.g., knowledge and motivation). Structural capital refers to the infrastructure in organisations, such as information systems, management processes and procedures, and organisational systems. Relational capital is the value derived from and created through continuous relationships with external economic actors.

5.15 Organisational Capabilities, Core Competencies, and Dynamic Capabilities

The relationship between organisational capabilities and competencies cannot be readily inferred from the lexicon used by practitioners. The theoretical objection to such rests on their distinctiveness. Competitive advantage may result from a firm's distinct capabilities; however, these capabilities are often insufficient to support a competitive advantage. Capabilities emerge when resources accomplish a specific task or set of functions. These capabilities may lie within functional areas such as Walmart's distribution, Apple's marketing and product **innovation**, and Zara's clothing production. Using these examples, it is clear how these capabilities enable these firms to perform at much higher levels than their peers.

Generally, firms must ascertain threshold competencies, the minimum required to compete in an industry. A proficiency that enables a firm to deliver customer value is consistent with the term core competence. These effects can be leveraged across various markets and be a source of competence-based strengths. Competence-based strategies are increasingly blurring interfirm boundaries, with collaboration becoming a growing market-based responsibility for securing resources and navigating turbulence. Collinson and Parcell (2001) describe five key organisational competencies: strategy development, management techniques, collaboration mechanisms, knowledge sharing and learning processes, and knowledge capture and storage. Successful organisational change is sustainable when core competencies are integral and aligned with strategy.

Information technology (IT) competencies can assist in implementing requisite entrepreneurial and adaptive actions (Chakravarty, Grewal, and Sambamurthy, 2013). These findings show that managers should consider multiple contingencies, both observed and unobserved, while assessing the effects of IT competencies on agility and firm **performance**, which is the essence of the latest arguments. Understanding the link between

IT competencies and **innovation** is essential for several reasons. First, IT is an enabler as organisations implement their renewal strategies. Second, the continued growth of digital business strategies requires higher functionalities. These digital strategies reshape existing processes into modular, cross-functional, distributed, and global, enabling the CEO to operate across traditional boundaries such as time and distance.

As the environment changes, capabilities must evolve and be managed dynamically. Successful organisations need to make timely responses to the environment using capabilities to coordinate competencies. This specific source of competitive advantage is referred to as dynamic capabilities. The term "dynamic" applies to the changing character of the environment and the strategic responses to such situations. The term "capabilities" refers to the specific organisational skills, resources, and functional strengths that can be a core component of the desired strategy. Teece et al.'s (1997) dynamic capabilities framework extends the RBV by incorporating environmental and technological change. Given this advancement, organisational capabilities can moderate the relationship between IT investments and **performance**.

As outlined previously, organisations need to be proactive rather than reactive in rapidly changing environments. To fulfil this objective, there is a requirement to integrate, build, and reconfigure internal and external competencies. Hence, the concept of dynamic capabilities remains suitable as it can help ascertain the capabilities necessary to lead to organisational success. The protection of output capabilities regarding the observable product or service is vital, whereas **innovation** capabilities, by contrast, are much harder to imitate. This reinforces the importance of being innovative in rapidly changing environments. Teece (2007) stresses that organisations with strong dynamic capabilities are intensely entrepreneurial.

5.16 Value Chain Analysis

Given that we have highlighted the importance of adding value from an internal perspective, the value chain provides some additional functional theory. Porter's value chain (see Figure 5.12) analysis seeks to provide a framework that describes the salient processes within and around an organisation that create a product or service. During the analysis, the user should be able to understand how value is made or lost in terms of activities undertaken and to diagnose strategic capability.

Value chain resources and activities are interdependent and must be evaluated as a whole, allowing for the optimisation and coordination of them to work together effectively and form a coherent strategy. The strategic and associated resource linkages are as crucial as the individual resources and activities.

5.17 Boston Consulting Group (BCG) Growth-Share Matrix

Sources of sustainable competitive advantage remain the holy grail of business and management education and practice. This chapter has considered a range of approaches enabling business leaders to stay on track during global economic crises and slowdowns. Now, the focus shifts to additional theories, which are somewhat dated but still provide an excellent platform for students and practitioners to understand the key components to consider. So, the following sections will review the BCG growth-share matrix, Ansoff, and Porter's generic strategies.

FIGURE 5.12 Value chain analysis

When making decisions about business objectives, the Boston Consulting Group's growth/share matrix (Henderson, 1979) (Figure 5.13) is a helpful tool for strategic investment decisions. Despite the blurring of discrete business units within some organisations, the analysis enables some attention to the cash flow of operations. Inherent assumptions include the margins generated by a product and respective cash flow generation resulting from the market share – the more significant the market share (relative to competitors), the greater the earnings potential. Sales and revenue growth require investment; the product portfolio should internally generate this cash. But we know that sales will only grow if there is effective marketing. High market share is desirable but requires additional investment. As businesses can only grow for a while, there must be trade-offs between earnings and money spent on them. Profitability is affected also by the product life cycle, and the user must take a holistic view of the product portfolio. Decisions need to be made about earnings from mature products being invested in other products of future earnings potential.

A balanced portfolio is highly desirable from a cash flow perspective (Figure 5.14). In summary, each quadrant presents varying challenges.

Question marks (high growth, low market share):

- The product requires a high expenditure to develop and launch, and it is unlikely to be profitable later. Further investments will be needed if the company wants to claim the market.

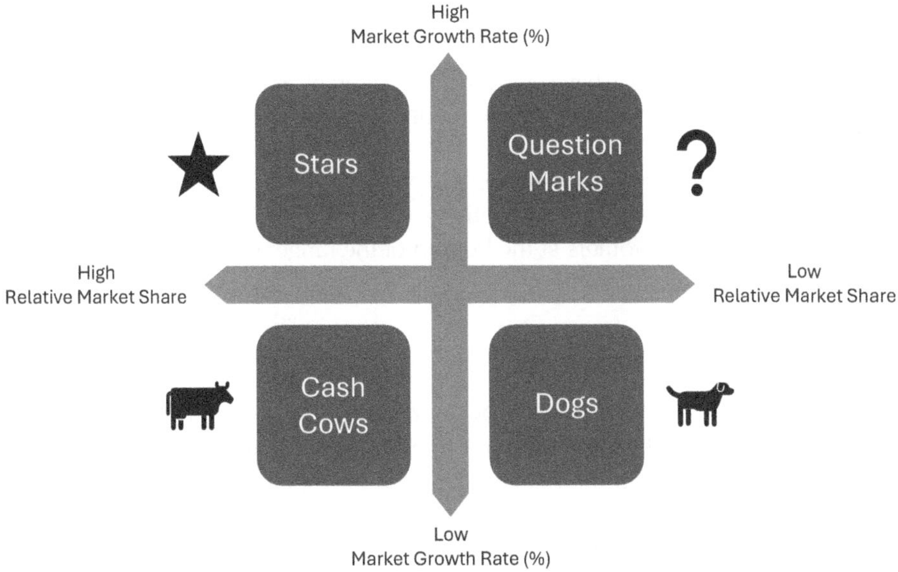

FIGURE 5.13 Boston Consulting Group (BCG) growth-share matrix

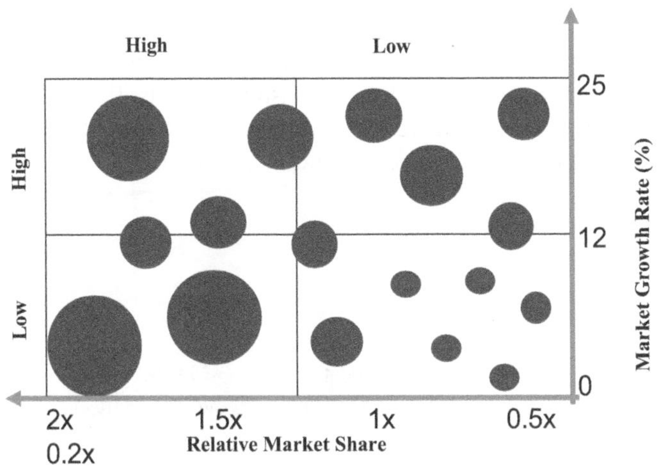

FIGURE 5.14 BCG matrix – balanced portfolio

Stars (high growth, high market share):

- Successful question marks become stars. However, investment is still necessary to sustain growth and maintain leadership positions. Only marginally profitable but becomes more profitable when growth slows down.

Cash cows (low growth, high market share):

- Mature products in well-established markets. As growth slows down, there is less need for high investment, which is most profitable. It should be used to fund other products.

Dogs (low growth, low market share):

- The previous cash cow may have enjoyed a loyal market, although it was largely replaced by a new rival. It is marginally profitable but should be withdrawn when it becomes a loss maker.
- Guard Dog: Blocking the competition.
- Guide Dog: Complements other activities.
- Sheepdog: Creating customers at the bottom of the range, who may trade up to one of its better products later.

5.18 Ansoff

The Ansoff Matrix (1957) guides CEOs in determining their firm's growth strategy (Figure 5.15). When faced with numerous opportunities, it is advisable to consider which products and markets are currently being targeted and should be targeted in the future. Outputs can be categorised into four distinct areas. Each option requires different strategies, actions, supporting resources, and skills.

5.18.1 Market Penetration

This is the most straightforward and least risky strategy to pursue. Focusing on existing products and markets means servicing existing customers and utilising existing product ranges to increase an organisation's share of existing markets. The added advantage is that there is prior knowledge of what works. Loyalty schemes could be promoted to existing customers, encouraging them to make additional purchases.

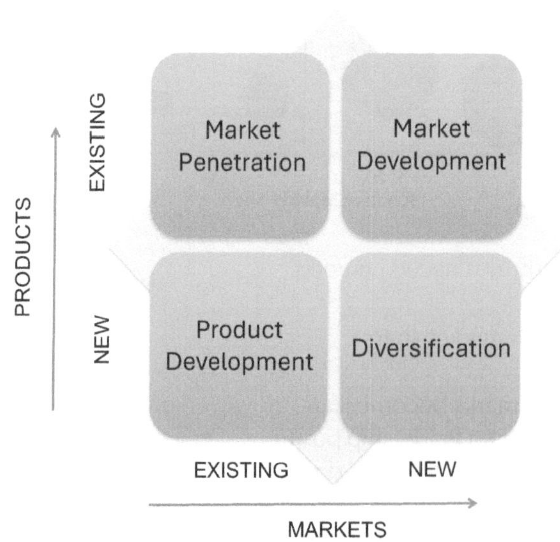

FIGURE 5.15 Ansoff matrix

5.18.2 Market Development

Like market penetration, the focus is on expanding existing products or services into new markets. This requires excellent marketing capability, as market research and marketing strategy must provide initial entry and effective organisational learning about the market. Accessing a new market takes time, but the high risk can translate to high returns.

5.18.3 Product Development

Introducing new products into existing markets is risky, but this can be mitigated as current customers are already known. Customers should be consulted during product development, and their feedback should be incorporated. Good ideas can be solicited from understanding existing customers. It is preferable to return to delighted customers and sell them something new rather than to find new customers.

5.18.4 Diversification

Contrary to market penetration, diversification is the riskiest strategy. With a focus on new products and services in emerging markets, there is also potential for high rewards. It may take time and resources to develop sufficient understanding to compete effectively. Diversification can be related (remaining in the same industry) or unrelated (competing in a new sector). When considering this growth strategy, the CEO must be realistic about strengths and weaknesses. Frequently, help is required from investors or through mergers and acquisitions.

5.19 Porter's Generic Strategies

During the 1980s, Porter's generic strategy and the full range of competitive strategies gained prominence. The approach became highly fashionable in Western business schools and among executives. Users sought to achieve two things. In the first instance, generic principles are used, and in the second, customised action plans are used (Mintzberg, 1992). The four quadrants (Table 5.3) built around low cost and differentiation are the primary types of competitive advantage. Initially, scholars considered differentiation and cost leadership as two separate strategies, i.e., pure strategy.

TABLE 5.3 Porter's (1980) generic strategy framework

Target Scope	*Advantage Low Cost*	*Advantage Product Uniqueness*
Broad (industry wide)	Cost leadership strategy	Differentiation strategy
Narrow (market segment)	Focus strategy (low cost)	Focus strategy (differentiation low cost)

5.19.1 Cost Leadership Strategy

- Successful firms tend to be the lowest-cost producers in the industry. This is achieved by maximising economies of scale and other cost advantages.
- Risks: Reducing the cost base may be impossible. Consider the supermarket, budget hotel, and budget airline sector.

5.19.2 Differentiation Strategy

- Successful firms tend to possess a differentiation strategy, offering their customers something unique and valuable. Customers are willing to pay higher prices.
- Risks: The higher prices must cover the additional costs. Imitation can be a problem.

5.19.3 Focus Strategy

- A focus strategy concentrates on a specific target segment and seeks a cost advantage or differentiation. Firms pursuing such a strategy will likely have lower volumes and consequently gain less bargaining power with their suppliers.
- Risks: It is relatively easy for a broad-market cost leader to adapt its product to compete directly.

5.19.4 Stuck in the Middle

Michael Porter argued that to be successful over the long term, the firm must select only one of his three generic strategies. Otherwise, pursuing multiple generic strategies will leave the firm "stuck in the middle" and prevent it from achieving a competitive advantage. This apparent dilemma has been extensively debated, and many scholars now see that there is no reason to discriminate against a mixed strategy. For example, insofar as the digital age is concerned, the application of Porter's generic strategy is not delineated. Moreover, with the growing influence of new products and services, Porter's generic strategies do not provide the full range of options to today's strategists and are not mutually exclusive. As the commercial world gets more complex, Porter's original blueprint created in the 1980s is limited. In today's dynamism and turbulence, firms now integrate the two elements and can pursue hybrid or combinative as opposed to pure strategies.

5.20 Improving Case Study Analysis

The need for students to score high marks in seminars, assessments, and exams is crucial, but over the years, marks may vary considerably. Table 5.4 summarises some of the issues for weak case study analysis among business school students, with details of issues, and suggestions to overcome these problems.

5.21 The Corporate I Don't Know Factor

The corporate "I don't know factor" is higher than ever because business leaders can lose direction in the global economic crisis and struggle to identify and focus on

TABLE 5.4 Scoring higher marks for case study analysis

Issues	*Details*	*Details to Overcome Problems*
1 Lack of practical experience	Limited real-world business experience hampers understanding and application of theoretical concepts.	Encourage internships, practical projects, and real-world business simulations.
2 Inadequate analytical skills	Weak critical evaluation, issue identification, and logical argument development skills.	Offer targeted analytical skill workshops and practice exercises.
3 Insufficient understanding of business concepts	Incomplete mastery of business concepts and frameworks needed for comprehensive analysis.	Provide in-depth coverage of business concepts and frequent application opportunities.
4 Poor time management	Failure to allocate sufficient time for thorough reading, research, and synthesis.	Teach effective time management strategies and emphasise the importance of thorough analysis.
5 Lack of confidence	Doubt in abilities leads to hesitation in presenting insights and second-guessing conclusions.	Build confidence through positive reinforcement, peer support, and practice presentations.
6 Limited exposure to diverse case studies	Narrow range of case studies results in difficulty approaching new scenarios.	Expose students to a wide variety of case studies from different industries and contexts.
7 Over-reliance on templates	Rigid adherence to templates inhibits critical thinking and creativity.	Promote adaptive use of templates, emphasising flexibility and contextual application.
8 Ineffective group dynamics	Poor communication, unequal contribution, and lack of collaboration in group work.	Facilitate team-building activities and workshops on effective group work techniques.
9 Difficulty in synthesising information	Challenge in distilling key points and integrating them into a cohesive argument.	Train students in synthesising information through structured exercises and examples.
10 Lack of feedback and guidance	Absence of detailed feedback and instructor guidance hinders understanding of weaknesses and improvement.	Implement regular, constructive feedback sessions and provide clear guidance and expectations.

growth opportunities appropriate for their business. They must look beyond tactical lower prices and cost-cutting to repair and rebuild value chain relationships. Many companies benefit disproportionately from their annual strategic planning efforts and rewards. Then, they complain about the lack of new ideas, along with power and political undertones.

So, why is there a mismatch between effort and result? The annual strategy review sometimes amounts to little more than a stage shows where business unit leaders present updates of last year's presentations and take few risks in announcing new ideas. This stage **performance** does not prepare organisations to face the strategic uncertainties ahead or serve as the focal point for creative thinking. The strategic analysis tools considered in this chapter suggest that executives should ask themselves "why" and "how." By asking why organisations will assess internal and external environments and, using a broad array of stakeholders, they will produce more challenging and innovative strategies. Another caveat relates to being too over-focused on extrapolating existing thoughts rather than new and stretching aspirations.

This necessitates a fresh approach to strategic analysis that incorporates the triple bottom line (TBL) of profit, people, and planet (Elkington and Rowlands, 1999). The point is echoed by Elkington (2018), who coined the TBL, 25 years previously, felt that his tool had become a mere accounting tool. The widespread adoption of TBL had not resulted in systemic changes or **innovation** in rethinking capitalism. So, he proposed a product recall.

In the context of this chapter, Elkington strongly advocates for a deeper, more critical evaluation of how sustainability is embedded into strategy. Strategic analysis is not just about identifying opportunities and threats, but also about questioning the underlying assumptions, frameworks, and tools that drive decision-making. Users should assess whether there is evidence of transformative thought driving change, or merely cosmetic. So Elkington's thesis is not a rejection of his TBL, 25 years previously, but a call for evolution to incorporate a regenerative perspective.

5.22 Chapter Key Takeaways

Some of the key takeaways from Chapter 5 on Strategic Analysis are as follows:

1. **Holistic Strategic Analysis:** Strategic analysis must integrate external and internal factors. Modern practice now needs to incorporate the sustainability phenomenon to ensure effective decision-making.
2. **VUCA and BANI:** These frameworks emphasise the uncertain nature of modern business environments. Strategic leaders must develop agility and resilience by aligning strategies with dynamic and unpredictable external forces.
3. **Triple Bottom Line (TBL) Approach:** Leaders are urged to move beyond the traditional focus on profitability. Incorporating social (people) and environmental (planet) goals alongside financial (profit) outcomes creates a more sustainable and forward-thinking strategy.
4. **External vs Internal Environment:** This chapter emphasises balancing external opportunities (e.g., technology **innovation**, market trends) with internal resources (e.g., core competencies) to form adaptive, future-proof strategies.
5. **Frameworks for Analysis:** Tools like SWOT, PESTEL, and Porter's Five Forces are essential but should be used flexibly. Over-reliance on rigid frameworks without contextual understanding can limit the effectiveness of strategic recommendations.
6. **Dynamic Capabilities:** To maintain a sustainable competitive advantage, firms must develop dynamic capabilities that enable them to respond swiftly to environmental changes and continually reconfigure their internal competencies.
7. **Scenario Planning:** Using scenario analysis allows organisations to prepare for multiple plausible futures, such as changes in environmental regulations or market conditions, which are significant in sustainability-related decisions.

5.23 Self-Reflection Questions

1 Outline the components of any organisation's growth strategy using appropriate strategy frameworks and tools.
2 Explain the importance of stakeholder analysis and critically discuss how it can enhance the identification of stakeholder interests to create a competitive advantage for the firm. Use examples to illustrate your answers.
3 Based on the growing influence of sustainability in strategic management, critically discuss how organisations can successfully incorporate sustainability into their corporate strategies to boost **performance**. Illustrate your answer with examples.
4 Outline the major differences in strategic **performance** measurement in the private and public sector organisations.
5 Explain the importance of value chain analysis and critically discuss how it can enhance organisational processes' effectiveness and create competitive advantage. Use examples to illustrate your answers.

References

Ansoff, H.I., (1957). Strategies for diversification. *Harvard Business Review, 35*(5), pp.113–124.
Barney, J.B. and Hoskisson, R.E., (1990). Strategic groups: Untested assertions and research proposals. *Managerial and Decision Economics, 11*(3), pp.187–198.
Chakravarty, A., Grewal, R. and Sambamurthy, V., (2013). Information technology competencies, organisational agility, and firm performance: Enabling and facilitating roles. *Information Systems Research, 24*(4), pp.976–997.
Collinson, C. and Parcell, G., (2001). *Learning to fly*. Capstone Publishing Ltd.
Dobbs, M., (2014). Guidelines for applying Porter's five forces framework: A set of industry analysis templates. *Competitiveness Review, 24*(1), pp.32–45.
Elkington, J., (2018). 25 years ago I coined the phrase "triple bottom line." Here's why it's time to rethink it. *Harvard Business Review, 25*(2–5), p.6.
Elkington, J. and Rowlands, I.H., (1999). Cannibals with forks: The triple bottom line of 21st-century business. *Alternatives Journal, 25*(4), p.42.
Henderson, B.D., (1979). The product portfolio: Growth share matrix of the Boston Consulting Group. *The Strategy Process: Concepts, Contexts, Cases*, pp.678–680.
Hesselbarth, I., Alnoor, A. and Tiberius, V., (2023). Behavioral strategy: A systematic literature review and research framework. *Management Decision, 61*(9), pp.2740–2756.
Hogan, S.J. and Coote, L.V., (2014). Organizational culture, innovation, and performance: A test of Schein's model. *Journal of Business Research*, 67(8), pp.1609–1621.
Hunt, M.S., (1972). *Competition in the major home appliance industry 1960–1970*, Unpublished doctoral dissertation, Harvard University, 1972.
Kaplan, R.S. and Norton, D.P., (2004). *Strategy maps: Converting intangible assets into tangible outcomes*. Harvard Business Press.
Kenny, G., (2023). *Strategy discovery: Achieving business resilience, engagement and performance*. Routledge.
Kim, W.C. and Mauborgne, R., (2005). How to create uncontested market space and make the competition irrelevant. *Harvard Business Review, 4*, p.13.
Kramer, J.P., Marinelli, E., Iammarino, S. and Diez, J.R., (2011). Intangible assets as drivers of innovation: Empirical evidence on multinational enterprises in German and UK regional systems of innovation. *Technovation, 31*(9), pp.447–458.

Leask, G. and Parnell, J.A., (2005). Integrating strategic groups and the resource based perspective: Understanding the competitive process. *European Management Journal, 23*(4), pp.458–470.
Mendelow, A., (1981). Environmental Scanning – The Impact of Stakeholder Concept; 2nd International Conference on Information Systems, Massachusetts, 407–417.
Mintzberg, H., (1992). *Five Ps for strategy in the strategy process.* H. Mintzberg and J.B. Quinn eds. Prentice-Hall International Editions.
Porter, M.E., (1980). *Competitive strategy: Techniques for analyzing industries and competitors.* The Free Press, Harvard Business Publishing.
Porter, M.E., (2008). *Competitive strategy: Techniques for analyzing industries and competitors.* Simon and Schuster.
Powell, T.C., Lovallo, D. and Fox, C.R., (2011). Behavioral strategy. *Strategic Management Journal, 32*(13), pp.1369–1386.
Schein, E.H., (1992). *Organizational culture and leadership.* Jossey-Bass Inc.
Teece, D.J., (2007). Explicating dynamic capabilities: The nature and microfoundations of (sustainable) enterprise performance. *Strategic Management Journal, 28*(13), pp.1319–1350.
Teece, D.J., Pisano, G. and Shuen, A., (1997). Dynamic capabilities and strategic management. *Strategic Management Journal, 18*(7), pp.509–533.
Wenger, E. and Snyder, W., (2000). Communities of practice: The organizational frontier. *Harvard Business Review, 78*(1), pp.139–145.
Wenger-Trayner, E. and Wenger-Trayner, B., (2014). Learning in a landscape of practice: A framework. In *Learning in landscapes of practice* (pp. 13–30). Routledge.
Williams, R., (1983). *Keywords: A vocabulary of culture and society* (2nd ed.). Oxford University Press.

6

CASE STUDY ANALYSIS

6.1 Learning Strategy Objectives

After completing this chapter, you will be able to:

1 **Knowledge-Based Objectives:**

- Identify, apply, and explain the concepts of external and internal strategic analysis in a case study context.
- Formulate strategies to move the organisation forward in its strategy journey.

2 **Skill-Based Objectives:**

- Identify and develop creative strategies based on the results of strategic analysis.
- Critically evaluate the strategic positions of organisations in different industries throughout their life cycles.

3 **Attitude-Based Objectives:**

- Cultivate a proactive attitude towards case study analysis, recognising the need to be adaptive to dynamic environments.
- Adopt well-balanced considerations in strategy decision-making about economic, societal, and environmental issues.

6.2 Introduction

Traditional case study analysis has been a cornerstone of business and management education since its inception at Harvard Business School in 1921. Harvard, which once claimed authorship of over 80% of the world's case studies, has played a pivotal role in shaping this educational tool. The prominence of case study analysis is evident, as most leading business schools ranked by Bloomberg Businessweek incorporate it as a primary teaching method. At Harvard Business School, a significant portion of class time

DOI: 10.4324/9781003516774-8

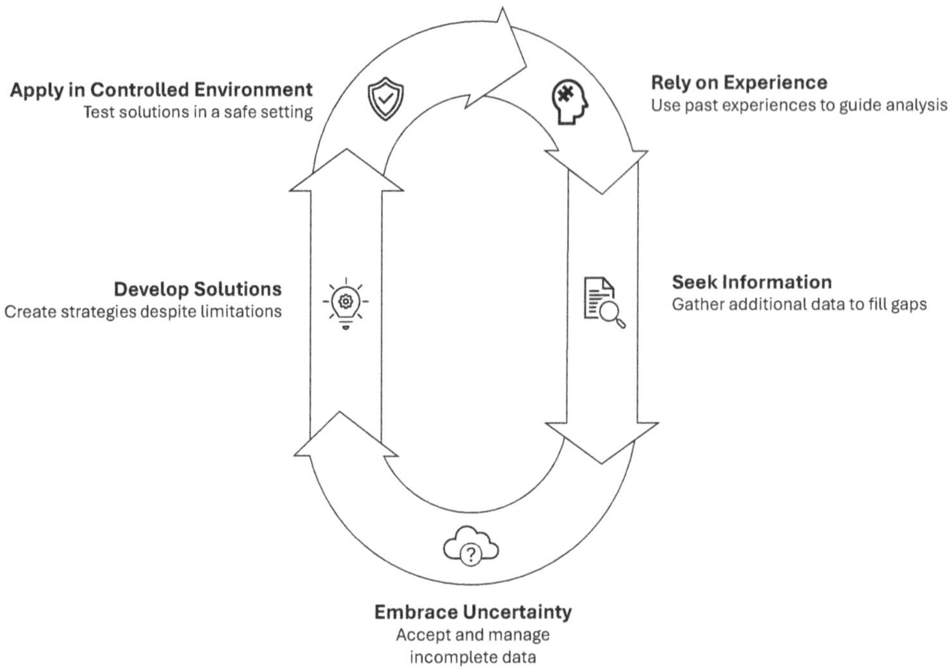

FIGURE 6.1 Making decisions in a classroom setting

is devoted to case studies, underscoring their critical role in preparing future business leaders.

Bringing the gap between the business school and the "real business world" helps students and executives test their knowledge of the curriculum in a controlled and safe environment. In the first instance, relying on experience, seeking additional information, and embracing uncertainty are the starting points in case study analysis (see Figure 6.1). The unit of analysis can range from an individual to a global firm. They have a common purpose of bringing reality to the classroom, and like reality, they do not contain all the necessary data to make decisions. This is a core skill for MBA, MSc, and executives to appreciate. They can figure out solutions knowing they are not in a real-world situation.

Other academic disciplines and professional bodies have increasingly adopted the business school case. Matching, exploiting, and assessing the numerous strategies organisations pursue have evolved case studies from descriptive to a more structured and realistic account of practice. Strategic fit (or lack of fit) can now be viewed through the lens of all industries and sectors in all countries.

Another benefit of case analysis is the development of essential strategic management skills (see Figure 6.2). These include strategic thinking, leadership and teamwork, analytical thinking, problem-solving, decision-making, global awareness, and communication. These practical development skills are one of the hallmarks of a business school education, available at undergraduate, postgraduate, MBA, and executive education levels. Case studies are now integral to graduate entry positions and are part of the consulting interview process. Case studies used at graduate assessment centres enable employers to observe candidates in action, either individually or in groups. Organisations deploy

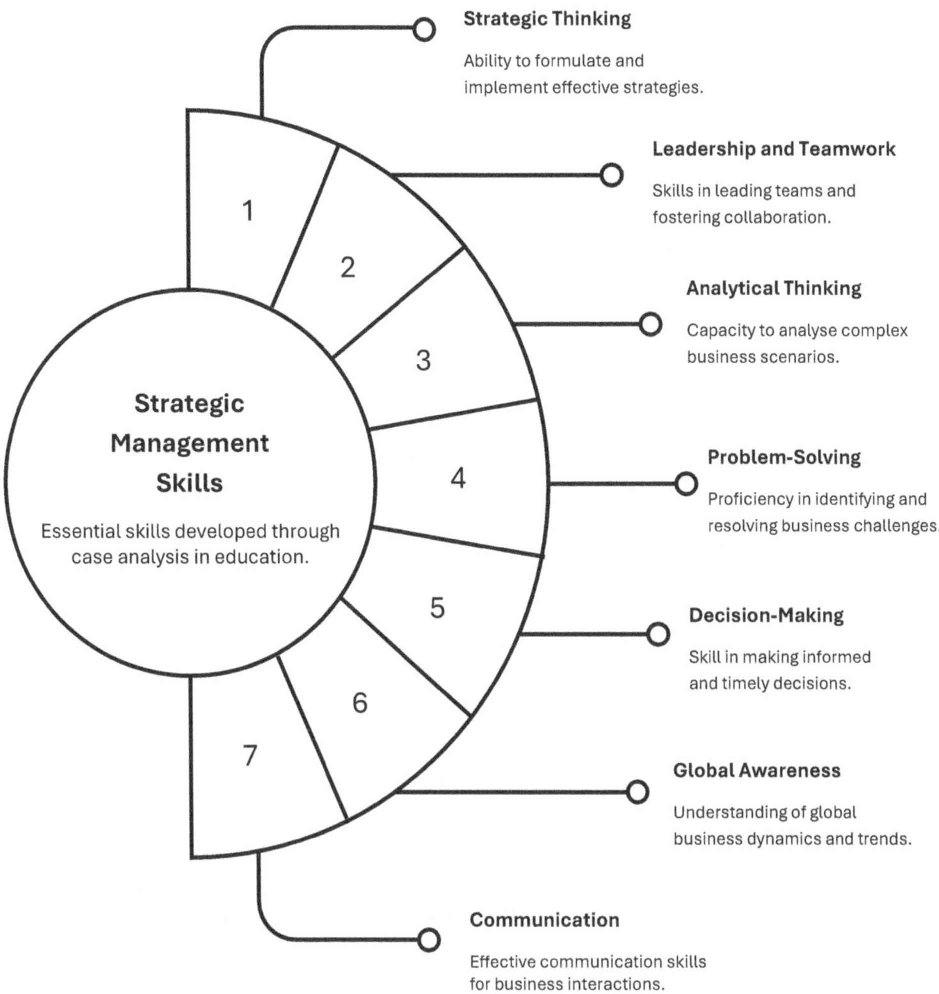

FIGURE 6.2 Essential strategic management skills

subject-related or general case studies, which are one of several steps to evaluate a candidate's ability in aptitude (strategic, creative, analytical, problem-solving) and employment skills (business, time management, working under pressure, oral communication).

The pandemic has given prominence to virtual assessment centres. Candidates use an interactive business case simulation and navigate through a scenario. Online assessors can evaluate **performance** and report back to the candidate. Like their face-to-face versions, candidates can also work in a group format. Case studies cover various industries and contexts, exposing the business environment and strategy challenges. Answers can be delivered in written, verbal, and online formats.

Case analysis requires you to examine a critical point in the life of an organisation. You are put in the position of a decision-maker. Essential decisions in a business situation must be made logically, objectively, and promptly. This is set against a background of noise and fluidity in the day-to-day environment; however, all case studies must contain at least one significant issue. In a case analysis, you must apply your analytical skills to identify and solve any problems that appear. Studying cases will help you develop the experience to make these decisions in the real world.

An additional benefit will occur as you become involved in the operations of fascinating and dissimilar organisational situations and dilemmas. You will become familiar with diverse organisational structures and business philosophies and apply alternative strategy techniques, which should broaden your knowledge. The entire process of preparing for case analysis will yield benefits in other ways. You will enhance your communication skills as you write and present your final report. The cases will allow you to use your initiative, decide on a course of action, and follow it through. Working in groups will develop your ability to work with others, a crucial skill in today's business world. Only with complete information will all the relevant information necessary to make critical decisions be available in the case; you will learn by doing.

An increasing number of strategic management courses now assess students, at least in part, by requiring them to answer case study questions. However, business and non-business students can find interpreting cases challenging. This chapter provides an outline of how to approach such case study questions. Students will gain practice in working with strategic management problems by assuming the role of decision-makers. The author outlines an approach for analysing, discussing, and writing about cases. Emphasis is placed upon outlining strategic options, making recommendations, and arriving at a conclusion.

Case analysis is flexible and can be used for semester-long projects, seminar classes, or shorter time frames. In these latter instances, issues are simplified, and the length is shorter. However, as Dobbs (2013) suggests, the variety of types and uses of case analysis can be challenging for students at all levels. Not only may the student need more experience managing others in a business setting, but they may also need to gain prior experience from which to draw. If not adequately supported, case analysis can result in an extemporised superficial analysis that lacks systematic rigour and proposes hasty, ill-informed decisions.

6.2.1 What Does the Case Study Provide?

Case studies provide insights from multiple situations and can be seen through various lenses (Williams, 2023). Figure 6.3 illustrates some of the perspectives to consider through the matrix representation. In terms of the academic literature, the sustainability dimension in case studies, while powerful, is in its embryonic phase (Edwards, Benn, and Starik, 2017). Notably, empirical evidence is lacking, despite the widespread adoption of the case study (Rosier, 2022).

A good case study can enrich the students' learning experience. In addition, the discussions held during seminars remain in the students' minds much longer than the contents of a 50-minute class. This highlights the difference in learning between surface and deep learning approaches (Guo, Yang, Zhang, and Gan, 2022). Business schools are in the public gaze for not producing work-ready graduates in sufficient numbers. So, rather than relying solely on traditional lectures, integrating case studies can help bridge the gap between theory and practical application. This will equip students with better critical thinking and problem-solving skills.

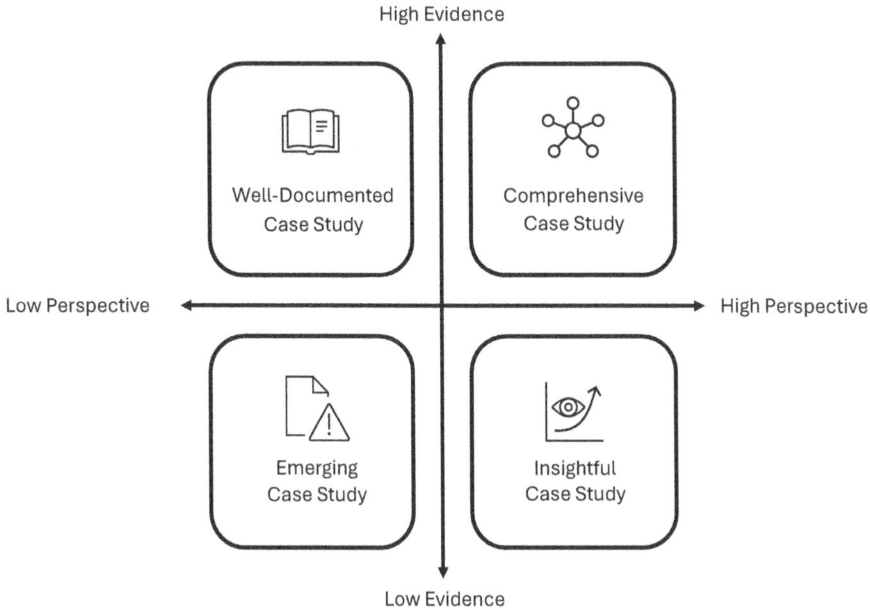

FIGURE 6.3 Case study matrix

The case study provides a snapshot picture of a management situation. The emphasis is usually on a situation presenting a challenge for management. Situations include large companies, small and medium-sized enterprises, and government organisations, where the student or executive is placed in a decision-making role. The case analysis will start with the reader assessing events that managers have had to deal with, together with changes in the internal and external environments. Issues and problems may relate to corporate, business, or operational level. The organisation's management may have initiated a response, such as a strategy renewal project, which either needs to be accelerated or has failed. The reader must utilise various strategic management tools and techniques to address these problems, as outlined in Chapter 5. The outline processes include analysis, identification of options, selection of a preferred option, and recommendations.

Case studies can help users understand how managers can make sense of an uncertain and increasingly complex world by considering various layers of influence, from macro-environmental issues to specific forces affecting their competitive position. The challenge is understanding the interaction of these different forces and how they impact an organisation. The exploration and identification of the various levels of resources, capabilities, and value-adding activities that organisations may draw upon to outperform the competition.

Case analysis is flexible, as it can be used for semester-long projects, which provide ample time for in-depth analysis. Alternatively, case analysis can be used for seminar classes or even shorter time frames. In these latter instances, issues are simplified, and the length is shorter. As Dobbs (2013) suggests, the variety of types and uses of case analysis can be challenging for students. Not only may the student need more experience managing others in a business setting, but they may also have no prior experience from which to draw. If not adequately supported, case analysis can result in an extemporised superficial analysis that lacks systematic rigour and proposes hasty, ill-informed decisions.

This chapter provides an overview of how to perform case study analysis, offering assistance through the introduction of a series of templates. Although most undergraduate students still need to gain business and, especially, leadership experience, modules in strategic management are taught in either the second or final year of undergraduate degree programmes. In the latter case, strategic management is used as a capstone subject to prepare students for work by consolidating and integrating their knowledge and skills. The lecturer's experience and style, together with the students' expectations, backgrounds, and abilities, influence how and what actual cases are employed.

Due to their experience and age, students often require assistance with analysis and navigating complex situations at the undergraduate level. The quality of the actual case depends on whether the case is realistic or based on the lecturer's (or author's) personal experiences. The lack of local cases (non-western) continues to frustrate students globally. Sometimes, the UG student may not even be a business and management student; they could be an engineering student. In such situations, students face the added burden of not having enough time to acquaint themselves with commercial awareness. This can be tackled by reading quality newspapers and business periodicals.

6.3 Case Study Analysis Steps

We now examine some practical steps from my case studies in classes, classroom discussions, and reports for formative assessments (monitoring student learning during the module) and summative assessments (evaluating student learning at the end of the module). When running executive education courses, vignettes (mini-cases) are commonly used during the programme, and case studies can be used as a capstone-type exercise towards the end of a programme. Over the years, sector-specific organisations have used case studies based on their scope of activities, financial firms finance-oriented, technology firms use IT-specific examples, and marketing organisations may use cases that seek to reposition firms by creating marketing campaigns.

Students should closely examine their significant issues to analyse the current situation. A common mistake is trying to identify every single problem facing the company. Then, prepare a long list to incorporate into the report. There are many ways for students to approach the analysis of business cases. Each instructor has their own ideas on the number and nature of the involved steps. A logical format should be used to analyse any business situation. Table 6.1 illustrates a generic ten-step procedure to begin.

Analysing a business situation needs a formalised plan of action. Case analysts should strive to comprehend the fundamental aspects of a specific business situation, enabling them to recommend targeted actions to enhance that situation. The entire process must be systematic. A strategic management case analysis should have systematic principles and procedures for examining a problem and making appropriate recommendations. The case method becomes an effective teaching device when students are encouraged to analyse the data presented and formulate their recommendations.

TABLE 6.1 Case study approach

Steps	*Activities*	*Questions to Consider About the Organisation*
1	Heritage, development, and growth review	Who were the founders? Who are the key individuals? What have been the critical incidents in the organisation's history? Has the development to date been successful? What have been the salient capabilities and competencies? What is the current situation? What are the big questions?
2	External analysis	What are the threats and opportunities?
3	Internal analysis	What are the internal strengths and weaknesses?
4	SWOT analysis	Define the problem. What problems need to be diagnosed? How can weaknesses be converted into strengths? How can threats be converted into opportunities?
5	Corporate strategy review	Is a corporate strategy renewal programme required?
6	Business strategy review	How are the SBUs position in their marketplace? What are the SBUs' value proposition? Are the SBUs on track to deliver their targets?
7	Option selection	Formulate the alternatives. What are the alternatives? Analyse the alternatives. What is the most appropriate option? What are the key risks?
8	Develop a strategic plan	What is the vision and mission?
9	Develop a strategic implementation plan	What barriers exist to implement the renewal strategy? What structures and control systems are required to implement the strategy? Is it affordable?
10	Recommendations	How can the strategic problem be solved? Recommend a solution.

Abbreviations: SBUs, Strategic Business Unit; SWOT, Strengths, Weaknesses, Opportunities, and Threats.

6.3.1 Case Overview

Imagine you are a seasoned strategy consultant tasked with dissecting an organisation and devising its future business strategy. Where would you commence this formidable endeavour? Your initial step would be to fully immerse yourself in the organisation's internal and external environments, understanding its services/products, processes, current situation, and other pertinent factors. You would strive to conjure a comprehensive mental portrait of the entire entity. With this holistic view, you can precisely address the specific components of the situation.

Your primary objective should be to capture an overarching sense of the case and grasp the scenario's essence. Begin by swiftly skimming the case study, highlighting its essential elements. Consider questions such as: What type of organisation is this? What broad factors are at play? What challenges is the organisation facing? How is its peer group performing?

Once you have this macro perspective, delve deeper with a meticulous read. Annotate critical statements and insights. The aim of this thorough examination is not only to understand the case in depth but also to identify preliminary problem areas. These issues will be explicitly defined later. In crafting the initial section of your case analysis, present a brief overview of the situation, setting the stage for your detailed analysis. Employing this systematic approach can ensure a robust and insightful case study analysis, laying the groundwork for strategic recommendations that are both informed and impactful.

6.3.2 Pre-Case Analysis

Although strategic management cases can be used in various ways, most instructors utilise them, often in conjunction with text material, to encourage students to apply principles and develop decision-making skills. This is intended to promote involvement, which fosters analytical skills and accelerates learning and understanding, rather than relying on rote memory. However, experience with this method – both as a student and as a teacher – suggests something needs to be added. In case analysis, many students need help sifting through the data to find helpful information. But case analysis offers a new dimension. Practice in making assumptions is precious since business executives regularly have to make "educated guesses." However, this may be one area for improvement in the case method for instructional purposes. The student may only carefully analyse the given data by making a solid assumption that overwhelms all other considerations.

Students can jump to recommendations and conclusions before reading the case. This section describes how forcing students to analyse more before preparing a formal case report can be beneficial. There are better ways to enhance case study analysis. These rather simplistic tools for today's dynamic environments do not provide the richness of insight. There can be a lack of understanding of incorporating the industry life cycle into the analysis. With all industries in **Transition**, a broader suite of tools should be deployed, as illustrated in Chapter 5.

6.3.3 Structuring the Analysis

It should be noted that some students need help knowing where to begin when given the "raw material," that is, the judgements or assumptions instructors usually expect students to create themselves. This can result in the frequent class experience of dominated, unstructured case discussions by students with limited conclusions. In other words, many students guess based on the average unstructured case analysis. To a lesser extent, treatment of a few different cases has led to similarly discouraging results. Students will provide superficial analyses by not incorporating the strategy frameworks and tools in Chapter 5. They may completely miss the underlying difficulties of which the current problem is only a symptom. As in business school marking criteria, the highest marks are awarded to students who perform extensive reading and demonstrate knowledge of modern material. So, preparation is everything.

6.3.4 Assessing the Situation

An exercise to propel students back to a foundational level in their analytical thinking requires them to submit a one-page paper titled "Assessing the Situation." In this exercise, students should articulate the scenario presented in the case using strategic management terminology, elucidating the underlying circumstances that contribute to the current issues and will influence potential solutions.

Business school case studies often focus on the big seven companies – Alphabet, Amazon, Apple, Meta, Microsoft, Nvidia, and Tesla. Each founder/CEO is charismatic, has shaped the organisational culture, has overcome critical incidents, and has created roadmaps for success. Their organisations have clearly defined goals, which enable the student to drill down on specific areas. They all face big questions in today's environment. Despite the differences in scale, smaller businesses face similar challenges, such as market positioning, organisational culture, and strategic growth. The key is to adapt the frameworks and insights gained from studying to other smaller enterprises. During and post-COVID crisis management, we have seen the importance of organisations establishing robust structures, systems, and processes. As described throughout this book, the sustainability agenda presents new challenges as well.

When assessing and working through the case study exercise, students should consider:

1 Clear Understanding and Application of Theoretical Concepts: Ensure the analysis demonstrates and incorporates a thorough understanding of the relevant strategic management frameworks and tools. Explicitly link these theories to the organisation's analysis, showing how you will inform the growth (or survival) strategy.
2 Depth of Analysis: Dive deep into the study, avoiding surface-level observations. Use the frameworks and tools discussed in your lectures to examine the organisation's internal and external environments comprehensively.
3 Strategic Insights: Your analysis should yield clear, actionable strategic insights. Avoid making generic strategies that could apply to any organisation in any sector. Instead, tailor your strategic recommendations to the specific context and needs of the organisation you are analysing. When formulating strategies, consider the organisation's resources, capabilities, and broader industry context.
4 Coherence and Structure: Ensure the report is well-structured, with a clear introduction, analysis, strategic plan or growth strategy, options, and conclusion. Each section should flow logically into the next, with clear subheadings and a coherent narrative.
5 Evidence-Based Arguments: Support your analysis and strategic recommendations with robust evidence from your study. Use examples from reputable sources to substantiate your points.
6 Clarity and Conciseness: Your report should be concise yet comprehensive despite the word limit. Avoid unnecessary jargon and ensure your writing is clear and accessible, focusing on pertinent information.
7 Professional Presentation: Ensure the report is professionally presented, with careful attention to formatting, grammar, and spelling. Use tables, figures, and appendices to supplement and clarify the text.

If the points are observed, the report then becomes the base on which a formal case analysis can be built. In many cases, if the situation assessment is done well, then the problem statement is clear, and the rest of the analysis is greatly simplified. It still requires imagination and logic but is not a vague guessing game.

6.3.5 Situation Analysis

After understanding the case and identifying the key problem areas, you should break the case into parts to critically evaluate all aspects of the organisation. Look closely at all case details, then try to pull this information into a more manageable form. The situation analysis stage involves analysing four general areas: the organisation, the customer, the competition, and the environment. Although these four areas of study are essential, one area that can create problems is financial analysis. While business schools subscribe to Bloomberg, FAME, Orbis (Osiris), and MarketLine software for their analysis and company information software, it is still necessary to appreciate financial data; the following is an outline to help you organise your situation analysis.

6.3.5.1 Company Analysis

Financial situation

a Balance sheet/income statement analysis

It would be best to analyse the financial statements vertically and horizontally. Vertical analysis involves calculating meaningful figures from one year's financial statements. For the balance sheet, each item may be expressed as a percentage of total assets. For the income statement, each item may be expressed as a percentage of sales. These figures can then be compared with industry figures, competitors, or other divisions of the same company.

Horizontal analysis compares items on the financial statements or calculations derived from the vertical analysis with those in other periods. A comparison of critical items over five years can be enlightening. For example, you might analyse sales trends over the past five years, calculating the percentage change from one year to the next. You might do the same for other vital items, such as cost of goods sold or net income. Not only can these figures be compared across years, but they can also be compared with industry trends, those of competitors, or other divisions within the same company.

b Ratio analysis

Calculating several financial ratios is essential to measure a firm's financial position accurately. Table 6.2 shows some of the more frequently used financial ratios, and Table 6.3 summarises profit measures. These ratios may be calculated for two or more years to identify any significant trends in the company's economic **performance**.

c Other quantitative analyses

You can conduct other quantitative analyses based on the information provided in the case. For example, break-even analysis is a helpful technique for analysing the relationship between fixed costs, variable costs, and revenue. Marketing profitability analysis examines the profitability of various segments of the company or different market segments. You should evaluate carefully all of the quantitative information you are given in a case and ask yourself, "What can I do with this data to make it more meaningful?"

d Overall financial assessment

After scrutinising all of the financial information in the case, you should be able to make some general statements regarding the firm's financial position. For example, you may have determined from your ratio analysis that the firm is in a precarious position relative to its liquidity. It would be best to draw attention to this, as it limits what the company can do in the short term and, thus, what you can recommend. You must concisely state the firm's financial position since it directly impacts future strategy.

6.3.5.2 *Problem Identification*

Now that you understand the case and have critically evaluated its essential elements, you are ready to formalise the problems in the organisation. Not only is this usually the most challenging part of the case analysis, but it is also the most crucial. Since the remainder of the case analysis revolves around solving the problems defined at this stage, it is essential to carefully consider the problem areas. At this stage, consider applying strategic management theory and practice. The amount of academic rigour and practice is increased at the postgraduate level. Students must often remember the differing programme and module outcomes at the undergraduate and doctoral levels. At the MBA level, I have found that the balance between theory and practice is skewed towards the latter. Conversely, students at the MSc level, with their varied backgrounds in prior business and management modules, require more substantial support in applying theory to practical situations.

An excellent way to start is to define all the problem areas in the case. Then, each of these should be reviewed, and the differences between the symptoms of problems and the actual problems themselves should be identified. Having a good grasp of theory can help identify the actual problems themselves. You may need to explore other functional areas to identify the underlying cause of the symptoms. A company may need help addressing issues such as increasing inventory costs, declining profitability, and poor customer service quality. After examining all aspects of the situation, you may conclude that the company's major problem is poor product management, particularly the lack of a formal product elimination strategy. As you carry out this process, you may find more than one problem in the case. In this situation, you must prioritise the problems into major and minor. Focus your case analysis on what you define as the one major problem. On occasion, you may identify two significant problems. If so, treat them separately; solve one entirely and then solve the other. In most situations, try to identify the most immediate problem and focus your analysis on it. However, you should not disregard minor problems; address them thoroughly at the end of the case analysis.

In writing up this section of your case analysis, which should follow what the instructor asks, you should define the primary problem (or, occasionally, problems). Also, list the appropriate symptoms. Following this statement of the major problem, list all the minor problems and the corresponding symptoms. Problem definition is also a matter of delineating a suitable framework to deal with what may be posed as an immediate question. The problem scope should be realistic and manageable. A good problem definition names the immediate problems and defines them in a way that calls for action-oriented answers.

6.3.5.3 *Statement and Evaluation of Alternatives*

Now that you have identified the primary problem, you are ready to solve it. Develop as many possible solutions as possible, then screen out illogical ideas until you have a set of realistic alternatives. You can then examine the advantages and disadvantages of these remaining alternatives to determine the best solution. The initial process of alternative generation is similar to idea generation in the creative process. The objective is to generate as many alternative courses of action as possible. The next step involves mentally eliminating each of these that is not feasible. This process should leave you with some realistic alternatives to be assessed more critically.

TABLE 6.2 Selected financial ratios

Ratio	*How Calculated*	*What It Measures*
(1) Liquidity ratios		
Current ratio	$\frac{\text{Current assets}}{\text{Current liabilities}}$	Measures the ability of the firm to meet short-term debt. The rule-of-thumb for this ratio is 2.
Quick (acid-test) ratio	$\frac{\text{Current assets} - \text{Inventory}}{\text{Current liabilities}}$	A more accurate measure of a firm's ability to pay off immediately its short-term debt.
Inventory to working capital	$\frac{\text{Inventory}}{\text{Current assets} - \text{Current liabilities}}$	Measures the extent to which the firm's working capital is tied up in inventory.
(2) Profitability ratios		
Return on net worth (return on equity)	$\frac{\text{Profit after taxes}}{\text{Net worth}}$	Measures the rate of return on stockholders' equity.
Return on assets (return on investment)	$\frac{\text{Profit after taxes}}{\text{Total assets}}$	Measures the return on total investment in the firm.
Net profit margin (return on sales)	$\frac{\text{Profit after taxes}}{\text{Sales}}$	Indicates return on sales.
(3) Leverage ratios		
Debt to assets ratio	$\frac{\text{Total liabilities}}{\text{Total assets}}$	Measures the extent to which borrowed funds have been used to finance the operation of the business.
Debt to equity ratio	$\frac{\text{Total liabilities}}{\text{Stockholders' equity}}$	Provides a comparison of the equity of the owners with the funds provided by the creditors.
Times interest earned	$\frac{\text{Profit before taxes \& interest charges}}{\text{Interest charges}}$	Measures the risk that a company might not be able to meet its interest payments.
(4) Activity ratios		
Inventory turnover	$\frac{\text{Sales}}{\text{Inventory}}$	Measures the number of times the average inventory is turned over in the year.
Fixed assets turnover	$\frac{\text{Sales}}{\text{Fixed assets}}$	Measures the sales productivity and utilisation of plant and equipment.
Total assets turnover	$\frac{\text{Sales}}{\text{Total assets}}$	Measures the sales productivity and utilisation of all the firm's assets.
Average collection period	$\frac{\text{Accounts receivable}}{\text{Total sales}} \times 365$	Measures the average collection period for accounts receivable.

TABLE 6.3 Summary of profit measures

Method	*Definition*	*Computation*
Payback period	Number of years until investment is recouped	If rate of flow is constant, $\text{Payback} = \frac{\text{Investment}}{\text{Net Cash Flow}}$ otherwise, the payback is determined by adding up the expected cash inflows until the total equals the initial investment.
Accounting (or unadjusted) rate of return	Ratio of average annual income after depreciation to the average book value of the investment	$\text{Average Annual Income} = \frac{\text{Average Annual Cash Flow} - \text{Average Annual Depreciation}}{\text{Half Initial Investment}}$
Net present value (NPV)	Difference between cash inflows and outflows discounted to the present at a given interest rate	$\text{NPV} = \sum_{t=1}^{T} \left[\frac{F_t}{(1+i)^t} \right]$ where F_t = net cash flow at time period t i = discount rate T = planning horizon
ROI (rate of return of the investment or internal rate of return)	Discount rate that makes the net present value of inflows and outflows equal to zero	The ROI is determined by solving the equation $\sum_{t=1}^{T} \left[\frac{F_t}{(1+i)^t} \right] = 0$ where i is the rate of return of the investment

In writing your case analysis, list these realistic alternatives, ensuring each relates to the significant problem you defined. Each alternative should be a potential solution to the central problem in the case; it should be a completely different way of solving the problem, independent of the others and mutually exclusive. Then, list the specific advantages and disadvantages of carrying out each alternative. Consider constructing a "T-account" for each alternative, listing the pros on one side and the cons on the other. If you identify multiple significant problems, then follow the same procedure for each. In a poor analysis, there needs to be a more explicit discussion of the pros and cons of each alternative. Problem and opportunity statements are the basis of your pro (opportunities) and con (problems) discussion. Different ones relate to specific options.

6.3.5.4 Recommended Solution and Justification

After following this logical approach to identifying potential solutions to the significant problem and evaluating the alternatives, you should be able to recommend a course of action. In this case analysis section, state your selected alternative and explain why. In cases where you defined more than one major problem and set of realistic options, select and justify an alternative for each issue. Remember that, ideally, up to one alternative should be chosen. If you select more than one, it is likely because (1) the other options in that set were not independent and mutually exclusive, or (2) your major problem statement is too general and should be more specific. Recommend the solution you think is most suitable, offering reasons for your decision. In your recommendations and implementation, be aware of constraints on the organisation. Some crucial constraints include the strength of competition, company resources, production capacity, budgets, and philosophies and capabilities of top management. It would be best if you reached a clear decision. Part of the skill of decision-making is to be forced to reach a decision under ambiguous circumstances and then be prepared to defend this decision. A good analysis reaches a decision that is logically consistent with the situation analysis that was done. This is the ultimate test of an analysis.

6.3.5.4.1 Implementation

The case analysis may be finished after you have recommended a solution. Sometimes, one of the questions for the case analysis explicitly asks for an implementation strategy. All you have accomplished so far is to decide on a specific course of action for the future. Now you must answer such questions as:

- How will it be accomplished?
- When will it be accomplished (short term, long term)?
- Who will do it?
- Where will it be done?
- How much is the projected revenue?
- How much is the projected contribution?

You may have a technical appendix at the end of your report in which you specify each part of your plan and the corresponding cost and revenue projections. Consider how these plans will impact the minor problems you identified earlier in the case analysis in your recommendations for the organisation. Address each of these minor problems and make appropriate recommendations for their solution as well. The final paragraph should tie a bow around your analysis. Briefly summarise how your recommendations will solve the organisation's major and minor problems. Suggest what the organisation should do in the future and how it will be better off because of it.

6.3.5.5 Writing the Report

Students who prepare written reports do a better job of analysing business problems. Writing an excellent report takes a particular skill. When instructors read reports, they verify whether students have a thorough understanding of the situation and whether their interpretations of the facts are reasonable. They also like to see papers that are objective, balanced, consistent, and decisive. The most common error students make in writing case reports is repeating the facts provided or merely regurgitating the lecture slides used by instructors. Instead of analysing the data in the light of the alternatives, students frequently repeat statements that appear in the cases with no apparent objective. Another area for improvement often observed in writing reports is the need for organisation. The result is a paper with no beginning and end, usually consisting of one long paragraph. To avoid this problem, some instructors require that reports be presented in outline form. The condensed nature of such reports sometimes makes them hard to follow, and the more readable narrative approach is preferred.

There is no optimum length for a written case analysis. It depends on the instructor's preference, usually measured in the number of words. The report should be long enough to adequately cover the subject and meet the module's learning objectives. Written reports must be neat, legible, and free of grammatical and spelling errors. Yet, students frequently submit work in a rush, ignoring that instructors expect specific minimum **performance** standards in written expression. Additionally, the conclusions are sometimes omitted, and the final report fails to address the instructors' questions regarding the weighting of marks.

Mini Case Study

Tencent – China

Strategic Partnership Implications for Universities: Lessons from Tencent's AI Move

Tencent, a Chinese multinational, is a world-leading internet and technology company that develops innovative products and services to enhance the quality of life for people around the world.

Tencent is a successful Chinese multinational technology conglomerate that provides internet value-added services, value-added telecommunication service business, online and mobile games, online advertising, technology development, cloud, and other business services:

- Founded in 1998
- 2024 revenue $91.9 billion
- 110,558 employees
- Global platform
- The world's largest video game publisher.

Part of Tencent's bold strategy involves integrating DeepSeek's artificial intelligence (AI) capabilities to strengthen its ecosystem and accelerate long-term growth. DeepSeek literally tore up the AI playbook when it dropped a large language model called R1 in January 2025. Even President Trump announced it was a wake-up call.

Tencent's approach shows that even market leaders need partners to scale fast.

It got me thinking about the implications of interactive challenges for universities, such as in the area of strategic partnerships.

Five things sprang to mind:

1 Industry-academia collaboration model
   - Instead of building and enhancing AI capability in-house, partner with tech companies like DeepSeek equivalents.
   - Use industry data to work on joint research projects that combine academic expertise with industry grand challenges.
   - Create fast-track higher education programmes to solve skill needs in academic settings.

2 Resource optimisation
   - Allocate AI infrastructure costs across the university ecosystem.
   - Share data resources between university research groups and partners.
   - Form joint ventures to share expensive AI computing resources with industry partners.
3 Curriculum impact
   - Co-develop AI courses with industry partners to enhance knowledge and skills for employment.
   - Use AI integration to shape internship programmes.
   - Design certification programmes validated by target industry practitioners.
4 Research benefits
   - Enable researchers to get access to real-world datasets through partnerships.
   - Seek joint patent development opportunities.
   - Reduce the timescale of commercialisation of university research.
5 Knowledge exchange acceleration
   - Leverage university strengths by forming cross-institutional AI labs.
   - Create faculty exchange programmes focused on AI strategy and implementation.
   - Build international partnership networks for sharing Generative AI to explore digital pedagogies.

Questions

1 Why has Tencent been such a successful organisation? Using some of the relevant strategy frameworks and tools for external and internal strategy analysis, outline its prospects.
2 What are the implications of interactable challenges for universities such as in the area of strategic partnerships? Suggest a roadmap for any university of your choice.
3 Outline some of the quantifiable economic benefits of university strategic partnerships.

Source: FT.com (2025).

6.4 Chapter Key Takeaways

The key takeaways from Chapter 6 on Case Study Analysis are as follows:

1 **Strategic Analysis Requires a Holistic Approach to Understand the Case Study's Core Issues:** It must go beyond financial metrics to include economic, social, and governance considerations essential in today's business environment.
2 **PESTEL and SWOT (Strengths, Weaknesses, Opportunities, and Threats):** They can be helpful tools, but they can be dangerous if incorrectly applied. If deployed correctly, they help to understand an organisation's macro- and micro-environments.
3 **The Triple Bottom Line:** Provides a more balanced view of the organisation, which enhances strategic decision-making. Strategic analysis should focus on financial **performance** and how organisations impact social equity and the environment.
4 **Scenario Planning:** Prepares organisations to cope with future uncertainty. Organisations must consider different sustainability-related scenarios (e.g., climate change

impacts or shifts in energy markets). Businesses can develop adaptive strategies that prepare them for potential disruptions.

5 **Resource-Based View:** Emphasises sustainability capabilities on the internal capabilities of an organisation. In the context of sustainability, companies must develop unique sustainability-driven resources (such as eco-efficient technologies or sustainable supply chains) that provide long-term advantages and are difficult for competitors to replicate.
6 **Porter's Five Forces:** Remains a critical strategic analysis tool, but in sustainable management, it must account for pressures like environmental regulation, social activism, and ethical consumerism. These external forces can significantly reshape competitive dynamics in industries.
7 **Integrated Strategy:** Key to balancing profit and purpose. Successful sustainable strategic management requires an integrated strategy that balances financial **performance** with social and environmental goals. By embedding sustainability into their core business strategies, organisations can drive sustainable growth and ensure resilience in the face of global challenges like climate change and resource depletion.

6.5 Self-Reflection Questions

1 Discuss the primary objectives of utilising case studies in business and education. How do they contribute to a deeper understanding of real-world business challenges?
2 Identify and elaborate on the essential steps in conducting a thorough case analysis. How do these steps ensure a comprehensive evaluation of the case?
3 What are the fundamental financial indicators and metrics used to evaluate an organisation's financial health? Explain the significance of each metric in the context of a case study analysis.
4 Analyse the importance of presenting and critically evaluating alternative strategic options in case study analysis. How does this practice influence decision-making processes?
5 Examine the advantages of integrating theoretical frameworks into the analysis of business cases. How does this approach enhance the depth and rigour of the study?

References

Dobbs, M.E., (2013). Internal analysis in practice: Templates for firm and case analysis. *Journal of the North American Management Society, 7*(1), p.40.

Dobbs, M.E., (2014). Guidelines for applying porter's five forces framework: A set of industry analysis templates. *Competitiveness Review, 24*(1), pp.32–45.

Edwards, M., Benn, S. and Starik, M., (2017). Business cases for sustainability-integrated management education. In G. George, M.R. Haas, H. Joshi, A.M. McGahan and P. Tracey (Eds.), *Handbook of sustainability in management education*, pp.45–66. Edward Elgar Publishing.

FT.com (2025). Tencent changes the messaging on its AI strategy. Available at: https://www.ft.com/content/9e7cbab3-0c1b-49ad-8f94-4d443a6a8ad0 (Accessed 15 January 2026).

Guo, J.P., Yang, L.Y., Zhang, J. and Gan, Y.J., (2022). Academic self-concept, perceptions of the learning environment, engagement, and learning outcomes of university students: Relationships and causal ordering. *Higher Education, 83*(4), pp.1–20.

Rosier, G., (2022). The case method evaluated in terms of higher education research: A pilot study. *The International Journal of Management Education, 20*(3), p.100660.

Williams, C., (2023). *Strategic business case analysis.* Routledge.

7

SUSTAINABILITY MEASUREMENT AND REPORTING

7.1 Learning Strategy Objectives

After completing this chapter, you will be able to:

1. **Knowledge-Based Objectives:**
   - Analyse and evaluate the key sustainability measurement frameworks to inform strategic decision-making and value creation.
   - Differentiate between the single and double materiality approaches to sustainability reporting.
2. **Skill-Based Objectives:**
   - Design integrated sustainability reporting systems that effectively capture salient economic, social, and governance (ESG) metrics.
   - Design and enhance data management systems to ensure accuracy, reliability, and assurance of sustainability reporting.
3. **Attitude-Based Objectives:**
   - Adopt a forward-looking perspective that integrates long-term sustainability risks and strategic planning.
   - Embrace a stakeholder-centric mindset that aligns investor priorities with the broader impacts.

7.2 Introduction

The sustainability measurement and reporting landscape is showing signs of maturity and is integral to informing strategy and investment decisions. But the obsession with metrics and indicators continues to evolve.

What was once a set of isolated compliance-based initiatives is now a system of frameworks, regulations, and tools that influence practice. This will raise the bar on transparency,

DOI: 10.4324/9781003516774-9

which is crucial to face the future of the planet's well-being. Ensuring organisations are prepared and positioned to tackle the demands of sustainability measurement and reporting needs mastering by the leadership team.

Navigating the regulatory and standard, and knowing what to focus on will help to avoid duplication of effort. The role of artificial intelligence (AI) and data science in sustainability measurement and reporting is increasing as it enhances process delivery in terms of efficiency, speed, and find sustainable growth opportunities (Chen, and Ge, 2025; Sariyer et al., 2024; Siddik et al., 2025). Sustainability measurement and reporting requires a new mindset! Sustainability indicators should be used, comparable over time and space (Tenuta and Cambrea, 2023).

At a more granular level, metrics are quantifiable, while indicators are more holistic and signal something of importance. The term "metric" originates from music and poetry, implying periodicity. The CEO should ensure all staff in the organisation agree on why they are recording each metric in the dashboard. Otherwise, indicators may be misleading and cause confusion. Reasons include:

- Measurement, strategy, articulation, alignment, and incentivisation in the wrong sustainability areas.
- Lack of focus on identifying sustainability objectives, rather than picking up the easy things to measure.
- Chase too many activities that can use up scarce resources.

The adage also comes to mind: you can't manage what you can't measure. Shifting beyond the economic perspective, the challenge is the growing recognition of environmental and social impacts. In a recent book, Archer (2024) emphasised the importance of examining the sustainability phenomenon from the inside. His behind-the-scenes look provides rich insights for any student seeking to enter the sustainability field. Chapter 2 – Measuring sustainability recounts many interviews and observations with executives on the topic.

Principles and standards now form the foundation for the measurement and reporting agenda. CEOs and their leadership teams are increasingly acknowledging the need to keep stakeholders informed. This chapter explores three indicators for measurement: ESG and for reporting through economic social and environmental (ESE). Key **performance** indicators (KPIs) and sustainable metrics are crucial for tracking progress towards sustainability goals and keeping stakeholders informed.

For example, in New Zealand, societal issues such as the outcomes for Māori businesses and their well-being are being integrated into the mindset of all. Māoris emphasise values, the plant, culture, and profitability. Sustainability reports in a Māori context can focus on an intergenerational vision spanning 50 years or more, reflecting the enduring nature of resources and opportunities for future generations. Incorporating traditional Māori values and concepts can be captured by sustainability reports. Picking the right KPIs will help the organisation obtain a clearer picture of its impacts.

On a much broader scale, the appetite for ESG data is voracious, driven by the rise of the sustainable investment market, which has brought concomitant increases in transparency and the detection of greenwashing practices. Now, with firmly established sustainable finance standards and policies, understanding ESG data has become a critical component for firms in navigating rating products.

The organisation for economic co-operation and development (OECD) rating uses 2,000 metrics and eight major ESG rating products. So, expanding fiduciary duty to include stewardship represents a significant advancement in governance. However, the OECD has been critical of some of the services of ESG data and ratings providers calling for more nuanced approaches.

Measuring the impact of sustainable strategies is essential for accountability and improvement. The selection of appropriate indicators will depend on relevance to sustainable goals, reliability, validity, and sensitivity to change. In the context of global markets and their cultural and institutional characteristics, transparent communication of sustainability efforts is crucial for building stakeholder trust.

Critically analysing sustainability reporting, the World Business Council for Sustainable Development elucidates that the focus is on internal and external stakeholders. The standard tool is the triple bottom line approach of profit, people, and planet. The impact of sustainability reporting on behaviour within the organisation (i.e., information inductance) is considered (e.g., Prakash & Rappaport, 1977). This can be related to strategic control systems (Simons, 1994), which affect **performance** evaluation.

Building on the foundations laid in the previous two chapters, this chapter explores the importance of strategic sustainability measurement and reporting in the modern era. Advisors now spend time obtaining fees from companies to advise them on what and when they must report to the various reporting bodies. Knowing what is necessary to disclose and what the companies can get away with has fuelled egregious spending on consultants for sustainability services.

Discussions in this chapter will consider the purpose, requirements, and reporting formats with thought to how such practices fulfil ethical responsibilities and contribute to long-term viability and competitiveness. Consideration is given to some of the current problems of Sustainability Measurement and Reporting, including lack of standardisation, materiality determination, integration with financial reporting systems, and stakeholder engagement.

Through a combination of examples, this chapter considers the Global Reporting Initiative (GRI), the Sustainability Accounting Standards Board, and the International Integrated Reporting Framework.

STRATEGY NUGGET

HSBC's Sustainability Risk Management: Balancing Global Finance and Environmental Responsibility

Introduction

In February 2025, HSBC, the global banking and financial services organisation, publicised its updated sustainability risk policies framework, which is fundamental to its future. With increasing stakeholder pressure to address environmental and social challenges, HSBC is taking a proactive lead in global sustainable finance.

"The primary role of risk management is to protect our customers, business, colleagues, shareholders, and the communities we serve while executing our business strategy and delivering sustainable growth," stated the bank's introduction to its sustainability risk policies.

A deep dive into challenges reveals HSBC's dilemma in balancing banking priorities with its increasing sustainability imperatives.

The Challenge

To accelerate its strategic priorities, in October 2024, HSBC informed the markets that it would restructure into four businesses – Hong Kong, UK, corporate and institutional banking, and international wealth, and premier banking. Decisions were made to retrenching from some of its M&A and equity businesses in Europe and the Americas would unveil $2.4 billion of savings over the next two years.

Regarding its sustainability priorities, the value creation platform had three pillars: **transition** to net zero, building inclusion and resilience, and acting responsibly. However, operationalising across 64 countries and territories increases the risk management level. So, in response, HSBC developed a coherent set of sustainability risk policies.

Jonathan Green, HSBC's Chief Sustainability Officer, revealed: "When you're operating globally, you need both principled and pragmatic policies. Too strict, you risk losing business to competitors with lower standards. Too flexible, and you face credibility issues with stakeholders and potential regulatory consequences."

HSBC's Sustainability Risk Framework

At the same time, the rapid proliferation in the importance of risk management led to HSBC developing a comprehensive risk management framework built around two categories of policies:

Core Net Zero-Aligned

- Energy
- Thermal coal phase-out.

Broader Sustainability Risk

- Agricultural commodities
- Forestry
- Mining and metals
- World heritage sites and Ramsar wetlands.The bank described its approach as "risk-based," focusing on "mitigating reputational, credit, legal and other risks related to our customers' environmental and social impacts."

Implementation Mechanics

The implementation of HSBC's sustainability risk reinforces the organisational system's complexity of embedding core sustainability considerations into a global financial institution:

1 **Front-Line Responsibility:** Business-facing relationship managers are responsible for identifying clients who take sustainability seriously.

2 **Expert Support:** Adopting a shared service technical mentality, specialists in the Sustainability Centre of Excellence assist relationship managers in navigating complex sustainability issues.
3 **Risk Function Oversight:** Independent scrutiny is provided by second-line risk professionals who can challenge assumptions and processes.
4 **Certification Reliance:** Where possible, HSBC relies on "dependable independent certification schemes" to authenticate client compliance with sustainability standards.
5 **Client Engagement:** For its net-zero-aligned policies, HSBC accentuated the importance of "engagement on client **transition** plans."
6 **Escalation Procedures:** In activities that could lead to material negative impacts, sustainability risk specialists and risk committees deploy an additional review and approval mechanism.

Questions

1 What strategies can financial institutions adopt better to balance their roles as enablers of economic activity and maintain their responsibility to address sustainability challenges?
2 Assuming you are the HSBC Chief Sustainability Officer, what metrics would you use to effectively measure the impact of HSBC's sustainability risk policies?
3 How should HSBC manage the tension between thinking globally and acting locally in implementing sustainability policies?

7.3 Purpose and Objectives of Sustainability Measurement and Reporting

Accountants seek to ensure that statements they verify are accurate, reliable, and free from material misstatement. Markets may agitate, with stakeholders of all forms demanding to know organisations' actual positions. Any guessing games about the outlook of geopolitical uncertainties require CEOs to explain the organisation's thinking in terms of sustainability. Organisations recognise that addressing sustainability risks is not just about appeasing rating agencies, but also about enhancing operational resilience.

In the accountancy profession, auditors evaluate how the organisation complies with accounting standards, laws, and regulations, which collectively help mitigate risks associated with non-compliance. Common risks can be strategic, financial, and/or operational, and the auditor seeks to assess the underlying controls. When audited accounts are published in the public domain, they foster transparency and gain public trust. Unfortunately, there are exceptions when fraud appears to be at the root of managerial malpractice. Recently, large-scale instances include Builder AI 2025, FTX 2024, Theranos 2024, and Wirecard 2022.

As previously mentioned, financial information is at the heart of **SSM**. It enables the CEO and board to assess scarce resources and allocate them to sustainability-themed projects. Aligning scarce resources with sustainability objectives relies on effective decision-making. The current financial markets continue to emphasise the importance of organisational risk management and resilience building.

A similar story applies to the Global South (see Figure 7.1), whose members face budgetary and developmental constraints. Governments use financial information for short-,

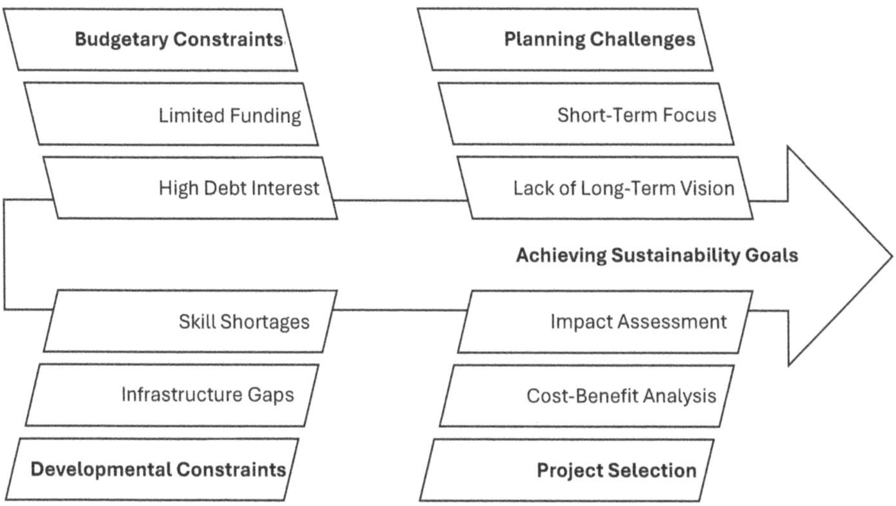

FIGURE 7.1 Challenges in Global South sustainable goals

medium-, and long-term planning to identify sustainability projects that generate the highest impact at the lowest cost.

Regarding the purpose and objectives of sustainability measurement and reporting, the onus is on distinguishing among the multiple frameworks to determine what produces valuable information for stakeholders. For analysts looking across industries, sustainability comparisons can be complex. Inconsistencies can make it challenging to gauge sustainability efforts.

Greenwashing is frowned upon, and CEOs now tread carefully when making grandiose marketing statements. Such exaggerations must be substantiated to ensure trust in sustainability reporting; stakeholders can become sceptical, leading to reputational damage. Sustainability statements must align with the overarching strategy.

7.4 Key Frameworks and Standards for Sustainability Measurement

The UN has well marketed Sustainable Development Goals (SDGs), but now, with ESG, companies are assessed by investors and other stakeholder groups. If they score poorly, they may be dropped from specialised investment funds. Like the US series "The Wire," analysts follow the money!

Leaders used to talk and issue glossy publications with smiling faces to show sustainability intent. However, the scope is rapidly disappearing for companies to fudge their SDG activities. While there was no immediate punishment, this is changing.

Now, with an ESG philosophy, companies will be continually assessed by stakeholders (and unfavourable results could lead to not getting their fair share of the market), so the time is now to move beyond intention. The array of rating products now ensures that organisations are under the spotlight.

ESG is a little broader than sustainability but can be more ambiguous and aspirational (e.g., it is challenging to measure ethics but easier to measure climate change). But the rating agencies have come to the fore to score businesses for investors. ESG challenges are business challenges, with their inconsistencies underscoring a crucial strategic reality.

Concerns about the absence of a standard for evaluating practices are being raised in the ESG space. This complicates users' understanding due to the growth of ESG scoring, ratings, and rankings providers in the marketplace. Second, most ESG products and insights focus on the score (the "how well you are doing" aspect) rather than what should be done with the data to improve the score.

Key Frameworks and Standards for Sustainability Measurement include:

- GRI
- International Sustainability Standards Board (ISSB)
- Integrated Reporting (IR) Framework
- United Nations SDGs Alignment
- Greenhouse Gas Protocol
- Carbon Disclosure Project
- Principles for Responsible Investment.

Table 7.1 overviews the key sustainability reporting frameworks and standards, highlighting their main features, strengths, and potential weaknesses. Many organisations use a combination of these frameworks to meet their reporting needs and stakeholder expectations.

TABLE 7.1 Summary of reporting standards and frameworks

Framework/Standard	*Description*	*Strengths*	*Limitations*
1 Global Reporting Initiative (GRI) https://www.globalreporting.org/	Popular and comprehensive framework for sustainability reporting covering economic, environmental, and social impacts with its universal, sector, and topic standards. To be transparent about impacts.	One of the world's most widely used. Can be used by any organisation, large or small, public or private from any sector or location.	Can be resource-intensive for some firms with its universal, sector and to implement. May lead to lengthy reports. Limited comparability due to flexibility.
2 International Sustainability Standards Board (ISSB) – In August 2022 the ISSB of the IFRS assumed responsibility for SASB standards https://www.ifrs.org/groups/international-sustainability-standards-board/	Tasked with creating a global baseline for sustainability reporting that is reliable for investors.	Provides insights into climate-related disclosures and financial materiality.	Companies have to adapt to new disclosure requirements. Need to align with IFRS S1 and IFRS S2.

(*Continued*)

TABLE 7.1 (Continued)

Framework/Standard	Description	Strengths	Limitations
3 Integrated Reporting (IR) Framework https://integratedreporting.ifrs.org/resource/international-ir-framework/	Promotes integrated thinking and integration of financial and non-financial information, including sustainability-related information into a single report.	Provides a structured approach to inform stakeholders of their strategy, governance, **performance,** and the future.	Lacks guidance regarding the interlinkages between financial and non-financial, which can be complex.
4 United Nations Sustainable Development Goals (SDGs) Alignment https://sdgs.un.org/goals	Popular framework for aligning business activities with 17 global sustainability goals.	Provides a common and strong message for sustainability aspirations. Helps connect business activities to societal and environmental goals.	Extremely broad in scope, may lack specific reporting guidance. Significant resources required for full-scale adoption.
5 Greenhouse Gas Protocol https://ghgprotocol.org/corporate-standard	Multi-stakeholder partnership that measures and manages greenhouse gas emissions.	Widely accepted corporate accounting and reporting standard. Framework based on five principles – relevance, completeness, consistency, transparency, and accuracy.	Focused solely on greenhouse gas emissions. Can be difficult to collect data to accurately measure.
6 Carbon Disclosure Project (CDP) https://www.cdp.net/en	Global independent disclosure system that provides new information to enable earth-positive decisions to protect future generations.	Used by investors, companies, cities, states, and regions to disclose environmental impact.	Lack of mandatory reporting and a focus on the reporting rather than action.
7 Principles for Responsible Investment (PRI) https://www.unpri.org/about-us/what-are-the-principles-for-responsible-investment	Network and principles for responsible investment practices.	Possess six principles developed by an international group of institutional investors reflecting ESG practice.	Can get complex as the issues by nation can differ. Getting investors to divest from "sin" companies can take significant effort.

Abbreviations: ESG, Economic, Social, and Governance; IFRS, International Financial Reporting Standards; SASB, Sustainability Accounting Standards Board.

7.5 Principles and Approaches to Measuring Sustainability

When assessing the sustainability phenomenon, accurate measurement and accounting help track the journey, whereby ESG is underpinned by risks and reputation. Stock markets reward short-term gains over long-term resilience, so a trick for the CFO is maintaining interoperability during the journey so that their organisations can report under multiple sustainable reporting frameworks. Figure 7.2 uses the iceberg analogy to reveal some of the ESG risks.

7.5.1 International Financial Reporting Standards

As mentioned in Table 7.2, the ISSB and International Accounting Standards Board provide oversight. The former acts as a conduit for investor-company dialogue. This partnership has resulted in the International Financial Reporting Standards (IFRS) S1, which outlines the general requirements for disclosing sustainability-related financial information. IFRS S1 objective is:

Companies are required to provide all sustainability-related risks and opportunities that could reasonably affect the company's prospects – its cash flows, access to finance, or cost of capital over the short, medium, or long term.

A pertinent question is how sustainability can affect a company's prospects. This book emphasises the benefits of sustainability but also incorporates risk to provide investors with a value narrative. A key feature for generating cash flows and tracking impacts, risks, and opportunities (IRO).

The prospects of a company are inextricably linked to:

- Stakeholders: Who it delivers value to.
- Society: Where it operates.
- Nature: Resources it draws upon.

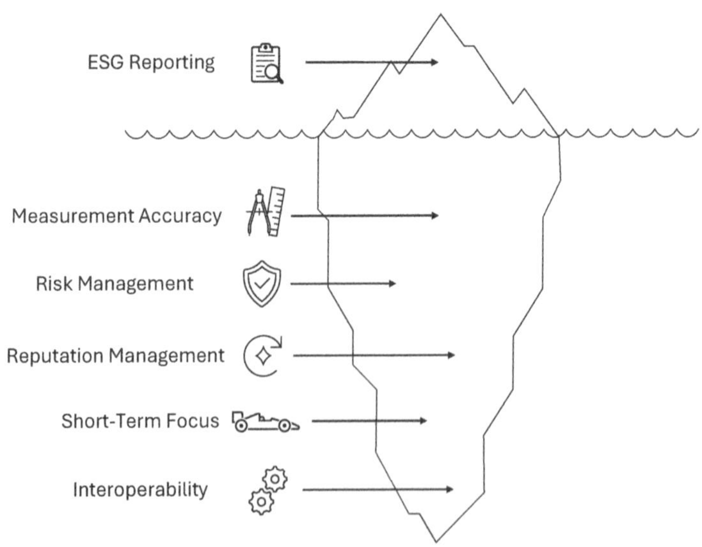

FIGURE 7.2 Sustainability's visible metrics are impacted by deeper factors

7.5.2 IFRS S1

The conceptual foundations provide a parameter for investor decision-making. The salient pillars include:

- Fair presentation
- Materiality
- Reporting entity
- Connected information.

Fair Presentation: Companies must ensure that they are not selective in their disclosures and that the reporting information is not misleading. They must also ensure that disclosures accurately and impartially represent their sustainability **performance** and impacts. Being objective means that accurate data and robust approaches must support disclosures.

Materiality: Companies can assess the materiality filter component using the following IFRS Accounting Standards definition of material.

Information is material, and if omitted, misstated, or obscured, it could reasonably influence investor decisions.

This provides a helpful connection with the financial statements, which aids the integrity of the statements.

EU materiality is broader than in the US, as the goal is to inform investors and a wider range of stakeholders. Unlike single material, the concept of double materiality involves the situation when there is impact material and financial materiality.

Reporting Entity: This concept emphasises that sustainability-related disclosures should incorporate all business activities reflected in the financial statements. Entities include subsidiaries, joint ventures, or other structures that contribute to the company's **performance**.

IFRS S1 allows the reporting entity to detail the breadth of their disclosures. This enables the investor to understand the company's sustainability risks and opportunities network. This approach should prevent selective reporting and provide greater assurance.

Connected Information: IFRS S1 asks for information relating to the connection between

- Sustainability risks and opportunities
- Disclosures on core content
- Sustainability-related financial disclosures and financial reports.

IFRS S1 uses a task force on climate-related financial disclosures (TCFD) to structure the content for governance, strategy, risk management, metrics, and targets.

The connected information typically includes general requirements, such as a source of guidance, location of disclosures, timing of reporting, comparative data, and a statement of compliance.

Applications for IFRS S1 should consider the application guidance and accompanying guidance, which contains material and connected information, and the latter on who the primary users are.

As a relatively new global standard, standardisation is sought by companies of all sizes and markets, utilising terminology and concepts derived from the accounting profession. Proportionately, companies should use reasonable and supportive information available without undue cost or effort. Help is provided with educational material, sources and illustrations, and **transitional** reliefs. To encourage companies to get started, reporting can focus just on climate.

7.5.3 IFRS S2

The IFRS S2 was effective for annual reporting periods from 1 Jan 2024. The emphasis is on climate-related risks and opportunities useful for investors who provide resources to the entity.

Specific climate-related risks include:

- Physical risks
- **Transition** risks
- Opportunities.

Organisations are expressly requested to disclose the:

- Governance practices, controls, and procedures the entity uses to monitor, manage, and oversee climate-related risks and opportunities.
- Entity's strategy for handling climate-related risks and opportunities.
- Procedures the entity uses to classify, evaluate, order, and monitor climate-related risks and opportunities, incorporating whether and how those processes are integrated into and inform the entity's overall risk management process.

TABLE 7.2 Integrated Reporting and Thinking Conference 2024, IFRS key takeaways

Takeaways	*Brief Comments*
IRF is a powerful tool for assisting companies to adopt IFRS S1 and IFRS S2	As in the case in any formal accounting standards, the onus on the preparer is to produce high-quality content for comparability and usefulness for capital markets.
Integrated Thinking helps companies overcome the silo mentality	Integrated thinking can catalyse a company's use of IRF and adoptions of IFRS S1 and IFRS S2.
Adopting IFRS S1 and IFRS S2 provides benefits for companies already publishing reports	Users of the information can rely on their quality to identify and compare material information on risks and opportunities.
Integrated Reports provide a context for investor-focused information	Material information on a company's business model, governance, risks and opportunities, **performance** and prospects provide reassurance for investors.
IRF continues to be an important resource for IASB and ISSB	Developments suggest that the IASB has built on the IRF and will produce a practice statement on Management Commentary.
The Integrated Reporting stakeholder community is vibrant, and IFRS wishes to encourage participation	A useful body of practice is developing that can be tested by investors and may inform strategic decision-making.

Abbreviations: IASB, international accounting standards board.

- Entity's **performance** regarding its climate-related risks and opportunities, including progress towards any climate-related targets it has set and any targets it must meet by law or regulation.

Source: IFRS S2.

In terms of progress for IFRS 1 and 2, at the Integrated Reporting and Thinking Conference 2024, the key takeaways were as shown in Table 7.2.

Mini Case Study

Singapore Airlines

Singapore Airlines: Charting a Sustainable Course in Global Aviation

Introduction

Singapore Airlines (SIA) is one of the most respected brands in the global aviation sector. The airline has strong foundations, robust balance sheet, industry-leading digital capabilities, and talent.

However, like other global airlines, the sustainability strategy dilemma is one of maintaining its business market position while addressing mounting environmental pressures.

SIA's CEO key messages include:

- Working towards a net-zero future
- Rethinking waste and resources
- Creating social impact
- Embracing technology in our sustainability efforts
- Caring for our planet, while connecting with the world.

SIA strategy for the future include:

- SIA Brand Promise Consists of Three Pillars: Service excellence, product **innovation,** and network connectivity.
- Portfolio Strategy: SIA and low-cost Scoot form the portfolio, and offer passengers a wider variety of options.
- Multi-Hub Strategy: Through investments in India, SIA now has a 25.1% stake in an enlarged Air India group.
- Partnership Strategy: SIA has already entered into agreements with Philippine Airlines, Air New Zealand, and All Nippon Airways.
- Investing in Digital Capabilities: Increasing Gen AI capability gives SIA a competitive edge. These include enhancing revenue generation, customer experience, operational efficiency, and employee productivity.

Clinching the 2023 Skytrax World Airline Awards for five consecutive years in 2023 is evidence of its success. For the year ended March 2025, the SIA group posted its highest net profit of S$2.78 billion, which included a one-off gain of S$1.1 billion.

SIA's Sustainability Commitment

The Group formulated multiple decarbonisation pathways that align with the International Air Transport Association (IATA) goal of achieving net-zero carbon emissions by 2050. This commitment falls within a broader sustainability framework that encompasses decarbonisation, waste management, and positive social impact.

Four-Pillar Approach to Emission Reduction

SIA's decarbonisation strategy aligns with the IATA's four-pillar framework:

1 Fleet Modernisation: SIA operates one of the industry's most fuel-efficient fleets, with an average fleet age of seven years. This compares to an average of 15 years. In addition, nearly 70% of the fleet consists of new-generation aircraft, including the Airbus A350 and Boeing 787. These planes are 25% more fuel-efficient than the older models they replace.
2 Operational Efficiency: SIA implemented 22 fuel-saving initiatives across its engineering, flight operations, and air traffic management business areas. This results in savings of 117,741 tonnes of CO2e for FY2023/2024. Operations also include less engine taxi procedures, optimal flap settings, and improved arrival sequencing at Singapore Changi Airport.
3 Sustainable Aviation Fuel (SAF): SIA is committed to replacing 5% of its total fuel requirements with SAF by 2030, using the critical lever of SAF as a key driver. In recognition of the need for global SAF supply to match demand, liaising with governments and industry partners is a priority. In May 2024, SIA signed an agreement with Neste to purchase 1,000 tonnes of SAF from its Singapore refinery.
4 Carbon Offsets: In addition to addressing direct emissions, SIA participates in the international civil aviation organisation (ICAO's) Carbon Offsetting and Reduction Scheme for International Aviation (CORSIA). This is a voluntary carbon offset programme for passengers and cargo customers. Using the CORSIA baseline, SIA has committed to achieving carbon-neutral growth from 2024.

Ground Operations and Resource Management

Aside from its air operations, SIA has made other breakthroughs, which include:

- Solar installations across all SIA-owned buildings in Singapore generate 5,379 MWh of renewable energy in FY2023/2024 (being 17% of total electricity consumption).
- Targeting a 10% reduction from FY2019/2020 levels in energy consumption at SIA-owned buildings by FY2029/2030.
- Water conservation through rainwater harvesting and groundwater recycling, contributing 25,204 cubic metres in FY2023/2024.
- Waste reduction initiatives, using digitised processes, material reuse programmes, and cabin waste management.

Questions

1. What strategies should SIA develop to meet in 2030, and 2050 sustainability commitments?
2. Compare the SIA sustainability strategy with any global airline of your choice. Identify its strengths and limitations.
3. In terms of the 194-page 2024/2025 SIA Sustainability Report, what are the implications for Sustainable Strategic Management?

SIA's sustainability report demonstrates the importance of managing with compliance in terms of the GRI and integrating long-term environmental and social goals with business strategies. As the sector evolves, other players will follow suit, placing emphasis on climate resilience, technological **innovation**, and resource optimisation to remain competitive and contribute to global sustainability goals.

Source: Singapore Airlines Sustainability Report (2024, 2025).

7.6 Corporate Sustainability Reporting Directive

The Corporate Sustainability Reporting Directive (CSRD) came into effect on 5 January 2023 and is a cornerstone of the EU Green Deal. It aims to guide companies in adopting a developmental model that supports the **Transition** towards sustainable environmental and social goals. The significance is huge in terms of transforming sustainability reporting from a voluntary to a mandatory organisational task.

The thrust extends beyond **performance** reporting and introduces disclosure obligations regarding governance, strategies, and objectives to foster more sustainable business models. Impact, risk, and opportunity are aligned with companies' businesses and value chains, which can enhance outcomes.

Public-interest entities that are already subject to the Non-Financial Reporting Directive (NFRD), such as large listed companies, banks, and insurance companies, must now comply with the CSRD. The first phase applies to large companies, as defined, which must produce their first CSRD reports by January 2025. Large companies not subject to NFRD status will need to produce NFRD for January 2026 and small medium sized enterprises (SMEs) in January 2027.

Companies will have to engage in strategic thinking by providing a coherent and holistic approach that incorporates both qualitative and quantitative information on a broad range of ESG topics.

Table 7.3 provides a structured comparison of how **CSRD**, **IFRS S1**, and **IFRS S2** differ in their approach to various aspects of sustainability reporting, strategic alignment, and stakeholder focus.

CSRD will require leadership teams to ensure that their **transition** plans align with the business model and strategy. Otherwise, politicians and citizens will see through any malpractice. There is extensive support for curbing greenwashing.

This requires embedding ESG in the strategy decision-making process, as considered by the leadership team. According to **SSM** principles, companies should integrate

TABLE 7.3 Structured comparison of CSRD, IFRS S1, and IFRS S2

Aspect	*CSRD*	*IFRS S1*	*IFRS S2*
Scope and applicability	Applicable to a broad range of EU companies, including large public-interest entities and, eventually, SMEs.	Designed for global use, applicable to entities already using IFRS accounting standards.	Focused specifically on climate-related disclosures and applicable to companies using IFRS standards globally.
Reporting focus	Emphasises double materiality, covering financial impacts and broader social/ environmental effects.	Primarily focuses on financial materiality, highlighting sustainability risks/ opportunities affecting financial **performance**.	Focuses on the financial implications of climate risks and opportunities, supporting investor decision-making.
Framework requirement	Uses European Sustainability Reporting Standards (ESRS) with detailed guidelines.	Provides principles-based guidance for general sustainability disclosures.	Provides more structured and detailed climate-specific reporting requirements, aligned with TCFD principles.
Integration with financial reporting	Integrated into management reports, creating a seamless link between financial and non-financial reporting.	Aims to align sustainability reporting with financial reporting, ensuring consistency.	Requires integration with financial reporting, particularly emphasising climate-related financial disclosures.
Assurance and verification	Mandates limited assurance initially, progressing to reasonable assurance over time.	Encourages assurance but does not mandate it, with practices driven by market and stakeholder expectations.	Assurance is not mandated, but external verification can enhance the reliability of climate disclosures.
Stakeholder consideration	Considers a wide range of stakeholders, including investors, employees, and the public.	Primarily targets investors and financial stakeholders, focusing on financial implications.	Aimed at providing climate-related financial information to investors and financial markets.
Alignment with global standards	Aligns with global frameworks like GRI, TCFD, and SDGs, while reflecting EU-specific goals (e.g., European Green Deal).	Draws on global standards such as TCFD and aims to create a globally consistent sustainability disclosure framework.	Aligns closely with TCFD, reinforcing climate-related financial disclosure principles in reporting.
Granularity of disclosures	Requires detailed disclosures on policies, strategies, targets, progress, and sector-specific information.	High-level principles allow for flexibility and adaptability to different company contexts.	Provides detailed guidance on climate risks, opportunities, strategy, governance, and metrics for thorough reporting.

(*Continued*)

TABLE 7.3 (Continued)

Aspect	*CSRD*	*IFRS S1*	*IFRS S2*
Materiality perspective	Double materiality approach, considering both financial impacts and external sustainability effects.	Focuses on financial materiality, addressing sustainability factors that impact financial statements.	Addresses financial materiality with a focus on climate risks and opportunities that impact financial health.
Level of detail	More prescriptive and includes sector-specific guidance for nuanced reporting.	Less prescriptive, allowing for company-specific reporting within a principles-based framework.	Structured to provide detailed climate-related disclosure requirements to align with financial reporting standards.
Strategic planning implications	Requires deep integration of sustainability into strategic planning, including long-term goals and action plans.	Encourages alignment between sustainability risks/opportunities and strategic priorities from a financial lens.	Supports strategic planning by addressing how climate-related risks/opportunities affect financial planning.
Impact on business strategy	Promotes a comprehensive approach where sustainability goals align with overall business strategy.	Influences business strategy mainly through financial risk and opportunity management related to sustainability.	Emphasises adjustments to business strategy based on the assessment of climate-related financial impacts.

Abbreviations: CSRD, Corporate Sustainability Reporting Directive; SDGs, Sustainable Development Goals; SMEs, Small Medium Sized Enterprises; TCFD, Task force on Climate-Related Financial Disclosures.

sustainability issues into their long-term business plans and strategies, ensuring that their operations align with their sustainability goals. As indicated throughout this book, this may involve modifying the company's supply chain, product design, marketing, and other areas to reduce environmental impact and promote social responsibility, as these are all subjects that companies are expected to report on in their sustainability reports. Therefore, in this regard, short-termism will become even less appropriate in meeting the expectations of today's stakeholders.

At a practical level, companies need to be able to deliver their CSRD in accordance with the guidance provided. Non-committal sustainability claims can no longer be made voluntarily. By January 2027, all companies will have to submit a CSRD. Companies operating across borders in global markets will encounter challenges when gathering data for their operations in different regions or markets. Consolidated reporting, such as calculating the gross scope of three greenhouse gas emissions and determining the potential financial effects of climate-related risks, will be challenging. The company may have its house in order regarding greenhouse gas emissions, but the responsibility will flow indirectly up and down its value chain. Ultimately, such issues will be the responsibility of the CFO.

This final section of this chapter provides an overview that captures the comprehensive and multifaceted approach companies take as they begin to deliver the required reports. Some high-impact strategies to consider include:

1. **Strengthen Regulatory and Reporting Frameworks:** Companies will be required to communicate through boards of statutory bodies to appraise and update reporting standards, addressing emerging and implementation challenges. A prerequisite for mandatory reporting requirements should ensure that frameworks provide clear guidance on disclosures for stakeholders.
2. **Promote Transparency and Accountability:** Supplementing strategy processes to ensure transparency in sustainability reporting through open data initiatives and digital reporting tools. Ensure companies publish detailed reports with independent verification for authenticity. Nurture a culture of best practice and continuous improvement by making reports publicly accessible and promoting stakeholder feedback.
3. **Empower Governance Structures:** Companies should enhance their internal governance structures to prioritise reporting and fulfil requirements. Ensure that the CEO and the Board have the expertise and authority to oversee and manage the formulation and implementation of new strategies. Reinforce the strategy capabilities of sustainability committees within the organisation to integrate ESG into core business strategies and decision-making processes.
4. **Raise Awareness and Foster a Sustainability-Focused Culture:** Use internal communication mechanisms to heighten awareness and educate employees and other stakeholders on the importance of ESG practices. Incorporate sustainability training into executive professional development programmes to instil a culture of responsibility. Promote ethical behaviour and integrity through organisation-wide initiatives and codes of conduct.
5. **Support Research and Knowledge Exchange:** Companies should invest in research to identify the most effective sustainability and ESG practices, industry-specific challenges, and potential **innovations**. Encourage collaboration between higher education institutions, corporate leaders, and policy experts to develop actionable insights. Establish platforms for sharing emerging trends to keep organisations at the forefront of ESG advancements.
6. **Implement Monitoring and Evaluation Mechanisms:** Develop and integrate robust monitoring systems to track **performance** metrics and report progress. Establish KPIs and metrics to regularly evaluate the effectiveness of current and future ESG initiatives. Adjust strategies based on data-driven insights to enhance sustainability practices continuously.
7. **Strengthen Financial Systems to Support ESG Goals:** Ensure the CFO aligns financial systems and investment portfolios with sustainability goals. Enhance collaboration between financial institutions and sustainability experts to ensure that capital flows support ESG-focused projects and practices.

Implementing these strategies requires harmonised efforts across the sustainability and ESG ecosystem. Continuous evaluation, adaptation, and learning are essential to address evolving sustainability challenges and maximise the impact of ESG reporting and strategies.

7.7 Chapter Key Takeaways

Some of the key takeaways from Chapter 7 on Sustainability Measurement and Reporting are as follows:

1 **Understand the Regulatory Environment:** Sustainability and ESG reporting are driven by a rapidly advancing regulatory landscape, where compliance is no longer an option. CEOs must be aware of standards such as the IR Frameworks, as well as European and global standards like IFRS S1 and S2, and CSRD. For large global firms, this means adapting to multi-layered compliance requirements to ensure comprehensive disclosures.
2 **Double vs Single Materiality:** The CSRD stresses double materiality, which entails organisations disclosing financially significant sustainability information and information that influences the environment and society. In contrast, IFRS S1 and S2 focus on single materiality, assessing sustainability issues only as they affect financial **performance**. Understanding this difference is crucial for firms operating in global markets or those catering to varied stakeholder expectations.
3 **Align Sustainability with Strategic Planning:** Preparing for sustainability reporting requires integrating sustainability considerations into long-term strategic plans. This involves embedding sustainability metrics in governance and decision-making processes. This shift from short-term to long-term planning can lead to more robust strategies that align with stakeholder expectations.
4 **Data Management and Quality Control:** Accurate data collection and reliable reporting processes are essential for reporting requirements. Establishing strong data collection frameworks that emphasise reliability and quality is crucial for sustainability reporting and reputation. With key metrics in vital areas of the business, they are robust and verifiable, enabling compliance and building stakeholder trust.
5 **Technology as an Enabler:** Leveraging AI, digital tools, and secure technology platforms are critical for streamlined data collection, analysis, and reporting. In addition to cost savings and productivity improvements, advanced reporting software and analytics tools can integrate sustainability data across silos.
6 **Governance and Accountability:** Effective governance structures that include sustainability oversight at the board and executive levels are essential. Assigning clear roles, accountability, and cohesion in sustainability reporting will support risk management frameworks. The CEO and Board can ensure that sustainability risks and opportunities are systematically identified, assessed, and managed.
7 **External Assurance and Stakeholder Engagement:** External assurance augments the integrity of sustainability reports, reassuring stakeholders about the reliability of disclosures. Engaging with stakeholders helps identify material issues and align reporting practices with their expectations. This practice builds trust and strengthens the firm's reputation as a transparent and responsible entity.

7.8 Self-Reflection Questions

1 What key elements define sustainable and ESG reports, and how do they differ?
2 How can a company identify salient Impact Risk and Opportunities (IRO) when assessing its existing sustainability business model?

3 What are the salient differences between IFRS S1 and IFRS S2, and what are the challenges associated with complying with the requirements?
4 Why does CRSD reinforce the importance of long-term strategic thinking? What are the implications for **SSM**?
5 What role does stakeholder engagement play in producing sustainability and ESG reports? What are the similarities and differences?

References

Archer, M., (2024). *Unsustainable: Measurement, reporting, and the limits of corporate sustainability*. NYU Press.

Chen, X. and Ge, L., (2025). Artificial intelligence and corporate ESG performance: Evidence from China. *Applied Economics Letters, 17*(2), pp.1–7.

Prakash, P. and Rappaport, A., (1977). Information inductance and its significance for accounting. *Accounting, Organizations and Society, 2*(1), pp.29–38.

Sariyer, G., Mangla, S.K., Chowdhury, S., Sozen, M.E. and Kazancoglu, Y., (2024). Predictive and prescriptive analytics for ESG performance evaluation: A case of Fortune 500 companies. *Journal of Business Research, 181*, p.114742.

Simons, R., (1994). *Levers of control: How managers use innovative control systems to drive strategic renewal.* Harvard Business Press.

Singapore Airlines (2023/24). Sustainability report. Available at: https://www.singaporeair.com/content/dam/sia/web-assets/pdfs/about-us/information-for-investors/annual-report/sustainabilityreport2324.pdf (Accessed: 15 January 2026).

Singapore Airlines (2024/25). Sustainability report. Available at: https://www.singaporeair.com/content/dam/sia/web-assets/pdfs/about-us/information-for-investors/annual-report/sustainabilityreport2425.pdf (Accessed 15 January 2026).

Tenuta, P. and Cambrea, D.R., (2023). *Corporate sustainability: Measurement, reporting and effects on firm performance (2022).* Springer.

PART III

Aligning Sustainability, Models, and Culture

8

UNSDGS AND SUSTAINABILITY ASSESSMENT

8.1 Learning Strategy Objectives

After completing this chapter, you will be able to:

1. **Knowledge-Based Objectives:**
   - Identify, apply, and explain the concepts of United Nations Sustainable Development Goals (UNSDGs) and sustainability assessment.
   - Compare and contrast the strategic sustainability prospects of an organisation pursuing the UNSDGs.
2. **Skill-Based Objectives:**
   - Identify and develop creative solutions to UNSDG challenges.
   - Critically evaluate the UNSDG journey of organisations in different industries.
3. **Attitude-Based Objectives:**
   - Cultivate a commitment to global responsibility to contribute positively to global challenges addressed by the UNSDGs.
   - Inspire active engagement and advocacy for the UNSDGs to influence policies and practices.

8.2 Introduction

In 2015, the UNSDGs were introduced by the United Nations (UN), comprising 17 goals and 169 targets to be achieved by 2030. The goals were universally announced as inclusive, with the scope for developed and developing countries to recalibrate outcomes regarding people, the planet, and profits. Using innovative strategies, global stakeholders in the UNSDG ecosystem were encouraged to attain these goals.

Under pressure from activists, some of the larger organisations in the private sector have taken on the challenge, but the rate of UNSDG achievements is behind schedule.

DOI: 10.4324/9781003516774-11

This presents a considerable opportunity for universities to use their intellectual capital and networks to support global stakeholders. In its sixth year of measuring 2,152 universities from 125 countries' progress towards the Sustainable Development Goal (SDG), *The Times Higher Education* (2024) found Australian universities to be taking sustainable development seriously. There are four Australian universities in the top 10 spots.

At the Heads of State and Government and High Representatives meetings at the UN Headquarters in New York, from 25 to 27 September 2015, a new agenda for sustainable development was announced. Recognising that billions of people live in poverty and are deprived of a life of dignity, the widely held perception was that the UNSDGs would help overcome the economic malaise and encourage businesses and society to seek solutions to address humanity's most pressing challenges.

However, as the global community grapples with unparalleled crises and shifting priorities, there is a mounting recognition that achieving these ambitious goals may require more innovative and collaborative approaches than previously anticipated. The evolving landscape demands a re-evaluation of strategies to ensure sustainable development and equitable progress.

8.3 Historical Development

Before delving into the UNSDGs, it is essential to have a clear understanding of their historical development, which dates back to the late 18th century. The term industrial revolution provides a context for transformations since the late 18th century. Over the last 250 years, human existence has witnessed and benefitted from numerous breakthroughs.

Looking briefly at the preceding four industrial revolutions as we enter the fifth phase (see Figure 8.1), the salient issues can be noted.

The first industrial revolution, which lasted from the late 18th to the mid-19th century, marked a shift from agricultural economies to industrialisation. This period saw the advent of mechanised textile production, steam engines, and significant advancements in iron production. Businesses received greater rewards as **innovations** drastically altered

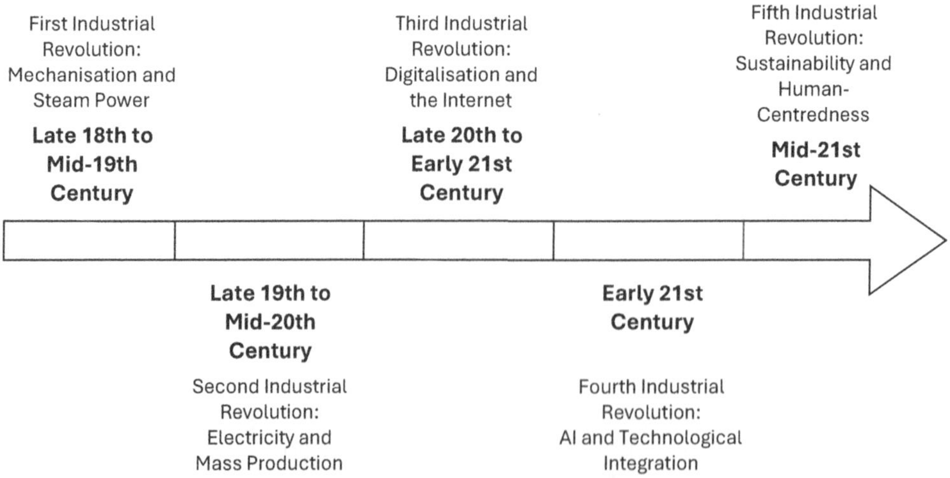

FIGURE 8.1 The evolution of industrial revolutions

the socio-economic landscape, leading to the rise of factories and jobs and benefiting stakeholders.

The second industrial revolution, which occurred between the late 19th and mid-20th centuries, brought further technological advancements to the marketplace. A defining characteristic is the widespread adoption of electricity, the internal combustion engine, aeroplanes, and assembly lines. This era witnessed the rise of mass production and the emergence of the modern corporation, driving further economic growth alongside significant societal changes. Mass production emphasises the economy of scale, which makes consumer goods more affordable. Similarly, the assembly line, popularised by figures like Henry Ford, epitomised this revolution.

In keeping with developments, the third industrial revolution, the digital revolution, continues disrupting approaches to how companies create winning strategies, innovate, and interact with stakeholders. This transformed how leaders managed their businesses; successful ones have evolved into US$ trillion companies. The semiconductor, personal computers, and the internet were at the heart of their successes. The digitisation of everything has profoundly affected forces such as the Internet of Things, where interconnected devices embedded with sensors, software, and other technologies can deliver numerous benefits to business and society, ranging from energy efficiency to disaster management.

As numerous companies illustrate, the fourth industrial revolution was a transformation era in which technologies incorporate physical, digital, and increasingly biological sciences. We now witness artificial intelligence (AI), which has dramatically changed commercial operations. Numerous applications make it challenging to think of many areas where AI won't change how we work. This is one of the top issues facing leadership teams. However, during such times, a key observation is the need to bring people along on the journey as well.

A growing perspective is the increasing influence of sustainability. The fifth industrial revolution builds upon the advancements of the fourth industrial revolution. We can witness governments worldwide exploring deeper and broader concepts of sustainability, human-centredness, and resilience. The Government of Japan (2015) aims to strike a balance between economic development and social issues resolution through systems that seamlessly integrate cyberspace (virtual space) and physical space (real space) at a high level. The human-centred society is a pillar of the government's vision of a future society for industry and the community.

Organisations that have adopted a human-centric approach will be better able to formulate and implement effective, sustainable development strategies. When coupled with machine learning, this perspective can enhance data-driven decision-making, resource allocation, and cost reduction, as well as optimisation of production processes, risk management, and customer engagement. Bad data can be a core strategic management blockage, leading to poor outcomes in implementing sustainability.

It emphasises the critical role of these assessments in shedding light on the environmental ramifications of organisational strategic endeavours. Critical assessments, including ecological footprint analysis, carbon footprint measurement, and life cycle assessments (LCAs), are explored to gain insights into the environmental impacts of corporate activities. These assessments serve as vital tools in identifying areas for enhancement and guiding strategic decision-making processes.

TABLE 8.1 The UN sustainable development goals

Themes the "5 Ps"	*SDGs*
People	**1** No poverty, **2** Zero hunger, **3** Good health and well-being, **4** Quality education, **5** Gender equality
Planet	**6** Clean water and sanitation, **12** Responsible consumption and production, **13** Climate action, **14** Life below water, **15** Life on land
Prosperity	**7** Affordable and clean energy, **8** Decent work and economic growth, **9** Industry, **innovation**, and infrastructure, **10** Reduced inequalities, **11** Sustainable cities and communities
Peace	**16** Peace, justice, and strong institutions
Partnership	**17** Partnerships for the goals

Abbreviation: SDGs, sustainable development goals.

Moreover, this chapter underscores that integrating sustainability considerations into strategic planning is pivotal for organisations aiming to align their objectives with broader societal goals. By integrating sustainability into their strategic frameworks, organisations enhance their operational efficiency and contribute to advancing the UNSDGs (see Table 8.1) and promoting sustainable development on a global scale. Organisations can proactively address environmental challenges through this integrated approach while fostering long-term prosperity for society and the planet.

8.4 Environmental, Social, and Governance

The environmental, social, and governance (ESG) perspective has now moved from being seen as doing good to running organisations well. Internal reporting includes the development of meaningful ESG risk reports. These will provide the basis for determining how the company should mitigate risk and for establishing its positioning in the marketplace.

Organisations now consider the intersection of profit and the planet closely, and the narrative varies. The concept is significant in strategic and financial management, where strategic decision-making evaluates marketplace opportunities. With the pivot from solely focusing on financial to sustainability stewardship, now sources of competitive advantage are sought.

The roles of the CFO and CSO continue to evolve, as regulatory and market volatility remain constant. The strategy frameworks and tools in Chapters 4 and 5 can help the leadership team navigate uncertainty and unlock new opportunities. By considering different scenarios, organisations can identify strong and weak signals of emerging trends and anticipate changes in ESG regulations.

This foresight enables them to prepare compliance strategies proactively, avoiding last-minute adjustments and potential penalties. Additionally, the CEO needs to be a strong communicator and able to influence key stakeholders through their thought leadership. Strong brand positioning and being viewed as a leader in sustainability are invaluable characteristics as well.

These are well-suited for considering strategies in a complex environment and implementing ESG initiatives. The CSO and the rest of the leadership team are seeking deeper structural commitments to ongoing challenges. According to London Business School (2025), markets are witnessing an ESG backlash. Unfortunately, in increasing cases, corporations' returns are not meeting stakeholders' targets.

Peeling beneath the surface reveals fault lines in organisations' sustainability strategies, which are easily identified by analysts who look for alignment between intent, operations, and action. Even those organisations that do not prioritise making strategic decisions based on planetary goals will face pressure from stakeholders to consider the risks resulting from climate change and zero-carbon, as well as the effects of these risks on their critical financial metrics, such as returns.

Leadership teams must cope with reporting demands to show they are ahead of regulatory changes and evolving stakeholder expectations. More specifically, the roles of CSO include ensuring that the organisation complies with ESG and sustainability regulations. From a strategic planning perspective, the alignment with ESG goals is sacrosanct.

From a corporate perspective, strategic risks provide a second line of defence for ESG strategic control. Middle managers must provide senior management with insights on the effectiveness of risk management and ensure the appropriate level of regulatory-aligned disclosures.

Evolution continues with the European Banking Authority (2025) drafting guidelines in a consultation paper to help financial institutions fuse ESG scenario analysis with risk management and strategic planning. Highlights include:

- Financial resilience and business model adaptation
- Addressing climate risk
- Large institution adoption in January 2026
- Small and non-complex institutions' adoption in January 2027
- Governance and data management.

8.5 Sustainability Assessments

Impact assessments cover tools for integrating environmental and social concerns into strategic decision-making processes. The following section examines the strengths and limitations of some existing impact assessment techniques to inform the evaluation of sustainability-related strategies. The implementation and evaluation of sustainability outcomes in the private and public sectors are essential processes that ensure government policies, programmes, and services effectively address the community's needs and deliver the intended outcomes.

These processes are particularly critical in the public sector due to their direct impact on public well-being, resource allocation, and the effectiveness of policies. Evaluation helps identify the strengths and weaknesses of sustainability initiatives, providing evidence-based insights that inform strategic and programme investment decision-making. This ensures that resources are used responsibly from a planetary perspective and that government actions are transparent and accountable to the public.

These sustainability assessment methods offer organisations a range of tools and approaches to evaluate and enhance their sustainability **performance** across various dimensions.

8.5.1 Life Cycle Assessment

During LCA, the user seeks to engage in thinking to encompass all three pillars of sustainability: (i) environmental, (ii) economic, and (iii) social. This involves conducting an assessment that considers environmental, economic, and social factors. The strategists can provide invaluable data for the CEO and Board to support sustainability initiatives by conducting an overarching LCA of a product, material, or process.

In terms of helping businesses, policymakers, and non-governmental organisations (NGOs), LCA can provide critical data for marketing, product and process design, and goal setting related to climate change and zero-carbon strategies. As explained in Chapter 1, in the circular economy, a circular model is preferred, and measurement is performed from inputs to outputs. Assessors will consider the metrics an organisation sets throughout the life cycle. These objective measures can track quantities such as volume, mass, or weight. This life cycle inventory assessment is interpreted in consideration of environmental and human health impacts.

Metrics can be applied to:

- Climate change
- Air pollution
- Water use
- Resource depletion
- Energy
- Radiation
- Land use.

Hotspots will be areas with a significant negative environmental impact. Then, these will become key segments of the sustainability strategy.

8.5.2 Environmental Impact Assessment

Environmental Impact Assessment (EIA) offers a comprehensive evaluation of a project's potential impacts. According to Morrison-Saunders (2023), the big idea in EIA is to "think before you act."

This can be depicted by systematically identifying future consequences of a current or proposed action.

The EIA approach helps analysts predict the likely future impacts of varying scenarios. This is particularly relevant for large-scale projects, such as airports, highways, and power plants, that will impact the natural environment and be applied to plans, programmes, and policies. Any environmental disturbance can worsen the delicate equilibrium, requiring remedial interventions if necessary.

8.5.3 Social Impact Assessment

A Social Impact Assessment (SIA) aims to manage the social issues associated with project implementation effectively. Vanclay and Esteves (2024) thoroughly investigate SIA in their 634-page state-of-the-art discussion. Experienced SIA practitioners worldwide offer valuable insights. Interestingly, one of the authors, Vanclay (2023), questions the merits of SIA and asks whether it is still fit for purpose. He notes that the SIA has evolved from being a sole regulatory tool to managing social issues throughout the life of a project.

Additionally, its scope can be limited, as not all potential consequences can be incorporated into the model. Its global nature will create issues relating to values, beliefs, and organisational culture. Different methodologies, including community participation, gender analysis, and stakeholder analysis, can highlight these social equity and inclusivity issues.

As a result, integrating diverse perspectives and adopting culturally sensitive approaches becomes essential in ensuring that assessments and subsequent actions are fair and just.

8.5.4 Carbon Footprint Assessment

A critical theme is the pursuit of a zero-carbon footprint. Concepts such as low-carbon living, carbon trade, and carbon tax remain among the foremost challenges of the sustainability phenomenon. The carbon footprint is a consequence of the ecological footprint, which measures the impact that human beings have on planetary ecosystems.

A carbon footprint can apply to the individual, organisational, and country levels. Greenhouse gas (GHG) emissions during the life cycle of a product or service can focus on a country's carbon footprint, which can be tracked through CO_2 emissions.

At the sector level, tourism needs to reduce its emissions by half by 2030 and attain net zero by mid-century (Gössling, Balas, Mayer, and Sun, 2023). Manufacturers face the brunt of customers who today demand cleaner, lower-carbon products. Ambitious electric vehicle (EV) car makers, such as Polestar, have announced that by 2030, they will have climate-neutral EVs across their value chain by 2040.

The three categories of GHG are:

Scope 1: Through organisational operations.
Scope 2: Indirect emissions acquired via external firms.
Scope 3: Indirect emissions that occur through business activity, such as employees travelling to and from work, tend to be the largest category.

Total GHG emissions can be calculated by:

Data x Emission Factor = Greenhouse Gas Emissions.

8.5.5 Ecological Footprint Analysis

The ecological footprint refers to the land area required to sustain a certain level of consumption. Examining how humanity exerts pressure on the planet's scarce resources can help shape policies worldwide. This biophysical metric effectively raises public awareness of environmental impacts resulting from production and consumption, or more precisely, on the planet's biocapacity.

Answers to the origin question of how much forest area is required to absorb CO_2 emissions from energy consumption (Fang, Heijungs, and de Snoo, 2014) will differ based on technological advancements, energy efficiency, and consumption patterns across different global regions.

Additionally, the varying capacity of different ecosystems to absorb carbon, as well as the distinct environmental policies and practices in place globally, contributes to these discrepancies. Understanding these differences is crucial for developing tailored strategies that address the unique ecological challenges faced by different communities and regions, thereby promoting a more sustainable and equitable use of the planet's resources.

The ecological footprint approach is widely applied in the agricultural sector to crops and livestock (Biagetti, Gislon, Martella, Zucali, Bava, Franco, and Sandrucci, 2023; Li, Zhou, Wang, Singh, Li, and Li, 2020). However, like most analyses, uncertainty and data quality are paramount, and their global nature may create challenges in obtaining localised figures.

8.5.6 Biodiversity Impact Assessment

The reduction of habitat globally is a significant threat to biodiversity conservation. Biodiversity loss impacts ecosystem functioning and has significant global economic and societal implications. Biodiversity loss and climate change are independent but interconnected issues that can exacerbate each other.

For instance, the loss of wetlands decreases the number of species that can thrive in these unique ecosystems. It impairs their ability to filter water and regulate flooding, thereby increasing the vulnerability of surrounding areas to extreme weather events.

On the other hand, rising temperatures and changing precipitation patterns due to climate change can dry wetlands, making them unsuitable for the species that depend on them and exacerbating biodiversity loss. Addressing these interconnected challenges requires comprehensive strategies that incorporate conservation efforts and climate adaptation measures, ensuring a balanced and sustainable future.

Although biodiversity loss remains a sustainability challenge, it must be given more attention in corporate priorities. In the World Economic Forum's 2023 Global Risks report, the next decade will be characterised by environmental and societal crises fuelled by ongoing economic and geopolitical trends.

With "biodiversity loss and ecosystem collapse" as one of the most pressing global risks over the next decade. The impacts on biodiversity include climate change, habitat loss, pollution, overexploitation of species, and invasive species.

Against this background, the EU published its EU Biodiversity Strategy for 2030 (2020), which is ambitious and long-term for protecting nature and reversing ecosystem degradation. However, as with the case of **SSM**, achieving the strategic goals will require overcoming significant challenges.

8.5.7 Social Return on Investment Analysis

Measuring Social Return on Investment (SROI) can enable organisations to track progress in social sustainability. The results can be used to help vulnerable members of society. The framework can generate monetised data, emphasising multi-bottom lines in the not-for-profit sector. By adopting traditional cost-benefit analysis, social returns using financial proxies can be compared against the input investments. Simply put, SROI is about value rather than money per se. Stakeholder engagement is pivotal so that beneficiaries can see changes.

Moreover, measuring SROI encourages transparency and accountability, requiring organisations to communicate their social impact and the outcomes achieved. This strengthens trust with donors, partners, and the community, providing valuable insights into what works and what doesn't, and enabling continuous improvement.

By highlighting the tangible and intangible benefits created, SROI helps organisations make informed decisions, prioritise initiatives that maximise social value, and advocate for policies and funding that support social good.

However, assigning monetary values to social outcomes is a subjective and problematic process. Estimating the value of financial proxies can vary significantly across sectors and regions. Other intangible aspects, such as community-themed metrics, such as well-being, may be underrepresented in the analysis.

8.5.8 Circularity Assessment

As previously mentioned in Chapter 1, the circular economy continues to emerge as a promising innovative solution to successfully and effectively achieve sustainability across the organisation. The multiple groupings of organisational variables that are in constant flux may make it more challenging to proactively respond to the depletion of natural resources and convert waste into inputs.

Approaches for circularity assessment involve evaluating how circular concepts fulfil salient guidelines. The evolution of the circular economy is a central aspect of the sustainability ecosystem. The circularity of products and services decouples economic growth from harming natural resources.

Circularity assessment can be systematically evaluated from the country level to the product level. Tools are structured to help appraise improvement points and interventions to enhance organisations' circularity and sustainability.

As the economic system **transitions** from a linear to a circular model, monitoring progress towards circularity is a key path to sustainability. Although commencing from a low base, the global economy is only 8.6% circular, short of the Paris Agreement goal (Patil, van Langen, and Ramakrishna, 2023).

This has seized the attention of businesses, the third sector, government, and NGOs, who measure progress through circularity metrics. The European Academies Science Advisory Council offers a list of more than 300 metrics to track progress in the circular economy (EASAC, 2016).

The European Environment Agency (2023) proposed the "Bellagio Process," which involves expert dialogue. This provides a richer insight into the circular economy, enabling stakeholders to track progress effectively. The seven principles are:

1 Monitor the circular economy.
2 Define indicator groups.
3 Follow the indicator selection criteria.
4 Exploit a wide range of data and information sources.
5 Ensure multilevel monitoring.
6 Allow for measuring progress towards targets.
7 Ensure visibility and clarity.

8.5.9 *Supply Chain Sustainability Assessment*

The effectiveness and efficiency of the supply chain encompass a continuum of operational processes, including planning, coordination, and control of inputs from materials, parts, and finished goods from the supplier to the customer. Organisations that successfully manage their supply chain as a cohesive entity and effectively measure and assess with appropriate tools and techniques will remain competitive and resilient in the current battle for survival.

Supply Chain Sustainability Assessment (SCSA) is a critical evaluative framework that quantifies and enhances a company's supply chain's environmental, social, and economic impacts. By upholding ESG standards across the supply chain, the focus is not only on sustainability but also on unintended consequences, such as adverse effects on employers or local communities.

The field of supply chains can include interchangeable terms such as:

- Green: Water usage, pollution, and GHG emissions.
- Ethical: Managing the social impacts.
- Responsible: Prioritises ethical practices, environmental sustainability, and social responsibility throughout all stages.

The size and risk of a supply chain will vary by organisation, based on the type of industry and the number of tiers within the supply chain. In a large and complex supply chain, assessing the risk of each supplier can be challenging. This makes it difficult for managers to prioritise an "intensive assessment" approach and determine the type of intervention that should prevail.

Each multidimensional assessment encompasses a systematic analysis of all phases of the supply chain, from raw material extraction to production, logistics, and end-of-life product management. The primary aim of SCSA is to identify and implement sustainable practices that reduce negative environmental impacts and promote positive societal outcomes.

By aligning supply chain operations with international sustainability standards, companies can simultaneously fulfil ethical obligations and gain a competitive edge in a market that increasingly prioritises ecological and social responsibility.

STRATEGY NUGGET

Counting the Cost of EU Sustainable Supply Chains

Introduction

Sustainability has altered the way firms approach the complex challenges they encounter in traditional strategic management, particularly in the realm of supply chain management.

This example, which stems from the EU's efforts to make supply chains more environmentally friendly, examines how changing rules and the growing importance of sustainability have become increasingly significant. In a changing situation, this nugget highlights some of the key problems and potential solutions.

Background and Context

The EU's Green Deal was established in 2019 with rules for businesses to follow in order to achieve climate neutrality by 2050. This commendable law encourages businesses to review their supply chains for environmental damage and human rights abuses. The Corporate Sustainability Due Diligence Directive (CSDDD) requires corporations to ensure that their supply chains don't harm their workers or the environment. Companies must follow this rule and others, such as the Corporate Sustainability Reporting Directive (CSRD). This places greater emphasis on digital and transparency.

Strategic Issues

This concentration on supply chains makes things more challenging for businesses in several ways. First, there are the additional costs of compliance, which can be substantial, especially for small businesses. For instance, one analyst said that one multinational corporation has already spent $18 million on automating carbon emissions data and expects to invest another $50–60 million over the next few years to completely comply with the CSRD.

The fact that marketplaces are worldwide makes it harder for companies because rules are different in different regions. The Netherlands-based boiler business BDR Thermea has faced challenges due to these external factors. Demand for their products fluctuates due to changes in national policies regarding heat pumps.

Because of this, some companies are being pushed to stop working with suppliers that cannot provide them with the data they need to comply with the CSDDD. This type of strategic decision-making is transforming the way people invest globally. The components coming together demonstrate the importance of the directions. One of the key principles of **SSM** is that sustainability should be integrated into all company plans.

Source: FT.com (2024).

Questions

1 Given the costs involved in complying with the EU's Green Deal, along with the number of national-level changes, how would you sell this project to the Board of your company?
2 How should CEOs balance the strategic aspiration to maintain global supply chains with new requirements to ensure suppliers in developing countries meet EU standards?
3 What are the challenges for boiler companies due to national regulatory inconsistencies on heat pumps?

8.6 SSM Selection in Practice

This section highlights some of the phenomenological issues in **SSM** and their influence on UNSDGs and sustainability assessment. Over previous decades, phenomenological issues in **SSM** have evolved from purely philosophical issues into a leadership approach in business.

This book seeks to immerse readers in the sustainability phenomenon but with a nuanced understanding of the ESG dashboard rather than merely looking at data. The issues of ESG problems need to be simplified to provide simplistic, reductionist solutions.

From a leadership perspective, we need to consider, namely (see Figure 8.2), (i) how firms behave in pursuing their sustainability strategy, (ii) how firms are organised in pursuing their sustainability strategy, and (iii) why firms differ in sustainability **performance**?

Collectively, these can be considered through a theoretical lens. Still, the breadth of **SSM**, as outlined in Chapters 3 and 4, suggests we need to consider examples to illustrate how theory can blend with practice to enhance understanding and rationale in strategic decision-making.

Table 8.2 illustrates each of the seven **SSM** schools, along with their assessment approaches and practical examples.

These examples demonstrate how different approaches to **SSM** can be applied in various contexts, highlighting the diverse methods and objectives that organisations pursue to achieve sustainability.

For example, if we examine the link between Global South Perspectives and COP29, Table 8.3 provides a summary of key outcomes. In terms of financial resources, the figures are staggering, but insufficient to engender the necessary change. The essential scaling up requires significant blended financial infrastructure change and risk-sharing mechanisms that are attractive for private capital. The $1.3 trillion per year will require financial

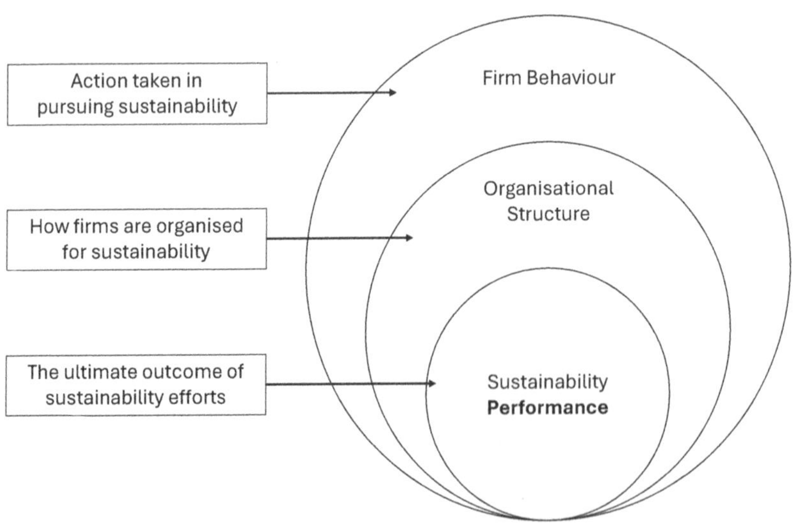

FIGURE 8.2 Sustainability strategy analysis

TABLE 8.2 **SSM** assessment approaches

Sustainable Strategic Management School	*Assessment Approach*	*Practical Example*
Traditional strategic management	Financial **performance** and competitive advantage.	Foxconn, a Taiwanese multinational electronics contract manufacturer, is known for producing devices for companies like Apple, Sony, and Del. But has been criticised in the past for focusing on maximising profits with staff suffering from well-being issues.
Corporate social responsibility (CSR) approach	Triple bottom line (people, planet, profit).	A multinational corporation implements a CSR programme that includes community development initiatives, environmental conservation efforts, and fair labour practices. For example, Unilever's Sustainable Living Plan focuses on improving health and well-being, reducing environmental impact, and enhancing livelihoods.
Environmental sustainability and green strategies	Environmental impact and promoting eco-friendly practices.	Tesla's focus on electric vehicles and renewable energy solutions, such as solar panels and energy storage systems, to reduce reliance on fossil fuels and lower carbon emissions.
Social **innovation** and inclusive business	Societal return on investment	The UN's Global Alliance for Clean Cookstoves aims to foster the adoption of clean and efficient cooking solutions in developing countries. The initiative seeks to reduce health risks associated with traditional cooking methods, such as indoor air pollution, which is a major cause of respiratory diseases.
Circular economy and cradle-to-cradle design	Circular assessment	IKEA's circular approach involves offering furniture take-back services, recycling materials, and designing products with sustainable materials that can be disassembled and repurposed.
Innovation and disruption	**Innovation** and disruptive technologies assessment	IBM Food Trust, which uses blockchain to trace food products from farm to table.
Global South perspectives	Inclusive and sustainable development	BRAC's integrated development programmes in Bangladesh, which combine education, healthcare, and economic development initiatives, tailored to the local context and aimed at lifting communities out of poverty.

execution complexity. Enabling environments across Global South markets will require the coordination of multiple stakeholder groups.

The onus is on Global South governments to move forward from incremental progress to systemic **transition** for effective sustainability action in the short, medium, and long term.

TABLE 8.3 Some key outcomes and implications of COP29

Key Outcome	*Details*	*Implications*
Climate finance agreement	Agreement to triple finance to developing countries, reaching $300 billion annually by 2035	Criticised as inadequate by many developing countries; seen as insufficient to meet the scale of their climate crisis
New collective quantified goal (NCQG)	Aim to secure $1.3 trillion per year in climate finance from public and private sources by 2035	Provides a framework for future climate financing but requires significant contributions from all sectors
Operationalisation of carbon markets	Full operationalisation of carbon markets under Articles 6.2 and 6.4 of the Paris Agreement	Enables international trading of carbon credits, potentially bridging financing gaps for energy **transitions**
Loss and damage fund	Decision to operationalise the loss and damage fund	Critical for addressing climate-related damages in developing countries, though funding remains inadequate
Nationally determined contributions (NDCs)	Countries must update their NDCs by February 2025, with several nations announcing early submissions	Encourages countries to set more ambitious climate targets, aligning with global efforts to limit warming
Support for least developed countries	Agreements include capacity-building support and financing for adaptation plans	Aims to help vulnerable nations build resilience against climate impacts, though more support is needed

Mini Case Study

Barbados' SDG Execution: Tourism, Resilience, and a Whole-Economy Transition

Context

Barbados is a 21 by 13–mile Small Island Developing State (SIDS) of approximately 270,000 people. Since 1969, it has been a stable parliamentary democracy and it is service-led and globally known for tourism, financial services, and creative industries.

The specificities of the postcolonial condition in the Caribbean Region are more about the neocolonial relations that continue to define economic and political relations, and current practices.

Recently, the government's push for climate finance and blended-capital partnerships, while safeguarding social inclusion, frames the SDG agenda as an investment philosophy, not a Public Relations (PR) communication exercise.

Performance Snapshot

Social outcomes (education access, basic health) are comparatively strong, but climate vulnerability, waste and water systems, imported-energy exposure, and marine ecosystem pressures threaten competitiveness. Post-pandemic debt dynamics and a concentrated tourism base amplify execution risk.

The Leadership Challenge

How can Barbados turn SDG intent into more investable pipelines that lift productivity, societal capital, and derisk climate and energy shocks, without overburdening and depleting the resources of the state?

Strategic Choices

1 Resilient Infrastructure First: Harden water, energy, and coastal assets; roll out distributed solar storage; expand reuse and leakage reduction; mandate resilience standards in permits/procurement.
2 Net-Zero High-Value Tourism 2030: Decarbonise tourism infrastructure, green certify suppliers, and localise more food and services to raise domestic value-add.
3 Blue/Green Economy Platforms: Develop and grow mangrove/reef restoration, offshore renewables pilots, and circular-waste ventures linked to ports and hospitality.
4 Data and Delivery: Create an SDG Delivery Unit and open-data backbone; tie ministry budgets to outcome targets; publish quarterly scorecards.
5 Financing Architecture: Use green/blue bonds; catastrophe-risk instrument; public-private partnerships (PPPs) with robust offtake; diaspora capital; prioritise projects with measurable savings (energy, water) and export earnings.

What Executives Can Learn

- Treat SDGs as a Strategy Cascade: Three national "big bets," each translated into bankable projects with owners, milestones, and unit economics.
- Manage Concentration Risk: Diversify demand (eco-, medical, education tourism; digital services) while deepening local supplier capabilities.
- Enhance Resilience to Strengthen Its Position in Regional and Global Markets: Firmly position Barbados as a low-carbon, climate-ready destination with high-level key **performance** indicators.

Questions

1 Barbados is a small island in the Eastern Caribbean, measuring 21 miles by 13 miles, with a population of 270,000. Being a country dependent on tourism, how does being a SIDS present unique challenges and opportunities for SDG implementation?

2 You should visit https://dashboards.sdgindex.org/ (pp. 112–113), and then explain which SDGs are most off-track for Barbados? Why do you think is the reason for this?
3 Which PPP structure best aligns investor returns with SDG outcomes?

Source: Sustainable Development Report (2025).

8.7 Chapter Key Takeaways

1 **The Evolution of Sustainability in Business Strategy:**
This chapter traces the evolution of sustainability from the 18th century, using the five industrial revolutions as context. Today's successful organisations recognise that sustainability isn't just "doing good" but is essential for running operations well. Business leaders must appreciate this historical progression to ensure that core SDG-themed strategies are not merely peripheral activities.
2 **The Shift from Compliance to Competitive Advantage:**
ESG considerations have evolved from being a source of regulatory compliance issues to becoming a key source of competitive advantage. Well-run organisations now view sustainability not merely as a cost centre, but as an opportunity for differentiation, **innovation**, and value creation. Leaders who proactively position their organisations as sustainability champions can unlock new market opportunities while mitigating some risks associated with climate change and regulatory changes.
3 **The Critical Role of Assessment Frameworks:**
Various sustainability assessment methodologies (LCA, EIA, Carbon Footprint Assessment, etc.) provide essential tools for assessing sustainability effectiveness.
4 **Integration of Sustainability into Core Business Models:**
This chapter reveals how frameworks like the triple bottom line or circularity assessment can help guide organisations towards fusing sustainability into their fundamental business models.
5 **The Multidimensional Nature of Sustainability Challenges:**
The challenges of climate change and biodiversity loss may be viewed as independent but if considered as interlinked issues, can produce synergistic effects. Organisations should ensure that their systems thinking capabilities are sufficient to decipher complex relationships.
6 **Strategic Decision-Making in a BANI (Brittle, Anxious, Non-Linear, Incomprehensible) Environment:**
Adopting to the ever-changing environment is an ongoing sustainability dilemma. Rigid, three- to five-year strategic planning horizons are ill-suited. The EU sustainable supply chains case show the importance of getting suppliers to confirm with CSDDD. Sustainability strategies must be built within the appropriate time frames.
7 **The Evolving Role of Leadership in Sustainability:**
C-suite executives, such as the CFOs and CSOs, must be able to influence key stakeholders with ease. Long-term value creation through sustainability must be transparent; otherwise, the organisation may be vulnerable to the "ESG backlash," which occurs when companies' sustainability claims don't match their actual **performance**.

8.8 Self-Reflection Questions

1 Analyse the importance of UNSDGs and critically evaluate the progress of one major organisation you are familiar with. How does this current practice influence the strategy decision-making processes?
2 Discuss the primary objectives of sustainable supply chain management. How do they contribute to developing strategies towards net zero, and what are some real-world business challenges?
3 Identify and elaborate on the key steps involved in conducting a comprehensive circularity assessment. How do these steps ensure a comprehensive evaluation of the circular economy?
4 What is the fundamental concept of the Triple Ps, which are used to evaluate an organisation's financial health? Explain each metric's significance in increasing shareholder tension between the CEO and the Board.
5 Examine the advantages and limitations of using one of the families of sustainability assessments to analyse business cases. How does this approach enhance the depth and rigour in evaluating and enhancing their sustainability **performance** across various dimensions?

References

Biagetti, E., Gislon, G., Martella, A., Zucali, M., Bava, L., Franco, S. and Sandrucci, A., (2023). Comparison of the use of life cycle assessment and ecological footprint methods for evaluating environmental performances in dairy production. *Science of the Total Environment, 905*, p.166845.

EASAC (2016). Indicators for a circular economy. *EASAC Policy Report 30.*

EU Biodiversity Strategy for 2030 (2020). Available at: https://www.eea.europa.eu/policy-documents/eu-biodiversity-strategy-for-2030-1 (Accessed: 28 August 2025).

European Banking Authority (2025). The EBA consults on guidelines on ESG scenario analysis. Available at: https://www.eba.europa.eu/publications-and-media/press-releases/eba-consults-guidelines-esg-scenario-analysis (Accessed: 28 August 2025).

European Environment Agency (2023). Measuring Europe's circular economy. Available at: https://www.eea.europa.eu/en/topics/in-depth/circular-economy/measuring-europes-circular-economy (Accessed: 2 September 2025).

Fang, K., Heijungs, R. and de Snoo, G.R., (2014). Theoretical exploration for the combination of the ecological, energy, carbon, and water footprints: Overview of a footprint family. *Ecological Indicators, 36*, pp.508–518.

FT.com (2024). Companies count the cost of compliance with green regulation. Available at: https://www.ft.com/content/276028dc-a492-44ec-9eee-58d9fb51c159 (Accessed: 15 January 2026).

Gössling, S., Balas, M., Mayer, M. and Sun, Y.Y., (2023). A review of tourism and climate change mitigation: The scales, scopes, stakeholders and strategies of carbon management. *Tourism Management, 95*, p.104681.

Government of Japan (2015). Report on the 5th Science and Technology Basic Plan. Available at: https://www8.cao.go.jp/cstp/kihonkeikaku/5basicplan_en.pdf (Accessed: 28 August 2025).

Li, M., Zhou, Y., Wang, Y., Singh, V.P., Li, Z. and Li, Y., (2020). An ecological footprint approach for cropland use sustainability based on multi-objective optimization modelling. *Journal of Environmental Management, 273*, p.111147.

London Business School (2025). What the ESG backlash reveals- and what comes next. *Forbes*, 25th March. Available at: https://www.forbes.com/sites/lbsbusinessstrategyreview/2025/03/25/what-the-esg-backlash-reveals-and-what-comes-next/ (Accessed: 28 August 2025).

Morrison-Saunders, A., (2023). *Advanced introduction to environmental impact assessment.* Edward Elgar Publishing.

Patil, R.A., van Langen, S.K. and Ramakrishna, S., (2023). Circularity assessment: Developing a comprehensive yardstick. In R.A. Patil and S. Ramakrishna (eds.), *Circularity assessment: Macro to Nano: Accountability towards sustainability*, pp.3–14. Springer Nature Singapore.

Sustainable Development Report (2025). Financing sustainable development to 2030 and mid-century. Available at: https://dashboards.sdgindex.org/ (Accessed 15 January 2026).

Times Higher Education (2024). Impact rankings 2024: Results announced. Available at: https://www.timeshighereducation.com/world-university-rankings/impact-rankings-2024-results-announced (Accessed: 28 August 2025).

Vanclay, F., (2024). After 50 years of social impact assessment, is it still fit for purpose? *Current Sociology, 72*(4), pp.774–788.

Vanclay, F. and Esteves, A.M. eds., (2024). *Handbook of social impact assessment and management.* Edward Elgar Publishing.

9

SUSTAINABLE BUSINESS MODEL INNOVATION

9.1 Learning Strategy Objectives

After completing this chapter, you will be able to:

1 **Knowledge-Based Objectives:**

- Identify, apply, and explain how organisations can use business models to achieve sustainable advantage.
- Compare and contrast the changing economics of sustainable business models.

2 **Skill-Based Objectives:**

- Design and implement sustainable business models through actionable and differentiated insights.
- Critically evaluate the causes of ineffective business model execution in different industries.

3 **Attitude-Based Objectives:**

- Overcome the fear factor in addressing change management challenges and global sustainability issues by overcoming resistance.
- Inspire active engagement by creating an innovative culture.

9.2 Introduction

Business model **innovation** is crucial for achieving both sustainability and financial **performance** (Geissdoerfer, Vladimirova, and Evans, 2018). The pertinent foundational knowledge of business model adoption in high-performing organisations reveals several traits. Some of these have been captured by Snihur and Markman (2023), who poignantly mention that research has thrived at the intersection of strategy, **innovation** management, and entrepreneurship. In their future directions, they include designing a business model for a more sustainable economy.

DOI: 10.4324/9781003516774-12

With markets in flux, organisations are compelled to deploy multiple business models, which make it imperative for the CEO to develop the requisite in-house knowledge to formulate and implement sustainability strategies.

The interest in business models continues to gain momentum as organisations adopt strategies around value capture and managing the supply and demand side of operations. The speed of change in markets compels transformation efforts to be breakthrough rather than solely incremental, with each incorporating differing risk levels.

Strong **performance** is a vital component of today's sustainability-themed organisation. Nonetheless, business model **innovation** comes at a cost and does not always lead to successful outcomes (Christensen, Bartman, and Van Bever, 2016). This can lead to wasted efforts, as organisations may allocate vast resources to invest in business transformation programmes to address critical gaps in strategic and operational processes.

However, outdated legacy operations and evolving customer needs can further block the creation of a resilient infrastructure. To remain competitive, obsolete technical and manual processes are costly to maintain, especially when it comes to implementing breakthrough changes. Organisational pushback may prevail, as staff knowledge acquired over time can act as a power base and will hinder unbiased opinions.

In such situations, fostering sustainable business model **innovation** becomes imperative to surmounting these barriers. New technologies must align with the environmental, social, and governance (ESG) objectives built into the transformation efforts. Today's pro-growth strategies require the removal of working in silos.

Reskilled staff need to feel comfortable working in sustainable practices that are incorporated into the transformation programme. Organisations must look to external stakeholders to ensure that what is being promised delivers value. Ultimately, transformation efforts must contribute to the triple bottom line (see Figure 9.1).

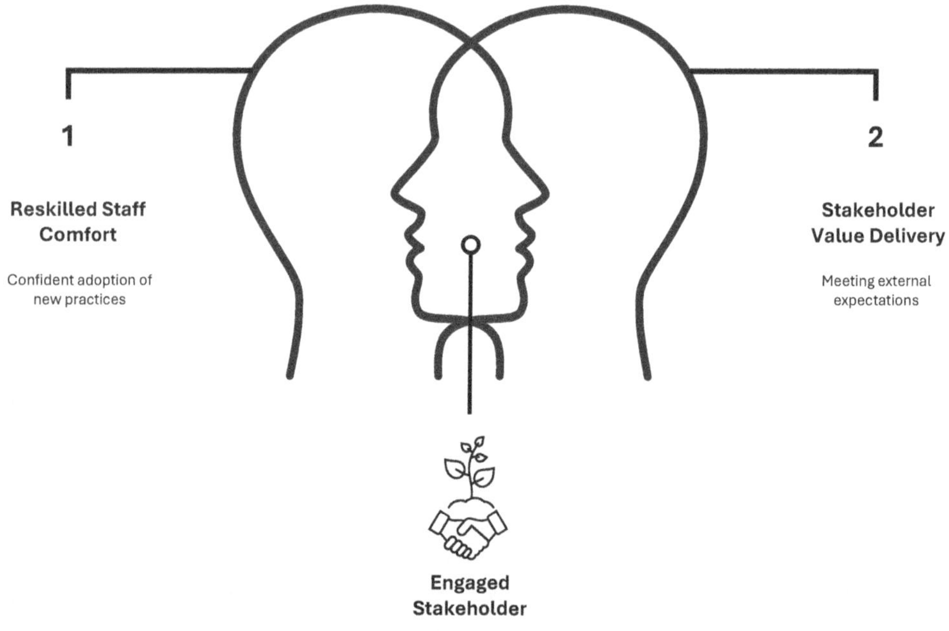

FIGURE 9.1 The synergy of reskilling, stakeholder value, and sustainability

Technology **innovation** and strategic insight present new pathways to the formation and delivery of business models. They are intertwined, with each influencing the strategist, and this symbiotic relationship is critical for researchers and practitioners. Organisational projects can involve reimaging their business models to obtain a competitive advantage. The rapid prominence of artificial intelligence (AI) has accelerated the rate of change and what is achievable. Unfortunately, this can change stakeholder expectations, with sustainability being a scapegoat. The rush towards sustainability is currently being met with organisations scaling back commitments.

In 2021, Danone's CEO was ousted by its activists, investors, and Board. Its financial **performance** could have been stronger than that of its peer group. The CEO mentioned that the company was more environmentally conscious. According to the *Financial Times* (2021), this was a classic example of a case study in the pitfalls of purpose. Since the pandemic, markets have witnessed internal friction with organisations of all sizes succumbing to the temptation to pursue sustainability-themed initiatives.

While **SSM** does incorporate significant change management programmes and direction, some organisations have had to correct their sustainability strategies. The luxury brand Burberry faced a backlash for its practice of burning unsold luxury stock to maintain brand exclusivity and scarcity. This situation shows the dilemma of environmental and ethical implications. McDonald's switched to paper straws to reduce plastic usage and lessen environmental impact. Unfortunately, stakeholders were unhappy when it was revealed that the paper straws were not recyclable. Both examples demonstrate the importance of ensuring that business models align positively with ESG objectives.

So, more than messaging is desirable with stakeholders' critical evaluation of sustainability strategies and business models. As in the case of **SSM**, strategies involve trade-offs; ultimately, an innovative business model is required to make money while doing good at the same time.

This chapter will explore the integration of sustainability and business models, examining how organisations can create value while advancing their sustainable goals and mission. It discusses innovative business models using a value proposition framework. By re-envisioning products, services, and processes, organisations can eliminate waste generation, extend product life cycles, and foster the regeneration of natural systems.

Additionally, this chapter explores the concept of shared value creation, which entails generating economic value while creating value for society and addressing societal challenges. Through initiatives that address social needs, mitigate environmental risks, and strengthen stakeholder relationships, organisations can unlock new sources of competitive advantage while contributing to the greater good. By exploring these innovative business models, this chapter aims to inspire organisations to adopt sustainability as a catalyst for both profitability and positive societal impact.

9.3 Business Models

Gaining prominence from the mid-1990s, business models are used by analysts to evaluate how an organisation approaches its business activities (Massa and Tucci, 2021). Business models for sustainability entail reframing organisations to embrace and adopt innovative processes that reflect current organisational design and change management practices.

Indeed, in their creation, they provide the architecture of how the organisation creates, delivers, and captures value and are a topic of considerable interest to leadership teams that realise this unit of analysis is distinct from the product, firm, industry, or network (Zott, Amit, and Massa, 2011). A well-crafted business model can be a source of competitive advantage by creating value for the organisation and all stakeholders, including society.

This paradigm shift reduces environmental harm and presents compelling opportunities for cost reduction and **innovation**. From a customer perspective, customer relationships, customer segments, and channels are considered. From a commercial perspective, revenue flows and operational cost structures underpin its viability. Ultimately, the key outputs are people, the planet, and **performance**, all of which are necessary for a positive and sustainable result.

By exploring innovative, sustainable business models, leaders can harness sustainability as a driving force for both profitability and positive societal impact. Considering two innovative business models, circular economy and shared value creation, inspires organisations to embrace sustainability as a moral imperative and a strategic opportunity for long-term profitability and positive societal impact.

The circular economy, a regenerative system aimed at minimising waste and maximising resource efficiency, often lies at the heart of sustainable business models. By reimagining products, services, and processes, organisations can design out waste, keep products and materials in use for longer, and regenerate natural systems. This reduces environmental degradation and presents opportunities for cost savings, **innovation**, and resilience.

By adopting a holistic approach to business model **innovation**, organisations can simultaneously enhance their bottom line and create a more sustainable and prosperous future for all stakeholders. The emphasis on value can alter the probabilities of success.

This is relevant as organisations are formulating and implementing multiple business models that cater to diverse consumer preferences, allowing them to tap into different market segments simultaneously. Uber operates a multi-sided business model that connects drivers and riders through a value exchange. The Uber platform serves as an intermediary, connecting drivers and riders, and earns revenue from each transaction. Uber's business capitalises on the benefits of the network effect, enabling it to scale quickly. This now numbers 5.4 million drivers available in 72 countries and 10,000 cities. Managing its multi-sided business model has brought sustainability challenges ranging from the negative effects of internal combustion engines on the road, and the legal status of its drivers.

As more organisations recognise the benefits of this approach, a proliferation of diverse and sustainable business models will emerge, catering to the evolving preferences of today's consumers. This suggests that business models may help drive product, process, and organisational **innovation**, which can assist the CEO in navigating different types of diversification strategies. These can include value-creating, value-neutral, or value-reducing. Examining these diversification strategies, value-creating addresses what stakeholders demand, value-neutral approaches may be acceptable during times of crisis, and value-reducing strategies may be a short-term tactical response to a market opportunity.

9.3.1 The Concept of Value

There are various elements of value (see Figure 9.2), but the overarching framework is often worth remembering. In terms of adopting a structured and visual approach, the following are pertinent.

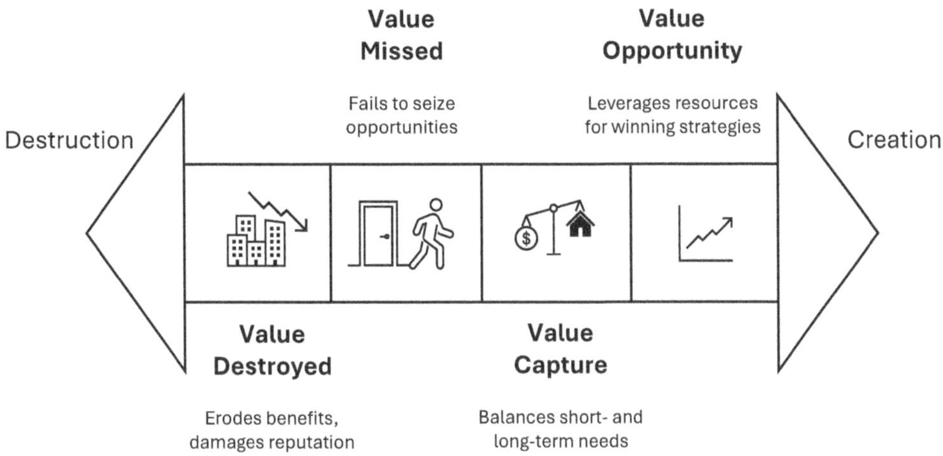

FIGURE 9.2 Value creation and destruction in business strategies

9.3.1.1 Value Capture

Organisations seek to deliver value to their customers. However, they must ensure that they secure value to deliver the triple-line metrics demanded by their stakeholders. Value capture from traditional business models that generate revenue must balance short- and long-term needs to ensure that the CFO has the financial resources to secure sustainable operations.

9.3.1.2 Value Destroyed

Sometimes, when a closer analysis of value is conducted, the business decision erodes the presumed benefits. This can occur with legacy systems and processes, which provide outputs that damage the brand's reputational standard. This risk is not solely economic but covers societal and environmental hazards.

9.3.1.3 Value Missed

In business, timing can be everything. An opportunity today may not be around for that long. The dynamic approach states that competitive advantage can be obtained by seizing opportunities. A closed-thinking organisation will not possess the attributes of customer and market insight, be resistant to change, and lack the agility to pivot.

9.3.1.4 Value Opportunity

There is a far-reaching consensus that the sustainability phenomenon worldwide presents significant opportunities for all. Many critics question who is benefiting the most, but this book seeks to consider how organisations can leverage their resources to create and implement winning strategies. By adopting sustainable approaches, organisations will be able to capitalise on their value opportunities.

Digital technologies remain at the forefront of transformation change programmes, but the success rate appears to be alarmingly low. Creating a business model in the absence of a strategic architecture can lead to trauma. As Phillips (2003) pointed out during the dot-com crash era, it is essential to recognise that a business model is not the same as a strategy. While a strategy outlines the long-term vision and plans to achieve specific goals, a business model is a framework through which an organisation delivers value and ensures sustainability and profitability.

As the sustainability market dynamics evolve, the business models must also incorporate flexibility and resilience to navigate uncertainties and emerging trends. Therefore, leadership teams are under pressure to innovate their products and services, as well as their fundamental business models. This means rethinking value propositions, customer relationships, and resultant revenue streams to align with sustainable practices that ensure long-term success and minimal negative environmental and societal impact.

Two decades later, the AI boom fundamentally transformed industries, with significant implications for **SSM**. Integrating AI into **SSM** processes offers unparalleled opportunities for enhancing efficiency, predicting trends, and optimising resource use, which are critical for sustainability. However, this technological advancement also presents an existential challenge to organisations that need to adapt.

Incorporating AI into **SSM** requires technical upgrades and a profound shift in organisational culture towards AI literacy and digital fluency. Organisations must develop strategies that align AI capabilities with their sustainability goals, ensuring that AI-driven insights inform decisions that balance economic growth with environmental and social responsibilities. Those who do not embrace this transformation risk being left behind, as AI becomes a pivotal factor in achieving organisational impact.

9.4 Business Model and AI

Business models combined with AI are a transformational combination with profound implications for sustainability. Integrating AI into business operations, organisations are able to squeeze resource allocation, reduce waste and enhance decision-making (see Figure 9.3).

Together with predictive analytics, the CEO can forecast organisational needs that can reduce the carbon footprint. As emerging technologies evolve, we can witness the relationship between business success and ecological well-being.

However, without considering the principles of **SSM**, the impact of the resultant business model can be vague and sometimes contradictory. Experience has revealed in my work that there are five ways organisations can unlock impact and add value to sustainability strategies:

1 Stop Chasing: Shrinking, local and international markets.
2 Rethink: What to do with loss-making sustainability activities, such as unfunded do-good initiatives.
3 Take: Tripartite perspective of stakeholders and include an external orientation.
4 Adopt: "Connected impact," the ability to demonstrate new knowledge/insight was applied in decision-making with measurable outcomes for a specific stakeholder group.
5 Change: Notion of impact to real transfer of value with economic, societal, and environmental responsibility

Organisations are grappling with integrating AI and business models into their strategies. The creative industries, such as music, are struggling with copyright issues, but

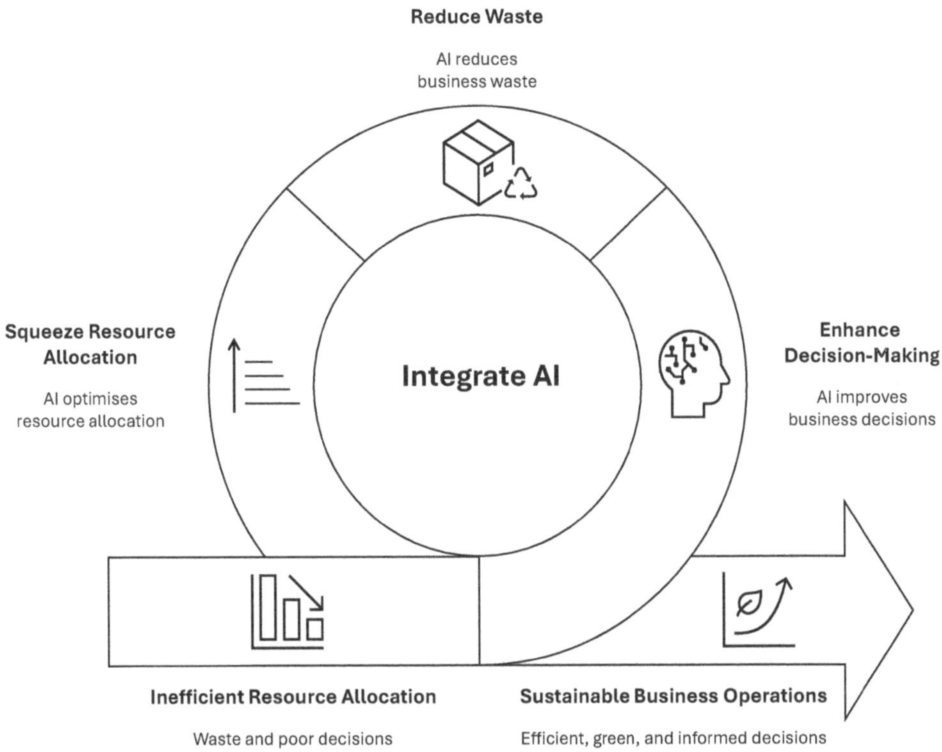

FIGURE 9.3 Artificial intelligence transforms business for sustainability

opportunities exist in the gaming industry. The use of AI has reduced the cost base, enhanced productivity, and positively affecting the bottom line.

The Chinese Tencent company uses generative AI, which speeds up the creation of video games with quicker development of three-dimensional backgrounds and scenes for games. This frees up resources and reduces budgets for game writers to write higher-quality, gripping storylines and develop game characters. Faster processes result in shorter spells between game releases, which boost revenues and share prices. AI-infused business models can also be applied to other sectors.

Conversely, universities have endured significant financial sustainability challenges and need renewal strategies. AI-infused business models present a significant opportunity for the higher education sector to redefine its relevance and impact in the commercial landscape.

By integrating AI, universities can enhance their research capabilities and drive **innovation** in delivering education, engaging with industry partners, and solving complex global challenges. AI can facilitate the development of personalised learning experiences, optimise operational efficiencies, and enable data-driven decision-making, making educational institutions more agile and responsive to ecosystem needs.

In the last two decades, impact remains one of the key challenges facing higher education. Universities have opportunities to solve sustainability challenges and identify technical solutions for organisations that don't know how to realise their return on investment (ROI). However, universities globally need business models to be constructed to realise the potential opportunities.

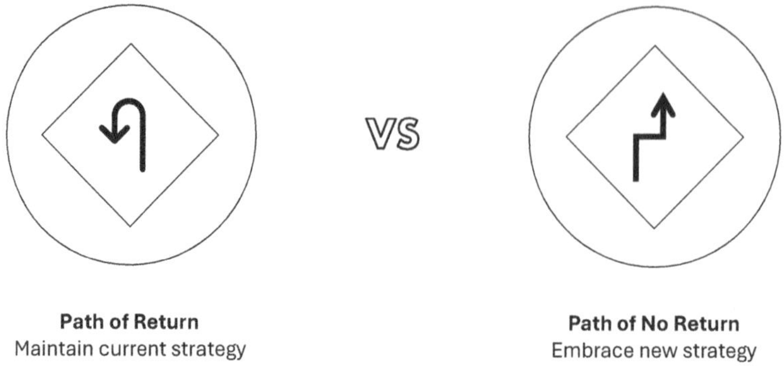

FIGURE 9.4 Choose the right path at the inflexion point

Moreover, by leveraging AI to create scalable solutions, universities can offer bespoke services to businesses and governments via executive education.

This helps them navigate the complexities of sustainability and achieve measurable ROI. Leadership teams must shape and drive end-to-end transformation across traditional boundaries within their ecosystems. This transformation requires a strategic shift in how universities conceive and implement their new business models, ensuring that AI is not just a tool but a core component of their value proposition.

The external orientation, particularly about ecosystem complexity, lies at the heart of **SSM**, which is crucial for sustainability, resilience, reputation, **innovation**, and compliance. Recently, ecosystems have become increasingly important, and this external dynamic plays a central role in **SSM**. Figure 9.4 represents a strategic inflexion point, a point of no return (Grove, 1997).

As sustainable development commences with asking and answering tough questions, the balance of forces that maintains the status quo must be broken to do things differently and not remain the same.

Sustainable business model **innovation** lies at the heart of the strategic planning exercise, as the goal is to create or reimagine a new and enhanced way of generating profit that protects people and the environment. So, business model literacy and architecting skills will be part of the CEO's toolkit, as they look to do things differently and better. Driving change across the shifting external environment necessitates a clear focus on identifying market opportunity signals that will grow the organisation.

Mini Case Study

Transforming Universities: Unlocking New Value with a Multi-Sided Business Model

Uber, the transportation and ride-sharing technology company, is well known for its multi-sided business model. The firm launched as a start-up in 2009, went public in 2019, and reported revenues of $43.98 billion in 2024.

Uber's competitive advantage stems from facilitating value exchange between passengers who need to reach their destinations and drivers who offer their vehicles for hire. Uber's business model is a platform that connects passengers and drivers as an intermediary. Then, it collects a percentage fee as revenue from each transaction.

Let us now imagine a university with a multi-sided business model. A good, innovative ecosystem will possess staff coordinating in unison, seamlessly integrating the university's mission of learning and teaching, research, and external services within its ecosystem.

This case applies this multi-sided business model to the learning and teaching mission. The value proposition approach helps to design the platform and assess stakeholders' needs.

The key elements of the proposed university's multi-sided business model for learning and teaching include the following:

1 Learners: Each higher education institution should provide an experience tailored to its target learner market. Learners benefit from a pain-free education experience and graduate with theoretical and practical knowledge to attain the standard of living they aspire to. By the end of the programme, they feel market-ready and confident about receiving a job offer from an appropriate employer. Increasing the role of universities in labour force participation is becoming progressively important.
2 Employers: Higher education institutions can offer employers convenient services for recruiting students. Nurturing ongoing mutually beneficial relationships will help employers access a strong candidate pipeline. They benefit from the platform's ease of use, lower recruitment costs, and shorter time to fill posts. The cyclic nature and ability to share resources offer both parties a superior value package.
3 University: A typical university has at least three significant challenges in pivoting towards a multi-sided business model. What is the university's value proposition? How does it create a platform that meets the needs of both learners and employers? How does it ensure that its programme portfolio fits its purposes? Starting with a value proposition approach will help shape the other two challenges. Universities' financial stability, enhanced quality, and learner outcomes are critical success factors.
4 Surge Pricing: Like Uber, which increases its prices during peak times, higher education institutions can implement a similar strategy. Job shortages in the labour market will drive up salary levels. This will increase the attractiveness of potential learners to enrol in university programmes, and the university can raise its fees accordingly.
5 Ecosystems: As ecosystems evolve, universities can become a more prominent player by influencing members and analysing not just what they're good at but what they're good for. The driving force should be to expose what they can do in terms of their value offer to constituents and be seen as a positive force for change. A primary objective is that each ecosystem member must deliver value to the target market.

Additional Benefits:

- **Network Effects:** Through network effects, the more learners register for programmes, the more attractive the platform becomes to employers, and vice versa. This self-reinforcing cycle enables a multi-sided business model to scale quickly.

- **Economies of Scale:** As the university expands, the cost per transaction decreases, enabling it to operate efficiently across its footprint, which can be local, regional, or global.
- **Value Creation:** Creating a robust value proposition will enable the university to strengthen its ability to capture value, which will be reflected in the triple bottom line of profit, people, and the planet.
- **Ecosystem Growth:** Understanding ecosystems is crucial for resilience, reputation, **innovation**, compliance, and growth. The continuous creation of partnerships will foster synergy and innovative capability.
- **Data-Driven:** A significant opportunity can arise from adopting a data analytics approach. The process should be cyclical, not linear, allowing ongoing enhancements of the multi-sided business model.

In conclusion, strategies and tactics are interdependent and should align with the overall university purpose. The multi-sided business model helps as it provides a robust approach to using heuristic **innovation** techniques to understand the salient problem and design a solution. For example, a change in purpose will lead to fresh discoveries and opportunities for all ecosystem members.

More specifically, transforming universities through an ecosystem approach will revolutionise the institution's impact by connecting learners, employers, and partners on a dynamic platform that drives revenue growth, enhances operations, and meets local skills.

Questions

1 Assume you are the CEO of a financial services bank. Outline how the multisided-platform model to connect borrowers, lenders, and financial intermediaries could work.
2 What strategic risks may emerge when universities compete as platforms rather than traditional educational institutions?
3 Assume you are the CEO of any organisation of your choice. Outline the implications of implementing "surge pricing" in your sector.

9.5 Integration of Sustainability and Business Models

Building on earlier ideas, ecosystems are giving rise to new business models that capitalise on sustainability-themed opportunities. Chapters 3 and 4 provide insights into the **SSM** phenomenon but stress that the seven schools are elements of a framework that explains the approaches to strategic management through a sustainable lens.

Individually, they can form differing dimensions to address the core of strategic management. Leadership teams can visualise the networks that are intertwined in their ecosystems. Then, business models can be formulated by mapping out operations from supply and demand perspectives that align with value propositions.

From a circular economy perspective, the integration of sustainability and business models is still relatively in its infancy. Organisations of all sizes are engaging in recycling to move from a linear takeaway economy to a circular economy. Business model adaptation plays a crucial role. For example, on the business model demand side, organisations can focus on value creation and get consumers willing to pay a higher price for recycled products and services.

Today's customers with heterogeneous preferences appear to be receptive to multiple business models, but value-for-money consumers remain a powerful group. This is particularly important given that the cost-of-living crisis may reduce consumer willingness to pay a premium for products and services.

This shift necessitates further adaptation of business models to incorporate sustainability at their core, enabling companies to reduce their environmental footprint and meet the growing demand from consumers for sustainable products and services.

For example, companies like IKEA and H&M have incorporated circular economy principles into their business models by offering products that are competitively priced, made from recycled materials, and encouraging customers to return used items for recycling or refurbishment.

Another example is Nike, with its long-term vision: creating a continuous loop without waste is the culmination of three decades of **innovation**, as seen in its Nike Grind initiative. Interestingly, Nike has recently reappointed a former executive who retired in 2020 after 32 years working at the company. This reinforces the need for the CEO to monitor key growth metrics, as well as sustainability.

Table 9.1 provides practical examples of an organisation's business model by Sustainable Development Goals (SDGs).

TABLE 9.1 SDG-themed business model

UNSDG	*Innovative Business Model*	*Example Organisation*
1 No poverty	Microfinance and mobile banking	Grameen Bank – Bangladesh
2 Zero hunger	Vertical farming and urban agriculture	AeroFarms – USA
3 Good health and well-being	Telemedicine platforms	Curoflow – Sweden
4 Quality education	Online learning platforms	Coursera – USA
5 Gender equality	Gender-lens investing	Invest Africa – Africa
6 Clean water and sanitation	Water purification technology	Pureaqua – South America
7 Affordable and clean energy	Pay-as-you-go solar energy	International Renewable Energy Agency (IRENA) – Abu Dhabi
8 Decent work and economic growth	Fair trade and ethical supply chains	Fairtrade – UK
9 Industry **innovation** and infrastructure	Circular economy	BNP Paribas Group – France
10 Reduced inequalities	Inclusive financial services	Triodos Bank – Netherlands
11 Sustainable cities and communities	Smart city technologies	InCitu – USA

(Continued)

TABLE 9.1 (Continued)

UNSDG	*Innovative Business Model*	*Example Organisation*
12 Responsible consumption and production	Sharing economy platforms	Airbnb – USA
13 Climate action	Carbon capture and utilisation	Climeworks – Zurich
14 Life below water	Sustainable fishing practices	Austral Fisheries – Australia
15 Life on land	Reforestation and ecosystem restoration	Ecosia – Germany
16 Peace, justice, and strong institutions	Green investment platform for strong institutions	Earthbanc – Sweden
17 Partnerships for the goals	Cross-sector sustainability alliances	World Business Council for Sustainable Development – Switzerland

Abbreviation: UNSDG, United Nations Sustainable Development Goal.

STRATEGY NUGGET

Jaguar Land Rover's (JLR) Strategy Bet

The Tata-owned JLR *Reimagine* strategy delivers a sustainability-rich vision of modern luxury by design.

JLR is transforming its business to achieve carbon neutrality across its supply chain, products, and operations by 2039. The company has detailed a roadmap to reduce emissions throughout its operations and value chains by 2030, utilising agreed, science-based targets.

Electrification is vital to this strategy, and before the end of the decade, the Range Rover, Discovery, and Defender lineups will each have a pure electric model. At the same time, Jaguar will **transition** to a completely electric lineup.

Fundamentally, JLR is a British company with two design and engineering sites, three vehicle manufacturing facilities, an engine manufacturing centre, and a battery assembly centre in the UK. They also have vehicle plants in China, Brazil, India, Austria, and Slovakia, as well as seven technology hubs worldwide.

JLR's aspirational transformation places the organisation in a risky position, particularly in balancing luxury with the cost pressure of electrification. Premium pricing is vital to absorb the investments in new battery technology, charging infrastructure partnerships, and supply chain decarbonisation.

Success will depend on JLR being able to differentiate its products from what the market wants.

Source: JLR (2024).

Questions

1 What are the significant risks to JLR's carbon neutrality goal by 2039, and how can this be best mitigated?
2 How should JLR prioritise its electrification timeline across its product range?
3 How can JLR ensure that it competes successfully in the electric vehicle market?

9.6 Innovative Sustainable Business Models

Changes in the global economy motivate the consumer desirability of sustainability-themed innovative products and services. Therefore, business model **innovation** is a strategic differentiator that can lead to rapid growth with healthy operating margins. In practice, this may be more complex, as organisations offer consumers choice. This is in stark contrast to Henry Ford's days, who kept choices to a minimum.

Despite the meteoric stock rises of the large technology companies, the bubble may have slowed down in terms of growth. So, while companies that enjoy AI-related benefits, the business fundamentals remain key and are subject to geopolitical and cost-of-living threats. Commentators continue to recalibrate their forecasts.

For instance, during the pandemic, affordability and value were key concerns for retailers. Many experts made pronouncements about the shape of the recovery path for different sectors. Suggestions proffered were:

What will the shape of recovery be: V, U, L, or Nike style "swoosh" shape?

- V: A quick upswing.
- U: A slower recovery for the next 18 months.
- L: Steep decline followed by slow recovery.
- I: Appears apocalyptic but should not be ignored.
- Swoosh: Downturn followed by slow up turn with GDP to surpass pre-COVID-19 levels.

Looking back, the pandemic left an indelible mark on the global economy, with specific sectors still struggling to regain their footing. The anticipated swift "V-shaped" recovery, where the economy would rebound just as quickly as it contracted, did not materialise uniformly across industries. Instead, what we are witnessing in some sectors could be better described as a "U-shaped" or even "L-shaped" recovery, where recovery is either slow or stagnating. The prolonged impact of the pandemic, coupled with ongoing economic uncertainties, a cost-of-living crisis, and supply chain disruptions, has made it difficult for certain industries to recover, particularly those highly dependent on consumer interaction or global logistics.

The hospitality and travel industries, for instance, have been severely affected. Many businesses within these sectors are still grappling with fluctuating demand, with changes in consumer behaviour and increased operational costs due to sustainability compliance issues. Marriott Hotels had to rethink its post-pandemic strategies, focusing on luxury, technology, and ESG strategy to meet new customer expectations. Similarly, the retail sector, particularly brick-and-mortar stores, has seen a slow recovery as the shift to e-commerce, accelerated by the pandemic, continues to dominate consumer preferences.

Retailers such as Macy's in the US and J.C. Penney have faced significant challenges and adopted various brick-and-mortar business models. Macy's, under its Chairman and CEO, Tony Spring, is pursuing a small-format strategy with store closures. These include, in March 2025, the 250,000-square-foot store in downtown Los Angeles. J.C. Penney seeks to maintain its store portfolio without the need to "shrink to grow." These varying strategies underscore the complex dynamics at play, where fear of ongoing economic instability intersects with the need for creativity and **innovation** to redefine business models in a post-pandemic world.

Organisations are increasingly being forced to reinvent themselves by formulating and implementing innovative, sustainable business models. However, the risk of failure can be high, so the journey needs to be carefully managed. The UNSDGs present opportunities for competitive advantage. However, observations in academic settings, business consulting, and workshops reveal a challenge in implementation deficit. Interpretation across the management team can be inconsistent with a failure to link actions with a value proposition that will create, deliver, and capture value for stakeholders.

When formulating a winning **innovation** strategy, various situations may arise. Are we looking at a piece of technology created in response to a focus on a customer need, or does the technology already exist, and the organisation is looking for a customer and an opportunity? These two contexts require differing approaches, such as the type of **innovation**.

- Product/Service: What improvements are required to existing products/services to serve customer needs better?
- New Market: Creating a product/service that enables existing tasks to be performed faster, cheaper, and better.
- Operational: Rethink existing value chain to reduce costs and waste.

Innovation and financing are closely intertwined in emerging markets, where societal challenges necessitate creative solutions and substantial financial resources. But despite an organisation pursuing a sustainability agenda, the investor wants to see strong risk-adjusted returns and social impact aligned with UNSDG.

When considering **innovation** and business models, the seminal business model canvas, developed by Alexander Osterwalder and Yves Pigneur (2010), incorporates nine blocks that cover the four main areas of business. Table 9.2 focuses on **SSM** issues that organisations need to consider within each area of the business model canvas to help guide strategic decision-making towards more sustainable business practices.

TABLE 9.2 Business model canvas, sustainability themes, and **SSM** issues

Areas	*Sustainability Theme*	***SSM** Issues*
Customer segments	Understand and segment customers based on their environmental and social values.	Communicate effectively with the end-user, and create a target offer for homogenous groups. Too often strategies are formulated with an inward focus, prioritising internal goals and perspectives over the actual needs and preferences of the end-user.
Value propositions	Craft value propositions that not only satisfy customer needs but also contribute to environmental stewardship and social equity.	Balancing sustainability with competitive advantage by designing value propositions that align with both environmental goals and market demands.
Channels	Optimise distribution channels to reduce carbon footprints and waste, while ensuring efficient delivery of products and services.	Incorporating sustainability into business model channels involves selecting and optimising distribution methods that minimise environmental impact while maintaining efficiency.

(*Continued*)

TABLE 9.2 (Continued)

Areas	*Sustainability Theme*	***SSM** Issues*
Customer relationships	Engage customers by building relationships rooted in transparency, ethical practices, and shared values around sustainability.	Building customer relationships with sustainability in mind means fostering transparency, trust, and long-term engagement by openly communicating the company's environmental and social initiatives.
Revenue streams	Develop revenue streams that are enhanced or generated through sustainable practices.	Incorporating sustainability into the revenue model requires identifying and capitalising on opportunities where sustainable practices can generate new income streams or enhance existing ones.
Key resources	Ensure that key resources are sustainably sourced, including renewable materials, ethical labour, and environmentally friendly technologies.	Key resources in a sustainable business model should prioritise renewable, ethically sourced, and environmentally friendly materials to ensure long-term viability and minimise ecological impact.
Key activities	Focus on activities that promote sustainability within the organisation's core operations.	Key activities in a sustainable business model should focus on integrating eco-friendly practices into core operations, such as adopting energy-efficient processes, reducing waste, and promoting circular economy principles.
Key partnerships	Forge partnerships with stakeholders who share a commitment to sustainability.	Key partnerships in a sustainable business model should be formed with organisations that share a commitment to environmental and social responsibility, ensuring that sustainability is embedded throughout the value chain.
Cost structure	Structure costs to support sustainable practices, balancing initial investments with long-term financial benefits.	The cost structure in a sustainable business model should account for both the short-term investments needed to implement sustainable practices and the long-term savings these practices can generate.

Abbreviations:

9.7 Strategy and Design

Design thinking can enrich the strategy process. In Chapter 2, Mintzberg's ten schools of strategy include the design school. Mintzberg's (1990) explanations are still pertinent in today's strategic planning processes. In his words, the design school strategy is "formed through a tightly controlled process of conscious human thought. Action follows, once the strategies have been fully formulated" (p. 175).

Design as a concept evolved from a purely aesthetic view to incorporate problem-solving. Consumer heterogeneity is one of the primary characteristics that differentiate successful sustainability-themed strategies. Heterogeneity in preferences necessitates tailored solutions that can inform the product or service portfolio. However, organisations today face a multifaceted landscape where sustainability challenges require inventive solutions that are both effective and efficient.

In this environment, human resources, one of the most valuable assets of any organisation, cannot be squandered. The success of sustainability initiatives depends heavily on the strategic alignment of strategy with the organisation's goals. When people-related resources are used in activities that are not strategically anchored to deliver successful outcomes, not only does the organisation miss out on the potential for breakthrough **innovations**, but it also risks losing its competitive edge in the market.

Leadership teams must recognise that, given the scarcity of resources, it is imperative to adopt a strategic approach to managing human resources too. By integrating strategy development, design methodologies, and problem-solving frameworks into their operations, organisations can ensure that their human resources are preserved and optimised for maximum impact. This careful stewardship of people-related resources drives **innovation**. It strengthens the organisation's ability to adapt and thrive in an era where sustainability is not just a goal but a necessity.

Design thinking offers tools to help the strategist with consumer-centric solutions. However, the availability of necessary guidance is lacking for the practitioner. Reflecting on the paucity of attempts to bridge the gap between strategy and design, Grimsgaard (2022), a comprehensive 650-page work, covers the foundations and more for anyone seeking help. Grimsgaard uses her design skills to simplify the strategy phenomenon. By providing a clear and actionable framework for linking design thinking to strategic processes, this work is highly relevant for time-pressed executives. The step-by-step approach can be used for the creation of innovative sustainable business models, and is illustrated in Figure 9.5.

By illustrating the difference between design attributes and corporate identity, the reader can translate knowledge from design to the problem-solving world of strategy.

Over the years, design and strategy specialists have collaborated with the client constituents and stakeholders to create a strategic plan with a truly shared vision. In some instances, the client will seek to develop a shared vision captured in a one-page infographic. Building on the strengths of the client, a values-based culture can be nurtured throughout the organisation. This illustrates the benefits of design and strategy elements, such as the following:

1 Comprehensive stakeholder involvement
2 Multi-method data collection
3 Visual facilitation and rapid reporting
4 Collaborative vision mapping.

By adopting this design-driven, participatory approach, organisations can develop a strategic plan that authentically embodies the collective aspirations of their diverse stakeholder groups. This approach will enhance the levels of buy-in from all stakeholders and also harness a wide range of interdisciplinary expertise to forge a more resilient and innovative strategy for the institution's future.

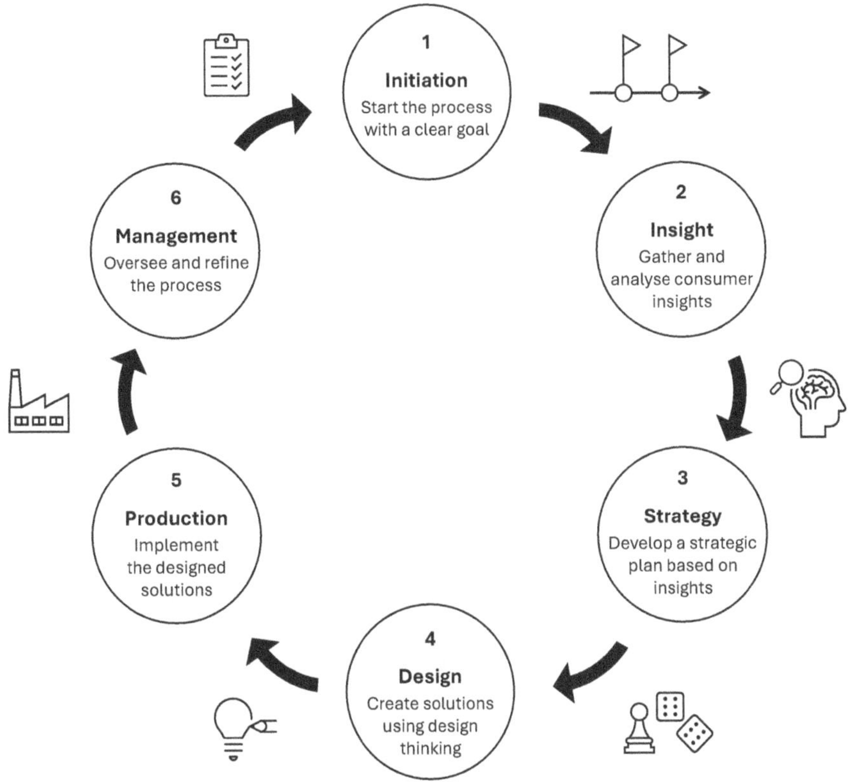

FIGURE 9.5 Design thinking and strategy cycle

Following this design-driven power approach is the IDEO design thinking framework. This human-centred approach is widely recognised and used across all industries. The design process and relevant activities are organised into the following areas:

- Empathise: Understanding the primary stakeholders' needs and activities. Deploy observations, interviews, shadowing, seek to understand, and non-judgemental mindset.
- Define: Identify the user's needs and problems activities. Understand objectives, decision-making, challenges, and constraints.
- Ideate: Challenge assumptions and create ideas activities. Workshops to share ideas, divergent and convergent mindset.
- Prototype: Create solutions. Activities involve proof of concept, mockups, and storyboards.
- Test Solutions: Activities include iteration; understanding viability, desirability, and feasibility; and reflective mindset.

This approach is structured but incorporates a flexible approach that can be applied to a broad set of sustainability challenges. This approach will encapsulate and translate findings from a quantitative to a qualitative realm to deliver an inclusive vision map for the client.

9.8 Chapter Key Takeaways

The key takeaways from Chapter 9, "Sustainable Business Model **Innovation**," are as follows:

1 **Sustainability as a Core Strategy:** Sustainable business model **innovation** requires integrating ESG objectives into the core strategic framework. This ensures that sustainability is not just a bolt-on but a central pillar of the business's operations, driving change throughout the organisation.
2 **The Circular Economy Is a Key Business Model:** The circular economy is a key concept in sustainable business models. It focuses on designing products and services that minimise waste, extend product life cycles, and regenerate natural systems. By doing so, businesses can reduce their environmental impact and tap into new cost-saving and **innovation** opportunities.
3 **Shared Value Creation:** This chapter emphasises the concept of shared value, which aligns economic value creation with social impact. By addressing societal challenges, such as environmental risks or gender inequality, businesses can unlock new sources of competitive advantage, benefiting both the company and the community.
4 **Value Proposition and Stakeholder Alignment:** Sustainable business models must create value propositions that align with both customer needs and sustainability goals. This requires engaging with stakeholders to ensure that business practices contribute to both business and social equity, thereby creating long-term value for all parties involved.
5 **Innovation and Technological Integration:** Technological advancements, especially AI, play a disruptive role in driving sustainable business models. AI can optimise resource use and improve productivity, all of which are critical for sustainability. However, businesses must also ensure that technology aligns with their sustainability goals to avoid unintended consequences.
6 **Business Model Flexibility and Resilience:** Sustainable business models need to be flexible and resilient to navigate uncertainties in market trends and environmental conditions. Organisations must be agile, adapting their operations, products, and services to evolving sustainability demands and consumer expectations.
7 **Addressing the UNSDGs:** Sustainable business model **innovation** can help organisations align with specific SDGs. From a societal perspective, strategies can be formulated and implemented that meet global sustainability challenges, such as poverty, climate action, and responsible consumption.

9.9 Self-Reflection Questions

1 What are the key elements that define a sustainable business model, and how do they differ from traditional business models?
2 How can a company identify opportunities for sustainable **innovation** within its current business model?
3 What are the potential risks and challenges associated with **transitioning** to a sustainable business model in pursuing the UNSDGs?
4 Why are ecosystems giving rise to the need for new sustainable business models?
5 What role does stakeholder engagement play in developing and implementing a sustainable business model?

References

Christensen, C., Bartman, T., Van Bever, D. and Snyder, E., (2016). The hard truth about business model innovation. *MIT Sloan Management Review, 58*(1), pp.31–40.

FT.com (2021). Danone board ousts Emmanuel Faber as chief and chairman. Available at: https://www.ft.com/content/8e7ae718-eb18-4d2f-bd18-59e6349540f2 (Accessed: 1 September 2025).

Geissdoerfer, M., Vladimirova, D. and Evans, S., (2018). Sustainable business model innovation: A review. *Journal of Cleaner Production, 198*, pp.401–416.

Grimsgaard, W., (2022). *Design and strategy: A step-by-step guide*. Routledge.

Grove, A.S. (1997). *Only the paranoid survive: How to exploit the crisis-points that challenge every company and career*. HarperCollins Business.

JLR (2024). JLR reveals honed go-to-market strategy. Available at: https://media.landrover.com/en-gb/news/2024/02/jlr-reveals-honed-go-market-strategy (Accessed: 15 January 2026).

Massa, L. and Tucci, C., (2021). Innovation and Business Models. *Oxford Research Encyclopedia of Business and Management*. Available at: from https://oxfordre.com/business/display/10.1093/acrefore/9780190224851.001.0001/acrefore-9780190224851-e-296 (Accessed: 28 August 2025).

Mintzberg, H., (1990). The design school: Reconsidering the basic premises of strategic management. *Strategic Management Journal, 11*(3), pp.171–195.

Osterwalder, A. and Pigneur, Y., (2010). *Business model generation: A handbook for visionaries, game changers, and challengers* (Vol. 1). John Wiley & Sons.

Snihur, Y. and Markman, G., (2023). Business model research: Past, present, and future. *Journal of Management Studies, 60*(8), pp.e1–e14.

Zott, C., Amit, R. and Massa, L., (2011). The business model: Recent developments and future research. *Journal of Management, 37*(4), pp.1019–1042.

10

LEVERAGING ORGANISATIONAL CULTURE FOR SUSTAINABILITY

10.1 Learning Strategy Objectives

After completing this chapter, you will be able to:

1 **Knowledge-Based Objectives:**

- Identify, apply, and deploy organisational culture to leverage sustainable advantage.
- Compare and contrast the various organisational cultures and how to create resilience in the desired corporate culture.

2 **Skill-Based Objectives:**

- Deploy a variety of managerial frameworks and tools to develop, manage, and reshape organisational culture in artificial intelligence (AI) environments.
- Critically evaluate the current organisational culture to use as a baseline for the future.

3 **Attitude-Based Objectives:**

- Avoid the fear factor in overcoming challenging organisational cultures.
- Inspire active engagement by inspiring and being a force for lasting change.

10.2 Introduction

SSM adopts a holistic perspective, which has been deconstructed throughout this book. Commentators' observations indicate that organisations tend to be isomorphic regarding structures and practices, which does not relate to the diversity of thought required. Sustainability challenges require new heuristics for successful problem-solving.

The macro-level aspirations in terms of **performance** can involve integrating sustainability throughout the organisation. At the commencement of the journey, board-level sustainability responsibilities are assigned within new procedural frameworks. However, ultimately, it's the organisation culture that can make or break success.

DOI: 10.4324/9781003516774-13

Leaders must understand the distinctions between leadership and management. Warren Bennis (1985) was often fond of saying, "The manager does things right; the leader does the right thing." This may imply that only leaders (or people who think they are leaders) are capable of or in a position to do the right (appropriate) thing, and that managers who serve them are merely capable of ensuring compliance within disciplined processes and not involved in refocusing organisational purpose. This shapes the organisational approach to sustainability.

Through my work with organisational leaders, I have found that the most successful transformational projects occur when culture is a driving force rather than a barrier to change. The necessity for a healthy organisational culture is obvious to any CEO when competing in the sustainability marketplace. But contextualisation is everything.

The well-known saying that culture eats strategy for breakfast has been proven time and again. Sustainability requires transforming the physical aspects of production systems and the attitudes of stakeholders. Jaganjac, Hansen, Lunde, and Hunnes (2024) contend that to implement sustainability projects effectively, a malleable structure and a green organisational culture grounded in a shared sustainability vision are essential. So, what is culture in this context?

UNESCO defines culture "as the set of distinctive spiritual, material, intellectual and emotional features of society or a social group, that encompasses, not only art and literature, but lifestyles, ways of living together, value systems, traditions, and beliefs" (UNESCO, 2001:3).

Building on this foundation, it is challenging to consider a more substantial and more impactful organisational dynamic to manage during any change programme.

A deeper examination of the epistemological frameworks of organisational cultures offers powerful insights. Yet, the knowledge of why it acts as a blockage remains embryonic in the academic literature (Assoratgoon, and Kantabutra, 2023). What we do know is that Schein's (1985) three multi-layered cultural framework of underlying assumptions and beliefs, norms and values, and artefacts shapes organisational behaviour. However, few researchers have considered how culture impacts the implementation process during sustainability processes (Jaganjac, Hansen, Lunde, and Hunnes, 2024). O'Reilly, Cao, and Sull (2024) call for a unified approach to understanding the relationship between organisational culture and **performance**.

Using four perspectives of ethics and responsibility (UNGC, 2022), strategic management (Baumgartner, and Rauter, 2017), systems perspective (Williams, Kennedy, Philipp, and Whiteman, 2017), and paradox theory (Hahn, Figge, Pinkse, and Preuss, 2018) illuminate a multi-layered cultural understanding. However, understanding of the deeper cultural levels is lacking in theory and practice.

Experiences suggest that it is not time to "bet the farm," with large-scale organisational change programmes becoming choked by self-inflicted legacy approaches (see Figure 10.1) prima facie, the traditional approach to strategy formulation and strategic planning provides a vision for the future. A plethora of points are observed, but three points are prominent:

- Leaders and their followers do not like uncertainty and cannot see round corners.
- Discursive approaches for internal communication messages get lost in the corporate noise, so followers do not see the tangible benefits.
- The mediating role of culture on the effect of **SSM** implementation is nascent.

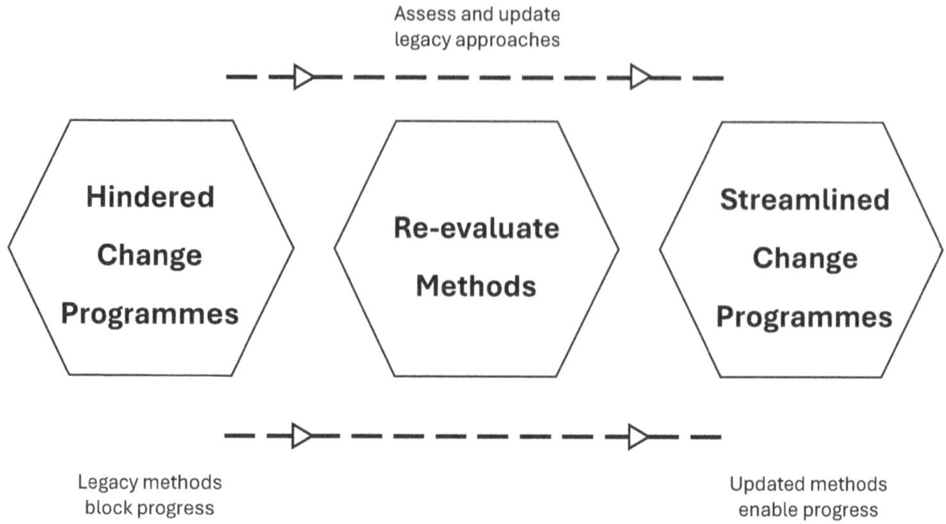

FIGURE 10.1 Overcoming legacy systems

Moreover, identifying critical bottlenecks assumes that there are clear-cut problems with straightforward solutions, like a puzzle. However, in complex institutional settings, challenges often arise from interconnected systems and multifaceted issues. Identifying bottlenecks requires a deep understanding of the underlying causes and the ability to address root causes rather than merely treating cultural symptoms with habitus effects, which can slow down change.

Despite recognising the imperative for sustainability, many organisations encounter implementation deficits due to various challenges, including resistance to change, competing priorities, and resource constraints. This is where **SSM** approaches can help. Yet, staff outside the C-suite may not be involved in strategic planning, so they lack exposure to or understanding of it. And yet, sustainability considerations require internal stakeholder involvement (information and ideas) and commitment to plans/strategies.

Organisational culture should be viewed as a behavioural process that involves staff at all levels. For instance, they understand boundary-spanning roles, which refer to positions within an organisation that operate at the interface between different departments, functions, or stakeholders, effectively bridging the gap between them.

These roles are essential for facilitating communication, collaboration, and coordination across organisational boundaries. Boundary spanners act as intermediaries or liaisons, facilitating the flow of information, resources, and ideas between different parts of the organisation or between the organisation and external stakeholders.

They play a vital role in breaking down silos, fostering cross-functional collaboration, and promoting **innovation**. By bridging internal and external boundaries, boundary spanners help organisations respond effectively to changing market conditions, customer needs, and competitive pressures.

In this chapter, we explore the critical role that organisational culture plays in shaping sustainable strategic initiatives. At the heart of any successful sustainability endeavour lies a culture that champions **innovation**, ethical conduct, and a steadfast dedication to long-term environmental protection and social responsibility.

This chapter delves into the various dimensions of organisational culture, examining how leaders can cultivate an environment that fosters innovative behaviours, creativity, risk-taking, and continuous improvement in pursuit of sustainability goals. By fostering a culture that values sustainability at its core, organisations can align their actions with their values, engendering a sense of purpose and collective commitment among employees. Change management strategies for successful implementation are also addressed, considering the many cases of reported implementation deficits.

10.3 Competing Values Framework

Cultural values can act as a stimulus for sustainability initiatives by shaping stakeholders' perceptions, behaviours, and interactions with nature. They help determine priorities and goals, leading to cultural perceptiveness that enhances the effectiveness and inclusivity of sustainability strategy. Differing praxis will help to overcome limitations in knowledge.

Our analysis reveals that organisational culture is a source of stimulation for stakeholders to display agreed-upon behaviours. Sustainability practices in the absence of a supporting culture will fail to deliver the necessary outcomes.

An integrating framework should encompass leadership, organisational culture, and strategy, and incorporate the different mixes of paradoxes and contradictions in the delivery of the desired state. As an organisation's needs evolve, additional values and expectations emerge, which create a complex terrain for institutional change. Approaches are needed that can help leaders at all levels navigate and address these ubiquitous challenges. Cameron and Quinn's (2011) Competing Values Framework (CVF) has stood the test of time with slight variations.

CVF comprises two dimensions. The horizontal axis shows the attention of the organisation, internal or external. The vertical axis portrays the organisation's level of flexibility – flexible or stable. Table 10.1 illustrates the four cultural quadrants and their corresponding cultural implications for gamification strategies.

By aligning gamification strategies with the CVF, organisations can effectively leverage diverse cultural strengths to foster a dynamic and cohesive work environment.

The matrix model is extremely useful for understanding the cultural shift necessary to develop and apply sustainability practices. A significant feature is its ability to locate an organisation or individual in terms of its current and preferred positions within the matrix, to consider the nature of the required journey, and the variables that need to be managed.

During conversations with CEOs, it is necessary to consider the organisational culture, governance, context, knowledge, skills, and mindsets that are required to play a winning (successful) game within a dynamic context. Figure 10.2 illustrates that two major dimensions are often identified: the "old" (current) and the "new" (emergent) games in the pursuit of realising sustainability value as it shifts from being a good to requiring contextual realisation and the delivery of measurable value.

Both games can be played to deliver high levels of value. However, the old way focuses on an internal (closed) approach without considering that sustainability practice is **transitioning** from a producer-led strategy towards a (more open) customer-focused approach whose goal is to deliver external and measurable impact.

TABLE 10.1 CVF and implications for gamification strategies

CVF Quadrant	*Cultural Focus*	*Gamification Strategies*
Clan culture	Collaboration and teamwork	**Team-Based Challenges:** Encourage collaboration through team goals and peer recognition. **Peer Recognition:** Use badges and points to recognise and reward teamwork and support.
Adhocracy culture	**Innovation** and flexibility	**Innovation Incentives:** Reward creativity with points for new ideas or solutions. **Exploratory Challenges:** Design tasks that encourage experimentation and risk-taking.
Market culture	Competitiveness and achievement	**Leaderboards and Competition:** Implement competitive elements like leaderboards to motivate high **performance.** **Performance Metrics:** Use gamified metrics to align individual achievements with organisational goals.
Hierarchy culture	Structure and control	**Structured Progression:** Use levels or tiers to reflect hierarchical advancement, providing clear pathways for growth. **Rule-Based Challenges:** Emphasise adherence to procedures through structured challenges.

Abbreviation: CVF, Competing Values Framework.

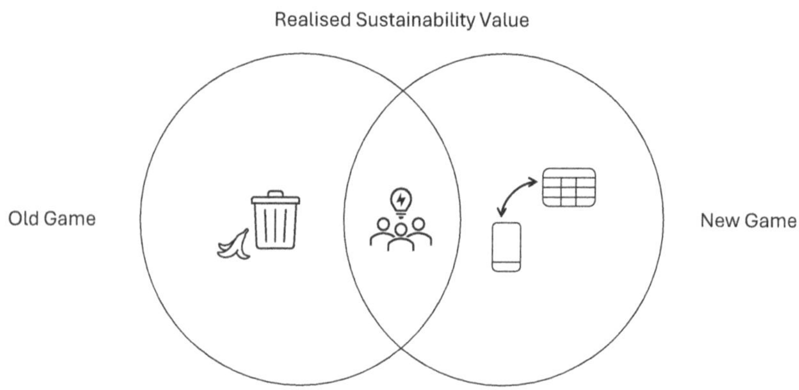

FIGURE 10.2 The delivery of measurable value

This indicates that organisations should understand their cultural profile and how it aligns with sustainability aspirations and cultivate subcultures to fill gaps. The challenge of implementing sustainable company values into everyday practice is not straightforward, and a lack of appropriate culture can be a barrier to the journey.

When considering organisational culture adaptation to the emerging sustainability ecosphere, the old ways of doing things no longer apply. In previous consulting engagements, the resulting old and new ways are dependent on the shared cultural perception of how "games" change when players choose to introduce new practices that change the nature of the game being played.

Interest in gamification has risen, as it enables organisations to design better, implement, and manage new practices (Robson et al., 2015). Industries such as financial services have been doing this for years, as higher sales levels result in bonuses. Now, with digital technologies, game-like experiences can create monetary and non-monetary benefits for stakeholders. In their conclusion, Robson et al. (2015) draw upon five summary guidelines:

- Understand the nature of the game.
- Identify the different roles.
- Gaming the game.
- Alter and change the experience.
- Identify the endgame for the game.

Gamification can be a key strategy to enhance staff and user engagement. Apps have been deployed in many organisations, including Nike and Duolingo, to create a dynamic and interactive approach to pivot culture. Incentivising target groups by keeping track of points in a competitive context can be inspirational. Leaderboards can help employees strive for excellence and continuous improvement in desired behaviours. However, maintaining the balance between competition and collaboration is vital.

10.4 SSM and Organisational Culture Challenges

The Sustainable Strategic Management journey needs to fuse with the organisation's aspirations. Throughout this book, various sustainability issues are characterised by organisational culture upheaval. Figure 10.3 uses the evolution of the butterfly to illustrate how the organisation must evolve. The necessary cultural change among the actors can act as

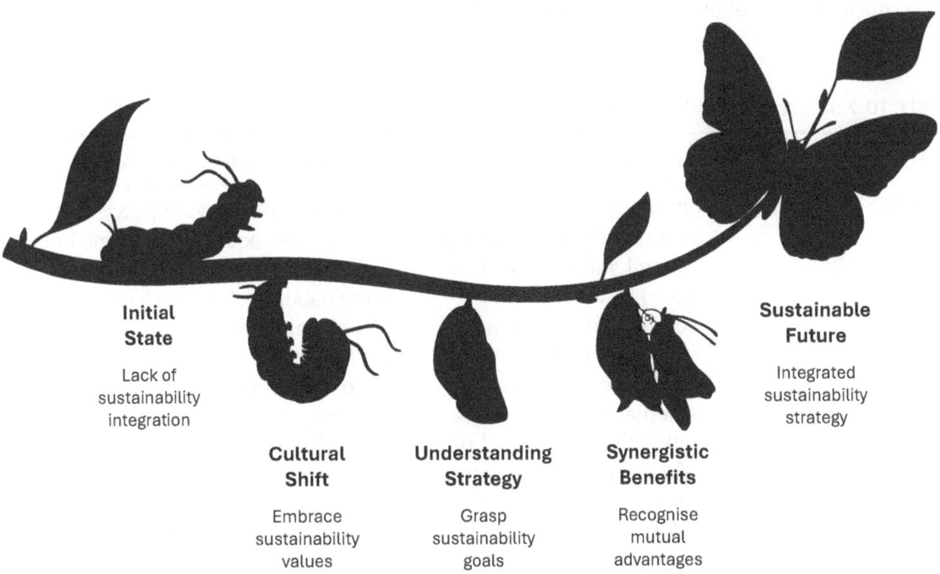

FIGURE 10.3 Embedding sustainability

a driver to support the sustainability strategy process. Otherwise, staff may not understand the sustainability strategy and the synergistic benefits for the organisation.

Integrating sustainability and culture is a critical issue for an organisation to attain its aspirations. In this context, organisations have become active in vocalising their communication messages to strengthen their ability to deliver on sustainability commitments.

Enabling culture will depend upon the external environment and the CEO's personal and world beliefs. This will shape the sustainability discourse. With business as usual no longer an option. A priority is to build adaptive capacity, foster a culture of **innovation** and creativity, and be responsive to changing circumstances, spotting emerging opportunities faster than their peer group. Nevertheless, it is incumbent upon the CEO to grapple with this, but why do strategies fall short in differentiating their offer?

In this perilous context, resistance to change and further blockages created by organisational culture necessitate investment in human capital to deliver quality higher education. Addressing resistance, fostering **innovation** and creativity, and promoting buy-in and engagement are critical for successfully implementing strategic initiatives.

However, the challenges faced in this process must be acknowledged and addressed effectively. By engaging end-users, adapting to the changing macro and micro economic landscapes, optimising resource allocation, managing change, and aligning with regulations, firms can overcome these challenges and navigate the complex landscape of strategic planning.

Cultural hardware, such as tangible items and physical elements, and cultural software, including intangible items like customs and norms, must be integrated to create a high-performing culture. Some organisations look to create biophilic workplaces to represent a physical manifestation of organisational culture. The workspace will reflect biophilic design principles, incorporating natural elements to reduce environmental impact and display alignment with the built environment. Another benefit is the positive impact on mental and emotional well-being. This, in turn, can help reduce staff turnover.

The effects of culture reach far beyond the strategy per se. Table 10.2 illustrates the integration of the seven schools of **SSM** with the CVF.

TABLE 10.2 Integration of the seven schools of **SSM** with the CVF

***SSM** School*	*Core Culture Issues*	*How to Overcome the Challenge*
Traditional strategic management	Culture focuses on hierarchy and stability, emphasising control and efficiency. Resistance to integrating sustainability as a core strategy persists.	Shift to a flexible leadership style that incorporates both top-down and bottom-up approaches. Provide training on sustainability's strategic value to align traditional goals with emerging societal and environmental expectations.
Corporate social responsibility (CSR)	Often perceived as an external compliance task rather than an integral part of the organisation, leading to superficial adoption.	Embed CSR into core organisational values by aligning it with the Clan and Adhocracy cultures, emphasising collaboration, shared purpose, and **innovation**. Engage employees and stakeholders in co-creating CSR initiatives to ensure buy-in and deeper integration.

(*Continued*)

TABLE 10.2 (Continued)

***SSM** School*	*Core Culture Issues*	*How to Overcome the Challenge*
Environmental sustainability	Green strategies may face cultural pushback due to their perceived high cost and operational disruptions, especially in market-focused cultures prioritising profit.	Foster Adhocracy by encouraging experimentation with green initiatives, highlighting long-term cost savings and brand advantages. Leadership should model commitment to environmental goals and incentivise sustainable practices across all departments.
Social **innovation** and inclusive business	Resistance to change in hierarchical cultures, where traditional power structures may obstruct inclusivity and social **innovation**.	Adopt a participative leadership style aligned with Clan culture to build trust and collaboration. Develop mentorship programmes and training to empower employees at all levels to contribute to inclusive and innovative initiatives.
Circular economy	Lack of alignment in market and hierarchy cultures where short-term profitability and rigid systems dominate, delaying circular strategies.	Introduce flexible processes within hierarchical systems to pilot circular practices. Build partnerships across functions (Adhocracy) and provide incentives for implementing circular economy projects, highlighting their potential for market differentiation and resilience.
Innovation and disruption	Fear of instability in hierarchical cultures and over-focus on immediate outputs in market cultures, limiting openness to disruptive **innovations.**	Create an Adhocracy-focused environment that celebrates calculated risks and experimentation. Establish cross-functional teams to test disruptive ideas and implement systems for iterative feedback and continuous learning.
Global South perspectives	Disregard for unique cultural and socioeconomic contexts, leading to misaligned strategies. Market-driven organisations may undervalue these perspectives.	Develop culturally sensitive strategies by fostering Clan culture's emphasis on inclusivity and shared purpose. Collaborate with local stakeholders and engage in knowledge exchange to ensure relevance and resonance with local needs and challenges.

10.5 Building a Sustainability-Driven Organisational Culture

When considering a sustainability-driven organisation culture, short-, medium-, and long-term perspectives are vital. The process should be transformative and requires active participation and commitment throughout the organisation. The emphasis needs to look beyond feel-good eco-friendly practices and embed sustainability into everyday practices.

A growing stream of publications in recent years has focused on the components that create a high-performing, sustainable form. Drawing on the management literature, Costa and Opare (2025) explain how organisations with strong corporate cultures that incorporate **innovation**, teamwork, and technology orientation enhance environmental **performance**. Efficient resource management practices can enhance sustainable

performance (Wang, Zhang, and Xu, 2022). Adopting a broader global supply chain lens, Osei, Papadopoulos, Acquaye, and Stamati (2023) found a positive relationship between organisational capital and external integration and sustainable supply chain **performance**.

A recurring theme in this book is that organisations first define clear sustainability goals and integrate them into their mission, values, and **SSM** processes. To help accelerate these processes, knowledge is key. With the proliferation of available heuristic consulting models, the hallmark of a successful global organisation remains the ability to identify, acquire, codify, capture, and reuse knowledge effectively and globally at a generic level, with local adaptation for different cultural contexts.

This ability ensures that in-house teams apply logical, systemic approaches to deliver value from sustainable problem identification and solution generation. This can be supported by front-end standard operating procedures to ensure buy-in through expectation management and project management skills. These can be adapted to traditional and now digital environments. The step-by-step guide can help staff comprehend complex routine operations. They deliver additional benefits by reducing miscommunication and assisting organisations to comply with increasingly sustainable and economic, social, and governance (ESG)–regulated environments.

The senior leadership team needs to display collaborative leadership skills to cope with its difficult cultures, systems, and behaviours. Relationships can be complex, which increases scope, risk and politics throughout the organisation. But the connectivity between individuals, organisations, and places is the lifeblood of the ecosystem. Fostering a culture of sustainability will necessitate transcending silos and deep-rooted behaviours. Collaborative leadership involves demonstrating both hard and soft skills, with trust at the epicentre. Open channels of communication, with transparency, can surmount some of the complexities of organisational culture. This can enrich the seamless exchange of ideas across the ecosystem.

Large organisations have come under scrutiny regarding the diffusion of culture, with subcultures emerging in various parts of the organisation. While sustainability may be viewed as a fad or a trend within organisations, new graduates who work in sustainability positions tend to possess key characteristics that include offering solutions in trendy or modern packages superficially influenced by the media. Such solutions can be the product where fad meets modernity, providing what appears to be curated and simplified products/services for a niche customer.

Additionally, the so-called "gig" economy, which often features employees with limited career progression, no succession planning, and "bottled" employee engagement, alongside short role cycles, will profoundly impact the organisation's transformation programme. Human resource managers in such a climate have a tough job, trying to engrain a new culture. Significant changes in traditional employment structures and changing lifestyle dynamics can lead to disengagement and a lack of continuity in crucial roles.

Sustainability professionals working on long-term projects may still face limited job security, which can hinder their ability to influence strategy. The dilution of influence develops and implements long-term sustainability initiatives. Projects requiring extended timelines, such as achieving carbon neutrality or **transitioning** to a circular economy, may suffer from high turnover and fragmented oversight. In times of transformation, human resources need to create flexible and meaningful engagement strategies. Otherwise, the movement of young talent between organisations will lead to the fragmentation of knowledge, making it harder to develop approaches over various time horizons (see Table 10.3).

TABLE 10.3 Cultural short-term, medium-term, and long-term key themes

Time Horizon	*Key Cultural Focus Areas*	*Strategies and Actions*	*Expected Cultural Outcomes*
Short-term	Sustainability mindset Leadership models with desired behaviours Cultural awareness and alignment	Develop and communicate a sustainability-focused vision, mission, and values. Create professional development opportunities for senior leadership in collaboration and trust-building. Launch internal communication campaigns to align employees with sustainability goals.	A shared understanding of sustainability across the organisation. Leadership alignment with cultural goals and norms.
Medium-term	Sustainability in subcultures Breaking down silos and fostering collaboration	Integrate sustainability principles into team and individual-level practices and subcultures. Establish cross-departmental initiatives to encourage collaboration and knowledge sharing. Use gamification and recognition programmes to incentivise desired cultural behaviours.	Subcultures aligned with overarching sustainability goals. Enhanced collaboration and knowledge exchange. Higher levels of trust.
Long-term	Enduring cultural transformation Institutionalising a culture of learning and adaptability	Codify sustainability practices into organisational SOPs and policies. Develop adaptive frameworks to address evolving sustainability challenges. Create feedback loops to continually refine cultural practices.	An organisational culture fully integrated with sustainability. Continuous cultural and operational improvement. Organisational culture is a key organisational asset.

Abbreviation: SOPs, Standard Operating Procedures.

10.6 Ethics

In a sustainability context, ethical issues may arise and be addressed by law. The once-commonly stated comment that ethics begins where the law ends is now blurred. The basis for distinguishing between right and wrong in any given situation is the values of the organisation. These values, which form an important constituent of the organisation's ethical system, are embedded in its brand and culture and are the manifestation of a system of artefacts, beliefs, and norms that the organisation considers right or wrong.

To set the scene in terms of what matters to working adults, the Institute of Business Ethics' (IBE) Our Ethics at Work (2024) survey is analysed. Each year, the IBE surveys a sample of working adults in different countries. In their 2024 survey, the sample included over 12,000 working adults in 16 countries.

For this, the focus is on Section 1 of the IBE report on organisational culture. The research study sought to understand employee perceptions of various ethic issues, using a scale ranging from acceptable to completely unacceptable.

Some key insights include:

1 How acceptable are these ethically questionable practices?

The first question contained a list of things that occur in the workplace. The most unacceptable behaviour was sexual advances towards a colleague (91%), and the other end of the scale was using the company's printer to print personal items (53%). Differing demographic groups viewed scenarios differently. Older colleagues, 55+, were less likely to find each of the eight actions acceptable. This contrasted with younger staff (18–34).

2 Is honesty practised at work?

The 2024 global average was 84%, with 80% of employees reporting that honesty is always or frequently practised. Interestingly, India scored the highest (91%), with the Netherlands lowest (77%). The USA and the UK scored 85% and 83%, respectively.

3 Do employees feel pressured to compromise their organisation's standards of behaviour?

The main observation was that around one in seven employees feel compelled to compromise on ethical behaviour. Again, India came top with 36% feeling pressurised. The UK and Germany scored the lowest at 9%.

4 Sources of pressure to compromise ethics.

Fifteen per cent of employees felt pressure to comply with ethical standards. The evidence suggests that the pressure originates from above, with indications that the problems are systemic and not easily fixable.

5 How common is awareness of misconduct at work?

Twenty-five per cent of employees reported being aware of misconduct at work. India (41%) scored the highest, with the UK and Germany (9%) scoring the lowest.

STRATEGY NUGGET

Patagonia: Unwavering Commitment to Sustainability

The US Patagonia's strong environmental culture aligns with its purpose and enables it to implement its ambitious sustainability strategies.

The founder, Yvon Chouinard, established a culture with environmental protection at its core, not as an adjacent consideration. The development of the culture includes analysing the company's hiring practices that prioritise environmental passion over industry experience, to its "Let My People Go Surfing" flexible work policy that connects employees with nature.

The strategic implications of Patagonia is how this culture enables the company to make counterintuitive business decisions that strengthened their market position: the "Don't Buy This Jacket" campaign that increased sales while discouraging consumption, their **transition** to 100% organic cotton despite initial supply challenges, and ultimately their decision to contribute all profits to environmental causes through the Patagonia Purpose Trust structure.

Questions

1. Perform an internal and external analysis of Patagonia to ascertain how the company's founder's values of profit do not have to come at a cost have been so successfully implemented.
2. Using Patagonia's annual reports, explain the importance of value chain analysis to its success. Critically discuss how it can enhance organisational processes' effectiveness and create a competitive advantage. Use examples to illustrate your answers.
3. With the growing influence of sustainability in strategic management, critically discuss how the CEO can successfully "Leveraging Organisational Culture for Sustainability." Illustrate your answer with examples from this chapter.

The findings of the IBE 2024 **Ethics at Work survey** reveal illuminating insights about the ethical nuances of workplace culture, which will have profound implications for fostering sustainability-driven organisational cultures.

The underlying philosophy of sustainability is the alignment of an organisation's ethical foundation with its long-term ESG. These survey results highlight the disparities in the ethical context across demographics and geographies. The common thread seems to be that a one-size-fits-all approach to culture may be insufficient. Human resource managers need to comprehend how corporate learning works.

For example, the generational divide in the acceptability of certain workplace behaviours underscores the need for nuanced strategies that address differing values and priorities. While younger employees may be more tolerant of minor ethical lapses, sustainability initiatives will require a rigid ethical framework.

The high levels of awareness of workplace misconduct in some countries, such as India, reveal regional variations in cultural challenges. These need to be investigated, as it may be due to India possessing higher levels of regulation and reporting expectations, which can highlight more breaches.

10.7 Cultural Issues in Emerging Regions: Overcoming Historical and Structural Legacies

This chapter has established that culture plays a central role in shaping the sustainability trajectories of firms. However, it can often present substantial impediments to transformative change. Many organisations operate under legacy systems where established practices and routines dominate decision-making. Such cultural inertia hampers the delivery of sustainability initiatives. For instance, organisational cultures steeped in hierarchical structures often fail to engage middle management and employees in meaningful ways.

A lack of inclusive dialogue within the organisation exacerbates this resistance. Decision-making is frequently top-down, with leadership imposing sustainability goals without involving other stakeholders in the process. As a result, employees may view these initiatives as externally driven mandates rather than shared organisational values.

At a regional level, cultural encounters can be deeply intertwined with historical legacies. Postcolonial societies, such as those in the Caribbean, still suffer from the indelible mark on their cultural and economic structures. Such structures, designed during colonial times to serve outsider powers, have created systemic resistance to new, locally driven economic paradigms. This will severely impact the ability to empower local communities, leading to a continued reliance on imported knowledge systems and practices. This can be at the expense of indigenous **innovation** and entrepreneurship.

Unfortunately, one of the cultural legacies persists in the power dynamics that continue to prevail in Caribbean societies. These practices remain deeply rooted in the plantation economy. Over the centuries, affluence and authority were concentrated in the hands of the privileged elite. These actions have cultivated an ingrained culture of a top-down management style.

Subsequently, the voices of indigenous communities and small-scale entrepreneurs are often not heard. Continued suppression will not only suppress **innovation** and growth but also perpetuate economic and social inequality. Governments in the region often call for assistance in creating a roadmap to achieve sustainable development.

Colonial history informs us that a deep-rooted mindset of dependency exists, wherein external source expertise is favoured over the development of local capabilities. For instance, the majority of business school curricula consist of Western tools and frameworks. Such models fail to reflect the unique social, cultural, and economic contexts of emerging regions.

This over-dependence on external frameworks undermines the development of locally adaptive solutions and perpetuates a cycle of economic sluggishness. The Caribbean's reliance on monoculture exports and tourism, both remnants of colonial economic strategies, further underscores the need for a cultural shift toward diversified and sustainable economic models.

10.8 Ethical Misalignments and the Role of Organisational Culture

Now, considering **transitioning** to ethical considerations, internal conflicts may arise when deploying frameworks due to systemic pressures. They may create transgressions that impede sustainability efforts, bringing them to the same level of importance as economic key **performance** indicators (KPIs). However, anecdotal evidence during conversations tends to suggest they are frequently espoused rather than actionable.

Vulnerable organisations may struggle to balance competing stakeholder priorities. In general, firms may promote commitments to environmental sustainability. However, the strategic narrative may include simultaneously engaging in practices that prioritise downsizing and cost-cutting tactical approaches over ecological preservation.

At the regional level, ethical misalignments are evident. The Caribbean's economic and social policies are shaped by external influences, including international financial institutions that provide capital for sustainable development projects. CFOs managing this workload may prioritise profitability over local development to repay the principal and meet interest payments.

In the eyes of some, this dynamic perpetuates a culture of exploitation, where the needs of local communities are subordinated to the interests of global financial markets. However, it is a challenge to move beyond the deep entrenchment of historical and structural legacies that shape both organisational and regional cultures.

Legacy practices create blockages, which slow down the transformation project. Many organisations in the Caribbean operate with structures and processes that were designed decades ago. CEOs and their teams are often resistant to change, as they are deeply entrenched in the current organisational DNA.

Regionally, the Caribbean's colonial history has left behind a complex web of social, economic, and cultural dependencies that continue to influence its development trajectory. The plantation economy, which prioritised wealth extraction for external powers, created a legacy of centralised economic management and resource dependency.

To overcome these challenges, both organisations and regions must adopt a new cultural paradigm that prioritises sustainability and ethical responsibility. This transformation is not without its challenges, as it requires significant shifts in mindsets, structures, and practices. However, by addressing the cultural issues outlined above, organisations and regions can pave the way for more sustainable and equitable futures by exploiting opportunities.

10.9 Future of Culture

This chapter has explored some of the organisational cultural landscape. A deeper examination reveals several key factors driving culture, but most have involved looking into the rearview mirror. Significantly, coping with tomorrow's uncertainties will involve a reset of organisational culture to align it with the necessary **innovation** and adaptive capabilities (Smith and Cox-Smith, 2023).

According to the Chartered Institute of Personnel and Development (2020), a key attribute of creating a supportive environment is organisational learning. In their research, they found that 98% of learning and development practitioners aim to foster a positive learning culture. This may appear to be obvious, but given current practice, is easily forgotten. Companies must invest considerable sums in today's and tomorrow's practice.

Conversation starters can challenge the juxtaposition of the current record profits within the banking sector against deteriorating progress towards the UNSDGs. Culture does not form part of the UNSDGs and is only mentioned in some cases as an indicator. However, looking to the future, with sustainability no longer a separate initiative, it needs to integrate seamlessly into the organisational DNA, highlighting how **SSM** practices must evolve alongside cultural transformation.

For instance, organisational culture will become more inclusive to members within its ecosystem. Effective governance models that incorporate diverse perspectives on sustainability will be implemented during strategic and tactical processes. Stakeholders will be brought in at the inception stage, rather than being presented with a case, after the strategy formulation stage. We are witnessing boards and major shareholders taking proactive stances in being involved in strategy making.

Balancing future desires will involve considerations of long-term impacts on future generations. The organisational culture has to ensure intergenerational equity. Executives need to deploy forecasting tools that can be interwoven with **SSM** assumptions to align practice with their cultural profiles.

Throughout this book, the importance of balancing **innovation** with human needs and within planetary boundaries is emphasised. With the rapid advancement of Gen AI, tomorrow's culture will involve a more nuanced approach that considers human well-being and ecological limits. This has to work in tandem with profit and growth outcomes.

Mini Case Study

Seven Myths of Organisational Culture in Sustainability Strategy Development

During consulting engagements, I've observed several myths that create harm when organisations develop and pursue their sustainability strategies (see Figure 10.4).

The following section explores each myth and provides practical approaches to overcome them:

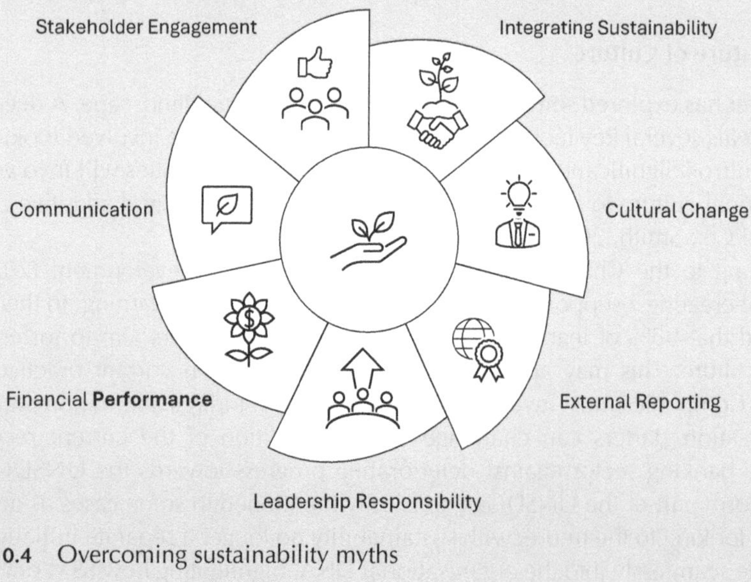

FIGURE 10.4 Overcoming sustainability myths

Myth 1: Sustainability is separate from core business strategy

Organisations still treat sustainability as a siloed initiative disconnected from their main business-as-usual operations. This creates internal pressure points for resource allocation.

Overcoming this myth:

- Fuse sustainability metrics with strategic planning processes and business KPIs.
- Strengthen the business case by quantifying both risks (regulatory, reputational) with opportunities (cost savings, market differentiation).
- Include sustainability goals in the leadership team's **performance** evaluations.

Myth 2: Cultural change requires a complete transformation

Leaders often believe that breakthrough, organisational-wide change is always necessary, making the task seem overwhelming for its staff.

Overcoming this myth:

- Position targeted interventions in high-impact areas rather than attempting to do everything.
- Enhance existing cultural strengths that align with sustainability values.
- Look for low-hanging fruit for visible "quick wins" to demonstrate progress and build momentum.

Myth 3: External reporting is sufficient for sustainability

Many organisations miss the opportunities to meet external reporting requirements rather than drive internal change.Overcoming this myth:

- The chief sustainable officer (CSO) should lead in evolving staff mindsets from compliance-focused to value creation.
- Include external reporting metrics with the organisational dashboard to drive operational improvements within a sustainability lens.
- Incorporate strategy feedback loops to strengthen strategic decision-making.

Myth 4: Top leadership team is solely responsible

Sustainability is often viewed as the exclusive responsibility of the C-suite or dedicated sustainability professionals. Overcoming this myth:

- Establish cross-functional sustainability committees with representatives from all business units at various levels.

- Empower sustainability champions to lead, contribute ideas, and take ownership of initiatives.
- Recognise and reward new staff for their ideas expressed during the recruitment process by creating experiments.

Myth 5: Sustainability conflicts with financial performance

Conversations within the organisation persist in the belief that environmental and social goals necessarily come at the expense of financial returns.

Overcoming this myth:

- Deliver workshops highlighting case studies of organisations showing that sustainability and financial success are not mutually exclusive.
- Use in-house integrated reporting outputs to link and show connections between sustainability and value creation.
- Focus initial efforts on initiatives with clear return on investment.

Myth 6: One-off communication campaigns are sufficient

Organisations often rely on occasional messaging rather than embedding sustainability into everyday core communication.

Overcoming this myth:

- Develop a consistent, ongoing communication-inspired narrative connecting sustainability to company purpose and values.
- Create multiple channels for two-way dialogue about sustainability challenges and solutions throughout the organisation.
- Make sustainability visible in daily operations through visual cues, newsletters, regular updates, and team discussions.

Myth 7: External stakeholders are less important than internal ones

Organisations sometimes focus exclusively on internal culture within their closed world, without adequately engaging external stakeholders.

Overcoming this myth:

- Identify members of the organisational ecosystem and develop tailored engagement strategies for each group.
- Establish deep partnerships with hard-to-reach community organisations.
- Use transparent feedback mechanisms to incorporate stakeholder perspectives alongside strategy development and implementation processes.

Questions

1. How should the CEO balance internal culture development with external stakeholder engagement to create a sustainability strategy that moves the organisation momentum forward?
2. Using appropriate academic literature, critically evaluate one of the seven myths, and suggest the key action you would take, and why it would work.
3. Identify the main stakeholders who are heavily influenced by organisational culture. Describe what their stake is in the business and outline three actions you should take.

10.10 Chapter Key Takeaways

Key takeaways from Chapter 10 on Leveraging Organisational Culture for Sustainability include:

1. **Culture Determines Sustainability Success:** The well-worn phrase "culture eats strategy for breakfast" underscores the importance of culture in sustainability transformations. CEOs that can create strong cultures incorporating **innovation** and shared values demonstrate higher levels of **performance**. Sustainability-themed projects without a supportive culture will fail to deliver the outcomes.
2. **CVF:** The CVF offers users a practical diagnostic to help understand the current cultural positioning. The internal/external focus is useful for creating a baseline for targeted sustainability interventions.
3. **Cultural Transformation Requires a Multi-Horizon Perspective:** The importance of designing a cultural change across distinct timeframes. Short term (sustainability mindset, leadership models with desired behaviours, cultural awareness, and alignment). Medium term (sustainability in subcultures, breaking down silos, and fostering collaboration). Long term (enduring cultural transformation, institutionalising a culture of learning and adaptability).
4. **Gamification Provides Leverage to Cultural Change:** Gamification is an underutilised tool for change with differentiated approaches aligning with CVF. Clan Culture (Collaboration and Teamwork), Adhocracy Culture (**Innovation** and Flexibility), Market Culture (Competitiveness and Achievement), and Hierarchy Culture (Structure and Control).
5. **Boundary-Spanning Roles Critical to Cultural Integration:** Operating within closed environments will not bring about cultural change. Designated staff need to operate at interfaces between departments and external stakeholders. Boundary-spanning roles will enhance key communication flows, break down silos, and encourage an innovative atmosphere.
6. **Ethics Plays a Role in Cultural Integration:** This chapter cites research showing ethical perception gaps between demographic groups and regions. One-size-fits-all approach is not conducive for cultural change. Executives need to create bespoke solutions that align with the values of the organisation.

7 **Seven Common Cultural Myths Impede Transformation:** This case study identifies critical myths that can block sustainable-oriented cultural change. Each myth requires specific interventions to overcome legacy thinking.

10.11 Self-Reflection Questions

1 Using the CVF, suggest how an organisation heavily dominated by a market focus can successfully integrate sustainability initiatives without compromising its core cultural strengths.
2 How would you design an integrated cultural transformation roadmap that addresses short-term and long-term sustainable integration? Make some recommendations for measuring cultural change.
3 Drawing on the IBE's findings presented in this chapter, analyse how a multinational corporation should approach cultural alignment for sustainability when operating across regions. Outline some of the key issues.
4 Design a comprehensive gamification strategy for a large organisation with multiple regional offices that would help shift from a predominantly hierarchical culture towards one that better supports sustainability, **innovation**, and collaboration.
5 As a senior CSO executive, how would you identify, develop, and empower boundary spanners to accelerate the integration of sustainability?

References

Baumgartner, R.J. and Rauter, R., (2017). Strategic perspectives of corporate sustainability management to develop a sustainable organization. *Journal of Cleaner Production, 140*, pp.81–92.

Bennis, W.G. and Nanus, B., (1985). *Leaders: The strategies for taking charge*. Harper & Row.

Cameron, K.S. and Quinn, R.E., (2011). *Diagnosing and changing organizational culture: Based on the competing values framework* (3rd ed.). Jossey-Bass.

Costa, M.D. and Opare, S., (2025). Impact of corporate culture on environmental performance. *Journal of Business Ethics, 196*(1), pp.61–92.

Hahn, T., Figge, F., Pinkse, J. and Preuss, L., (2018). A paradox perspective on corporate sustainability: Descriptive, instrumental, and normative aspects. *Journal of Business Ethics, 148*, pp.235–248.

IBE (2024, 18 September). Ethics at work: 2024 International survey of employees. Available at: https://www.ibe.org.uk/knowledge-hub/eaw-futureoftheworkplace/

Jaganjac, B., Hansen, K.W., Lunde, H. and Hunnes, J.A., (2024). The role of organizational culture and structure in implementing sustainability initiatives. *Business Ethics, the Environment & Responsibility, 34*(4), pp.1239–1254.

O'Reilly, C., Cao, X. and Sull, D., (2024). Organizational culture archetypes and firm performance. *Journal of Business Research, 182*, p.114780.

Osei, M.B., Papadopoulos, T., Acquaye, A. and Stamati, T., (2023). Improving sustainable supply chain performance through organisational culture: A competing values framework approach. *Journal of Purchasing and Supply Management, 29*(2), p.100821.

Robson, K., Plangger, K., Kietzmann, J.H., McCarthy, I. and Pitt, L., (2015). Is it all a game? Understanding the principles of gamification. *Business Horizons, 58*(4), pp.411–420.

Smith, S. and Cox-Smith, S., (2023). *Future cultures: How to build a future-ready organization through leadership*. Kogan Page Publishers.

UNESCO (2001). *UNESCO Universal declaration on cultural diversity*. UNESCO.

United Nations Global Compact (2022). *Guide to corporate sustainability: Shaping a sustainable future*. United Nations Global Compact.

Wang, Y., Zhang, S. and Xu, S., (2022). Impact of efficient resource management practices on sustainable performance: Moderating role of innovative culture-evidence from oil and gas firms. *Frontiers in Psychology, 13*, p.938247.

Williams, A., Kennedy, S., Philipp, F. and Whiteman, G., (2017). Systems thinking: A review of sustainability management research. *Journal of Cleaner Production, 148*, pp.866–881.

PART IV

Sustainable Leadership

11

PURPOSE-DRIVEN LEADERSHIP

11.1 Learning Strategy Objectives

After completing this chapter, you will be able to:

1. **Knowledge-Based Objectives:**
   - Define and explain the concepts of purpose-driven leadership and its role in changing how businesses can better align with employee engagement.
   - Evaluate how CEOs can integrate the purpose of sustainable values into an organisational blueprint for doing good.
2. **Skill-Based Objectives:**
   - Design and implement purpose-driven business models that balance economic, societal, and environmental goals.
   - Critically assess the causes of ineffective leadership practices in managing organisational change.
3. **Attitude-Based Objectives:**
   - Embrace a mindset with focus, purpose, transparency, and fairness to deploy values-based decision-making.
   - Cultivate a culture to build trust for integrating purpose into leadership strategies to drive sustainable outcomes.

11.2 Introduction

Organisational leaders are caught in a dilemma between profit orientation and societal goals, and are caught in the crosswinds (Blocker, Cannon, and Zhang, 2024). Encouragingly, purpose-driven leadership is emerging as a transformative force for modern firms, shifting from other leadership styles to one that addresses an inspiring organisational purpose.

DOI: 10.4324/9781003516774-15

The role of purpose-driven leadership emphasises aligning organisational goals for each actor. Specifically, managers should lead with a clear purpose and involve all organisation members in implementing their purpose (Florez-Jimenez, Lleo, Ruiz-Palomino, and Rey, 2024).

From a leadership perspective, addressing ESG issues is a topic of growing interest in the sustainability field. Purpose can be conceptualised within an overarching, relevant, and shared ethical vision of an organisation's fundamental values (Bhattacharya, Sen, Edinger-Schons, and Neureiter, 2023).

Building on one of the core themes of this book, companies are expected to recognise and take responsibility for their actions in their ecological footprint. Stead (2025) highlights the need to revolutionise business from an ecological perspective by advocating for the integration of sustainability and spirituality to ensure environmental and societal well-being alongside long-term organisational viability, emphasising that Porter alone is insufficient to bring about the required changes.

A degrowth philosophy will be a challenge for today's hard-pressed CEOs, who face pressure from investor scepticism, employee concerns, and customer expectations when they hear the term degrowth. At the country level, the GDP focus as a proxy for human economic development will be hard to alter. Stead (2025) strongly argues for a shift into ecological economics, acknowledging the limitations of nature and promoting sufficiency over growth.

Costanza (2010) asserts that ecological economics acts as a bridge that incorporates psychology, anthropology, archaeology, and history (see Figure 11.1). This has been a constant message during conversations with sustainability activists during my research for this book. But in business schools, neoclassical economics prevails, so the profound social-ecological-economic change together with degrowth strategies will take time (Bärnthaler, 2024).

Research indicates that such leadership is essential for navigating the complexities of sustainability and driving change (Gartenberg, 2021). Interactions with stakeholders are critical for building enduring support for ensuring sustainability efforts (Nakra, and Kashyap, 2025).

Leadership today requires a departure from traditional command-and-control approaches. On the one hand, readers can find voluminous statements that are critical of the conventional approach; however, few examine this through the lens of sustainability. In response, this chapter advocates that leaders must embrace a distributed model of decision-making that empowers employees at all levels. This shift is especially relevant in

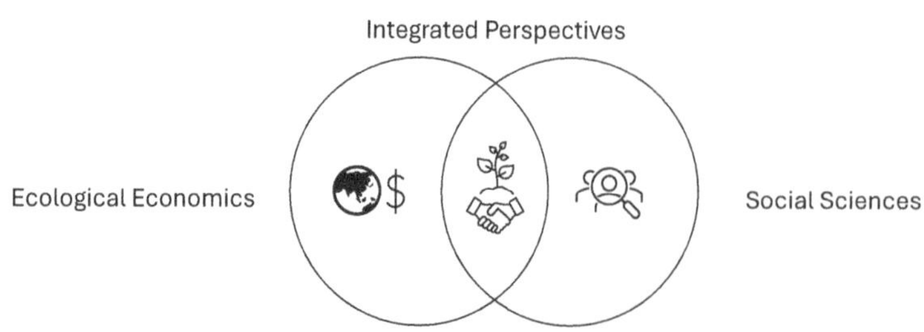

FIGURE 11.1 Ecological economics as a unifying bridge

the sustainability world, where uncertainty demands rapid adaptability and shared values incorporated into desired outcomes.

By now, purpose-driven leadership transcends cutting carbon emissions and achieving net-zero but reimaging the organisation from the outside in rather than the inside out. Using the framework and tools in Chapter 5, external analysis will identify new opportunities. These may require a more explicit articulation of the desired strategy, which can help redefine purpose.

So, mere ambition is insufficient as leaders increasingly prioritise values and societal impact, but followers don't always want to follow. Gleeson (2024) uses metaphors from his experiences in sports, the military, and entrepreneurship and contends that purpose-driven leaders must inspire and transform organisations by aligning individual and organisational values.

Inspiration is often one of the missing ingredients that can impose huge costs. Without staff buy-in to the purpose, the **transition** can buckle under the strain. Failure to address this can erode followers' faith and may lead to a slow-motion catastrophe.

11.3 Organisational Trauma

In this context, change management is persistent, but strategy, technology, and the market offer can cause leaders to suffer fatigue. To address this phenomenon, the job demands–resource model pioneered by Bakker and Demerouti (2007) is helpful. Job demands and job resources impact staff well-being (including leaders) and can lead to poor job **performance**, stress, and burnout.

Sustainability-driven organisations often face even higher burnout risks due to purpose-driven pressure and resource constraints of the working environment. The signs remain, but the triggers intensify, especially around workload, boundaries, and purpose.

Job stress and burnout result from a mismatch between staff's daily demands and the resources they have available (see Figure 11.2). This is especially acute in sustainability strategy initiatives, where there is a lack of time and resources. Psychologically, the concept of purpose-driven leadership is intertwined with the idea of meaningful work, which is linked to the variability of **performance** levels in terms of employee engagement and outcomes.

Sustainability strategies are often underfunded, and initiatives are implemented at the margins with goodwill. This can only go so far before problems set in. Weak signals remain, but the triggers will intensify, especially around workload and purpose.

So, what makes an organisation function during such times? My interactions with clients constantly reveal that what at first appears to be a cohesive leadership team often reveals more dissimilarities than similarities in strategy lexicon. One of my mantras with clients is that consensus should not always be taken for granted, as the path forward is not linear, and critical friends can add insight when looking around corners. It is known that management consultants are often appointed to deliver what the CEO wants, when their ideas need legitimising.

During these times, the organisation's unending leadership is paramount. The simultaneous occurrence of multiple change initiatives complicates matters. Leadership teams must recognise that black swan events will disrupt the anticipated strategy trajectory, necessitating a shift from existing strategies in existing and new markets.

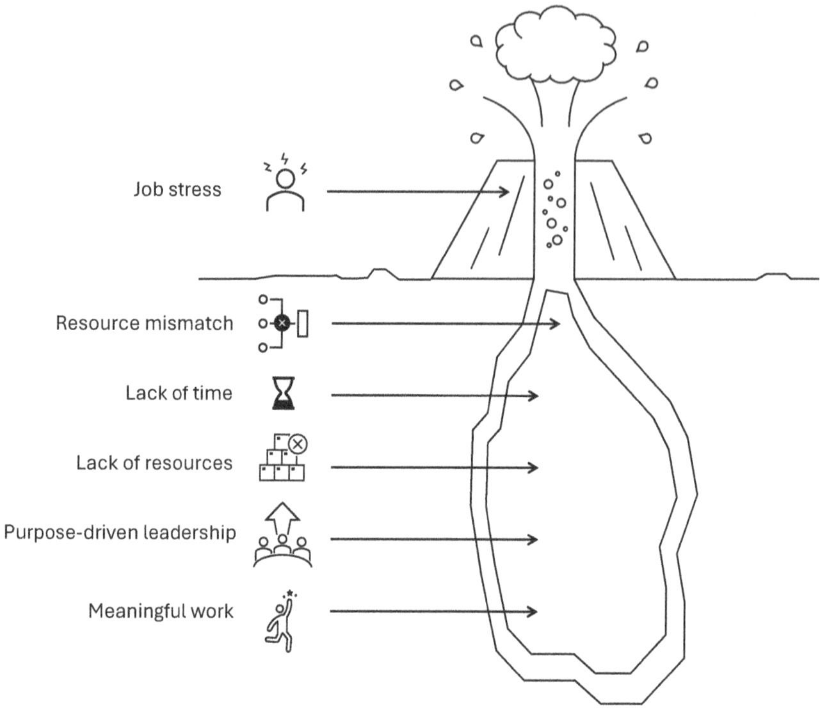

FIGURE 11.2 Job stress and burnout

Now, with firms slashing headcount, organisational pain prevails. This, along with change management, can lead to organisational change fatigue, paralysing the **SSM**. Middle managers who understand their markets become frustrated and leave, increasing staff attrition, and they take their knowledge with them.

11.4 The Influence of Artificial Intelligence

In terms of purpose, leaders need to possess a laser-like focus on providing direction to guide their followers. However, with artificial intelligence (AI) being a disruptive force that transforms work, calls are being made for a fundamental rethink of how leaders make the **transition**.

McKinsey's (2025) "The state of AI report" provides some invaluable insights for organisational leaders. Encouragingly, McKinsey finds that when CEOs take personal responsibility for AI governance, AI pioneers are three times more likely to report revenue growth and twice as likely to achieve cost savings, and are tackling the hurdle of creating the necessary structure and processes.

McKinsey finds that organisations are embracing AI at different paces, with companies with revenues larger than $500 million changing more quickly than smaller organisations. The pace of change is critical as organisations seek to generate value from their AI investment. As momentum builds, the use of AI is spreading across various business functions, which in turn impacts the hiring process.

This rewiring process changes existing workflows and will shift hiring practices. The best leadership teams look into the future to forecast how the automation of jobs in the next 5, 10, and 20 years will influence the demands of their skilled workforce. This can be illustrated by the way robotics, drones, and autonomous vehicles have created new products and services, displacing jobs.

AI possesses the inherent ability to enhance productivity levels, reduce operational costs, and boost growth. Aside from the technology-related jobs such as software engineering, data science, and machine learning, AI is also transforming professional fields. AI-driven personalisation and operational efficiency can benefit organisations.

For example, in Chapter 7, the focus was on strategic sustainability measurement and reporting, and firms are already using AI to assess their sustainability disclosures. In healthcare, AI-powered tools can help automate time-consuming, repetitive tasks, allowing medical professionals to spend more time on making faster and more accurate diagnoses. In banking and finance, AI-driven algorithms can help detect fraudulent transactions, automate core processes, and improve the personalisation of customer services and products. Meanwhile, predictive analytics optimise core business processes, such as the supply chain.

As AI evolves, leadership teams will need to develop new competencies. First and foremost, they must create a deeper appreciation of AI technologies and their implications for the organisational climate. Additionally, leaders will need to strike a balance between technological integration and ethical considerations, ensuring transparency, fairness, and inclusivity in AI-driven decision-making processes.

This influences the role of leadership. During this era of rapid technological advancement, effective leadership requires more than traditional decision-making skills. Speed is a critical resource to drive **innovation**. AI derives its potency from the fact that a sustainability-driven world requires new ways of doing things, and theories taken for granted are now proven to be false and costly.

Leaders who integrate AI into their strategies gain a significant competitive edge by making informed, data-driven decisions. If we consider the philosophy of **SSM**, then many traditional assumptions in strategic management need to be radically revised in light of the changing external context. But the CEO must understand that, like technology, AI is an enabler of strategic planning.

STRATEGY NUGGET

Unilever and Accenture Join Forces to Establish a New Industry Standard in Generative AI-Powered Productivity

In an effort to drive Unilever efficiencies and improve business agility, Unilever and Accenture are collaborating. The proposed multi-year programme will offer fresh perspectives with new industry standards in generative-AI-powered productivity.

In November 2023, Unilever announced its global AI Lab, Horizon3 Labs, to accelerate the generation of new AI concepts, designs, and projects. Unilever's CEO reports that they have already introduced 500 AI applications across their organisations. The goal is to enhance levels of efficiency. By adopting this initiative, the CEO sees the organisation accelerating and obtaining the desired scale to be a leader. The priority is to deliver faster growth and drive productivity and **performance**.

Accenture enables Unilever to overcome a range of productivity challenges, barriers, and enablers that lead to higher levels of returns. GenWizard provides an illustration of what technology can do for the corporate strategist.

This enables the CEO to operate in the rapidly emerging Generative AI environment, successfully making it easier to form collaborations. The adoption of Generative AI is providing significant opportunities to explore the interplay between strategy and technology.

Source: Accenture (2024).

Questions

1 Unilever's CEO reports that they have already introduced 500 AI applications across their organisations. How should the leadership team balance the rapid scaling of AI with ensuring that deployments are aligned with corporate strategy?
2 What are the risks for Unilever's partnership with Accenture for AI implementation?
3 What specific leadership qualities and organisational structures should the CEO deploy to lead Gen AI at scale?

11.5 Sustainable Strategy Toolkit (4) – Triple A Leadership Framework

Modern leadership requires more than technical competence or traditional management approaches. Over the years, my work with clients, guiding organisations through leadership development, suggests that the use of three pillars – Accountability, Authenticity, and Agility – can help firms (see Figure 11.3).

The three pillars of the Triple A Leadership Framework provide a blueprint for navigating the **transition**. With some of the complexities of organisational challenges, while fostering a culture that thrives on purpose, trust, and adaptability.

The Triple A Framework: A Leadership Paradigm outlines three essential dimensions of leadership:

- Accountability: This is generally one of the cornerstones of trust and empowerment within organisations. In the most prominent organisations, senior staff may not be held accountable.

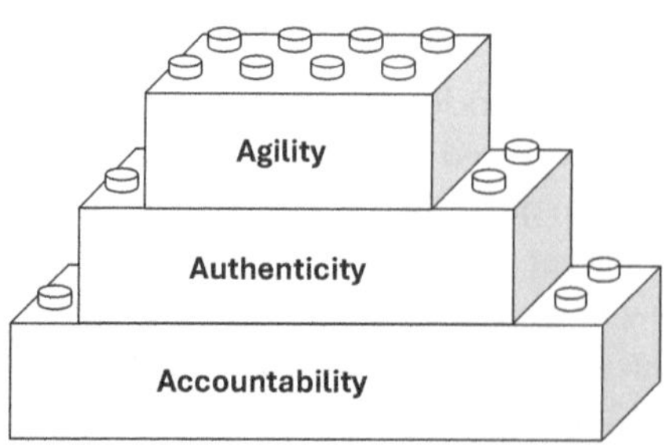

FIGURE 11.3 Triple A leadership framework

- Authenticity: The practice of leading with integrity and aligning actions with values. Gen Z places importance on leaders being authentic in their actions and words.
- Agility: Possessing the ability to adapt and innovate in the face of environmental shifts. Each element works in synergy to create leaders who are effective but also inspiring, purpose-driven, and capable of delivering sustainable organisational success.

11.6 Accountability

The first point of friction is fundamental to leadership. Accountability affords the foundation for trust and collaboration. Yet, in my experience, accountability often falters in blame-centric cultures, where individuals fear reprisal and **innovation** stagnates. Instead, accountability must be reframed as an empowering force that aligns team responsibilities.

Key strategies for fostering accountability include:

- Modelling Accountability: Leaders should take full responsibility for their actions and incorporate open practices into decision-making. Being transparent about successes and failures will help to inspire a culture of trust and transparency.
- Empowering Teams: The culture should encourage employees to take the initiative without fear of blame, which helps foster creativity and ownership. Accountability becomes a shared ethos rather than a top-down mandate.
- Transparent Communication: Leaders must maintain open, consistent dialogue, ensuring individual and organisational goals are aligned. Clear metrics and progress assessments further reinforce accountability. The balanced scorecard remains a successful framework for effective communication.

11.7 Authenticity

In an era where employees value purpose and transparency, authenticity has emerged as a critical leadership trait. Authentic leaders align their actions with stated values, fostering trust, engagement, and a sense of belonging.

Key strategies for fostering accountability include:

- Acting with Integrity: Authentic leaders should operate with sincerity, honesty, and clarity. Their actions reflect their principles, ensuring alignment between their leadership behaviours and organisational missions.
- Understanding Context: Authenticity should be fused with cultural and historical awareness. For instance, leadership in the Global South requires sensitivity to the region's unique socio-economic and political realities.
- Personalised Approaches: Leaders should adapt their styles to address the individual needs and aspirations of their team members. Recognising and valuing these differences foster stronger, more assured teams.

11.8 Agility

Uncertainty is now the norm, and leaders who can adapt to shifting landscapes will be able to maintain the momentum of the journey. Agility, the third pillar of the Triple

A model, is about creating organisations that view change as an opportunity rather than a threat.

Key dimensions of agility include:

- Rapid Decision-Making: Agile leaders can implement quicker learning cycles, make iterative adjustments to strategy, and adapt to meet evolving demands. This ability to pivot ensures resilience in volatile markets.
- Technological Enablement: Agile organisations leverage AI and digital tools to enhance their adaptability and deliver value to stakeholders. Collaborative technologies, for example, support faster decision-making and improve team communication.
- By cultivating agility, leaders can transform disruption into growth, positioning their organisations to innovate and thrive in challenging conditions.

So, how can we make it happen?

Integrating the Triple A Framework

The Triple A Framework is not just a theoretical construct; it is an actionable model that leaders can implement to drive transformative change. Key steps include:

- Building a Culture of Accountability: Embed accountability into organisational processes, behaviours, and metrics to foster a sense of shared responsibility.
- Fostering Authentic Leadership: Encourage leaders to reflect on their values, align them with organisational goals, and communicate them transparently.
- Promoting Organisational Agility: Invest in training, technology, and collaborative structures that enable teams to respond quickly to change.

The Triple A Framework offers a powerful roadmap for redefining leadership in a complex and rapidly evolving world.

11.9 Ethics

An ethical framework will help the leadership team make decisions that are consistent with the organisation's purpose. This alignment fosters trust and credibility among employees and stakeholders, as they can see that actions align with the stated values and principles. Using already agreed-upon guidelines during ethical dilemmas will help ensure that leaders can navigate complex situations where they must balance competing stakeholder interests.

Ethics-based leadership in the age of AI emphasises the importance of human-centric approaches. Leaders must advocate for the development of AI technologies that enhance human capabilities rather than replace them. This perspective not only aligns with organisational purpose but also contributes to a broader societal good by prioritising human dignity and welfare.

Despite the increasing importance attributed to ethics-based leadership, evidence remains limited. CEOs struggle to translate their ethical principles into practical action. However, an ethical framework is indispensable for purpose-driven leadership in the context of AI. It guides leaders in making informed decisions, addresses potential biases, fosters stakeholder trust, navigates complex ethical dilemmas, and promotes a human-centred approach to technology integration. This alignment ultimately strengthens the organisation's commitment to its purpose while responsibly harnessing the transformative power of AI.

The ethical application of AI presents a complex and multifaceted problem for which corporate leaders must adopt a thorough and proactive approach. Effective, purpose-driven leadership must close the gap between the idea and the forward momentum of the company.

Fundamentally, building a strong AI ethical framework can help. Establishing strict governance systems and procedures to support an AI ethical and responsible culture results in a structured environment. In this sense, working with external stakeholders, leaders can ensure that the transforming potential of AI is used in a way that is consistent with the principles of the company and the larger society's good.

Leaders have a responsibility to lead in determining the ethical course of these technologies, as the acceptance of AI maintains the pace. By doing this, they may help to build a fairer, egalitarian, and sustainable future in addition to shielding their companies from the hazards and unanticipated effects of AI.

TABLE 11.1 Leadership and AI implications from IBM's CEO Report

Challenge	*Leadership Implications*	*Action Steps for CEOs*
1 Talent and skills	Assess workforce readiness and Generative AI skill gaps.	Investment in capacity building in reskilling and training programmes. Identify new emerging AI-related roles. Foster an organisation culture of lifelong learning.
2 **Innovation** and customer-centricity	Enhance **innovation** pace, while maintaining the trust of the customer.	Use Generative AI for new personalisation strategies. Communicate transparently about data use. Engage customers in co-creation processes.
3 Ecosystem partnerships	Don't place over-reliance on unproductive partnerships.	Audit partnerships. Focus on mutually aligned high-quality, collaborations. Leverage partners' expertise in AI projects.
4 Decision-making dynamics	Maintain effective AI processes among C-suite leadership team to foster collaboration and **innovation.**	Conduct constructive conversations with clear purpose. Focus on EDI perspectives in decision-making. Align incentives for staff to encourage mutually beneficial collaboration.
5 Vision and culture	Ensure staff buy into vision and culture and look for resistance to change brought about by AI and employee scepticism.	Build an inspirational shared vision aligned with organisational values. Invest in interventions to enhance capacity building in strategic thinking. Address employee concerns about roles in AI playbook.
6 Technology and transformation	Align AI short-term focus with long-term investment and growth.	Prioritise long-term sustainable AI technology strategy. Align Generative AI investments with strategic priorities. Balance long-term opportunities with quick wins.

Abbreviations: AI, artificial intelligence; EDI, equality diversity and inclusion.

Consistent with these ethical dilemmas, Jobin, Ienca, and Vayena (2019) pronounced five principles:

- Transparency
- Justice and fairness
- Non-maleficence
- Responsibility
- Privacy.

Table 11.1 provides a clear and actionable framework for addressing the six hard truths identified in the leadership and AI implications IBM's CEO Report (2024).

With a purpose-driven leadership approach, organisations can achieve higher levels of talent attraction and retention, as well as a more motivated workforce. The CEO plays a critical role in nurturing this sense of purpose, by crafting an environment where staff feel enthused by aligning professional success with achieving the company's goals.

11.10 United Nations Sustainable Development Goal Purpose-Driven Leadership Issues

Table 11.2 reframes the challenges with a focus on purpose-driven leadership, emphasising the need for visionary, ethical, and inclusive approaches to achieving each United Nations Sustainable Development Goal (UNSDG).

TABLE 11.2 Purpose-driven leadership conversation starters for each of SDGs 1–17

SDG	*Purpose-Driven Leadership Conversation Starters*
SDG 1: No poverty	Insufficient alignment of poverty reduction efforts with human dignity and empowerment; lack of commitment to equitable policies.
SDG 2: Zero hunger	Inadequate attention on reducing hunger as a moral necessity; failure to provide inclusive food systems that balance economic, social, and environmental aims.
SDG 3: Good health and well-being	Neglect of holistic approaches to health that give mental, physical, and social well-being top priority above reactive healthcare interventions.
SDG 4: Quality education	Limited investment in education as a societal equaliser; lack of leadership focus on lifelong learning as a transforming instrument for individuals and societies.
SDG 5: Gender equality	Opposition to creating inclusive societies that celebrate diversity; neglect of gender equality as a fundamental organisational and social guiding principle.
SDG 6: Clean water and sanitation	Insufficient emphasis on water stewardship as a shared responsibility; lack of integration of water access goals with community well-being.
SDG 7: Affordable and clean energy	Focus on short-term energy advantages over sustainability; weak leadership vision for switching to renewable energy as a moral obligation to next generations.
SDG 8: Decent work and economic growth	Lack of dedication to equitable work conditions and human-centred development with low priority of sustainable practices benefiting workers and communities.

(*Continued*)

TABLE 11.2 (Continued)

SDG	*Purpose-Driven Leadership Conversation Starters*
SDG 9: Industry, **innovation**, and infrastructure	Lack of a visionary attitude to **innovation** as a tool for society benefit and inadequate attention on infrastructure for fair access.
SDG 10: Reduced inequalities	Ignorance of eliminating inequality as necessary for social cohesiveness and justice with little leadership attention on systematic inclusion hurdles.
SDG 11: Sustainable cities and communities	Lack of innovative urban design to produce inclusive, safe, and sustainable environments; insufficient integration of citizen voices in decision-making.
SDG 12: Responsible consumption and production	Responsibly inadequate leadership attention on ethical production systems with weak prioritising of circular economy models as a road to sustainability.
SDG 13: Climate action	Lack of urgency in seeing climate action as a moral imperative with inadequate leadership alignment with long-term planetary and human health goals.
SDG 14: Life below water	Limited support for the inherent importance of marine habitats with neglect of embedding sustainability of oceans as a non-negotiable goal in government.
SDG 15: Life on land	Poor attention on fostering harmony between human activities and environment with vision on biodiversity as fundamental for human survival weak leadership.
SDG 16: Peace, justice, and strong institutions	Lack of collaborative approaches to institutional reforms; insufficient prioritising of integrity and transparency as pillars of government.
SDG 17: Partnerships for the goals	Limited cooperation driven by shared purpose; insufficient leadership focus on partnerships that fit transforming society aspirations.

Abbreviations: SDGs, Sustainable Development Goals.

11.11 Serendipitous Inspiration

What we cannot comprehend by analysis, we become aware of in awe Heschel (2001)

- A cognitive dilemma exists whereby leadership teams must lead with vision, manage resources effectively, and provide inspiration to their teams. Figure 11.4 shows the circle of serendipitous inspiration in leadership.

Dow (2009) states that serendipitous inspiration can allow room for happy accidents:

- Serendipitous inspiration refers to the process of finding valuable insights, solutions, or opportunities by chance or accident.
- It often arises unexpectedly, outside of planned objectives or structured processes.
- Serendipitous inspiration can provide fresh perspectives and fuel **innovation**, leading to positive outcomes for organisations.

Serendipity, the act of finding something valuable or delightful when you are not explicitly looking for it, has long been recognised as a powerful catalyst for **innovation** and creativity. In the context of purpose-driven leadership, serendipitous inspiration can play

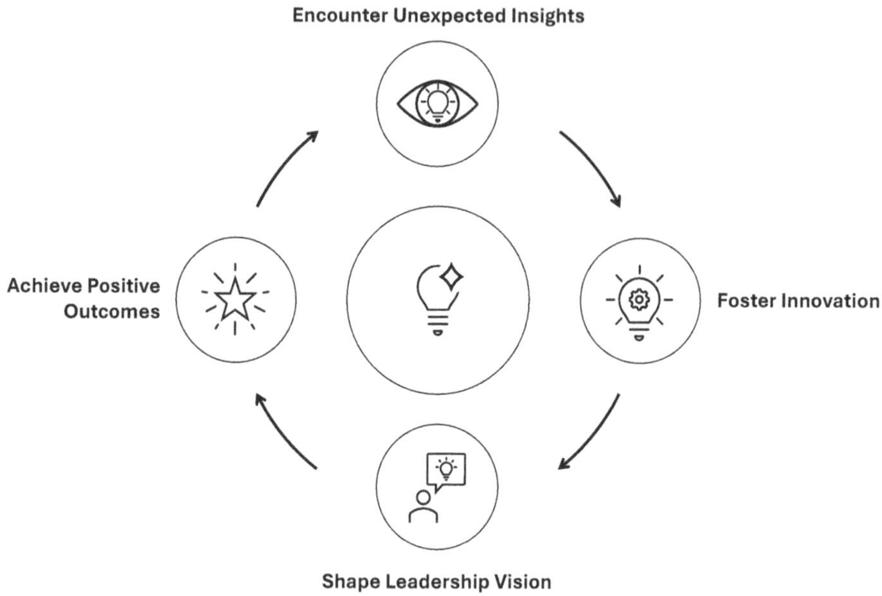

FIGURE 11.4 The cycle of serendipitous inspiration in leadership

a crucial role in shaping the vision and goals of leaders. This section explores how serendipity contributes to and helps the development of purpose-driven leadership.

Over the years, there has been evidence in serendipitous inspiration in medical discoveries:

- Insulin
- Lysergic acid diethylamide, commonly known as LSD
- Superglue
- Pacemaker
- X-rays
- Radioactivity
- Penicillin.

Business **innovation**

- Serendipity has been studied in diverse fields, including human-computer interaction, library and information science, and molecular chemistry.
- More recently, there has been a spike in interest in this topic in management studies.

Organisations must explore innovative approaches to sustain long-term success in a world where complexity and uncertainty dominate. During work with clients who struggle with a lack of creativity, my approach introduces the concept of serendipitous inspiration as a transformative tool for achieving effective strategic planning outcomes. This idea emphasises the role of unplanned discoveries or "happy accidents" in driving **innovation**, enhancing problem-solving, and fostering a culture of adaptability.

Traditional strategic planning can become a process where leadership teams prioritise the **transition** journey. The bureaucratic process that pursues efficiency can lead to what

Max Weber (2001) calls an "iron cage," in which complying and controlling rather than discovery hold sway. This metaphor illustrates if society becomes so focused on efficiency, it will stifle creativity. Organisations need to think of themselves as social places of work, so that they optimise processes striving to attain sustainability targets.

Leadership teams can be more creative in the range of ideas they propose during strategic planning retreats. Serendipitous inspiration refers to the discovery of valuable insights, solutions, or opportunities that occur by chance rather than through structured or deliberate actions. Historically, numerous groundbreaking **innovations**, such as Penicillin, X-rays, and the pacemaker, originated from unexpected discoveries. In the organisational context, serendipitous inspiration emerges when leaders create environments that allow for exploration, creativity, and collaboration.

When leaders face a cognitive dilemma, they must provide vision and inspire their teams. While they cannot predict every challenge or opportunity, they can foster conditions that encourage serendipity to thrive. This requires shifting from rigid strategic planning practices to one that embraces flexibility and openness.

By incorporating serendipitous inspiration, organisations can uncover innovative solutions to complex challenges.

11.12 Creating an Environment to Embrace Happy Accidents

Organisations can foster serendipitous inspiration by:

- Celebrating and Learning from Uncertainty: Encouraging teams to view unexpected outcomes as opportunities for growth.
- Promoting Collaboration: Breaking down silos and facilitating cross-disciplinary interactions to spark new ideas.
- Embracing Technology and Data: Leveraging digital tools to uncover insights and trends that may not be immediately obvious.
- Allowing Unstructured Time: Providing space for creativity and exploration outside of strict deadlines and objectives.
- Fostering an Inclusive Culture: Ensuring that diverse perspectives and ideas are valued, creating a fertile ground for **innovation**.

These practices align with sustainable planning by ensuring that strategies remain adaptable and inclusive.

By integrating the principles of serendipitous inspiration into sustainable strategic planning, organisations can enhance their ability to adapt, innovate, and thrive. In summary:

- Gain a new way of tackling the cognitive dilemma of how to lead teams and, at the same time, provide serendipitous inspiration.
- Discover the advantages of planning for happy accidents and integrating them into your differentiation strategies.
- Leave with an understanding of the causes of bad strategies and overcoming your blind spots.

Table 11.3 presents the core elements of purpose-driven leadership and provides practical strategies for implementation.

TABLE 11.3 Purpose-driven leadership, insights, and actionable **SSM**

Aspect of Purpose-Driven Leadership	*Key Insights*	*Actionable* **SSM**
Clarity of purpose	The North Star directing decisions and motivating teams.	Clearly state your authentic goal.
Authenticity	To establish credibility and confidence, match actions with values.	Ensure choices and values align with seven **SSM** framework.
Vision that inspires action	Link daily responsibilities to more general objectives to inspire involvement and output.	Share the vision at every strategy level with good clarity.
Empathy and emotional intelligence	Recognise and attend to the needs of staff members and stakeholders.	Listen actively, create inclusive environments, and gently resolve issues.
Purpose embedded in strategy	Include environmental and social objectives into output corporate plans.	Match operations to long-term sustainability and equality objectives.
Modelling desired behaviour	Lead by moral behaviour that is consistent by means of openness. Model ethical decision-making and responsibility in every action.	Model ethical decision-making and responsibility in every action.
The ripple effect	Motivational creativity and social impact outside of company lines.	Advance behaviours that add value for society and stakeholders.

Mini Case Study

Hitachi News Release

Hitachi's New "PLEDGES" Sustainability Plan

Tokyo, 27 June 2025 "PLEDGES," a new sustainability strategy, was unveiled by Hitachi, Ltd., to promote sustainable management further.

Hitachi's new management strategy, "Inspire 2027," outlines its goals for sustainable growth and helping to realise a harmonious society where happiness, the environment, and economic progress are all in balance. The strategy is based on seven pillars that underpin this bold strategy.

Background

Following its founding tenet of "Contributing to society through the development of superior, original technology and products," Hitachi has spent its entire 110-year history tackling social challenges.

Its new management plan, Inspire 2027, reflects this attitude by emphasising social challenges and utilising Hitachi's strengths in IT, Operational technology (OT), and products to create corporate value further and deliver benefits to society. Given the rapid evolution of the global competitive landscape, Hitachi views sustainability as a crucial component of competitiveness. Hitachi will enhance its sustainable management and make sustainability the central focus of its business strategy to achieve sustainable growth.

Seven strategic pillars make up the sustainability strategy, or "PLEDGES," which is essential to both Hitachi's corporate expansion and the realisation of a sustainable society. Hitachi's approach and tactics for building a group management basis for sustainable growth are outlined in the first six pillars: Planet, Leadership, Empowerment, and Diverse Viewpoints, Governance, and Engagement, and Sustainability for All. The last pillar, represents Hitachi's commitment to utilising its business operations to benefit society per the six pillars mentioned above.

For each strategic pillar, KPIs and targets are established; some of these serve as evaluation indicators to determine executive compensation for the short-term, medium-term, and long-term periods, starting in FY 2025.

- **Planet:** Green Transformation (GX): Hitachi has a long-term environmental vision that outlines the path for the Hitachi Group, as it believes it is critical to address environmental concerns that are becoming increasingly serious globally. Hitachi's three strategy pillars – "Decarbonisation," "Circular Economy," and "Nature Positive" – are part of this vision. The company will support group-wide activities aimed at becoming a global leader in GX to assist in safeguarding the environment and promoting human well-being.
- **Leadership, Empowerment, and Diverse Views:** Developing organisational culture, using diverse views, and strengthening human capital. More substantial human capital and an organisational culture that promotes growth and challenges are, in Hitachi's opinion, crucial for fostering **innovation**. On the basis of this strategy, Hitachi will work to improve the development of the next generation of leaders who will spearhead change and to promote an organisational culture that supports personal development and challenges. In addition, Hitachi aims to contribute to society by fostering an inclusive workplace culture that enables staff members to grow and develop alongside one another.
- **Governance:** Strengthening the organisation's resilience is essential to achieving sustained growth, as the business environment of the Hitachi Group is constantly evolving. Throughout the group, governance will enhance safe and secure work environments and foster a corporate culture where all employees conduct themselves honestly and fairly.
- **Engagement:** Collaboration with procurement partners, particularly those upstream, will be a key feature of Hitachi's sustainable procurement practices. Addressing societal and environmental concerns at each stage of the value chain will be a priority.
- **Sustainability for All:** The seventh pillar represents Hitachi's dedication to utilising business principles and operations grounded in the preceding six pillars to provide benefits to all. With sustainability at the heart of its operations, Hitachi aims to accelerate its social **innovation** business, centred on Lumada, to deliver value across the globe.

Source: Hitachi (2025).

Questions

1 How does leadership play a role in embedding PLEDGES sustainability strategy into Hitachi's overarching corporate strategy, and what are the risks if senior leadership is not fully committed?
2 Given Hitachi's emphasis on value chain engagement and sustainable procurement, what leadership competencies are needed to drive sustainable strategy within the organisation?
3 Why are diverse leadership perspectives essential when formulating sustainable strategies, particularly for a global company like Hitachi? How does this affect the implementation of PLEDGES?

11.13 Chapter Key Takeaways

11.13.1 There are seven key takeaways on purpose-driven leadership:

1. **Purpose as Strategic Integration:** Leaders implementing purpose-driven leadership will help advance the conventional economic perspective narrative by incorporating ESG goals into the company's values. This alignment can motivate a cohesive organisational vision that acts as a "North Star" for tactical and strategic decisions.
2. **Triple A Leadership Framework:** This comprehensive strategy requires balancing the key forces behind agility, authenticity, and accountability. Among the benefits are responsibility, which fosters trust through open accountability; authenticity, which aligns behaviour with values; and agility, which enables quick adaptability to changing external circumstances.
3. **AI's Transformative Role:** The transformative power of AI is reshaping organisational needs, giving human-centric methods top priority. Getting it incorrectly could cause organisational trauma. Leaders must reconcile ethical issues with the integration of AI to build workforce confidence.
4. **Organisational Resilience:** Through proactive measures that ensure crisis management aligns with organisational values, purpose-driven leaders can strengthen organisational resilience. This kind of strategy will enable companies to navigate interruptions while maintaining a commitment to environmental objectives.
5. **Hybrid Work Evolution:** The post-pandemic shift to continuous hybrid work requires leaders to reassess organisational productivity measures, such as being present outside of conventional office hours. Leaders must create a welcoming atmosphere that respects both in-office and remote efforts on par.
6. **Ethical Framework for Decision-Making:** Strategy decision-making in purpose-driven companies requires a robust ethical framework. One advantage is being able to negotiate environmental challenges. The structure should stress openness, fairness, accountability, and privacy.
7. **Serendipitous Inspiration:** Effective purpose-driven leaders will find it beneficial to establish settings that encourage "happy accidents" and lead to unanticipated discoveries. Leaders can find creative solutions to complex sustainability challenges by embracing uncertainty, fostering cross-disciplinary collaboration, and allowing for unstructured thinking time.

These takeaways encapsulate how purpose-driven leadership make organisational **transition** by aligning economic goals with environmental and social impacts, fostering ethical technological integration, building resilient cultures, and inspiring **innovation** through both structured processes and creative serendipity.

11.14 Self-Reflection Questions

1. How would the Triple A Framework (accountability, authenticity, agility) match or contradict the leadership style of your company now?
2. How does your company handle AI deployment, and how might you improve ethical governance in this regard?

3 How successfully does your company generate conditions for "serendipitous inspiration," and what obstacles might be stifling sustainability **innovation**?
4 How may burnout or organisational trauma affect your sustainability projects? What tools might help to solve these problems?
5 Which of the UNSDGs poses the most significant challenge to your company's leadership? And how may a purpose-driven strategy close this disparity?

References

Accenture (2024). Unilever and Accenture join forces to establish a new industry standard in generative AI-powered productivity. Available at: https://newsroom.accenture.com/news/2024/unilever-and-accenture-join-forces-to-establish-a-new-industry-standard-in-generative-ai-powered-productivity

Bakker, A.B. and Demerouti, E., (2007). The job demands-resources model: State of the art. *Journal of Managerial Psychology, 22*(3), pp.309–328.

Bärnthaler, R., (2024). Problematising degrowth strategising: On the role of compromise, material interests, and coercion. *Ecological Economics, 223,* p.108255.

Bhattacharya, C.B., Sen, S., Edinger-Schons, L.M. and Neureiter, M., (2023). Corporate purpose and employee sustainability behaviors. *Journal of Business Ethics, 183*(4), pp.963–981.

Blocker, C.P., Cannon, J.P. and Zhang, J.Z., (2024). Purpose orientation: An emerging theory transforming business for a better world. *Journal of the Academy of Marketing Science, 53,* pp.1–27.

Costanza, R., (2010). The need for a transdisciplinary understanding of development in a hot and crowded world. In R. Bhaskar, C. Frank, K.G. Høyer, P. Naess and J. Parker (eds.), *Interdisciplinarity and climate change: Transforming knowledge and practice for our global future,* pp.136–148. Routledge/Taylor & Francis.

Florez-Jimenez, M.P., Lleo, A., Ruiz-Palomino, P.A.B.L.O. and Rey, C., (2024). How to make organizations highly resilient: The role of purpose-driven leadership and shared purpose. In *Academy of Management Proceedings* (Vol. 2024, No. 1, p.14975). Valhalla, NY: Academy of Management.

Gartenberg, C., (2021). Purpose-driven companies and sustainability. In G. George, M.R. Haas, H. Joshi, A.M. McGahan and P. Tracey (eds.), *Handbook on the business of sustainability,* pp.24–42. Edward Elgar Publishing. https://dx.doi.org/10.2139/ssrn.3786823

Gleeson, B. (2024). Forbes. Available at: https://www.forbes.com/sites/brentgleeson/2024/11/05/5-strategies-for-becoming-a-purpose-driven-leader/ (Accessed: 9 December 25).

Heschel, A.J., (2001). *I asked for wonder: A spiritual anthology* (Edited by S. H. Dresner). Crossroad.

Hitachi (2025). Hitachi's new sustainability strategy "PLEDGES". Available at: https://www.hitachi.com/New/cnews/month/2025/06/250627.html

IBM Institute for Business Value (2024). 6 hard truths CEOs must face: How to leap forward with courage and conviction in the generative AI era. Available at: https://www.ibm.com/thought-leadership/institute-business-value/en-us/report/2024-ceo (Accessed: 29 August 2025).

Jobin, A., Ienca, M. and Vayena, E., (2019). The global landscape of AI ethics guidelines. *Nature Machine Intelligence, 1(9),* pp.389–399.

McKinsey's (2025). The State of AI: How organisations are rewiring to capture value. Available at: https://www.mckinsey.com/capabilities/quantumblack/our-insights/the-state-of-ai-how-organizations-are-rewiring-to-capture-value (Accessed: 29 August 2025).

Nakra, N. and Kashyap, V., (2025). Responsible leadership and organizational sustainability performance: Investigating the mediating role of sustainable HRM. *International Journal of Productivity and Performance Management, 74*(2), pp.409–426.

Weber, M. (2001). *The protestant ethic and the spirit of capitalism.* Routledge Classics.

12

LEADERSHIP IN SUSTAINABLE ECOSYSTEMS

12.1 Learning Strategy Objectives

After completing this chapter, you will be able to:

1. **Knowledge-Based Objectives:**
   - Identify, apply, and explain how to collaborate with partners and develop sustainable ecosystems.
   - Understand the implications of the shift from markets to ecosystems.
2. **Skill-Based Objectives:**
   - Design and develop sustainable ecosystems through actionable and differentiated insights.
   - Critically evaluate the causes of ineffective ecosystems and their implications for execution in different industries.
3. **Attitude-Based Objectives:**
   - Overcome the fear factor in addressing change management challenges and global issues outlined in the United Nations Sustainable Development Goals.
   - Inspire active engagement by creating an innovative culture.

12.2 Introduction

The adoption of the ecosystem concept is seen as a rational approach to enhance the odds of **transition** success. This applies in biology and now in business organisations. In the sustainable context, the leadership team must commit to forming stronger and new relationships. The creation of stronger and more resilient supply chains is crucial for enhancing sustainability and ensuring implementation and success (see Figure 12.1).

Operating as a leader within an ecosystem requires a multifaceted approach that is adaptive to address the complex environment. In such situations, employees must adjust

DOI: 10.4324/9781003516774-16

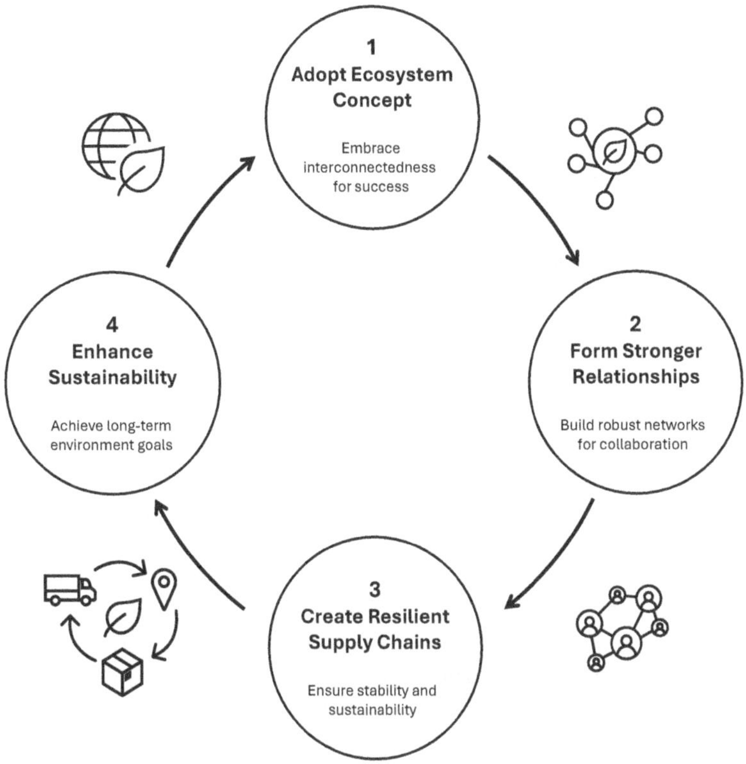

FIGURE 12.1 Ecosystem approach to sustainability

management practices in response to the receipt of new information and changing conditions to drive **innovation** (Foss, Schmidt, and Teece, 2023). Having distinguished **SSM** with its focus on economic, social, and governance, and linked with taking advantage of opportunities, approaches must be different from when pursuing closed strategies (Altman and Tushman, 2017). By partnering with the actors in the ecosystem the role of the orchestrator needs to be articulated (Lingens, Miehé, and Gassmann, 2021; Shen, Shi, Parida, and Jovanovic, 2024).

Within the wider ecosystem, tremendous opportunities exist to fulfil new visions and missions. This chapter begins by considering the damage that working in organisational silos creates. Today's pro-growth strategies require value propositions that are attractive to stakeholders. Times have moved forward beyond the old economic model of stakeholders as merely the firm and the customer; we now operate in a multi-stakeholder marketplace. A crucial currency is one of value, and this chapter considers several examples.

The shift from markets to ecosystems is encapsulated in the **SSM** imperative. The World Economic Forum "Sustainomy" approach (2024) stresses that ecosystems require more than business success. This necessitates a revaluation of traditional global systems and values for everyone's benefit.

If, as argued, organisations must adapt to and extend relationships beyond boundaries, the switch from one-to-one to one-to-many requires changes in strategy philosophy. Leaders have to place themselves at the centre of discussions about ecosystems and what it specifically means for the organisation.

Sustainable ecosystems consist of independent enterprises and actors. Ultimately, an ecosystem's ability to support itself without external influence makes it sustainable. This interdependent system of organisations contains value systems. The digitisation effects of inter-organisational networks and platforms can make the context complex. In a manufacturing environment, the end-to-end system begins with raw material suppliers and extends to the end-customer (Kohtamäki, 2019).

12.3 Theoretical Foundation

The pressure for a swift recovery from the pandemic reinforced the importance of connecting organisations to solve grand sustainability challenges. World-leading dynamic **innovations** are part of an interconnected ecosystem. Sustainability requires building a future that is greener, safer, and healthier than before for all members of society.

The ecosystem concept has emerged with some vigour but still lacks clarity. Commencing with biological systems of living organisms, the adaptive approach has been extended to business and management. This captures terms such as industrial ecosystem, digital ecosystem, business ecosystem, and **innovation** ecosystem (Tsujimoto, Kajikawa, Tomita, and Matsumoto, 2018). Table 12.1 provides some definitions of ecosystems in practice.

Using ecosystems for value creation presents opportunities for leaders to develop effective sustainability strategies. The business world has witnessed the dominance and the criticality of platforms. This **transition** reconceptualises leadership from a position of authority within their firm to one within a collective of organisations.

The shift from individual products and services to platforms operating within an ecosystem presents challenges for leaders. The external focus beyond firms' boundaries requires the ability to influence others towards a shared vision (Nambisan, Zahra, and Luo, 2019).

Cognitive forms of leadership, which incorporate unconscious and perceptual processes, require leaders to develop new capabilities to sense opportunities, mobilise resources, and transform the ecosystem. By cultivating dynamic sensing mechanisms and synthesising disparate data streams, leaders can detect weak signals before peers in their environment.

TABLE 12.1 Definitions of ecosystems

Ecosystem Term	*Academic Definition*
Industrial ecosystem	A system of interconnected industrial actors and processes that integrate material and energy flows to minimise waste and environmental impact while maximising economic value (Boons and Howard-Grenville, 2009).
Digital ecosystem	A socio-technical environment where digital technologies, platforms, and users interact dynamically to create value, share resources, and innovate in real-time (Zahra and Nambisan, 2012; Iansiti and Lakhani, 2020).
Business ecosystem	A collaborative and competitive network of diverse organisations, including firms, suppliers, distributors, and customers, that co-create and co-evolve to sustain competitive advantage and adapt to market changes (Jacobides, Cennamo, and Gawer, 2018).
Innovation ecosystem	A network of actors, institutions, and resources that collaboratively foster knowledge flow, technology development, and the commercialisation of **innovation** to drive economic growth and competitiveness (Autio, Nambisan, Thomas, and Wright, 2018).

During the last two decades, theoretical research in ecosystems has been invaluable in strategic management. Organisations operate through networks that possess bilateral inter-organisational relationships (Shen, Shi, Parida, and Jovanovic, 2024). While ecosystems comprise multi-lateral, non-hierarchical relationships (Jacobides, Cennamo, and Gawer, 2018), leaders have to reconcile seemingly contradictory objectives through higher-order thinking.

12.3.1 Theory of the Firm

A hallmark of **SSM** is consideration of how value is created and captured, with implications for sustainability and the firm. From a value creation perspective, leaders must carefully balance the value they create for their firm and the ecosystem. Failure to strike the right balance will lead to trust issues. This can impair progress, as ecosystem partners will bring their specific strengths to the ecosystem.

By shedding light on the redefinition and repositioning of organisational dynamics in the context of sustainability, ecosystems can help overcome the growth sclerosis in emerging regions. For nearly a century, the firm has played a crucial role in economic growth theories. But within an ecosystem, firms are no longer isolated entities and are dependent on their members.

The **SSM** pioneering journey aims to reconceptualise traditional strategic management within the unique socio-economic sustainability landscape. The modern firm has several internal drivers that operate at deeper levels and require working in a more disciplined manner, which is only sometimes intuitive. These unique characteristics present both challenges and opportunities, prompting a reevaluation of the baseline assumptions underlying the theory of the firm (TOF).

TOF originated from the static neoclassical theory of the firm (Coase, 1937), which relates to a series of theories that include transaction cost economics (Williamson, 1989), production theory (Holmstrom, and Tirole, 1989), and incomplete contract theory (Hart, 1988).

While the seminal work of Coase establishes a solid foundation for the TOF, in which fellow economists have been able to hypothesise about the existence, behaviour, structure, and relationships, it has limitations in some areas in explaining firm behaviour.

TOF is a leading paradigm in the economics literature, but from a sustainability perspective, it still needs to be completed in its current form. The significant limitations and implications of the TOF in understanding firm behaviour in environments where a myriad of externally imposed nuanced practices make the nature and purpose of firms differ from post-industrialised Western profit-focused enterprises. Business ecosystems contain groups of independent and complementary organisations that share resources.

Despite the growing literature, the strategic leadership role in ecosystems remains underdeveloped, creating an opportunity for **SSM**. Modern practice necessitates new frameworks and tools for managing ecosystems and the diverse range of actors across firm boundaries. Specifically, how can leaders influence members? The concept of strategic leadership needs to be recast to cope with the more complex hierarchical levels and various project leads.

The sustained application of an ecosystem approach in public and private strategy decision-making underscores the importance of governance. A diversity of approaches

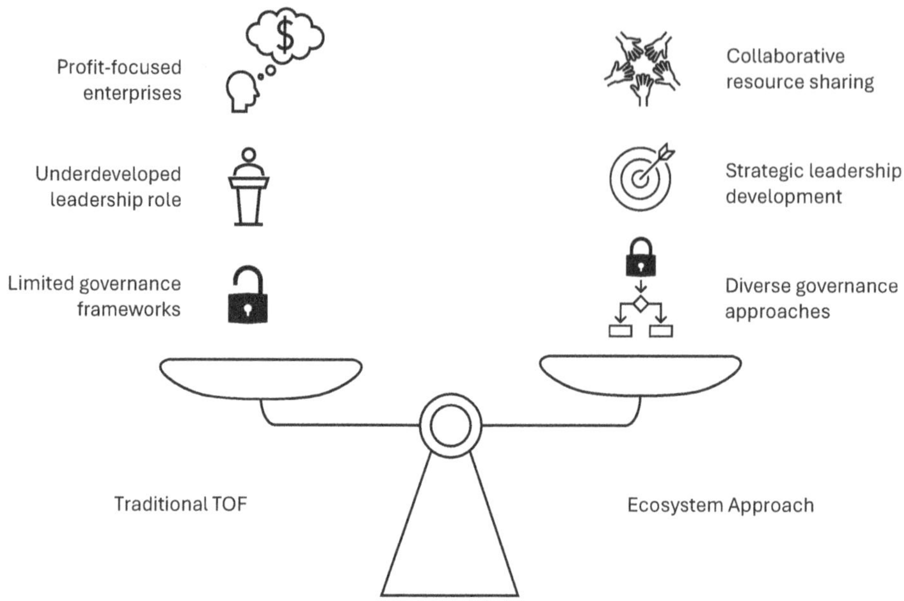

FIGURE 12.2 TOF and business ecosystem cycle

is required, in which individuals and institutions, as well as public and private actors, collaborate to address their challenges. Regulatory frameworks with a balance of direct government regulation, market-based approaches, decision-making processes, and awareness-raising approaches. With the development of new technologies, digitally driven governance approaches will bring new opportunities by supporting communication and generating alternative forms of engagement. In summary, Figure 12.2 illustrates the TOF and business ecosystem cycle.

12.4 The Business Ecosystem Concept

Over the last two centuries, the concept of management has evolved from efficiency and control. Today, Management 5.0 is set to redefine leadership by shifting the focus towards a more holistic, adaptive, and interconnected approach. Leaders will embrace technology, sustainability, collaboration, and continuous learning, creating more agile, human-centred, and purpose-driven ecosystems that benefit all stakeholders in an ecosystem context.

So how did we get here? Table 12.2 summarises the **transition** from Management 1.0 to Management 5.0, highlighting the key focus, management style, and key concepts for each stage.

Ecosystems are driven by a hub firm, with members nestled within the value system. The structure can include market or networked forms. Well-cited thriving business ecosystems include the magnificent seven of Amazon, Alphabet (Google's parent company), Apple, Meta, Microsoft, Nivida, and Tesla. Each firm leverages its ecosystems to provide and fulfil sustainability opportunities. The strategists can craft customer-centric models, with solutions (see Figure 12.3).

TABLE 12.2 Journey management 1.0 to 5.0

Management Stage	*Time Period*	*Key Focus*	*Management Style*	*Key Concepts*
Management 1.0	Late 19th century – early 20th century	Efficiency and control	Top-down, hierarchical, authoritarian	Scientific management (Frederick Taylor) Bureaucracy (Max Weber) Administrative theory (Henri Fayol)
Management 2.0	Mid-20th century	Motivation and human needs	Collaborative, human-centred, participative	Hawthorne effect (Elton Mayo) Maslow's hierarchy of needs theory X and Y (Douglas McGregor)
Management 3.0	Late 20th century	Strategy, leadership, organisational culture	Visionary leadership, strategic management	Competitive strategy (Michael Porter) Management by objectives (Peter Drucker) Excellence in management (Tom Peters)
Management 4.0	Early 21st century	Digital transformation and **innovation**	Agile, flexible, adaptive	Agile methodology Lean management Digital transformation Disruptive **innovation**
Management 5.0	Present and future	Human-centric leadership, sustainability	Holistic, collaborative, adaptive	Human-centric leadership sustainability and UNSDGs AI and automation collaborative ecosystems lifelong learning

Abbreviations: AI, artificial intelligence; UNSDGs, United Nations Sustainable Development Goals.

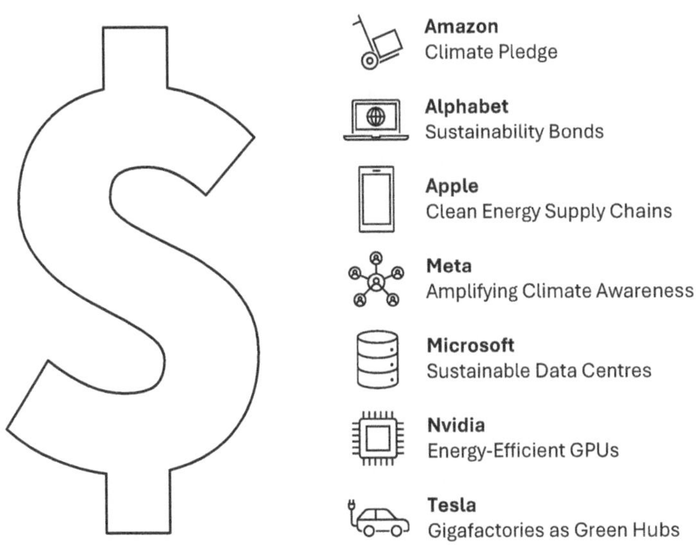

FIGURE 12.3 Tech giants' green initiatives

Collaboration is required and must be led from the top. However, in today's digital world, all staff, regardless of whether they hold formal leadership roles, possess leadership responsibilities. This chapter examines how visionary and adaptive leaders are crucial for organisations aiming to thrive in today's dynamic and ever-changing business landscape. Leadership for sustainable ecosystems will address how formal organisation design impacts the **innovation** of its members and, thus, strategic capability to innovate for sustainability.

In addition, managing cooperative strategy with other businesses and collaborative endeavours between industry and government is an essential topic. Exploring the concept of ecosystems within sustainability will highlight the intricate web of relationships and interactions among various stakeholders, including businesses, communities, governments, and the environment.

It underscores the importance of viewing sustainability challenges through a systems-thinking lens, recognising the interconnectedness of social, environmental, and economic factors. This illustrates the importance of adopting an ecosystem mindset to identify new opportunities and manage risks effectively. Amidst the intricate complexities of our contemporary world, nurturing sustainability within ecosystems is imperative for success.

Mini Case Study

Green Banks

One of the pressing issues for the Global South is the lack of available funding for sustainability projects. Given their inherent risks, climate projects can deliver uncertain returns, but they still require financing. Regional needs vary, so structured public-private conversations differ.

Traditional sources of private capital are unable to fill the gap. However, green banks offer a new source of funds. Green lending practices evolve by providing access to capital and enhancing market conditions to finance sustainable infrastructure development.

Green banks are typically capitalised by the government at the state or federal level, rather than private depositors. These funds are used to make loans to individuals and organisations with lower credit scores than banks typically lend to. The financial instruments are innovative, using policy frameworks and technological advancements.

Such loans can help fill gaps in energy programmes, so they play a pivotal role in accelerating the **transition** to cleaner energy and fighting climate change. The Australian Clean Energy Finance Corporation (CEFC) is arguably the world's largest green bank. In 2023, its CEO, Ian Learmonth, announced that the Australian government seeks to reach 82% renewable energy by 2030 and allocated A$20.5 billion to the CEFC to achieve this goal.

In the US, the number of not-for-profit banks has tripled since 2019. For example, the New York Green Bank is a division of the New York State Energy Research and Development Authority, operating as a state-sponsored financial institution. Capitalised with $165 million in public funds the bank seeks to increase green investment in NY.

TABLE 12.3 Typical characteristics of green banks – US Protection Agency (2025)

Programme Types	*Local or State Agencies, or Not-for-Profit Entities*
Target sectors	Commercial, residential, public, transportation
Potential funding sources	Bonds, public and private, rate payer, philanthropy
Security required of borrower	Determined by lender and nature of disbursement/ programme
Repayment mechanism	Typically, monthly or quarterly loan repayment
Funding needs	Typically, sponsors must provide an advance of upfront funding
Enabling legislation requirement	May be required

Source: FT.com (2024a).

Questions

1 The CEFC is arguably the world's largest green bank. You are to visit its website to perform a brief strategic analysis, then demonstrate how the bank attained its premier position.

2 Consider the concept of green banks, how can they help Global South Governments deal with tourism climate change issues?

3 Using any green bank of your choice, provide an example of an innovative strategy that reconciles economic success with environmental stewardship.

12.5 Value Creation in Ecosystem Leadership

Leadership teams must understand the interdependencies and information flows within the ecosystem. In such a dynamic environment, much must be learned about the underlying mechanisms, processes, and desired outcomes. Navigating ecosystems demands a distinctive set of leadership capabilities, which includes a shift from a linear to a networked approach.

Ecosystems expose organisations to interconnected risks, including reputational, regulatory, and operational risks. There are undoubtedly many reasons for the various ecosystem dynamics, but setting the tone for value creation among members is imperative. So, understanding the roles and interests of all actors is paramount.

Ecosystems are ripe for collaboration rather than competition. The key traits of trust, shared vision, and alignment need to be present. However, ecosystems will have dominant players that influence the flow of resources, which in turn impacts power dynamics.

Ecosystems require governance structures that maintain an equilibrium between control and collaboration. Leadership teams must define roles, responsibilities, and value-sharing mechanisms during the **transition** journey.

In summary, the ecosystem engagement strategy is illustrated in Figure 12.4. The following section delves into each step, and begins:

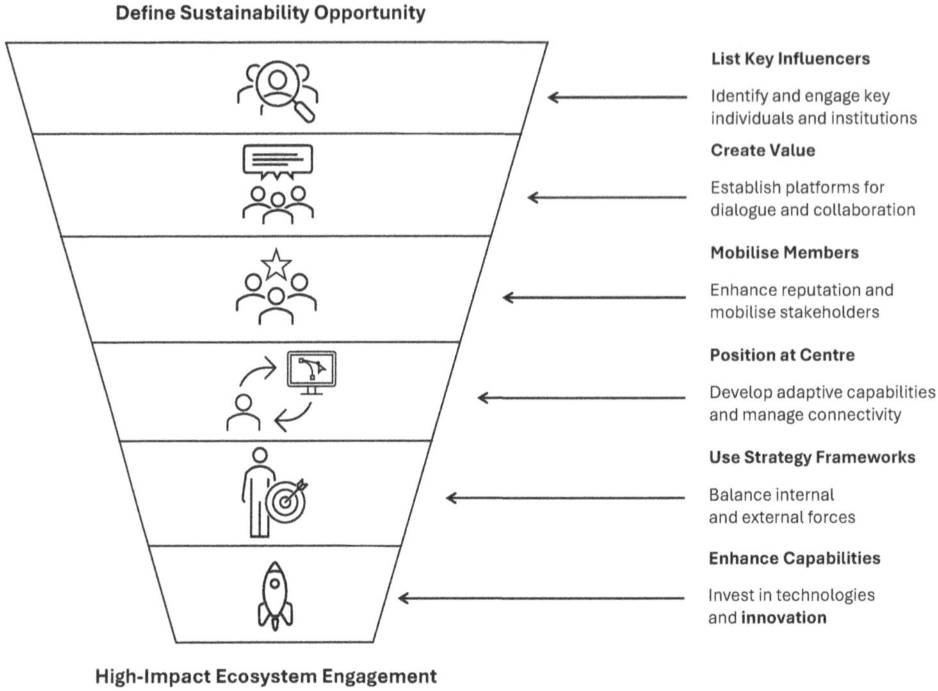

FIGURE 12.4 Ecosystem engagement strategy

Define the sustainability opportunity that you seek to exploit.

- Who will be affected, and who cares?
- Do you possess the resources and power to solve this problem?
- Where are the current gaps in your strategy?

Then

1 List individuals and institutions.

- Who are the key influencers and essential for success?
- Who are the gatekeepers? Who need to be mobilised?
- How do they help you achieve your goals? What can you do for them?

2 Value creation.

- What do you bring to the table?
- Facilitate platforms for dialogue.
- Orchestration, people, practices, information.

3 Members.

- How can the organisation enhance its reputation and positioning among stakeholders?
- How can members be usefully mobilised?
- What can members do for you?

4 Position yourself at the centre.

- Create adaptive capabilities within the organisation.
- How do you design and make the hub?
- How to manage connectivity between internal and external ecosystem members?

5 Use strategy frameworks and tools.

- How do you balance internal and external focus on your strategy?
- Create an impactful architecture that is fit for purpose.
- Look for opportunities to convert existing threats into new value pools.

6 Enhance high-impact capability.

- Invest in technologies that enable seamless integration across the ecosystem.
- How to build elements of **innovation** into your strategy processes?
- Incorporate problem-solving and solution framing heuristics into key processes.

12.6 Leadership Strategies for a Sustainable Ecosystem

The benefits of new partnerships can help integrate societal and environmental activities, creating an energised network of engaged actors. Forming novel ecosystems will help leaders gain access to new consumers.

During a recent conversation, I was told a story about how bureaucracy was choking the creativity of an organisation. It had more than 100 main committees and subcommittees and was unable to make strategic decisions based on market data. Instead, decisions were made based on data derived from committees, and such data could be biased due to the composition of the committees. Now imagine if this organisation was operating in a complex ecosystem!

Deiser (2023) captures this elegantly by extolling: "Cumbersome, bureaucratic decision processes are poison for collaboration and co-creation, which thrive on flexibility, agility and speed."

Figure 12.5 shows Deiser's (2021) three subdomains dimensions – ecosystem strategy, ecosystem organisation, and ecosystem relationships. These three subdomains are broken down into nine capability domains for effective business ecosystem leadership.

The subject of complex, interconnected systems has become a critical competency. The following sections will explore the concept of ecosystem leadership within the framework.

12.6.1 The Shift to Ecosystem Thinking

As emerging technologies dismantle the value chains of existing industries, conventional thinking needs to permeate traditional boundaries. No longer can organisations operate as isolated entities. Instead, they must form novel alliances and partnerships to complete value propositions, design compelling business models, and ensure excellence throughout the customer journey.

Evidence demands a new understanding of leadership, preferably one that extends beyond the individual leader to encompass organisational capabilities for ecosystem

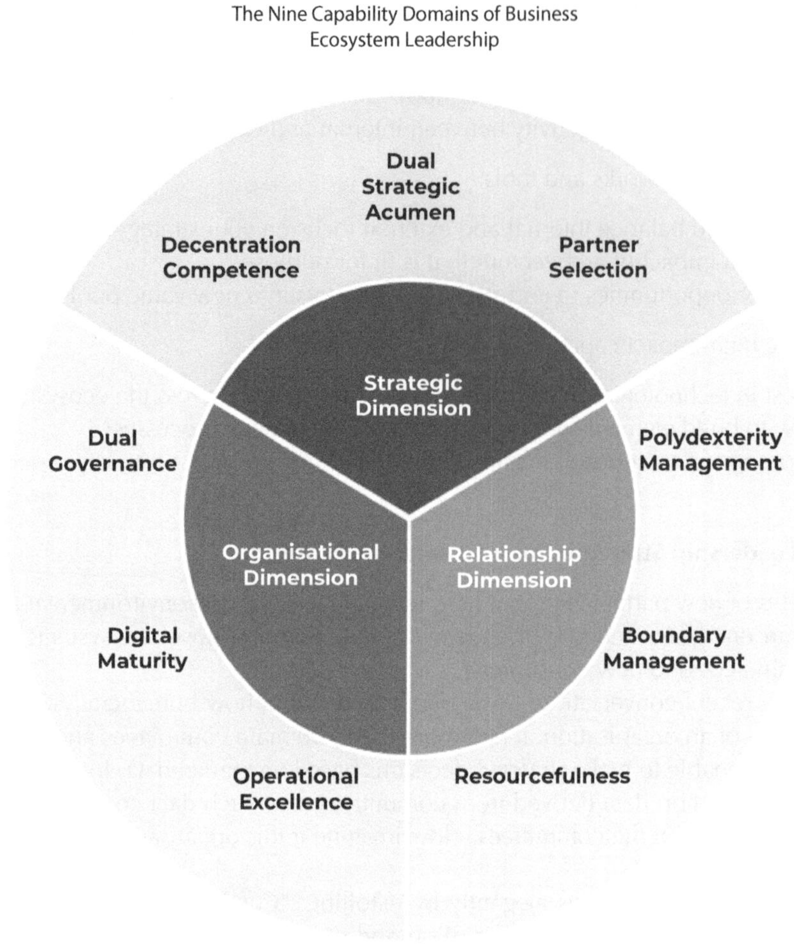

FIGURE 12.5 Ecosystem leadership: A framework for 21st-century organisations (reprinted with permission)

Source: Deiser (2021).

engagement. Today's collaborative approaches to governance and value creation render traditional and rigid command-and-control practices obsolete.

Despite the plethora of theories of organisational leadership, ecosystem leadership is different. While winning the hearts and minds is vital, ecosystem leadership is a capability that requires designing, operating, and building relationships within dynamic and increasingly digital ecosystems.

This capability works within three critical dimensions:

- The Strategic Dimension: How organisations think about and formulate strategy in ecosystem contexts?
- The Relationship Dimension: How organisations manage complex cross-boundary relationships?

- The Organisational Dimension: How internal structures and processes enable ecosystem participation?

Each dimension requires specific capabilities that organisations need to develop to lead effectively in ecosystem contexts.

12.6.2 The Strategic Dimension of Ecosystem Leadership

Decentration Competence: Ecosystem leaders must transcend the self-interest of their organisation in favour of a superordinate view of the ecosystem's strategy, operations, and **performance**. This requires stepping out of a self-centred frame of reference to see the world as a network of interrelations, namely "decentration competence."

Ironically, overcoming self-interest first requires a thorough awareness of one's own capabilities and purpose. Only a strong self-identity provides the basis for credibly defining a position within the ecosystem while relinquishing control when necessary. This strong identity enables an unbiased appreciation of ecosystem partners and a decentralised view of overall system dynamics.

Dual Strategic Acumen: Ecosystems, by definition, are based on value propositions that can only be delivered through collaborative efforts of interdependent stakeholders. This creates two levels of strategy – the ecosystem's strategy and each participant's strategy, which follow different rationales yet must be integrated.

Organisations with dual strategic acumen understand both their business rationale and the ecosystem's purpose. They excel at combining their strategy with the ecosystem's strategic requirements, creating synergies rather than conflicts between these two strategic thrusts.

Strategic Partner Selection: The composition of partners has a critical impact on ecosystem **performance**. The ever-increasing strategic opportunities will require different types of partners who can embrace the cultural implications of potential collaborations.

Throughout this book, the managerial concepts of soft factors such as leadership values, and agility will impact intellectual property (IP) ownership, sustainability product/service fit, and market positioning. Cultural due diligence acts like a glue to bind the ecosystem loosely.

12.6.3 The Relationship Dimension of Ecosystem Leadership

Polydexterity Management: The ability to display polydexterity competencies to effectively engage concurrently is pivotal. The leadership team must cope with the idiosyncrasies of each partner while maintaining flexibility in strategic decision-making.

Ecosystem participants often differ substantially in size, operating models, and roles. They may include major digital platforms, large incumbent enterprises, specialised niche players, research organisations, and startups, each operating under different regulatory environments with different ownership structures and cultures.

Strategic partnerships can take many forms, ranging from joint ventures, licensing agreements, to co-branded collaborations and shared IP frameworks. Each relationship presents its own risk, and the firm needs to assess if it is to operate in an orchestrator or participant-based position.

Boundary Management: Ecosystems work more effectively when the interactions of boundary-spanning activities are frictionless, fuelling creativity and **innovation**. Otherwise, there could be territorial battles over space and the capture of value. Effective boundary management recognises these challenges and designs a cross-institutional process that benefits each member.

Skilled leaders can determine the degree of openness during conversations. Protecting as much IP as possible should be the mantra during meetings but needs to be balanced with the ownership of co-created assets and the interests of all parties.

Resourcefulness: It extends beyond leveraging internal assets to identifying and accessing resources throughout the ecosystem, including talent, market access, financing sources, technology, data, and manufacturing capacity. The quality of access to these resources depends on relationship dynamics, trust levels, and cultural compatibility among partners.

Effective ecosystem leaders build boundary-spanning communities of practice and shared platforms to develop resourcefulness. These social frameworks facilitate relationship-building, enhance collaboration, build trust, and provide privileged access to key decision-makers and top talent across the ecosystem.

12.6.4 The Organisational Dimension of Ecosystem Leadership

Operational Excellence: Unlike traditional corporations, which have legally codified governance mechanisms, ecosystems lack a formal "constitution" at the outset. The interdependent nature of relationships between semi-autonomous players creates fluid contractual frameworks that require dedicated roles, policies, and mechanisms to connect ecosystem rules with each participant's operating systems.

Organisations must simultaneously optimise their contributions to the ecosystem while aligning their internal structures with external collaboration requirements. This dual focus requires internal roles and responsibilities dedicated to ecosystem leadership, with sufficient authority to drive the structural and cultural agility necessary for effective participation.

Digital Maturity: Digital technologies serve dual roles in ecosystem contexts, enabling new product and service offerings, as well as supporting ecosystem architectures and operations. This makes digital maturity indispensable for successful ecosystem engagement.

Digital maturity encompasses both "hard" dimensions (technical infrastructure, networks, software, cybersecurity) and "soft" dimensions (digital literacy and creativity). Organisations lacking digital sophistication not only jeopardise ecosystem operations but also limit their benefits from participation, making them less attractive partners.

Dual Governance: Within complex ecosystems, members capture more value when efforts are agile and accountability is ensured from all participants. This helps shape the enabling internal governance frameworks that provide adequate autonomy while maintaining strategic purpose.

Simultaneously, the ecosystem itself needs mechanisms that cope with value sharing, membership selection criteria, and rule changes. Working across boundaries, leaders must excel in horizontal negotiation and influence to achieve system-wide agreements.

Building Ecosystem Leadership Capabilities: Organisations that systematically develop their ecosystem narrative can gain a first-mover advantage and a competitive edge for their sustainability strategy. Having experts in-house dedicated to overcoming the aforementioned challenges can help keep the sustainability journey on track.

Key activities that enhance ecosystem leadership capabilities may include:

- Acting as a hub to hosting platforms that encourage ecosystem member conversations.
- Getting the core messages of the ecosystem strategy and management in mission statements and leadership development.
- Benchmarking diagnostic assessments of current ecosystem capabilities.
- Organising boundary-spanning events for communities with shared interests.
- Institutionalising collaborative strategy processes with external stakeholders.
- Creating dedicated boundary-spanning roles to exploit potential synergies.
- Investing in emerging ecosystem-enabling technologies.

12.6.5 Conclusion: The Imperative for Ecosystem Leadership

Developing these capabilities requires the traits of purpose-driven leadership, strategic, structural, and cultural acumen; institutionalised change architecture; and committed change leaders.

The driver of this process must be cross-functional, integrating an understanding of strategy, organisational development, IT, customer experience, and the political acumen needed to deal with friction and drive change. In essence, ecosystem leadership encompasses the comprehensive skill set required of 21st-century leaders.

Organisations that master the nine capabilities of ecosystem leadership position themselves not only for enhanced **performance** today but also for sustainable evolution in an increasingly interconnected business landscape. The future belongs to those who can lead beyond boundaries.

12.7 Strategic Foresight in Ecosystem Environments

As discussed in this book, **SSM** requires leaders to detect emerging trends and changes in ecosystems. This will provide early warning signs about shift in stakeholder behaviour, artificial intelligence, and regulatory changes. Strategic foresight tools enable users to prepare for multiple futures, so that leaders can create contingency plans to strengthen resilience (Table 12.4).

Strategic foresight is a valuable tool for ecosystems.

A road map for embedding strategic foresight skills during **transition** should comprise:

Phase 1: Foundation (0–6 months)

- Create a cross-functional foresight team of people from customer-facing, R&D, strategy, and sustainability areas.
- Teach senior staff fundamental foresight techniques (scenario planning, horizon scanning).
- Initiate an initial environmental scanning programme with an eye towards signals indicating disturbances to ecosystems.
- Plot the present and future ecosystem and note important uncertainties.

TABLE 12.4 Strategic foresight tools with their advantages and best use cases

Tool	*Advantages*	*When Best to Use*
Environmental scanning	Provides insights into external trends (e.g., regulatory, social, and market changes) affecting sustainability.	For ongoing monitoring of external forces influencing long-term strategy.
Scenario planning	Prepares organisations for multiple futures by exploring uncertainties and potential impacts.	During strategic planning to develop flexible strategies for sustainability and resilience.
Delphi method	Gathers expert consensus on complex or uncertain topics, ensuring informed decision-making.	When addressing complex challenges requiring expert insights, such as climate or policy changes.
Horizon scanning	Detects early signals of change to anticipate opportunities or threats.	In long-term planning to stay ahead of shifts in markets or regulations.
Trend analysis	Identifies and interprets emerging patterns to inform **innovation** and strategy.	For **innovation** and developing sustainable product or service offerings aligned with consumer trends.
Causal layered analysis (CLA)	Explores underlying assumptions about sustainability that shape organisational strategies.	Effective in workshops aimed at challenging existing narratives about sustainability and exploring transformative changes.
Futures wheel	Maps out cascading effects of decisions to assess long-term impacts.	In brainstorming sessions to visualise consequences of sustainability initiatives.
Three horizons framework	Balances immediate actions with long-term goals, fostering **innovation** and sustainability alignment.	For integrating short-term actions with a long-term vision in strategic planning.
Backcasting	Starts with desired future outcomes to design pathways for achieving them.	When setting ambitious goals like carbon neutrality or net-zero emissions.
Policy gaming	Simulates various scenarios to evaluate policies or strategies under different conditions.	In policy development or stakeholder engagement initiatives to test responses to sustainability challenges.
Roadmapping	Aligns technology and strategic objectives with long-term sustainability goals.	For planning how to integrate emerging technologies into sustainability strategies.
Visioning workshops	Engages stakeholders to build a shared vision for a sustainable future.	At the start of strategic initiatives to ensure alignment and buy-in from diverse stakeholders.

Phase 2: Integration (6–12 months)

- Include foresight instruments in the strategic planning process.
- Create three to four thorough future models, emphasising the evolution of ecosystems.
- Design an "ecosystem radar" to track faint signals constantly.

- Initiate regular discussions among stakeholders on the evolution of future ecosystems.
- List "no-regret" actions with value in several contexts.

Phase 3: Institutionalisation (12–24 months)

- Provide official control linking vision to decision-making.
- Create measurements of ecological resilience to assess strategic choices.
- Provide official procedures for converting ideas into projects related to **innovation**.
- Develop systems of foresight that span ecosystems and involve key allies.
- Establish methodical review systems to change presumptions and situations.

STRATEGY NUGGET

Coca-Cola Corporate Backtracking

In contrast to its original goal of collecting and recycling one bottle or can for every one sold by 2030, Coca-Cola pushed back its goal to recover 70–75% of each can and bottle sold by 2035.

Coca-Cola is among an increasing number of firms reassessing their sustainability objectives.

The markets anticipate this trend in 2025, as competitive pressures intensify, which place pressure on margins. So, it increases the risk of greenwashing allegations, compelling corporations to adopt more pragmatic sustainability objectives.

Coca-Cola's recent reversal on its sustainability objectives has significant implications for purpose-driven leadership, particularly in terms of corporate accountability and stakeholder confidence.

Consequences for purpose-driven leadership include:

1. Deterioration of trust and credibility.
2. Changes in corporate responsibility behaviour.
3. Effect on employee engagement and morale.
4. Heightened regulatory oversight and activism.
5. Requirement for a clear purpose and effective communication of the strategy.

Coca-Cola's rethinking of its sustainability objectives highlights the decisions Boards will be increasingly confronted with as they face rapidly evolving business challenges. Adapting the sustainability approach involves balancing short-term versus long-term results.

Questions

1. In the sense of "More Corporate Backtracking" by Coca-Cola, what are the implications for purpose-driven leadership?
2. Do you believe that more multinational organisations will seek to address greenwashing fears by reducing the numbers in their objectives?
3. Assume you are a sustainable strategy consultant. What advice would you provide to a multinational client who is facing stakeholder pressure about its financial and sustainability **performance**?

Source: FT.com (2024b).

12.8 Chapter Key Takeaways

Some key takeaways from Chapter 12 on "Leadership in Sustainable Ecosystems" include:

1. **The Paradigm Shift from Markets to Ecosystems:** From conventional marketplaces to linked ecosystems, the corporate world has undergone drastic changes, calling for a complete rethink of leadership styles. This shift calls for a change from closed methods to open, cooperative solutions using alliances outside of organisations. Modern corporate success increasingly relies on the ability to coordinate intricate multi-stakeholder ecosystems rather than controlling single-market sectors.
2. **Ecosystem Leadership Calls for a Three-Dimensional Capability:** Three fundamental aspects define effective ecosystem leadership: the organisational dimension (how internal structures enable ecosystem participation), the relationship dimension (how organisations manage complex cross-boundary relationships), and the strategic dimension (how organisations formulate strategy in ecosystem contexts). Every dimension requires specific skills that must be acquired systematically.
3. **Digital Change Support Ecosystem Success:** Digital technologies support ecosystem structures and operations, as well as new product and service offerings, thereby playing dual roles in ecosystem settings. Companies lacking digital sophistication not only compromise ecosystem operations but also reduce their advantages from involvement, which makes them less appealing allies. Digital maturity covers technical infrastructure as well as digital literacy and creativity applied all throughout the company.
4. **Ecosystem Leaders Must Go beyond Organisational Self-Interest:** In favour of a superordinate vision of the strategy, operations, and **performance** of the ecosystem. This "decentralising competency" calls for seeing the world as a network of interrelations outside of a self-centred frame of reference. Ironically, this capacity results from a strong organisational identity that allows confident involvement free from continual control.
5. **Governance Needs to Operate at both the Ecosystem and Firm Levels:** Dual governance is essential in complex ecosystems. Organisations must have systems in place that provide sufficient autonomy while also maintaining strategic intent. The ecosystem itself simultaneously requires systems for rule updates, value exchange, and membership choice. To achieve system-wide agreements instead of relying solely on hierarchical power, leaders must excel in horizontal negotiation and influence.
6. **Dynamic Ecosystems Demand Strategic Foresight:** Strategic foresight helps executives anticipate changes in ecosystems, identify new trends, and recognise early warning signals concerning shifts in stakeholder behaviour, technological advancements, and legislative changes. This capacity helps companies to build contingency plans, enhancing ecosystem resilience, and being ready for several futures. In this context, especially useful tools are scenario planning, horizon scanning, and backcasting.
7. **Value Creation Must Be Balanced between the Ecosystem and the Business:** Leaders must delicately strike a balance between value for their company and for the ecosystem from a value creation standpoint. Ignorance of this equilibrium would result in mistrust that could hinder development, as ecosystem partners provide particular skills necessary for the prosperity of the society. Effective ecosystem engagement

plans outline sustainability potential, identify key influencers, articulate value generation mechanisms, and help the company position itself strategically within the network.

12.9 Self-Reflection Questions

1 How should the Chief Sustainability Officer decide whether their company should present itself as an ecosystem orchestrator instead of a participant? What skills should be cultivated in enhancing the organisation's strategic ecosystem positioning?
2 Arguably, ecosystem leadership needs "decentralised competence" to balance environmental concerns with corporate ones. Which basic conflicts surface in this balancing act, and how could they be effectively controlled?
3 Based on this chapter's examination of digital maturity as a necessary ecosystem competency, create a framework for CEOs to assess their company's digital readiness for ecosystem participation. Which holes would most greatly compromise the success of an ecosystem?
4 How may reporting on sustainability measures be included in ecosystem management? Analyse carefully possible strategies and their consequences for Chief Sustainability Officers.
5 This chapter stresses that "ecosystems work more effectively when boundary-spanning activities are frictionless and fuel creativity and **innovation**" (p. 34). How can companies create efficient boundary management strategies that safeguard important intellectual property while still encouraging open **innovation** inside sustainable ecosystems?

References

Altman, E.J. and Tushman, M.L., (2017). Platforms, open/user innovation, and ecosystems: A strategic leadership perspective. In J. Furman, A. Gawer, B.S. Silverman and S. Stern (eds.), *Entrepreneurship, innovation, and platforms*, pp.177–207. Emerald Publishing Limited.

Autio, E., Nambisan, S., Thomas, L.D.W. and Wright, M., (2018). Digital affordances, spatial affordances, and the genesis of entrepreneurial ecosystems. *Strategic Entrepreneurship Journal, 12*(1), pp.72–95.

Boons, F. and Howard-Grenville, J., (2009). *The social embeddedness of industrial ecology*. Edward Elgar Publishing.

Coase, R.H., (1993). The nature of the firm (1937). *The nature of the firm: origins, evolution, and development*, pp.18–33.

Deiser, R., (2021). *How to succeed in business ecosystems. A capability framework for business ecosystem leadership*. CFFO Press.

Deiser, R., (2023). The art of business ecosystem leadership. *Developing Leaders Quarterly*. Available at: https://futureorg.org/wp-content/uploads/2023/08/The-Art-of-Business-Ecosystem-Leadership.pdf (Accessed: 12 September 2025).

FT.com (2024a). US green banks take off. Available at: https://www.ft.com/content/34adcbd5-13d4-4df4-b494-5c3a2d7a949f (Accessed: 12 September 2025).

FT.com (2024b). Coca-Cola draws fire after watering down environmental targets. Available at: https://www.ft.com/content/75d5fb6d-2bc8-4621-a955-9c70897541cd (Accessed: 12 September 2025).

Foss, N., Schmidt, J. and Teece, D., (2023). Ecosystem leadership as a dynamic capability. *Long Range Planning, 56*(1), p.102270.

Hart, O.D., (1988). Incomplete contracts and the theory of the firm. *The Journal of Law, Economics, and Organization, 4*(1), pp.119–139.

Holmstrom, B.R. and Tirole, J., (1989). The theory of the firm. *Handbook of Industrial Organization, 1*, pp.61–133.

Iansiti, M. and Lakhani, K.R., (2020). *Competing in the age of AI: Strategy and leadership when algorithms and networks run the world.* Harvard Business Review Press.

Jacobides, M.G., Cennamo, C. and Gawer, A., (2018). Towards a theory of ecosystems. *Strategic Management Journal, 39*(8), pp.2255–2276.

Kohtamäki, M., Parida, V., Oghazi, P., Gebauer, H. and Baines, T., (2019). Digital servitization business models in ecosystems: A theory of the firm. *Journal of Business Research, 104*, pp.380–392.

Lingens, B., Miehé, L. and Gassmann, O., (2021). The ecosystem blueprint: How firms shape the design of an ecosystem according to the surrounding conditions. *Long Range Planning, 54*(2), p.102043.

Nambisan, S., Zahra, S.A. and Luo, Y., (2019). Global platforms and ecosystems: Implications for international business theories. *Journal of International Business Studies, 50*, pp.1464–1486.

Shen, L., Shi, Q., Parida, V. and Jovanovic, M., (2024). Ecosystem orchestration practices for industrial firms: A qualitative meta-analysis, framework development and research agenda. *Journal of Business Research, 173*, p.114463.

Tsujimoto, M., Kajikawa, Y., Tomita, J. and Matsumoto, Y., (2018). A review of the ecosystem concept—Towards coherent ecosystem design. *Technological Forecasting and Social Change, 136*, pp.49–58.

US Environmental Protection Agency (2025). Available at: https://www.epa.gov/statelocalenergy/green-banks (Accessed: 12 September 2025).

Williamson, O.E., (1989). Transaction cost economics. *Handbook of Industrial Organization, 1*, pp.135–182.

World Economic Forum (2024). To create a 'sustainomy' businesses must focus on the ecosystem, not just the market. Available at: https://www.weforum.org/stories/2024/06/to-create-an-economy-that-works-for-all-businesses-must-focus-on-the-ecosystem-and-the-market/(Accessed:28August 2025).

Zahra, S.A. and Nambisan, S., (2012). *Entrepreneurship and strategic thinking in digital ecosystems.* Academy of Management Perspectives.

13

OVERCOMING ORGANISATIONAL PUSHBACKS

13.1 Learning Strategy Objectives

After completing this chapter, you will be able to:

1 **Knowledge-Based Objectives:**

- Analyse and evaluate the various organisational resistance to sustainability initiatives.
- Compare and contrast the economic implications of sustainable business models, focussing on how they must address stakeholders' concerns and mitigate pushback.

2 **Skill-Based Objectives:**

- Design and develop sustainable business models that anticipate and proactively address sources of organisational resistance.
- Critically evaluate the causes of implementation deficit challenges and enhance the resilience of organisational staff in the face of dynamic market conditions.

3 **Attitude-Based Objectives:**

- Overcome the staff fear factor in managing change and addressing global challenges through sustainability initiatives.
- Inspire active engagement by developing leadership skills to inspire and drive a forward-thinking mindset throughout the organisation.

13.2 Introduction

Organisational pushbacks in a sustainability context cost organisations considerable sums in their triple bottom line metrics. Frameworks such as the circular economy can help alleviate some of the planet's waste issues, but implementation issues can frustrate. Implementing circular economy strategies impacts the micro-levels, such as the firm and consumers and involves trade-offs (Schroeder, Anggraeni, and Weber, 2019).

DOI: 10.4324/9781003516774-17

Institutional resistance can be attributed in part to fear of **innovation** and adherence to the dominant social paradigm (Goudie, 2005). Several determinants influence individuals' attitudes and willingness for change. The dominant social paradigm is a socially embedded (behavioural) driver of environmental choices (Kilbourne, Beckmann, and Thelen, 2002).

Organisations need to make internal adjustments, which can prove challenging for staff to accept. The dialectic between strategy formulation and implementation has become a central discussion around the organisation pushback, as we live in an ecological crisis.

13.2.1 Overview of Common Challenges

During any change management programme, leaders may face pushback for various reasons, including fear of the unknown, trust and communication, cultural inertia, and negative prior experiences. This chapter provides insight from the academic literature, practice, and client engagements into the pushback leaders can face when implementing sustainability-related projects.

Organisations pursuing sustainability objectives can face resistance and pushback from internal and external stakeholders, posing significant challenges to implementation. Internally, resistance may stem from entrenched organisational cultures, where traditional profit-centric mindsets clash with the perceived costs and uncertainties associated with sustainability initiatives.

Employees and managers accustomed to established practices may resist change, fearing disruption to familiar workflows or potential job insecurity. Moreover, resistance may manifest from the perceived trade-offs between short-term financial gains and long-term sustainability goals, leading to scepticism about the feasibility and profitability.

Leaders are now wary of implementing sustainable projects with overly ambitious goals, fearing negative backlash. Investors who focus solely on short-term returns may view sustainability investments as detracting from profitability, prioritising immediate financial results over longer-term sustainability benefits. Similarly, customers accustomed to inexpensive and convenient products or services may resist changes that result in higher prices or inconvenience, especially if sustainability considerations must be effectively communicated or perceived as imposing sacrifices.

Veblen's theory, named after economist Thorstein Veblen, illustrates this. Contrary to traditional economic principles, the Veblen (2017) effect describes a phenomenon where the demand for luxury goods increases as prices rise. Chanel, LVHM handbags, signal status, and exclusivity justify pricing points.

This effect is driven by the desire for conspicuous consumption, where high prices signal exclusivity, status, and prestige. Luxury electric vehicle (EV) cars were typical examples of Veblen goods. However, the global EV luxury car industry presents an interesting case where today's demand decreases as prices increase, contradicting the Veblen effect. This discrepancy suggests that the EV market is now driven by value for money.

During the writing of this book, the luxury *EV* slowed down, and consumers reinstated traditional priorities, such as **innovation** and technological reliability. To assist readers in overcoming the challenges of adopting a sustainable strategic approach to managing a firm, this chapter will demonstrate how to navigate resistance by employing proactive approaches that foster buy-in and collaboration.

Understanding these dynamics during **transition** is crucial for companies operating in luxury and EV markets, as it influences pricing and marketing strategies. While luxury brands often leverage the Veblen effect to justify high prices and enhance exclusivity, the EV industry may need to focus on different marketing strategies that emphasise sustainability and **innovation** rather than status symbols.

Internally, promoting a culture of sustainability through education, training, and incentives can overcome resistance by aligning individual and organisational values with sustainability goals. Externally, transparent communication, stakeholder engagement, and partnerships can build trust and legitimacy, mitigating resistance by addressing concerns and demonstrating the mutual benefits of sustainability initiatives. By acknowledging and addressing pushback and resistance, firms can cultivate resilience and drive transformative change towards sustainable practices, ultimately reaping long-term rewards for both business and society.

STRATEGY NUGGET

Moving Beyond Economic, Social, and Governance Compliance

Heightened market tensions around "forced" economic, social, and governance (ESG) adoption reveal a critical organisational strategic blind spot. When companies treat sustainability as a compliance issue rather than a market opportunity, we see (1) lower returns, (2) market bubbles, and (3) mission creep.

A possible solution?

Seek strategic ESG integration that drives both purpose and profit. This involves adopting **SSM** principles to **transition** from compliance to a competitive advantage successfully. Actionable strategies include:

- Operational Excellence: Embed sustainability operational metrics into core strategy key **performance** indicators. Incorporating executive compensation into carbon reduction targets can stimulate behavioural change.
- Investor Relations Strategy: Communicate the ESG return on investment (ROI) story with supporting CFO approved data-driven narratives. Demonstrate how sustainability initiatives will reduce costs, mitigate risks, and capitalise on new market opportunities.
- Business Model **Innovation:** Use **SSM** approaches to identify where ESG can strengthen the competitive moat.
- Stakeholder Alignment: Move beyond doing nice things via corporate social responsibility (CSR), to a broader base stakeholder value creation model. This should include hard-to-reach stakeholders, such as communities.

Some industry-specific implications:

- Tech companies will leverage ESG for talent acquisition and retention in competitive recruitment markets.
- Manufacturing can use sustainability to drive supply chain resilience and cost optimisation.
- Financial services can position their ESG expertise as a client advisory differentiator.

The bottom line:

Companies that can integrate ESG strategically rather than reactively will capture their share of the $30 trillion global ESG investing market.

Can you afford to miss the opportunity?

What's your experience with ESG integration challenges? Share your insights in the comments below.

Questions

1 Can organisations afford to miss the ESG opportunity? Provide some insight to your views.
2 How can organisations use **SSM** to crack the ESG code to create their competitive moat?
3 How can companies demonstrate the ROI of their sustainability initiatives to investors and other stakeholders?

13.3 Understanding Organisational Resistance

13.3.1 Types of Pushback

In prior consulting engagements, I have witnessed pushbacks, which can take several forms, including active or passive resistance. In a sustainability context, resistance can encompass both overt objections and subtle non-compliance. The nature of pushbacks, however well-prepared one may be, continues to take me by surprise.

These can consist of resistance at all levels throughout the organisation. Sometimes, even senior leadership team members may need to pay closer attention to the benefits of implementing a sustainability strategy, which can provide the organisation's lifeline. The paradox is that overcoming a nuanced understanding of organisational power and politics is key, and this takes on greater importance in the face of exogenous shocks.

Such a situation can translate to a source of inertia, market irrelevance, and demise. To overcome this, organisations need to reconfigure operating dynamics to overcome resistance.

Resistance during engagements can be visible, deliberate, and even hostile. Instead of vocal objectives for the key messages delivered in meetings and forums, behaviour can take several surprising forms.

When considering why this may occur, it often comes back to a fear of job insecurity in newly structured organisations, a perceived loss of personal and department autonomy, and even misalignment with personal values. Maintaining open channels for employees to voice concerns and suggestions can help mitigate this threat.

Passive resistance is much more challenging to notice. Actions are subtle and less visible. There may be a failure to appreciate the broader benefits of the espoused sustainability strategy, which appears as a lack of visibility at regular in-house Zoom meetings, with minimal effort being made to execute key tasks. When individuals attend meetings, there is a surprising lack of awareness or understanding of the key planks of the sustainability strategy.

TABLE 13.1 Symptoms of organisational resistance

Symptom	*Diagnosis*	***SSM***
1 Misalignment with core values	Ensuring that proposed changes align with organisation's core values. When employees see that new initiatives resonate with shared beliefs, they're more likely to support them.	Stakeholder engagement audit to identify specific gaps between stated values and actual behaviours.
2 Perceived lack of involvement	Engage staff meaningful in the planning process to foster a sense of ownership.	Include bottom-up approaches to feel the pulse of the organisation.
3 Fear of change	Address employees' fears with clear communication, and support.	Action research methods with the use of tools such as Padlet can get feelings out in the open.
4 Lack of trust	Deploy approaches that build trustworthiness.	Create structured opportunities for vulnerability and collaborative problem-solving across hierarchical levels.
5 Concerns about workload or resources	Ensure project tasks and resources are built into existing workloads.	Establish a transparent governance system for resource allocation decisions with clear criteria for project approval and continuation.
6 Prioritise open communication	Ensure staff understand and appreciate the big picture and how they fit in.	Implement a "psychological safety index" to measure and improve environments where candid dialogue flourishes.
7 Empower staff	Engage them in the process and respect their need for control over their work.	Implement a structured decision rights framework that clearly delineates where employees have authority to act independently versus where consultation is required.

13.3.2 Root Causes of Resistance

From my experience, Table 13.1 provides a list of some pushback issues.

The industry focus influences how emerging technologies are integrated into core processes. Digital platforms enable interfunctional systems that can provide new sustainability strategies. Research reports that organisations with integrated sustainability practices achieve measurable **performance** outcomes (Bhattacharya, Nand, and Castka, 2019, Xie et al., 2024; Sariyer et al., 2024; Morgan, Fok, and Zee, 2024).

13.3.3 The Onion Model for Problem-Solving

Working with clients has revealed that problem-solving must be pitched at the appropriate level. Figure 13.1 illustrates that dealing with the problem/symptoms and process may only scratch the outer layer of the onion. This is pertinent when previous change management projects have stalled the **transition**. We can see that layers 3 and 4 deal with human behaviour and environmental cause and effect, where perception may be stronger than reality. Staff often know what could work but rarely talk about it.

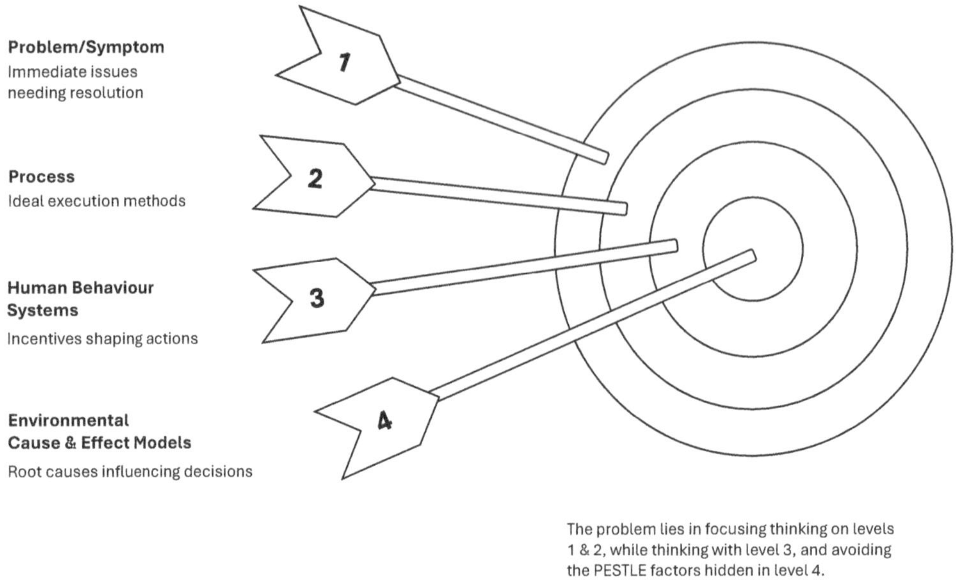

FIGURE 13.1 Systemic thinking and levels of problem-solving

13.4 Aligning Strategic Implementation

Since the advent of the pandemic, organisations have experienced heightened complexity. To overcome this, investment in human resources and digital technology is justified as a necessary strategy for coping. However, individual personal values influence levels of strategic engagement throughout the organisation, which can be positive or negative.

13.4.1 Internal Stakeholder Resistance

The human-environment sustainability relationship plays a crucial role in organisational alignment. However, shattered (and even shaken) business models need new practices, and workforce strategies must be redefined in ways that could not have been predicted pre-pandemic.

Today's environment requires strategic engagement to create adaptive processes in people and organisations. There is a delicate balance between people and systems, as they are both driven by pressure for change and stability. Such conflict must align with adaptive outcomes at the individual and organisational levels.

Employee well-being is paramount, but toxicity levels in businesses and the workplace are increasing. Figure 13.2 illustrates evidence of blame games, deteriorating relations at higher levels, poor customer service, and quiet quitting harm both employee well-being and the bottom line.

13.4.2 External Stakeholder Challenges

Strategic engagement depends on several factors, including overcoming individual and firm proclivities, social capital, and structural issues. However, the key is the ability to

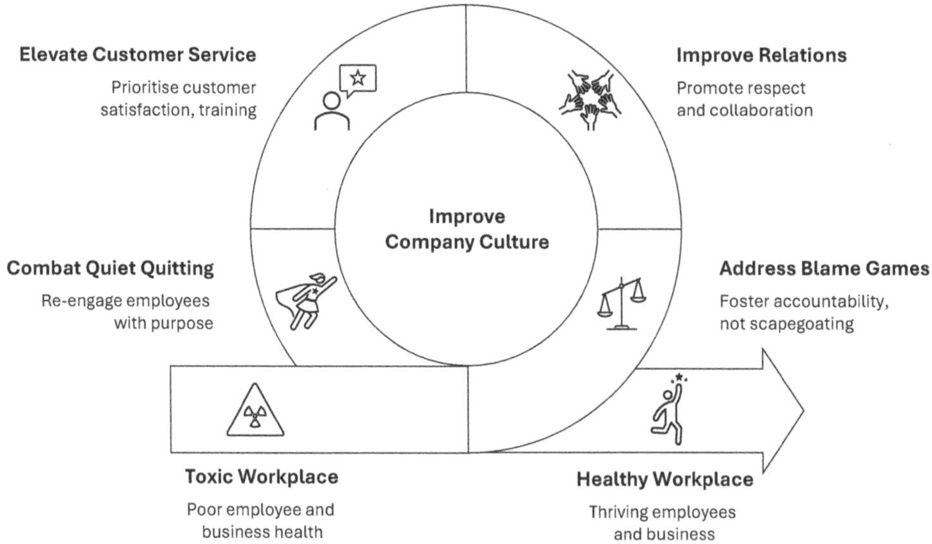

FIGURE 13.2 Eliminating workplace toxicity

interact with the complex external environment. Therefore, the firm needs to develop simple-to-use heuristics to engage strategically in which uncertainty is accepted. This presents learning and development opportunities within the firm to reduce surprises (what you don't know, you don't know).

Key factors include:

- Media and Public Opinion: Greenwashing scepticism about the authenticity of sustainability claims.
- Consumer Resistance: Resistance to higher prices for "green" products.
- Investor Resistance: Balancing short-term profit focus with long-term sustainability rewards.
- Regulatory Challenges: Changing government policy that impacts the incentives for sustainability.
- Supply Chain Partners: Can be difficult and costly to convince suppliers to adopt green practices.
- Market Competition: The growth mantra exists, and market share needs to be protected.
- Communities: Sustainability strategies can have unintended consequences on their communities.

13.4.3 Cultural and Structural Barriers

Organisations don't need the ill effects of toxicity reducing productivity. Research has shown that avoiding a toxic worker (or removing them) is more beneficial than replacing an average worker with a superstar worker (Housman and Minor, 2015).

At the institutional level, external pressures can create a risk-averse culture that drives strategic behaviour. This can lead to a lack of thought and practice diversity, culminating in a paucity of effective strategising within the organisation. A seemingly successful institution can swiftly hit the buffers.

An HR detox and modernisation approach can be a useful de-cluttering exercise, by eliminating all unnecessary and harmful HR practices and processes. This will contribute to a healthy recovery of HR learning and development capability. The responsibility approach will move beyond making employees cognitively aware and help manifest this learning in the workplace.

More specifically, the approach consists of three elements: culture-driven and will improve engaged employees' opportunity-spotting, collaboration-building, and strategic planning and thinking.

The CEO needs to ensure that the staff:

- Gain a new way of reducing the organisation's toxicity levels and recognising the implications for the Learning and Development pipeline.
- Feel comfortable with the organisation's DNA, which aligns with the immune system to prevent nasty external shocks from entering and harming the firm.
- Understand ways of assessing bureaucracy and trauma in the digital environment.

Benefits include:

- Gain a new way of thinking about alignment and recognising the importance of the human-environment sustainability relationship.
- Uncover the personal values that are acting as barriers to developing winning new strategies.
- Leave with new heuristics for leading the organisation's strategic engagement – complexity-related initiatives.

Mini Case Study

The €60 Billion Novo Nordisk Wake-Up Call 30 July 2025

€60 billion. Wiped out. In one day. That's what happened to the Danish drugmaker Novo Nordisk yesterday, a company that had everything going for it just 12 months ago.

The impact has been felt in Denmark, with the country having to slash its annual growth forecast to 1.4% from 3%, largely due to events at Novo Nordisk.

My take on events. The shocking reality? Novo Nordisk had a first-mover advantage in the obesity drug market. Ozempic became a household name. The stock price shot up 300% in three years, and market leadership appeared to be secure. Then, Eli Lilly made a competitive move.

A key lesson for business executives: First-to-market means nothing if you can't execute at competitive speed. So, what did Lilly do differently?

Moved at "double speed" to commercialise and built direct-to-consumer channels faster. Scaled manufacturing more aggressively and better understood market dynamics. The result? Lilly's Mounjaro just overtook Ozempic in weekly prescriptions for the first time. Market share between the two companies has now flipped. This situation does not only apply to the pharma industry. It can apply to any market leader who thinks their moat is unbreachable.

Novo's Incoming CEO Maziar Mike Doustdar made the comment: "Setbacks don't define companies. Our response does." Takeaways:

- By the time you're responding to setbacks, you're already behind.
- The companies winning today aren't necessarily the first movers. They're the fast implementors.
- Check your last organisational strategy review. How many times did you discuss competitor speed vs your speed?

Questions

1 What are the key takeaways from The €60 Billion Novo Nordisk Wake-Up Mini Case Study for leadership teams?
2 How should the CEO stress-test the current assumptions of the competitive strategy?
3 What three strategy tools should the strategist use to determine whether their competitors are moving faster than they think?

13.5 The Role of Equity, Diversity, and Inclusion

The term Equity, Diversity, and Inclusion (EDI) gets used but can come with baggage. The bandwagon has existed for decades, but attaining diversity is not always meaningful. Staff brought in with an EDI mission can leave if lived experiences in the organisation are not in alignment.

13.5.1 Equity

Equity refers to the principle of fairness and justice in allocating resources, opportunities, and benefits. It stresses that all individuals have equal access to these elements, regardless of their economic, societal, and environmental circumstances. Equity in a sustainability-themed culture involves addressing systemic inequalities and promoting social justice to achieve desired outcomes.

At the individual level, attention should be placed on social structures and systems in which people live. No staff member should feel like a misfit within their organisation, and adjustments may need to be made to help overcome the thorny issues of sense of belonging and value (Milton, Yhnell, and Jones, 2025).

13.5.2 Diversity

Diversity is a key plank of sustainability (see Figure 13.3), which moves beyond equity. By harnessing the collective wisdom of diverse communities, encompassing gender, age, sexual orientation, ethnicity, religion, beliefs, and disability, we collectively create solutions that benefit both people and the planet. Since the 1990s, neurodiversity has been defined as the way the brain processes information, encompassing conditions such as autism, dyslexia, dyscalculia, and dyspraxia. Research findings suggest up to a fifth of individuals are neurodivergent.

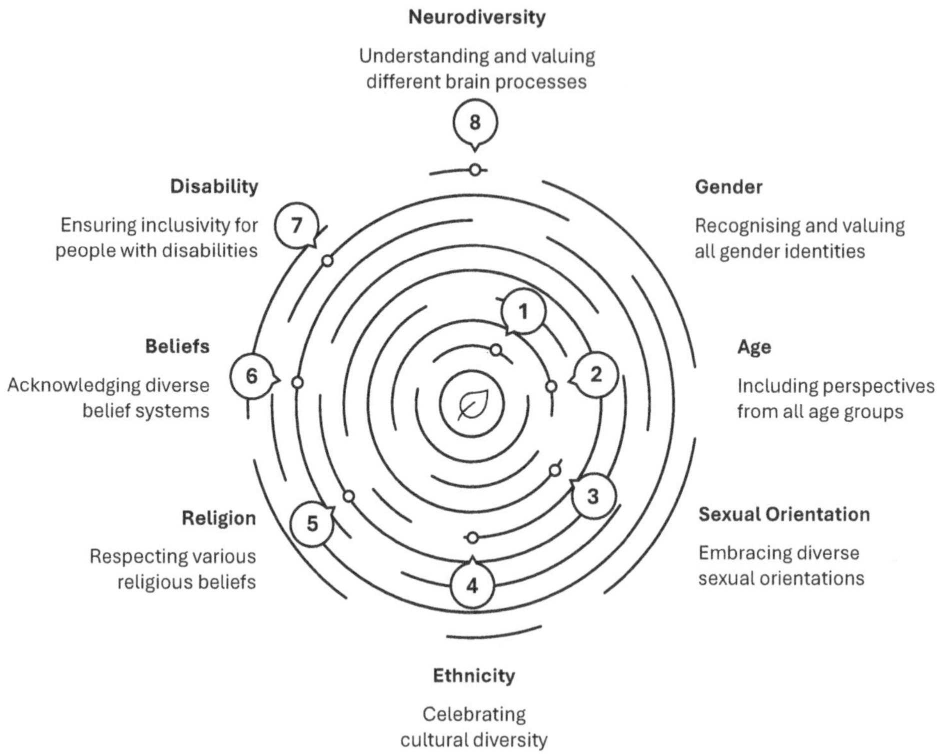

FIGURE 13.3 The pillars of diversity and sustainability

Organisations can benefit from a neurodivergent workforce. Individuals with ADHD may excel in creative thinking and problem-solving. However, they may face difficulties in traditional learning assessments and workplace structures that do not accommodate their learning styles.

Insights into the economic aspects of workplace diversity for organisations in differing contexts are crucial. Research focussing on evidence from US firms, by Nadarajah, Atif, and Gull (2022), reported that firms in highly individualistic states are less likely to adopt workplace diversity policies, adversely impacting **performance**.

13.5.3 Inclusion

According to Forbes (2024), women control 85% of purchases, which underscores their business importance and the necessity of their inclusion. Women's networks will provide direct access to valuable consumer sentiment and market trends related to sustainability preferences. Such nuances provide the strategic intelligence that traditional market research often overlooks. Being inclusive during strategy processes will enrich sustainable strategies.

Diversity can refer to the constituents, perspectives, and combinations of individuals. However, inclusion refers to the extent to which staff feel they belong, are valued, and are accepted. So, while diversity refers to simply having representation, inclusion refers to being invited to conversations about strategy.

According to Romansky, Garrod, Brown, and Deo (2021), the academic literature has grown at a pace that allows for a closer examination of practice through a process lens. Randel (2025) uses the input-mediator-output framework at the individual level of inclusion:

- Input: How alignment and signalling influence inclusion.
- Mediator: How change, learning and power.
- Output: **Performance**, well-being, and commitment.
- Input: Willingness to engage with diverse colleagues.

By having a leader with a deep understanding and experience in EDI, the organisation can align its EDI strategy with overall sustainability objectives, enhancing its reputation and competitiveness. A common observation during client engagements is the scarcity

TABLE 13.2 Issues, pitfalls, and solutions of EDI implementation

Issue	*Pitfall*	*Solution*
1 Homogenous talent acquisition teams	Recruitment teams that lack diversity tend to hire candidates who resemble themselves, perpetuating a lack of diversity.	Recruitment teams look for "outsiders" to be part of the recruitment process.
2 Limited sourcing channels	Relying solely on traditional sourcing methods can lead to a lack of diversity in candidate pools.	Look to include stakeholders who are hard to reach and get them involved in shortlisting candidate pools.
3 Biased job descriptions and screening processes	Job descriptions and screening processes can unintentionally include biased language or criteria, deterring diverse candidates.	Use inclusive language in job descriptions and implement blind resume screening to eliminate personal biases.
4 Inadequate training on diversity and inclusion	Recruiters and hiring managers often lack training on diversity, equity, and inclusion, leading to missed opportunities to recognise diverse talents.	Provide ongoing training on unconscious bias, microaggressions, and inclusive hiring practices.
5 Poor candidate experience	A poor candidate experience can deter diverse candidates from applying or accepting offers.	Ensure that all stages of the hiring process are welcoming and inclusive, from job descriptions to onboarding.
6 Tokenism and lack of inclusive environment	Hiring for diversity without creating an inclusive environment can lead to tokenism and high turnover rates among diverse employees.	Foster an inclusive workplace culture that values diversity and supports the growth of all employees.
7 Lack of data-driven insights	Not tracking diversity metrics can hinder efforts to improve EDI recruitment strategies.	Regularly collect and analyse data on diversity metrics to identify areas for improvement and measure the impact of EDI initiatives.

Abbreviation: EDI, Equity, Diversity, and Inclusion.

of specialists with an in-depth understanding of EDI issues across various sectors, which hinders organisations from creating authentic experiences aligned with their strategy. Possessing current legislation and best practices related to EDI will help ensure that the organisation remains compliant with legal requirements.

Organisations wishing to address the EDI challenges will create an infrastructure that supports the necessary values. However, during assignments, significant pitfalls in EDI recruitment policies have been observed. Often, solutions are not rocket science, but it is disturbing that a high number of organisations continue to deploy ineffective processes to attract and retain diverse talent.

Using EDI as a strategy to overcome organisational pushback involves several key approaches that address resistance effectively while fostering a more inclusive and equitable workplace environment.

Table 13.2 illustrates some of issues, pitfalls, and solutions of EDI implementation.

13.6 Strategies for Overcoming Organisational Pushback

When considering strategic decisions, the internal habits and behaviour will determine what gets implemented. In determining new sources of competitive advantage, Table 13.3 illustrates common strategies and suggests some actions. The CEO should seek to fix damaged value creation processes to deliver the value all stakeholders demand.

TABLE 13.3 Strategies for overcoming organisational pushback

Strategies	*Action*
1 Clear communication and education	Articulate the business case: Clearly communicate how sustainability initiatives align with the organisation's mission and goals, highlighting their positive impact on culture, reputation, and bottom line. Provide ongoing training and education on pushback issues to dispel misconceptions and build support among employees and leaders.
2 Engage stakeholders and build trust	Involve employees: Encourage employees to take ownership of sustainability efforts, making them active participants rather than passive recipients. Leadership commitment: Leaders should demonstrate their commitment to sustainability through actions and decisions, building trust and confidence among employees.
3 Address resistance with empathy	Acknowledge emotions: Validate the emotions of those experiencing pushback and create safe spaces for open dialogue. Empathetic leadership: Train leaders to be empathetic and facilitate constructive conversations about sustainability.
4 Implement accountability systems	Establish clear policies: Develop and communicate sustainability strategies aligned with best practices. Hold stakeholders accountable: Implement systems to hold individuals and departments accountable for advancing sustainability initiatives.
5 Blend internal and external support	Internal champions: Identify internal sustainability champions and advocate to support initiatives. External expertise: Utilise external experts for specialised training and support to enhance internal efforts.

13.6.1 Conclusion

By employing these strategies, organisations can effectively address organisational pushback and create a more inclusive environment where EDI initiatives are valued and supported. This approach not only enhances organisational culture but also contributes to long-term success by fostering a diverse and engaged workforce.

Over the last six decades, the prevailing view of sustainability has been that it's a good thing to do, as it enables organisations to achieve a greater balance with nature. The alignment with ESG and strategy will result in a higher-performing organisation.

Since the pandemic, the organisational infrastructure has evolved with digitally interconnected services and products. Across sectors the media has reported on winners and losers. Accordingly, the final section of this chapter, and the book, critiques the sustainability strategies of high- and low-performing organisations in a comparative approach.

13.7 Strategy Innovation Toolkit – (5) Sustainability Strategy Matrix

The final toolkit in this book provides a holistic view of the organisation's sustainability approach and current positioning. The strategic toolkit is presented in the form of a 2×2 matrix, which helps users to map their journey (see Figure 13.4).

The matrix is organised along two critical dimensions, which present varying degrees of success:

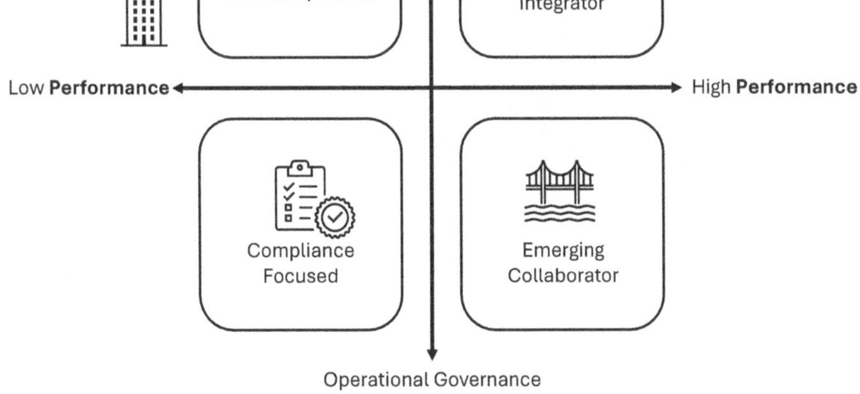

FIGURE 13.4 Sustainability strategy matrix

Matrix Dimensions:

1 X-Axis: Strategic Focus (Internal vs Ecosystem)

- Context matters, and it is strategically important to possess an in-depth knowledge of the organisation's maturity in terms of its focus. The X-axis considers the extent to which an organisation's sustainability efforts are internally and externally focused.

2 Y-Axis: Governance Integration (Operational vs Strategic)

- An appropriate governance framework and structures, ranging from operational to strategic integration at the C-suite level, will ensure that sustainability is integrated into practice.

The Four Quadrants:

1 Compliance Focused (Under-Performing Companies)

Characteristics tend to be:

- Restricted, internally orientated sustainability policies
- Loose governance frameworks
- Short-term, compliance-driven orientation
- Restricted stakeholder involvement
- Insignificant sustainability metrics/reporting
- Minimal emphasis on sustainability **innovation**.

Strategic Implications: Companies in this quadrant typically underperform financially and in their sustainability metrics, with limited market differentiation and **innovation** potential for their products/solutions.

2 Emerging Collaborator (**Transition** Companies)

Characteristics tend to be:

- Seeking new external collaborations
- Developing a formalised industry ecosystem perspective
- Operational-level sustainability focus
- Incremental approach to external engagement
- Developing sustainability supply chain practices
- Increasing external disclosures in reports.

Strategic Implications: These companies attempt to build external networks but lack the internal governance and coordination structures to fully capitalise on market opportunities.

3 Internal Optimiser (**Transition** Companies)

Characteristics tend to be:

- Strong internal sustainability governance

- Board-level responsibility established
- Executive compensation linked to sustainability
- Robust measurement of triple bottom line metrics
- Limited external ecosystem engagement
- Internally driven **innovation** for sustainability.

Strategic Implications: These companies have strong internal sustainability foundations but are not fully leveraging external partnerships and industry ecosystem opportunities.

4 Ecosystem Integrator (High-Performing Companies)

Characteristics tend to be:

- Comprehensive sustainability governance
- Extensive multi-stakeholder collaboration
- Market-led sustainable **innovation** & R&D investment
- Comprehensive green supply chain sustainability
- Long-term strategic orientation
- Industry-wide ecosystem perspective of their sector.

Strategic Implications: The evidence shows these companies significantly outperform on both business and sustainability metrics, with measurable advantages in operational efficiency, market share, and revenue growth.

Strategic Recommendations for CEOs

1 Governance Transformation:

- Establish board-level responsibility for sustainability.
- Link executive compensation to sustainability metrics.
- Implement robust measurement and disclosure of non-financial information.

2 Ecosystem Engagement:

- Develop extensive stakeholder engagement processes.
- Collaborate with government agencies, academic institutions, and sustainability groups.
- Extend sustainability focus throughout the supply chain.

3 Strategic Reorientation:

- Shift from short-term to long-term orientation.
- Integrate sustainability with core business strategy.
- Adopt an industry-wide ecosystem perspective on sustainability.

4 **Innovation** Integration:

- Increase R&D investment focused on sustainability.
- Develop eco-**innovation** capabilities.
- Use collaborative approaches to drive sustainable **innovation.**

FIGURE 13.5 Turn the dial to 11!

By strategically moving towards the "Ecosystem Integrator" quadrant, technology companies can unlock significant business value while advancing meaningful sustainability outcomes. Now it's time to turn the dial to 11! (Figure 13.5).

13.8 Chapter Key Takeaways

Some of the key takeaways from Chapter 13 on organisational pushbacks are as follows:

1 **Resistance Is Layered rather than only Surface Level:** Most failed environmental projects fall short since they just treat symptoms rather than underlying problems. The "onion model" discussed in this chapter shows that good intervention calls for removing layers from surface symptoms to more underlying cultural and environmental causes. Although staff members often know what might work, they rarely express it; set up safe environments for these kinds of talks.
2 **Most Resistance to Sustainability Is Based on Fear:** Benevolent concerns underneath reasonable arguments and spreadsheets are job security concerns, autonomy threats, and personal value conflicts. Before embracing change intellectually, people emotionally digest it according to their particular adaption curve (Figure 13.2). See this emotional trip instead of focussing simply on the business case.
3 **Conventional Companies Still Mired in the "Dominant Social Paradigm":** This chapter emphasises how fear of **innovation** and loyalty to antiquated paradigms frequently lead to institutional opposition. To allow significant sustainability transformation, leaders must purposefully question these mindsets. Though alternative models like the circular economy aid, micro-level implementation problems can impede advancement.
4 **Passive Resistance More Dangerous than Active Opposition:** While subtle non-compliance – missed meetings, low effort, pretended ignorance of initiatives – is more difficult to resist, vocal objectors can be addressed constructively. Look for these warning signals: poor awareness of important components of a sustainability strategy, little effort on assigned responsibilities, and obvious missing from pertinent meetings.
5 **Empty Vacuums in Leadership under the C-Suite Doom Implementation:** The chapter emphasises a crucial realisation: structural improvements by themselves cannot foster strategic leadership capabilities at middle management levels. Translating vision into reality depends on cross-functional leadership development programmes with sustainability concentration.
6 **EDI Might Be Strong Sustainable Enablers:** This chapter shows EDI is a strategic instrument for overcoming sustainability pushbacks, not only a parallel endeavour. Different points of view produce more creative environmental ideas. But meaningless diversity

hiring without inclusion causes more problems than it solves; lived experiences must align with stated values.

7 **Resistance of External Stakeholders Calls for Various Strategies:** From media mistrust to supply chain partner hesitation, this chapter lists seven separate forms of external resistance. Each calls for focused plans instead of generalisations in communications. Especially remarkable is the change in premium markets – such as EVs – away from status symbols towards stressing dependability, actual value, and **innovation**.

This chapter offers an interesting structure for evaluating sustainability maturity and conquering organisational opposition. Most importantly, it shows how addressing the human aspects of change management and organisational culture contributes to the sustainability implementation more than just systems and policies.

13.9 Self-Reflection Questions

1 How may the "onion model" shown in Figure 13.1 assist sustainability leaders in spotting and handling more underlying levels of organisational resistance than only surface-level manifestations?
2 What interventions are available for CEOs to overcome opposition to sustainability projects using EDI approaches as tools?
3 Digital transformation projects are key drivers of sustainability initiatives. You are to outline how leaders can avoid possible risks and overcome particular forms of opposition to sustainability projects.
4 How should a Chief Sustainability Officer use the Sustainability Strategy Matrix to assess their organisation's current position and develop a practical roadmap towards becoming an "Ecosystem Integrator"?
5 How should the CEO move beyond doing nice things via CSR to a broader base stakeholder value creation model?

References

Bhattacharya, A., Nand, A. and Castka, P., (2019). Lean-green integration and its impact on sustainability performance: A critical review. *Journal of Cleaner Production, 236*, p.117697.

Forbes (2024). Who runs the world? Women control 85% of purchases, 29% of STEM roles. Available at: https://www.forbes.com/sites/digital-assets/2024/03/07/who-runs-the-world-women-control-85-of-purchases-29-of-stem-roles/ (Accessed: 3 September 2025).

Goudie, D., (2005). *Sustainability planning: Pushing against institutional barriers* (Vol. 81). WIT Press. Available at: https://www.witpress.com/Secure/elibrary/papers/ECO05/ECO05023FU.pdf

Housman, M. and Minor, D., (2015). Toxic workers. Harvard Business School Strategy Unit Working Paper, (16-057).

Kilbourne, W.E., Beckmann, S.C. and Thelen, E., (2002). The role of the dominant social paradigm in environmental attitudes: A multinational examination. *Journal of Business Research, 55*(3), pp.193–204.

Milton, E., Yhnell, E. and Jones, K., (2025). An overlooked EDI issue… can valuing the diversity of third space professionals support a more sustainable future in higher education? *Journal of Learning Development in Higher Education,* (33). https://doi.org/10.47408/jldhe.vi33.1241

Morgan, Y.C., Fok, L. and Zee, S., (2024). Examining the impact of environmental and organisational priorities on sustainability performance in service industries. *International Journal of Productivity and Performance Management, 73*(8), pp.2480–2507.
Nadarajah, S., Atif, M. and Gull, A.A., (2022). State-level culture and workplace diversity policies: Evidence from US firms. *Journal of Business Ethics, 177*(2), pp.443–462.
Randel, A E., (2025). Inclusion in the workplace: A review and research agenda. *Group & Organization Management, 50(*1), pp.119–162.
Romansky, L., Garrod, M., Brown, K. and Deo, K., (2021). How to measure inclusion in the workplace. *Harvard Business Review, 27,* pp.1–7.
Sariyer, G., Mangla, S.K., Chowdhury, S., Sozen, M.E. and Kazancoglu, Y., (2024). Predictive and prescriptive analytics for ESG performance evaluation: A case of Fortune 500 companies. *Journal of Business Research, 181,* p.114742.
Schroeder, P., Anggraeni, K. and Weber, U., (2019). The relevance of circular economy practices to the sustainable development goals. *Journal of Industrial Ecology, 23*(1), pp.77–95.
Veblen, T., (2017). *The theory of the leisure class*. Routledge.
Xie, X., Khan, S., Rehman, S., Naz, S., Haider, S.A. and Kayani, U.N., (2024). Ameliorating sustainable business performance through green constructs: A case of manufacturing industry. *Environment, Development and Sustainability, 26*(9), pp.22655–22687.

INDEX

Note: **Bold** page numbers refer to tables and *italic* page numbers refer to figures.

For Product Safety Concerns and Information please contact our EU representative GPSR@taylorandfrancis.com Taylor & Francis Verlag GmbH, Kaufingerstraße 24, 80331 München, Germany